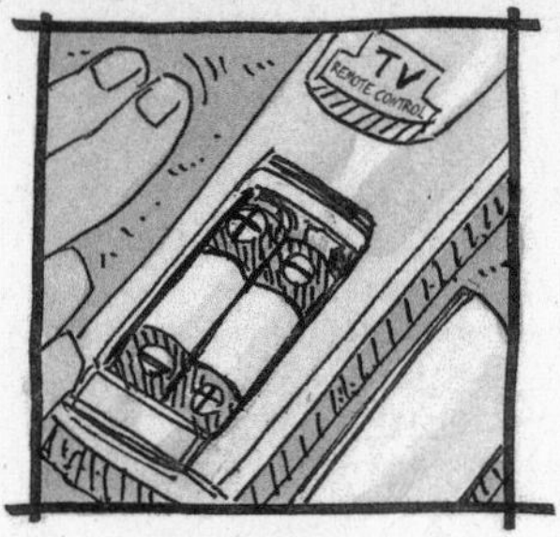
TV
REMOTE CONTROL

岸本斉史

Recently, the batteries in my TV and DVD player remote control have started running out of juice, responding sluggishly when I press the buttons and not powering on easily. However, they do still eventually turn on, so I keep telling myself "Eh, it's still okay..." and procrastinating. And then I noticed something. Once the remote stops working at all, if I open up its battery case and rub the batteries, it starts working again! You all should try it too!

It's true... though it would be faster just to change the batteries.

—Masashi Kishimoto, 2010

Author/artist Masashi Kishimoto was born in 1974 in rural Okayama Prefecture, Japan. After spending time in art college, he won the Hop Step Award for new manga artists with his manga **Karakuri** (Mechanism). Kishimoto decided to base his next story on traditional Japanese culture. His first version of **Naruto**, drawn in 1997, was a one-shot story about fox spirits; his final version, which debuted in **Weekly Shonen Jump** in 1999, quickly became the most popular ninja manga in Japan.

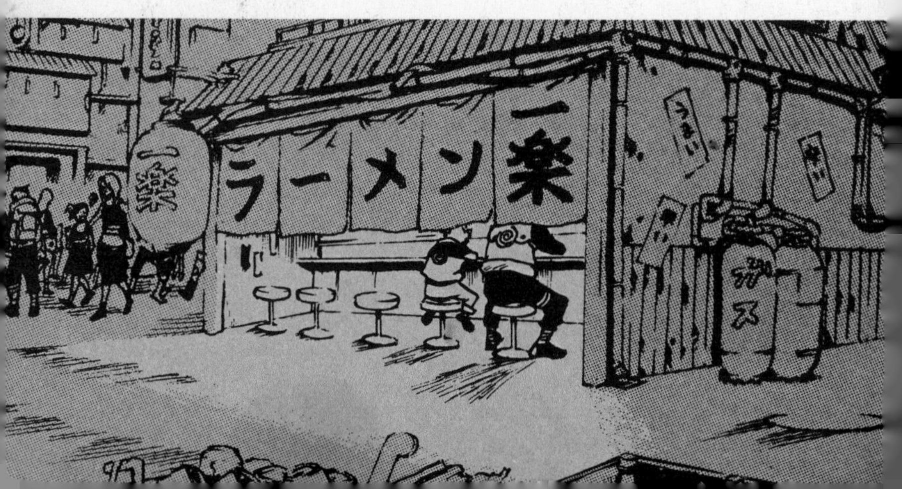
一楽
一楽
ラーメン

NARUTO VOL. 50
SHONEN JUMP Manga Edition

This graphic novel contains material that was originally published in English
in SHONEN JUMP #88–91. Artwork in the magazine may have been
slightly altered from that presented here.

STORY AND ART BY MASASHI KISHIMOTO

Translation/Mari Morimoto
Series Touch-up Art & Lettering/Inori Fukuda Trant
Additional Touch-up Art & Lettering/Sabrina Heep
Design/Sam Elzway
Series Editor/Joel Enos
Graphic Novel Editor/Megan Bates

Printed in the U.S.A.

Published by VIZ Media, LLC
P.O. Box 77010
San Francisco, CA 94107

10 9 8 7 6 5 4 3 2 1
First printing, February 2011

www.viz.com

THE WORLD'S
MOST POPULAR MANGA

www.shonenjump.com

SHONEN JUMP MANGA EDITION

NARUTO

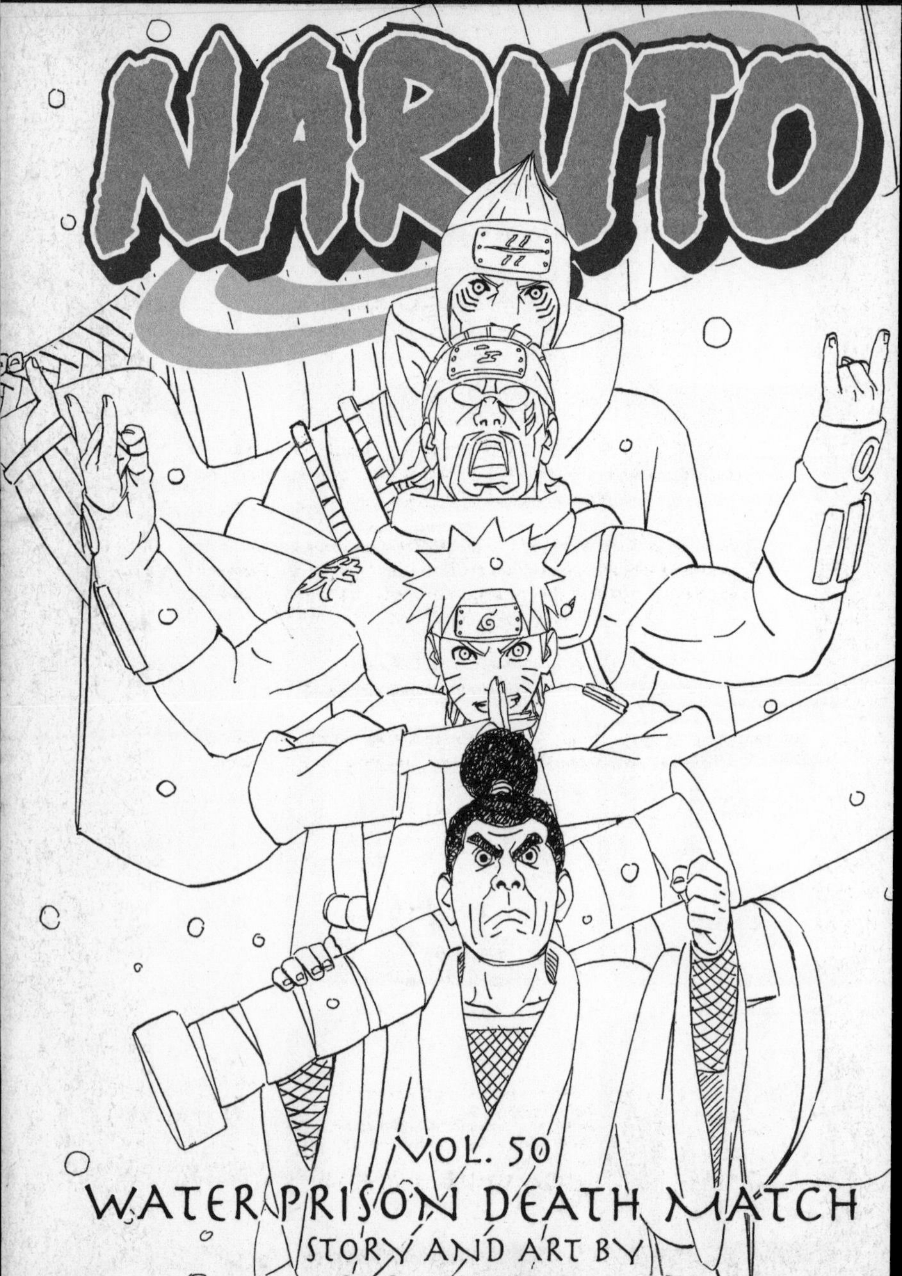

VOL. 50

WATER PRISON DEATH MATCH

STORY AND ART BY

MASASHI KISHIMOTO

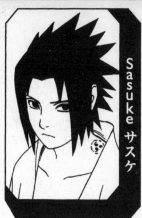
Sasuke サスケ

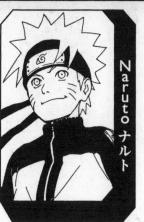
Naruto ナルト

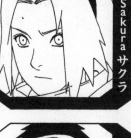
Sakura サクラ

Kakashi カカシ

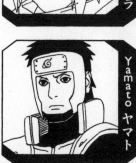
Yamato ヤマト

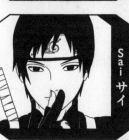
Sai サイ

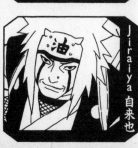
Jiraiya 自来也

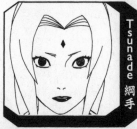
Tsunade 綱手

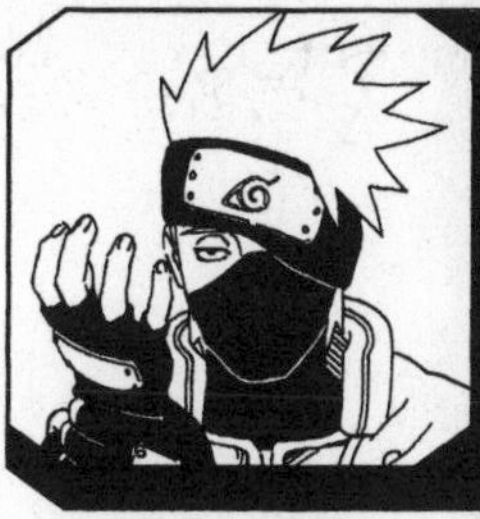

CHARACTERS

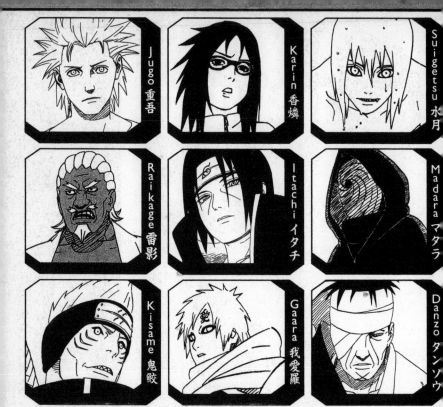

Jugo 重吾

Karin 香燐

Suigetsu 水月

Raikage 雷影

Itachi イタチ

Madara マダラ

Kisame 鬼鮫

Gaara 我愛羅

Danzo ダンゾウ

THE STORY SO FAR...

Naruto, the biggest troublemaker at the Ninja Academy in the Village of Konohagakure, finally becomes a ninja. Along with his classmates Sasuke and Sakura, he grows and matures during countless trials and battles. Sasuke, unable to give up his quest for vengeance, leaves Konohagakure to seek the renegade ninja Orochimaru, from whom he hopes to gain immense power.

Two years pass. Naruto battles against the Tailed Beast-targeting Akatsuki. Elsewhere, after winning the epic battle against his brother Itachi, Sasuke learns the truth about Itachi's perceived betrayal of their clan. He allies with the Akatsuki and sets out to destroy Konoha.

Ultimately, Naruto saves his village. But Danzo of the Black Ops is appointed the Sixth Hokage in Tsunade's place. And the Raikage—leader of the Cloud Village—summons a meeting of the five other leaders. Sasuke attacks, and engages in battle with the Raikage!!

NARUTO

VOL. 50
WATER PRISON DEATH MATCH

CONTENTS

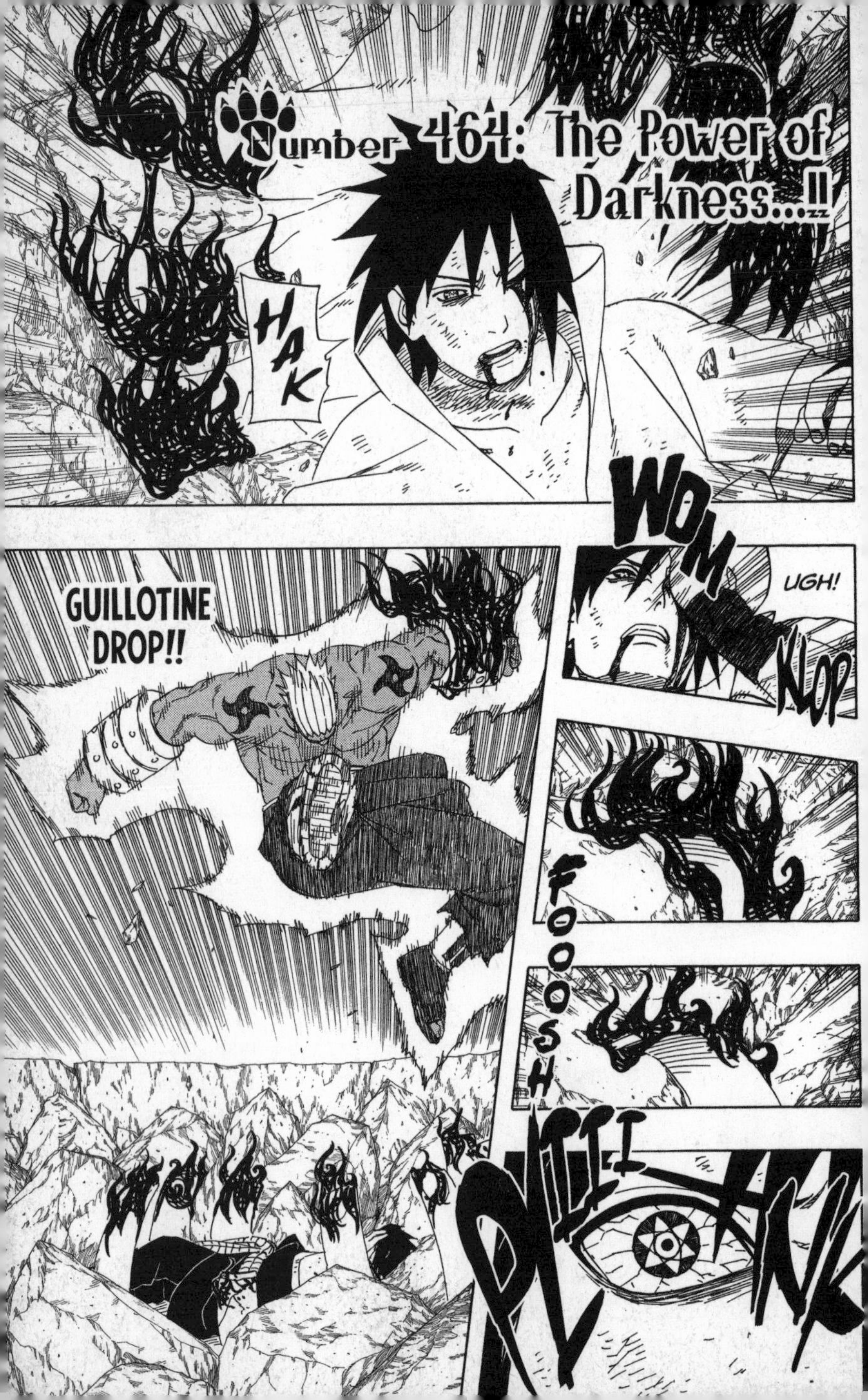
Number 464: The Power of Darkness...!!
HAK
WOM
UGH!
KLOP
FOOOOSH
GUILLOTINE DROP!!

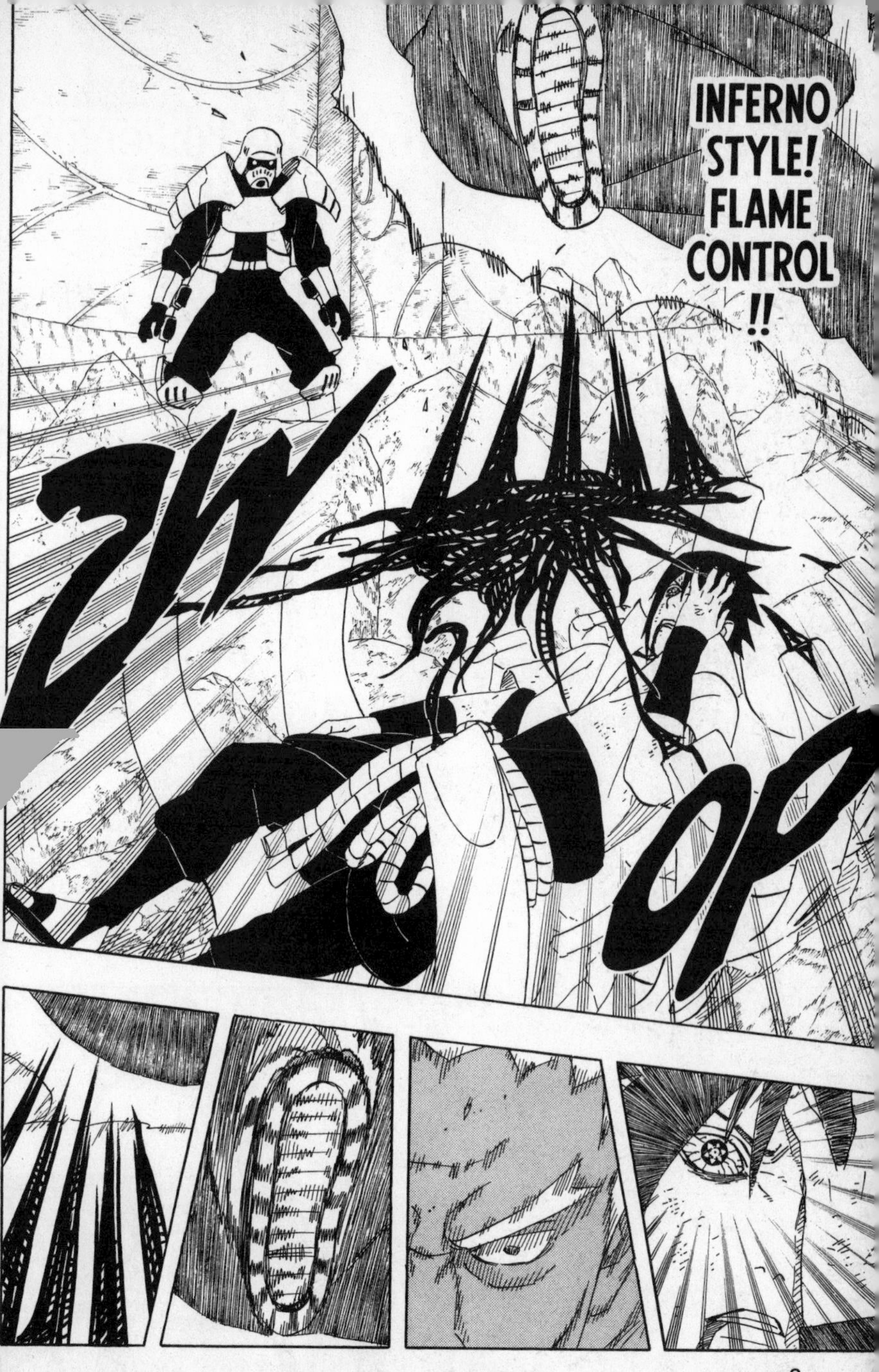
INFERNO STYLE! FLAME CONTROL!!
ZWOOP

READ THIS WAY

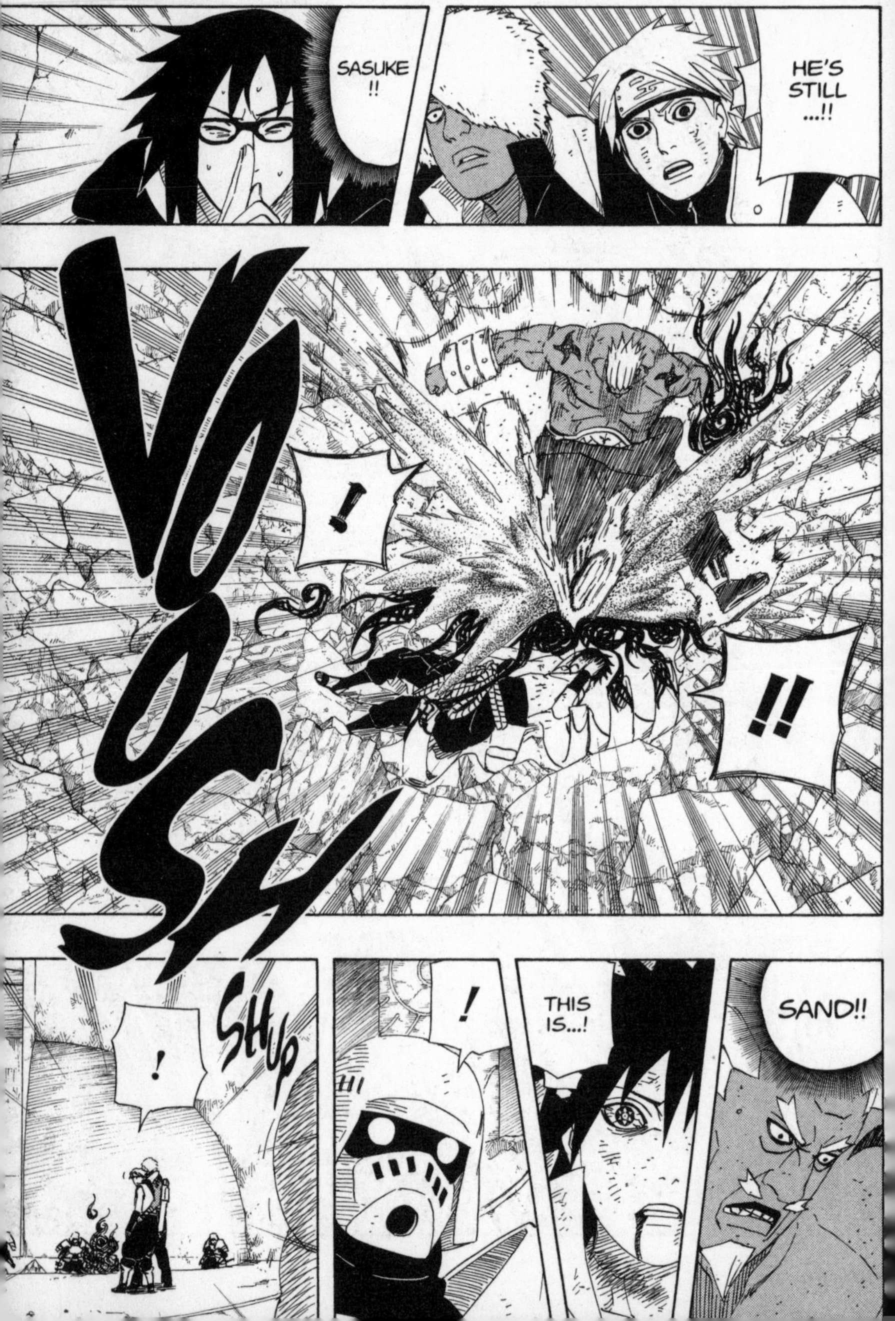
HE'S STILL ...!!
SASUKE !!
VOOSH
!
!!
SAND!!
THIS IS...!
!
SHUP
!

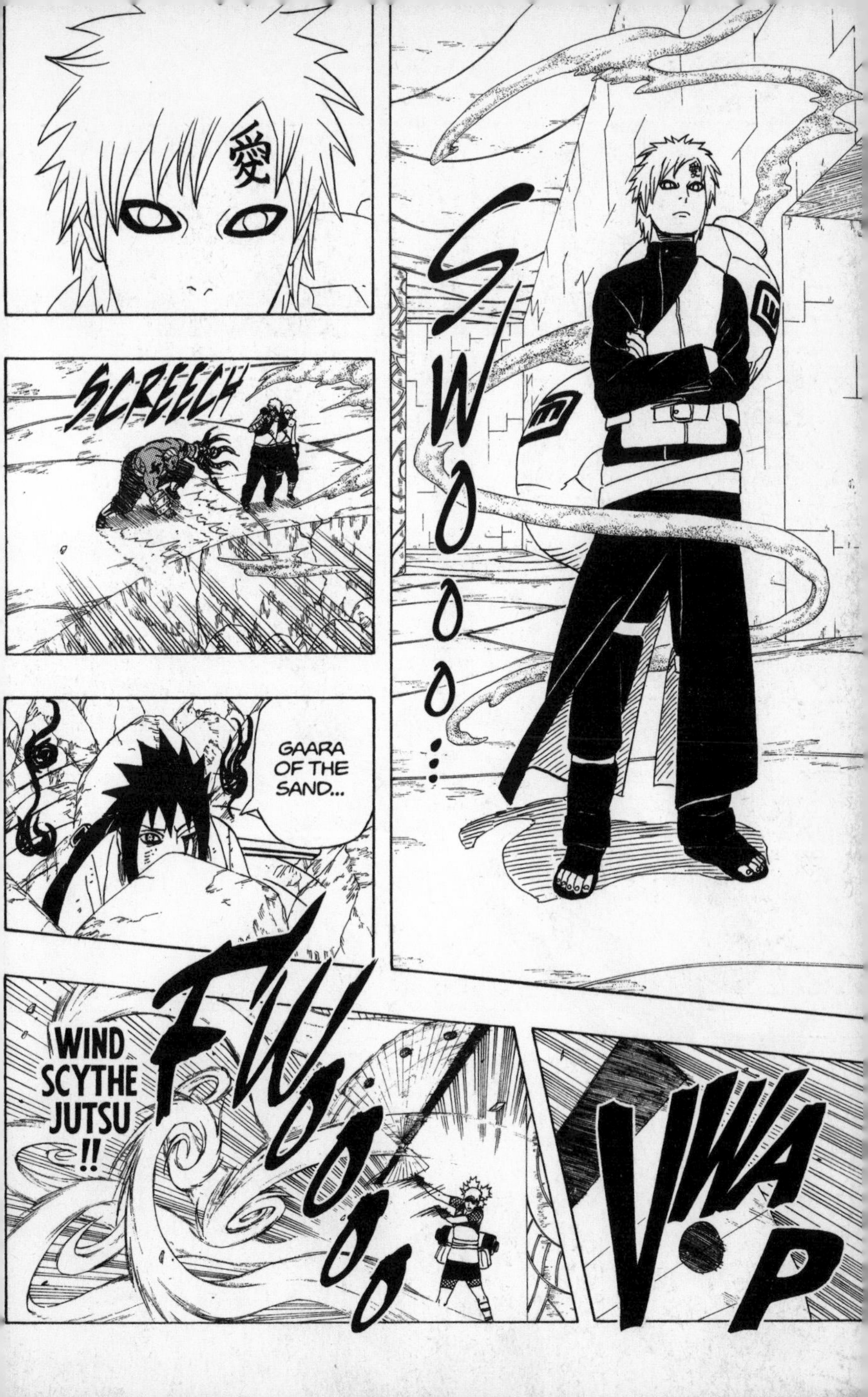
SWOOOO...
SCREECH
GAARA OF THE SAND...
VWAP
WIND SCYTHE JUTSU!!
FWOOOOO

READ THIS WAY

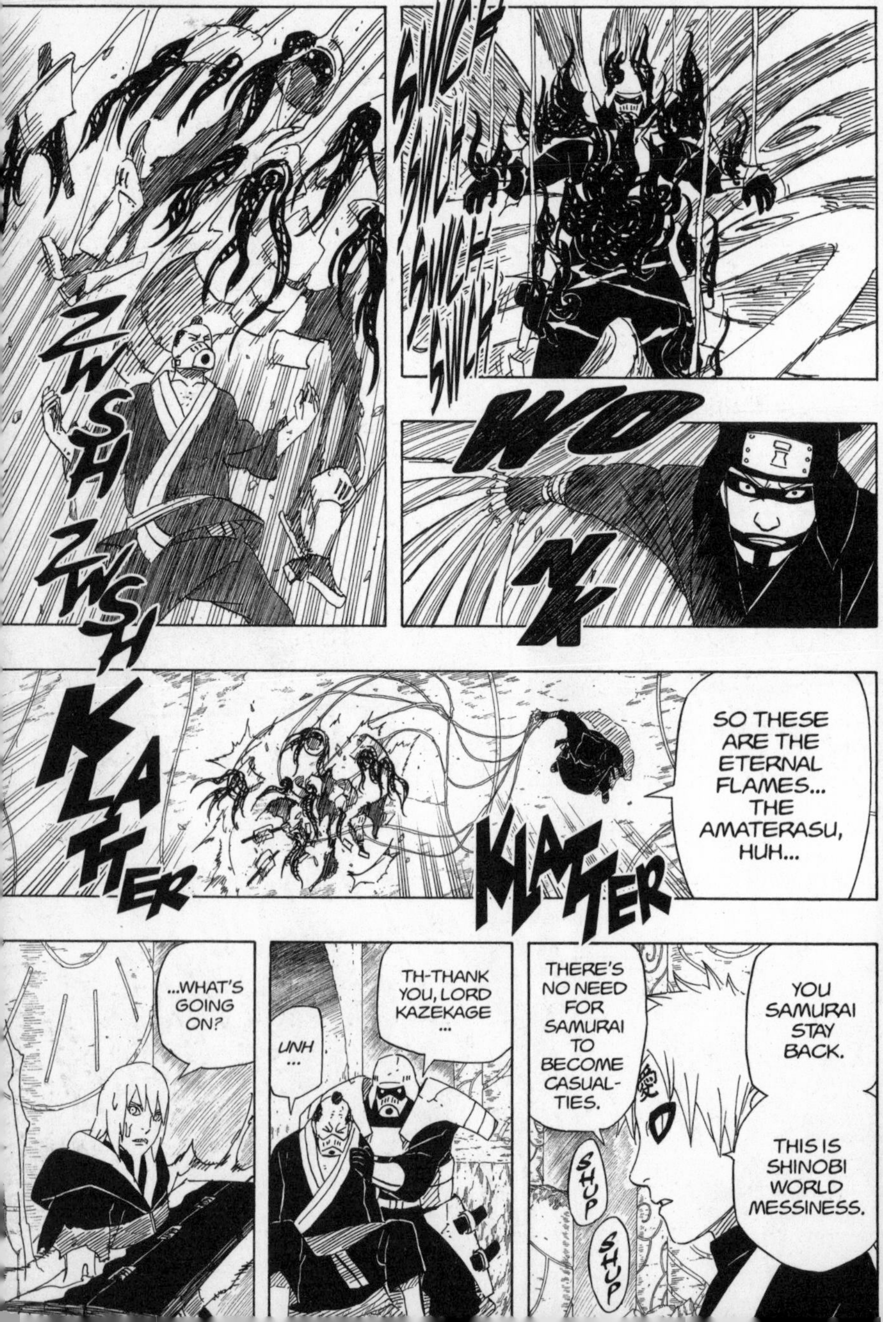

SWCH
SWCH
SWCH
SWCH
WONK
ZWSH
ZWSH
SO THESE ARE THE ETERNAL FLAMES... THE AMATERASU, HUH...
KLATTER
KLATTER
YOU SAMURAI STAY BACK.
THIS IS SHINOBI WORLD MESSINESS.
THERE'S NO NEED FOR SAMURAI TO BECOME CASUALTIES.
SHUP
SHUP
TH-THANK YOU, LORD KAZEKAGE ...
UNH ...
...WHAT'S GOING ON?

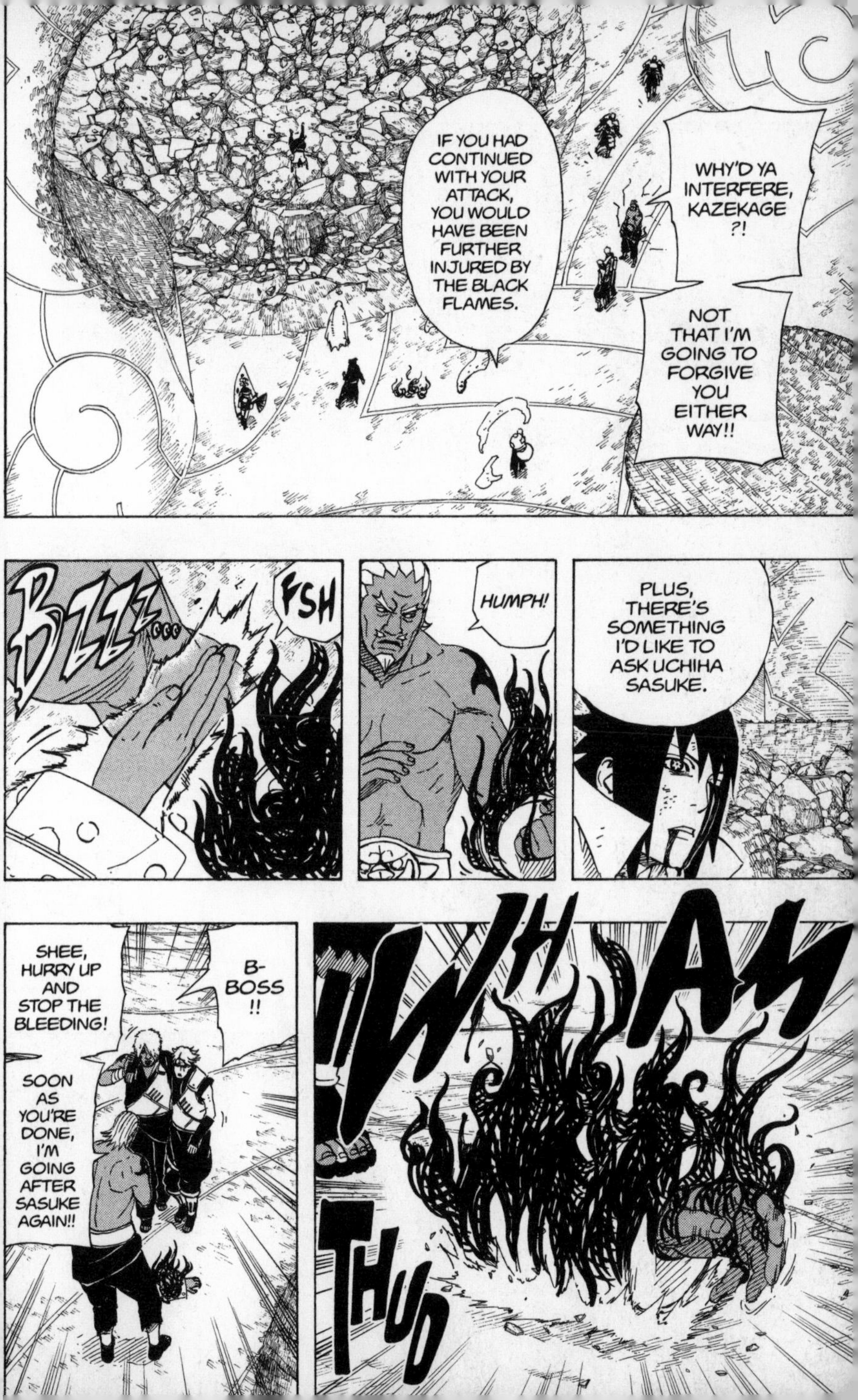

WHY'D YA INTERFERE, KAZEKAGE?!
IF YOU HAD CONTINUED WITH YOUR ATTACK, YOU WOULD HAVE BEEN FURTHER INJURED BY THE BLACK FLAMES.
NOT THAT I'M GOING TO FORGIVE YOU EITHER WAY!!
PLUS, THERE'S SOMETHING I'D LIKE TO ASK UCHIHA SASUKE.
HUMPH!
FSH
BZZZ...
WHAM
THUD
B-BOSS!!
SHEE, HURRY UP AND STOP THE BLEEDING!
SOON AS YOU'RE DONE, I'M GOING AFTER SASUKE AGAIN!!

READ THIS WAY

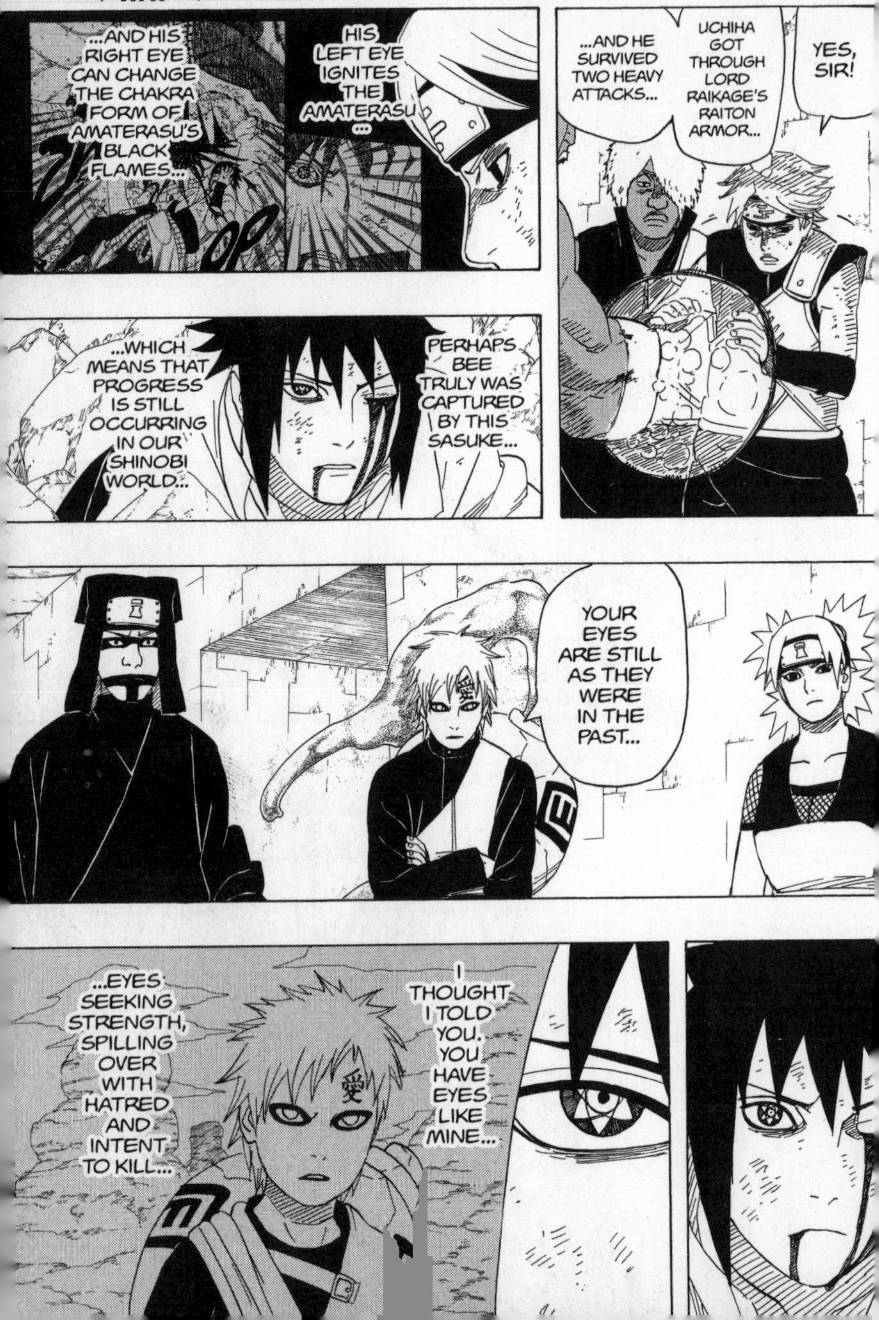
YES, SIR!
UCHIHA GOT THROUGH LORD RAIKAGE'S RAITON ARMOR...
...AND HE SURVIVED TWO HEAVY ATTACKS...
HIS LEFT EYE IGNITES THE AMATERASU...
...AND HIS RIGHT EYE CAN CHANGE THE CHAKRA FORM OF AMATERASU'S BLACK FLAMES...
PERHAPS BEE TRULY WAS CAPTURED BY THIS SASUKE...
...WHICH MEANS THAT PROGRESS IS STILL OCCURRING IN OUR SHINOBI WORLD...
YOUR EYES ARE STILL AS THEY WERE IN THE PAST...
I THOUGHT I TOLD YOU. YOU HAVE EYES LIKE MINE...
...EYES SEEKING STRENGTH, SPILLING OVER WITH HATRED AND INTENT TO KILL...

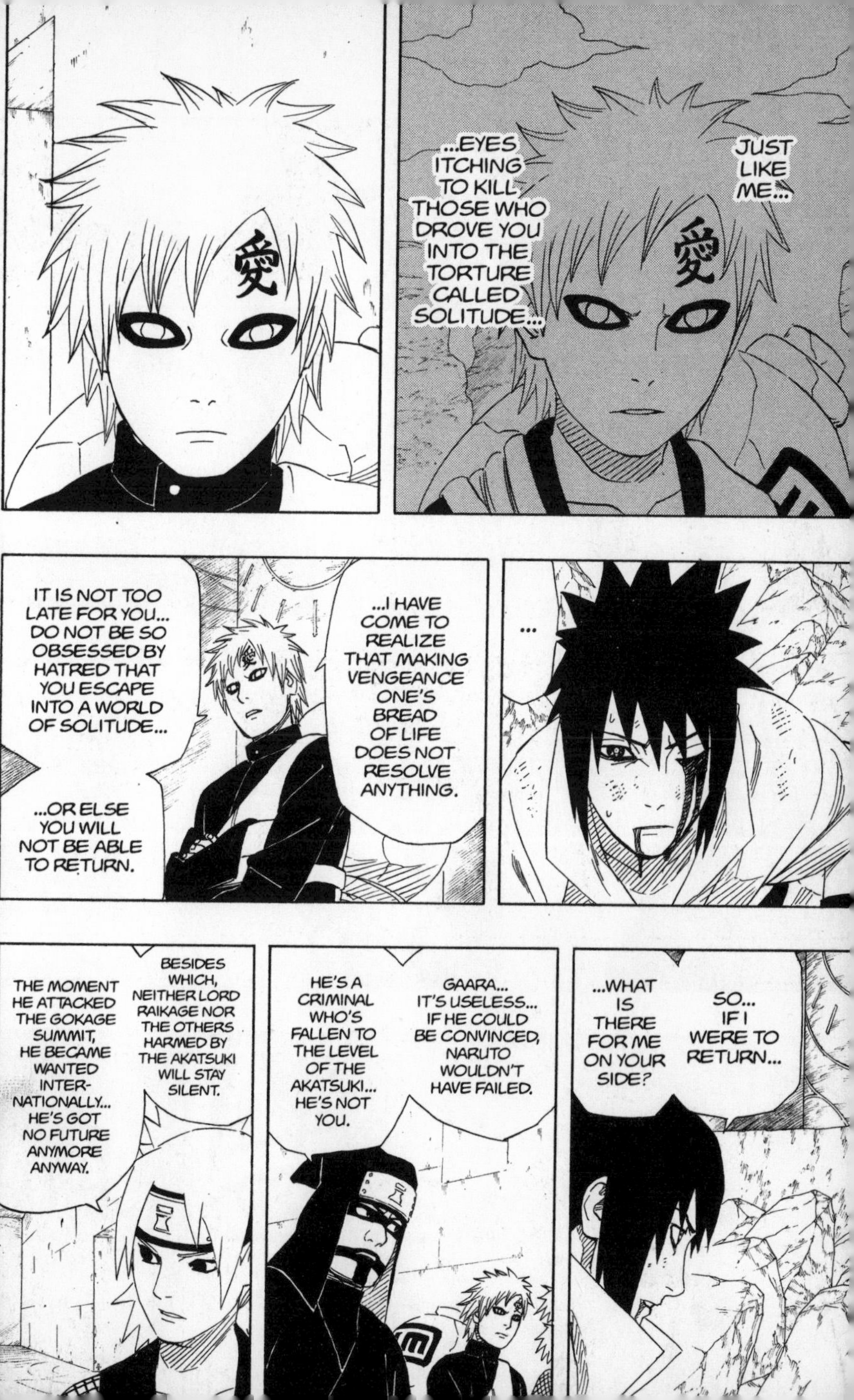
JUST LIKE ME...
...EYES ITCHING TO KILL THOSE WHO DROVE YOU INTO THE TORTURE CALLED SOLITUDE...
...
...I HAVE COME TO REALIZE THAT MAKING VENGEANCE ONE'S BREAD OF LIFE DOES NOT RESOLVE ANYTHING.
IT IS NOT TOO LATE FOR YOU... DO NOT BE SO OBSESSED BY HATRED THAT YOU ESCAPE INTO A WORLD OF SOLITUDE...
...OR ELSE YOU WILL NOT BE ABLE TO RETURN.
SO... IF I WERE TO RETURN...
...WHAT IS THERE FOR ME ON YOUR SIDE?
GAARA... IT'S USELESS... IF HE COULD BE CONVINCED, NARUTO WOULDN'T HAVE FAILED.
HE'S A CRIMINAL WHO'S FALLEN TO THE LEVEL OF THE AKATSUKI... HE'S NOT YOU.
BESIDES WHICH, NEITHER LORD RAIKAGE NOR THE OTHERS HARMED BY THE AKATSUKI WILL STAY SILENT.
THE MOMENT HE ATTACKED THE GOKAGE SUMMIT, HE BECAME WANTED INTER-NATIONALLY... HE'S GOT NO FUTURE ANYMORE ANYWAY.

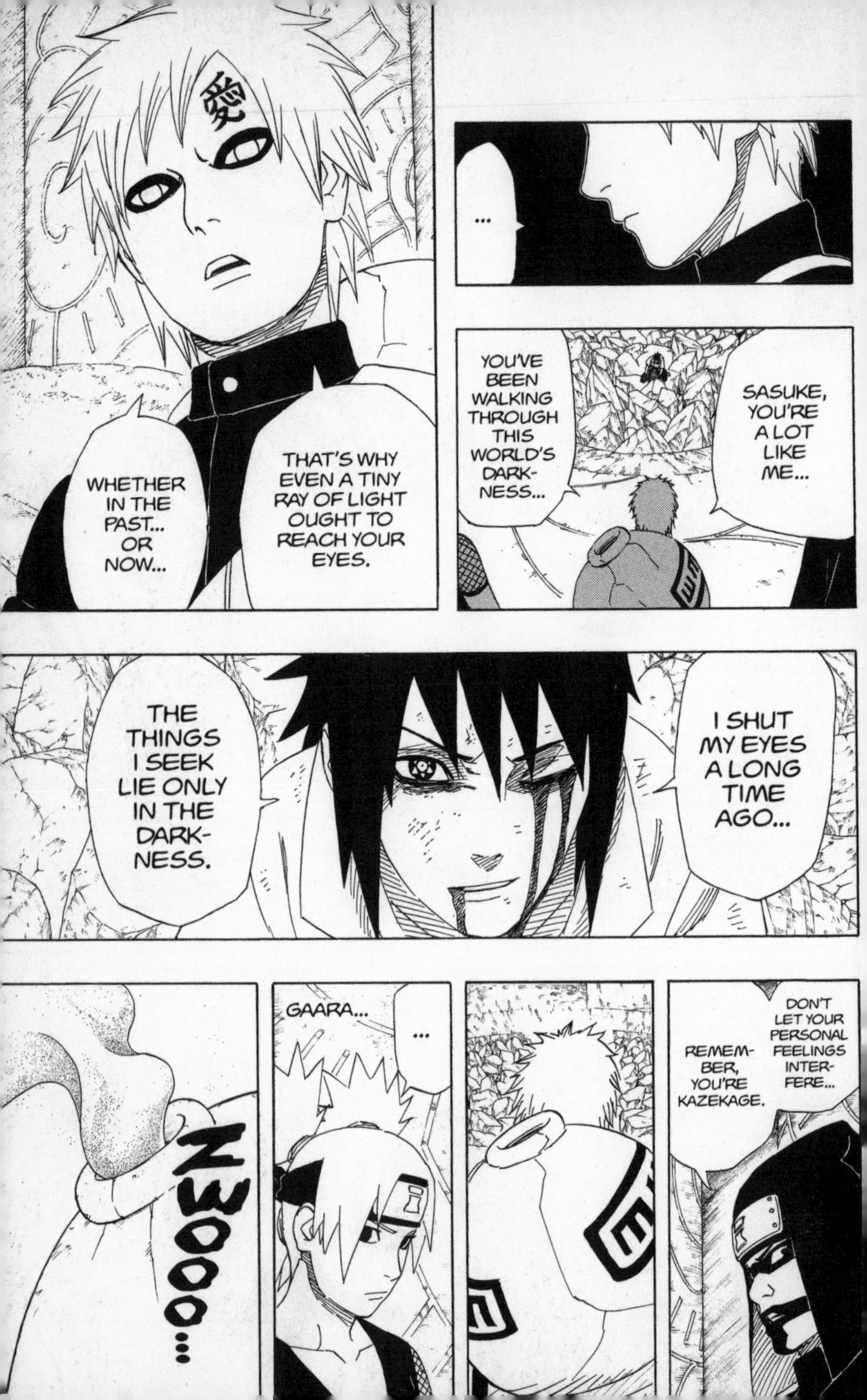
...
SASUKE, YOU'RE A LOT LIKE ME...
YOU'VE BEEN WALKING THROUGH THIS WORLD'S DARK-NESS...
THAT'S WHY EVEN A TINY RAY OF LIGHT OUGHT TO REACH YOUR EYES.
WHETHER IN THE PAST... OR NOW...
I SHUT MY EYES A LONG TIME AGO...
THE THINGS I SEEK LIE ONLY IN THE DARK-NESS.
DON'T LET YOUR PERSONAL FEELINGS INTER-FERE...
REMEM-BER, YOU'RE KAZEKAGE.
GAARA...
...
ZWOOOO...

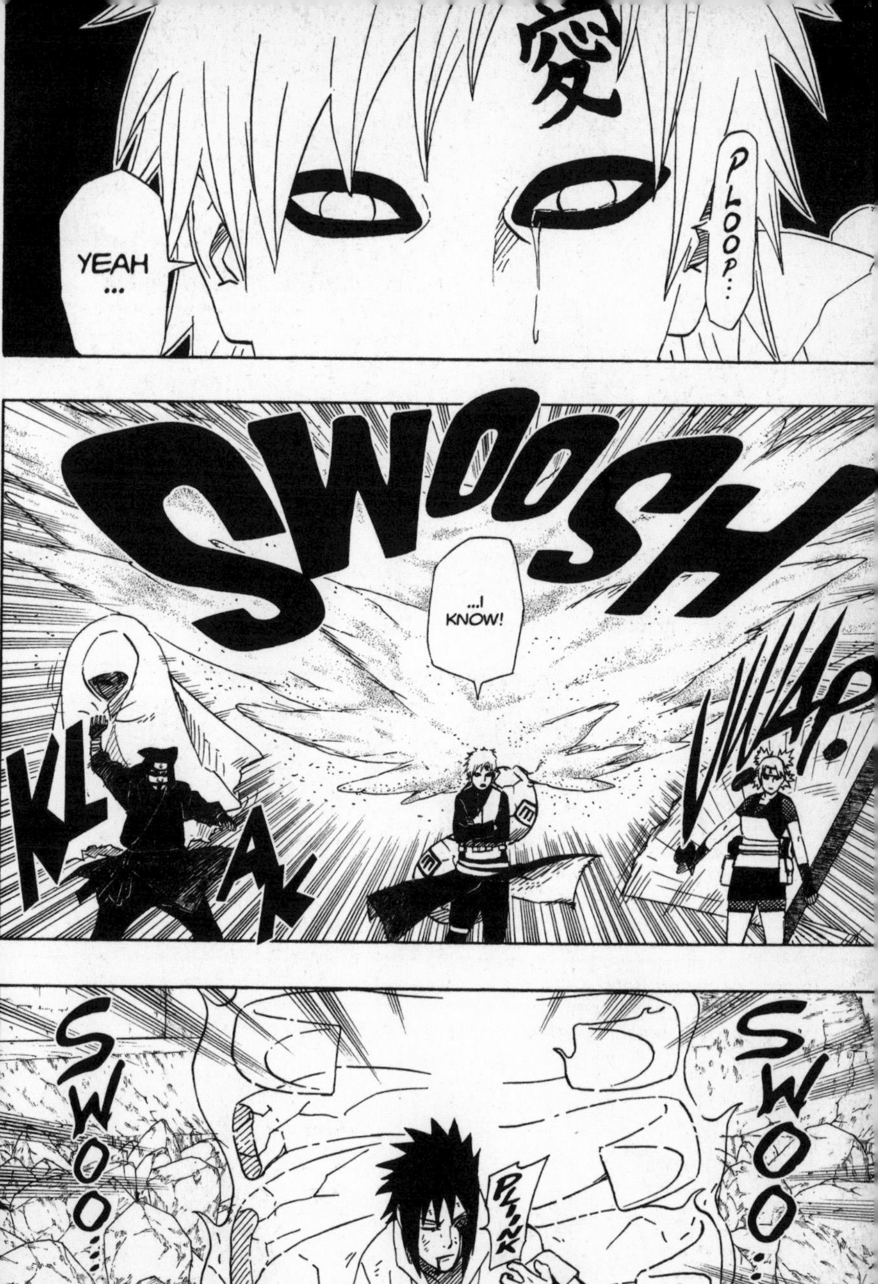
愛
PLOOP...
YEAH ...
SWOOSH
VWAP!
...I KNOW!
KLAK
SWOO...
PLINK
SWOO...

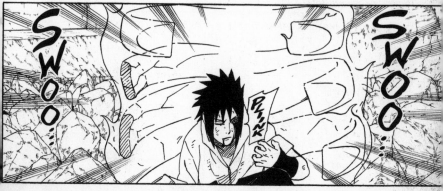

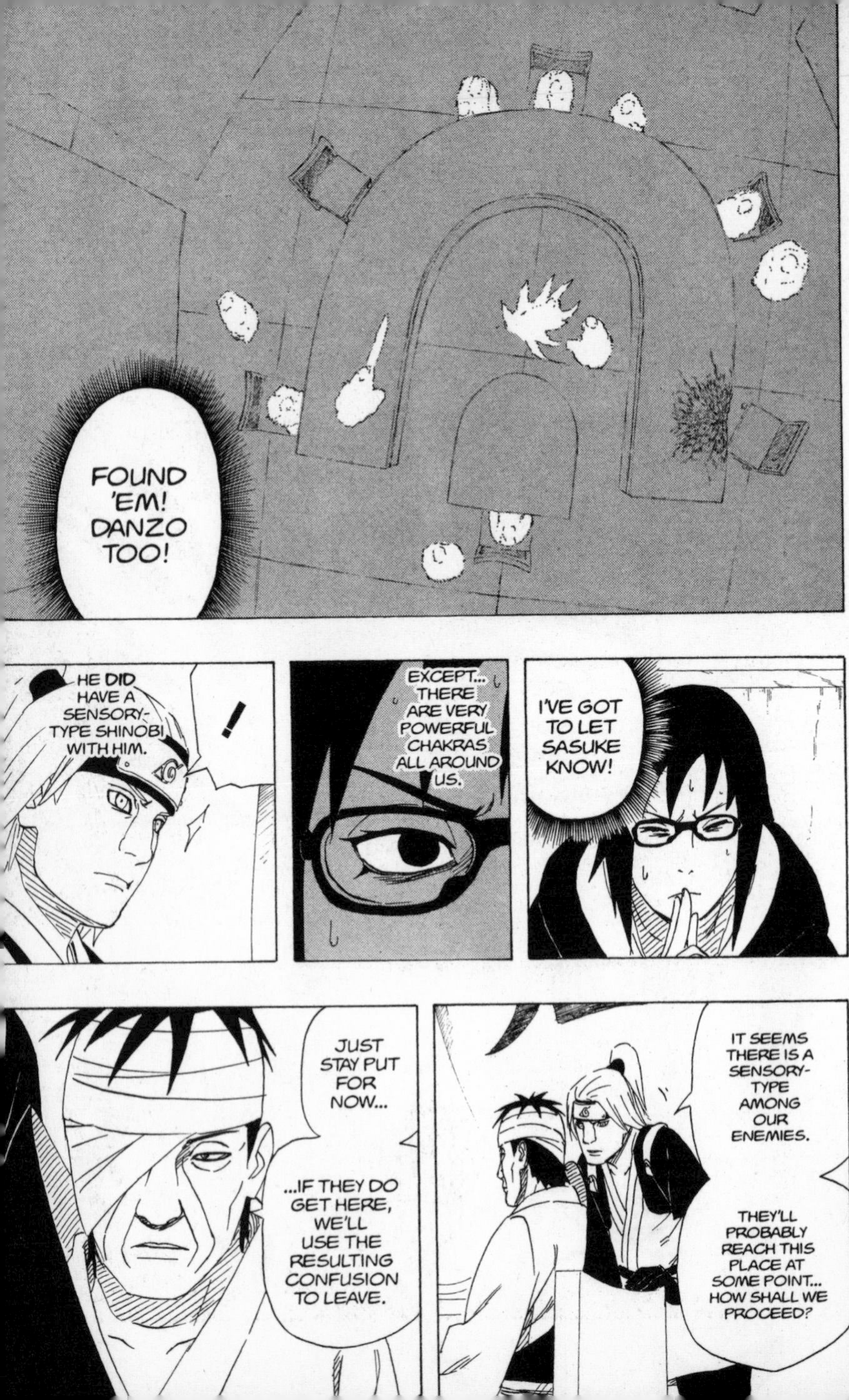
FOUND 'EM! DANZO TOO!
I'VE GOT TO LET SASUKE KNOW!
EXCEPT... THERE ARE VERY POWERFUL CHAKRAS ALL AROUND US.
HE DID HAVE A SENSORY-TYPE SHINOBI WITH HIM.
!
IT SEEMS THERE IS A SENSORY-TYPE AMONG OUR ENEMIES.
THEY'LL PROBABLY REACH THIS PLACE AT SOME POINT... HOW SHALL WE PROCEED?
JUST STAY PUT FOR NOW...
...IF THEY DO GET HERE, WE'LL USE THE RESULTING CONFUSION TO LEAVE.

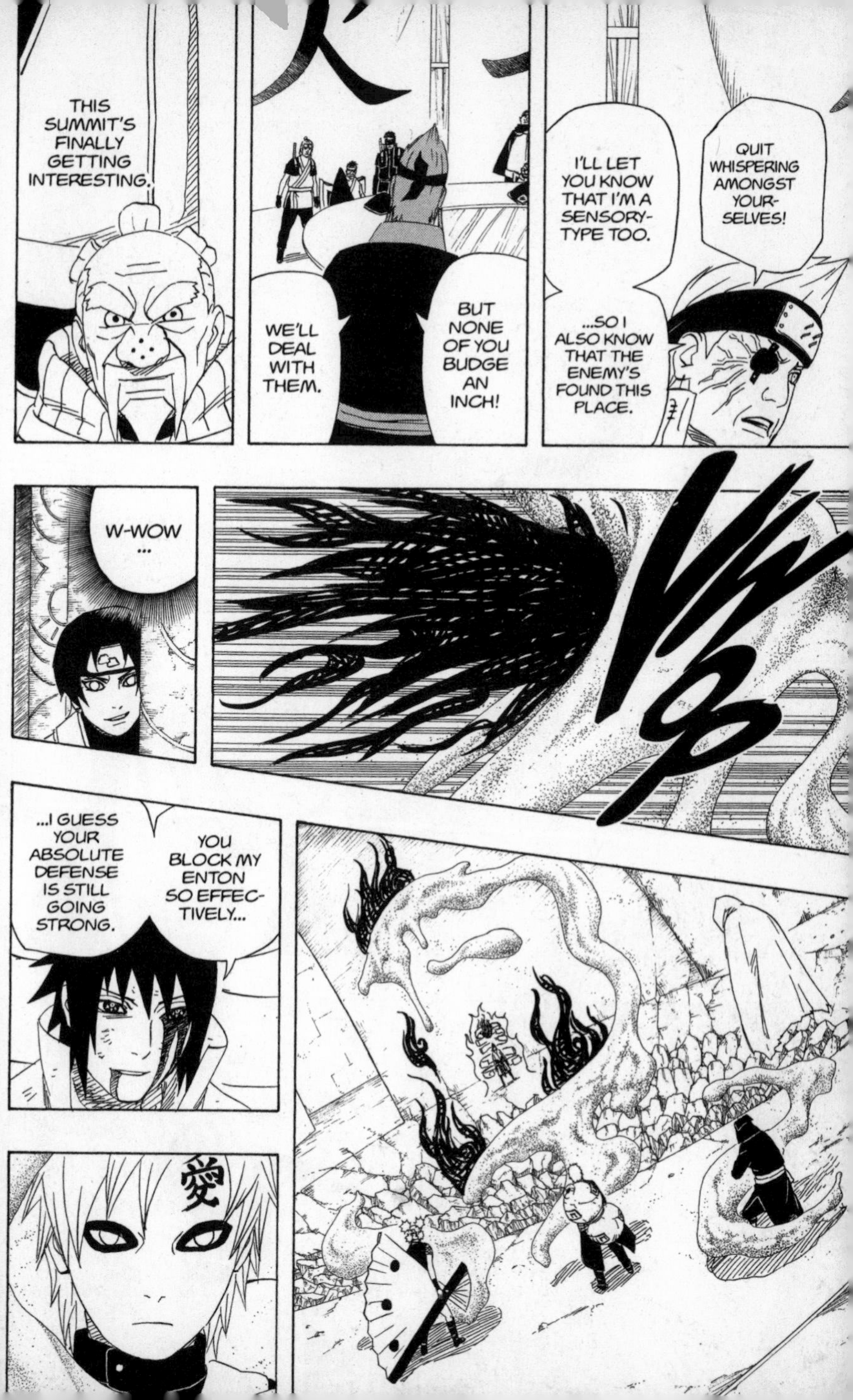
QUIT WHISPERING AMONGST YOUR-SELVES!
I'LL LET YOU KNOW THAT I'M A SENSORY-TYPE TOO.
...SO I ALSO KNOW THAT THE ENEMY'S FOUND THIS PLACE.
BUT NONE OF YOU BUDGE AN INCH!
WE'LL DEAL WITH THEM.
THIS SUMMIT'S FINALLY GETTING INTERESTING.
W-WOW ...
YOU BLOCK MY ENTON SO EFFEC-TIVELY...
...I GUESS YOUR ABSOLUTE DEFENSE IS STILL GOING STRONG.

READ THIS WAY

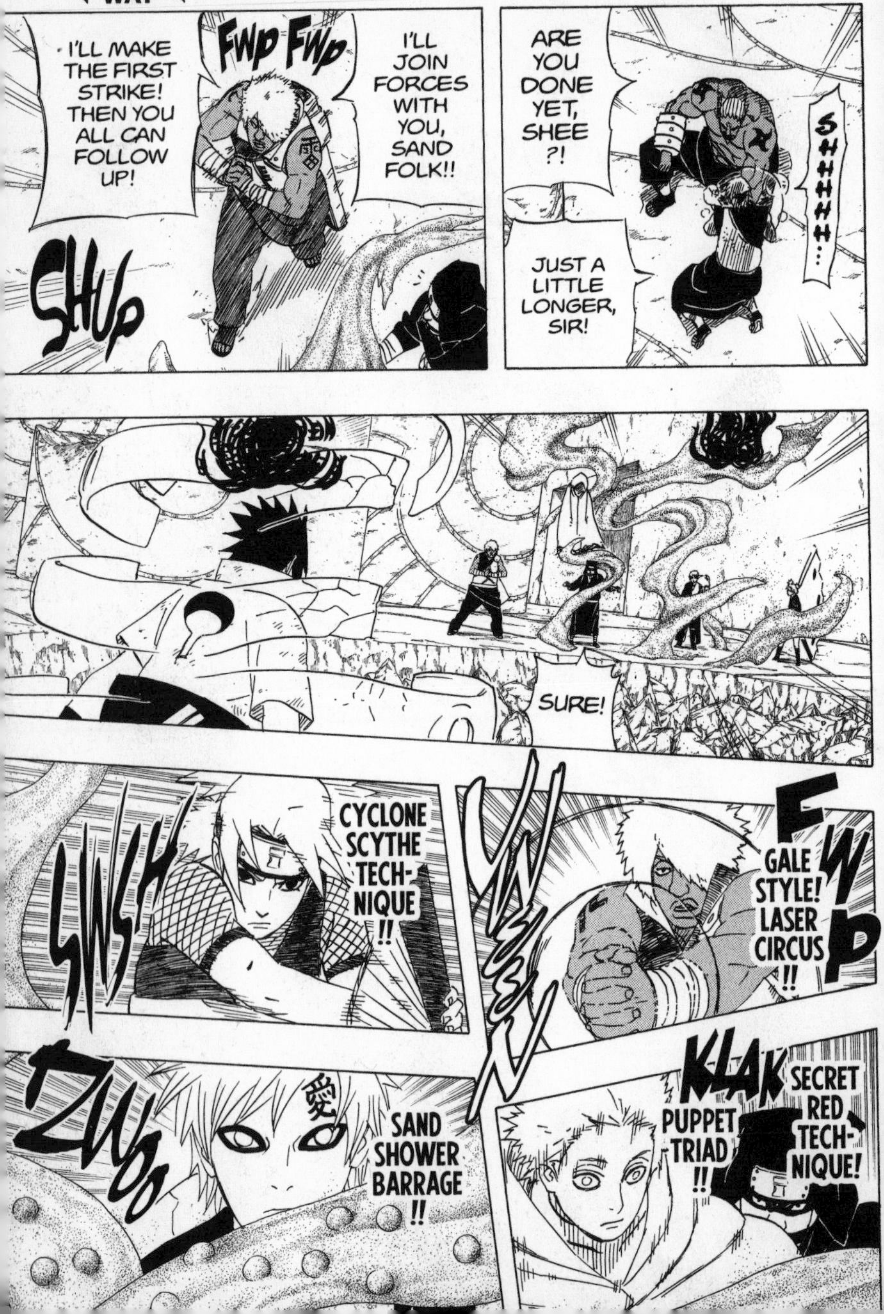
ARE YOU DONE YET, SHEE?!
SHHHHHH...
JUST A LITTLE LONGER, SIR!
I'LL JOIN FORCES WITH YOU, SAND FOLK!!
FWP FWP
I'LL MAKE THE FIRST STRIKE! THEN YOU ALL CAN FOLLOW UP!
SHUP
SURE!
FWP
GALE STYLE! LASER CIRCUS!!
CYCLONE SCYTHE TECHNIQUE!!
SWSH
SECRET RED TECHNIQUE!
KLAK
PUPPET TRIAD!!
SAND SHOWER BARRAGE!!

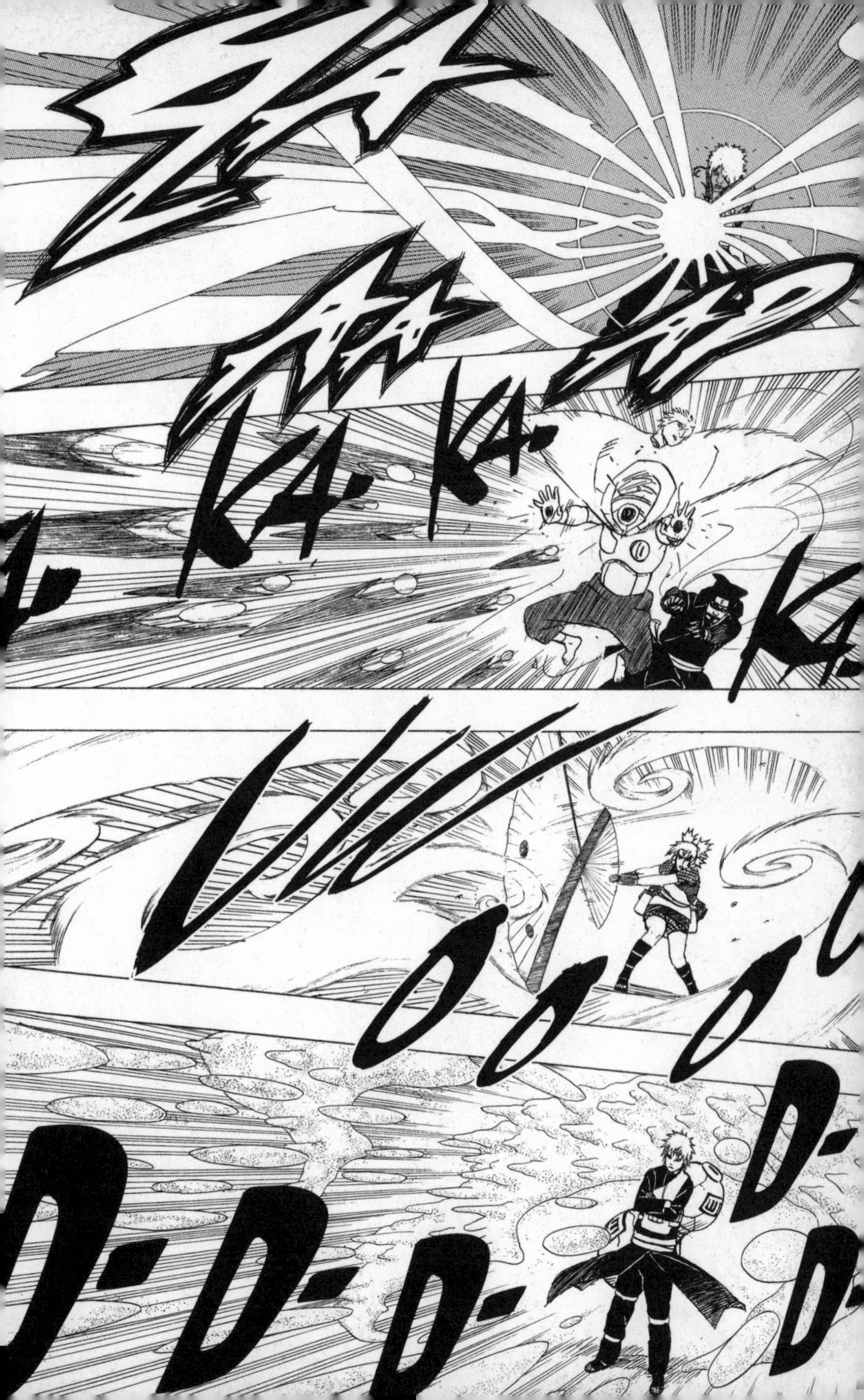
KA-KA-KA-KA-
VWOOOO
D-D-D-D-D-D-D-

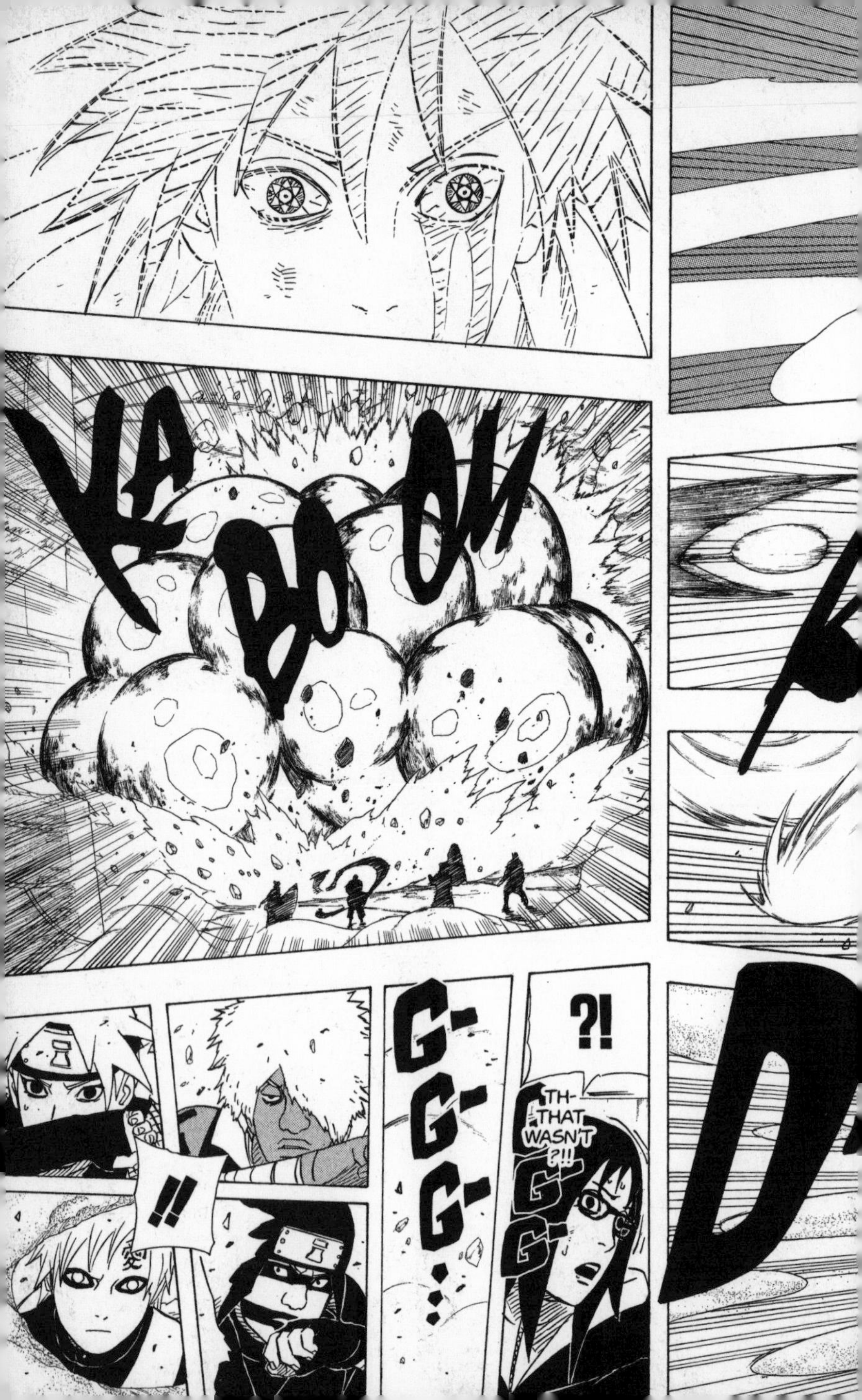

KA BO OM
?!
TH- THAT WASN'T ?!!
G- G- G-...
!!

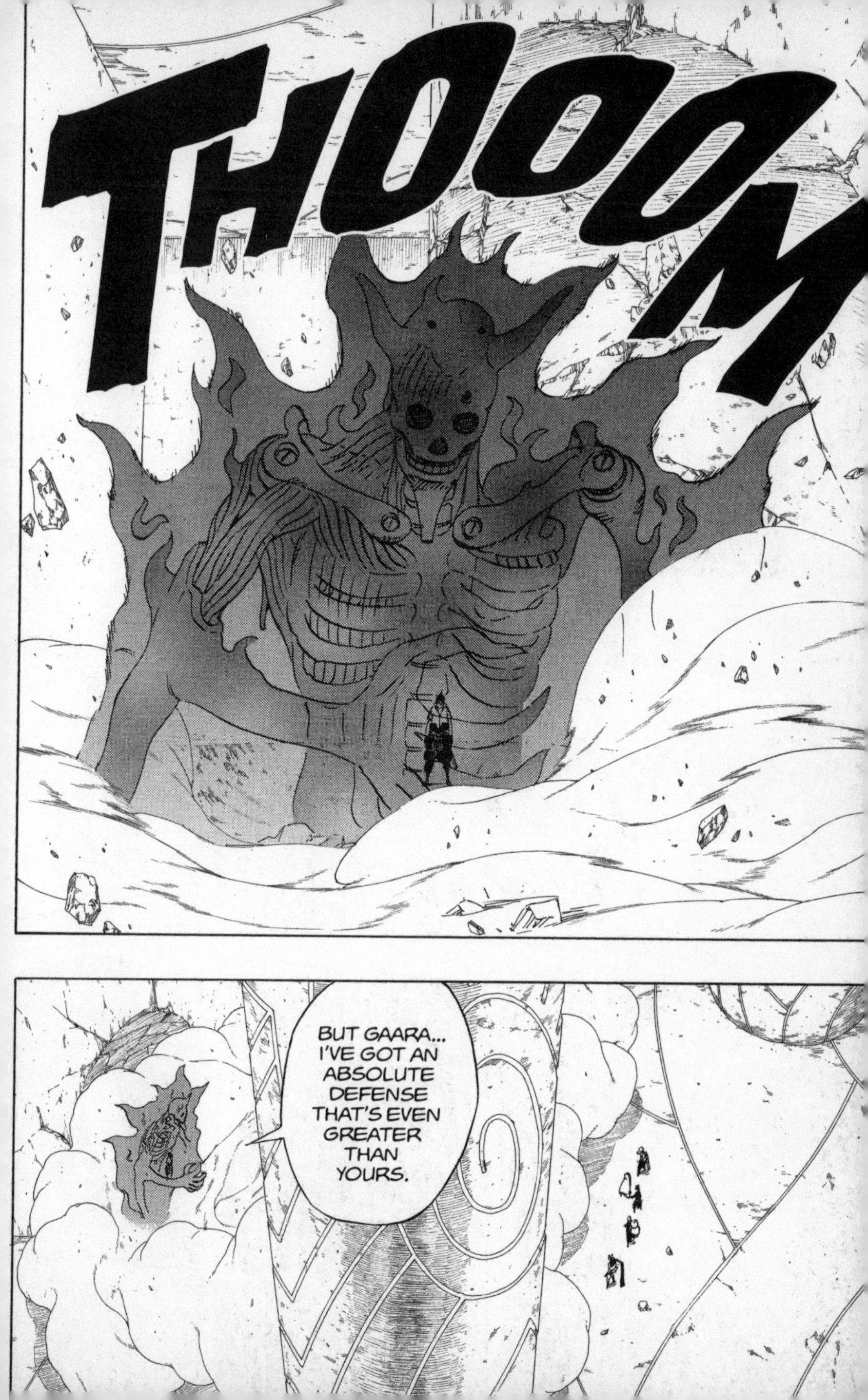
THOOOM
BUT GAARA... I'VE GOT AN ABSOLUTE DEFENSE THAT'S EVEN GREATER THAN YOURS.

READ THIS WAY

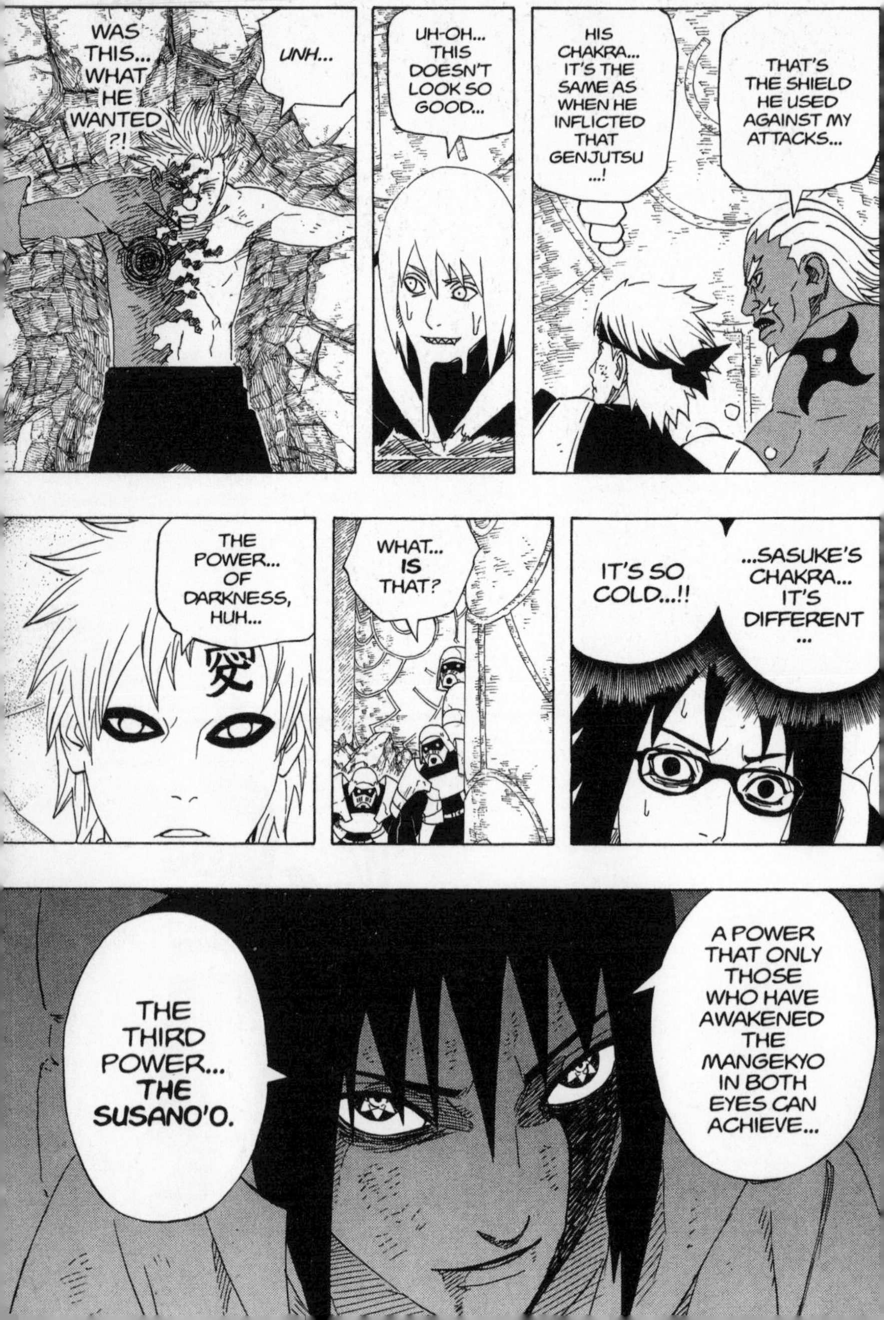
THAT'S THE SHIELD HE USED AGAINST MY ATTACKS...
HIS CHAKRA... IT'S THE SAME AS WHEN HE INFLICTED THAT GENJUTSU ...!
UH-OH... THIS DOESN'T LOOK SO GOOD...
UNH...
WAS THIS... WHAT HE WANTED ?!
...SASUKE'S CHAKRA... IT'S DIFFERENT ...
IT'S SO COLD...!!
WHAT... IS THAT?
THE POWER... OF DARKNESS, HUH...
A POWER THAT ONLY THOSE WHO HAVE AWAKENED THE MANGEKYO IN BOTH EYES CAN ACHIEVE...
THE THIRD POWER... THE SUSANO'O.

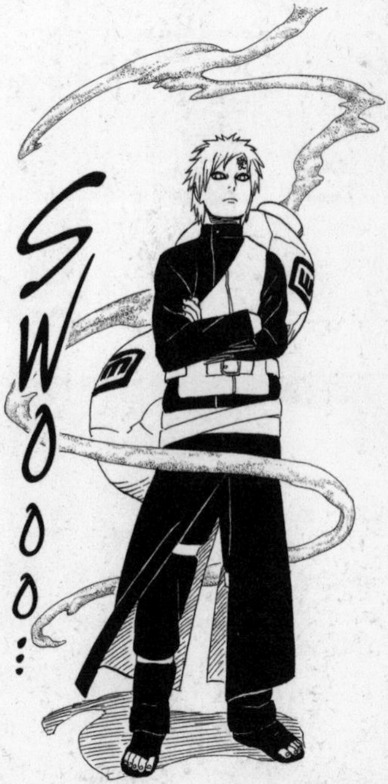
SWOOO...

Number 465: The Summit Hall Attacked!

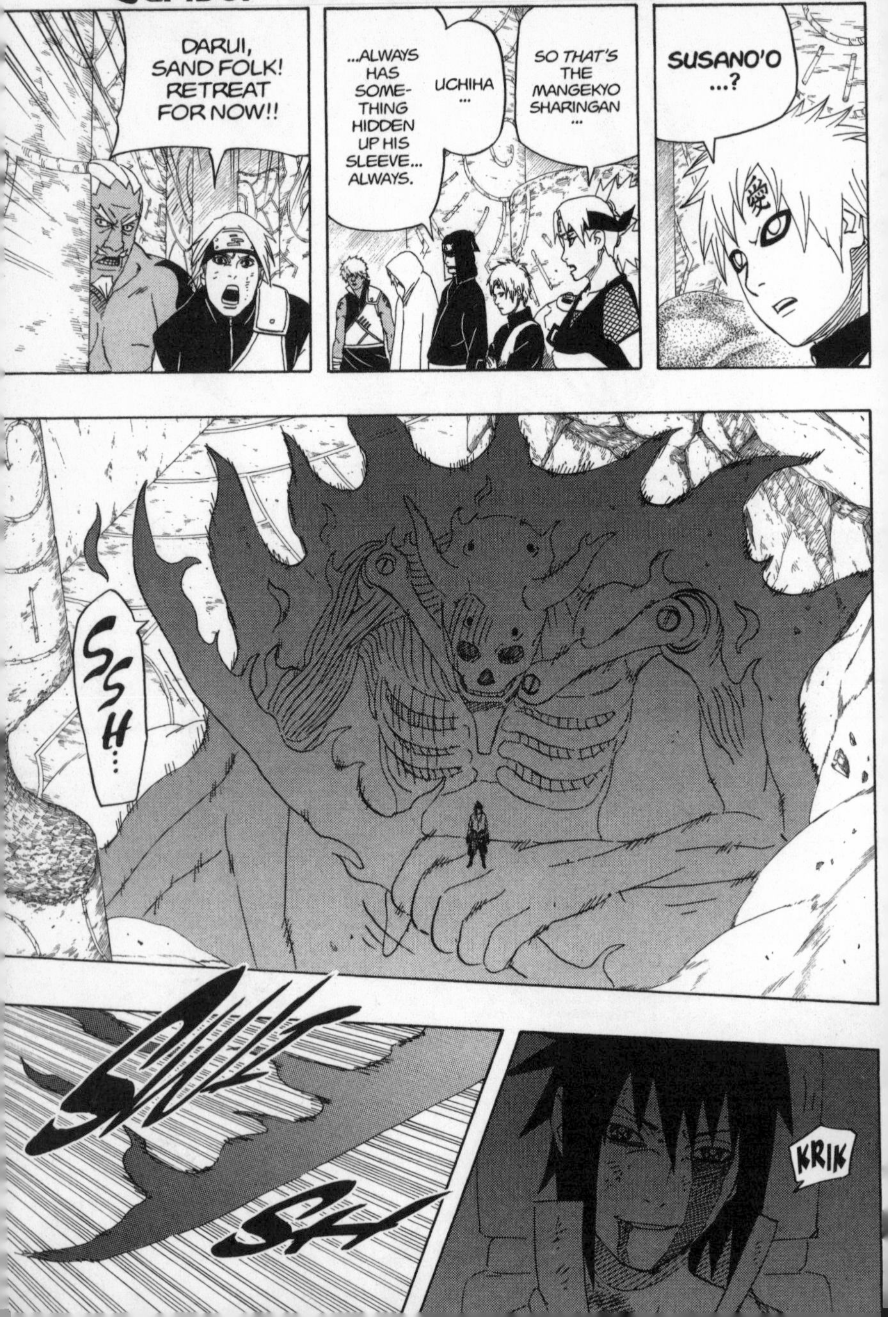
SUSANO'O ...?
SO THAT'S THE MANGEKYO SHARINGAN ...
UCHIHA ...
...ALWAYS HAS SOMETHING HIDDEN UP HIS SLEEVE... ALWAYS.
DARUI, SAND FOLK! RETREAT FOR NOW!!
SSH...
KRIK
SH

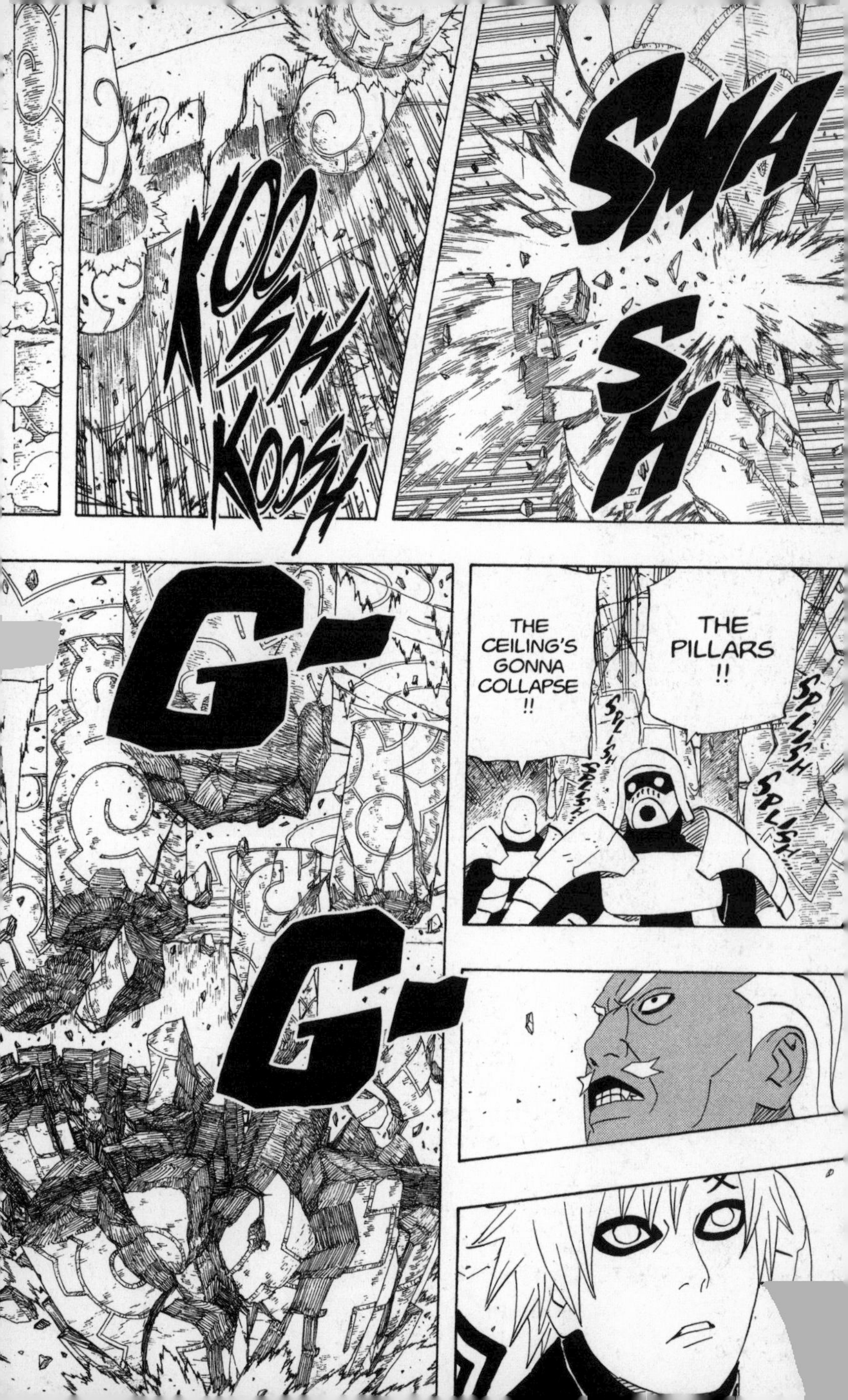
SMASH
KOOSH KOOSH
THE PILLARS !!
THE CEILING'S GONNA COLLAPSE !!
SPLISH SPLISH...
SPLISH SPLISH...
G-G-

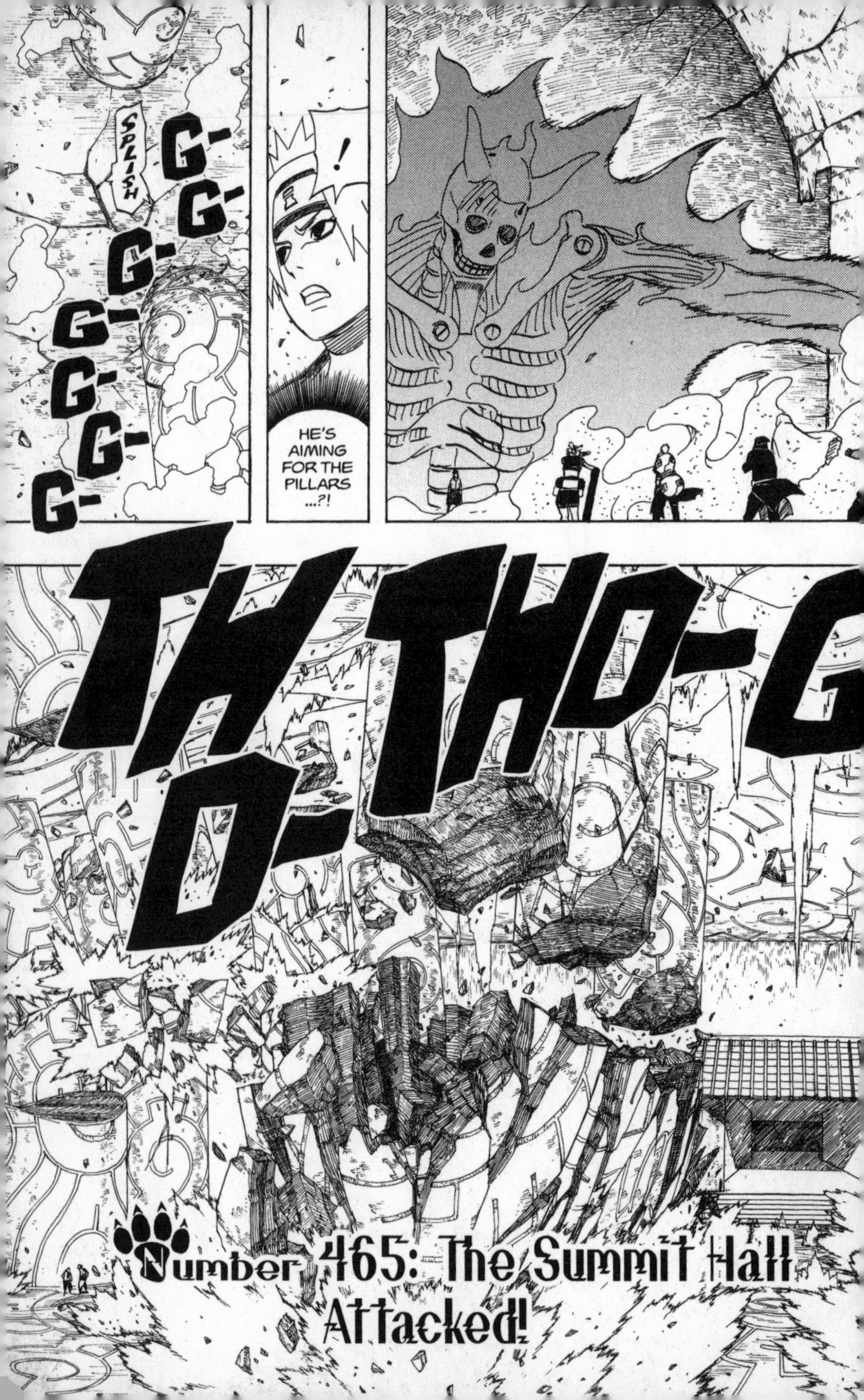

!
HE'S AIMING FOR THE PILLARS ...?!
SPLISH
G-G-G-G-G-G-G-G-
TH-THD-G
D-
Number 465: The Summit Hall Attacked!

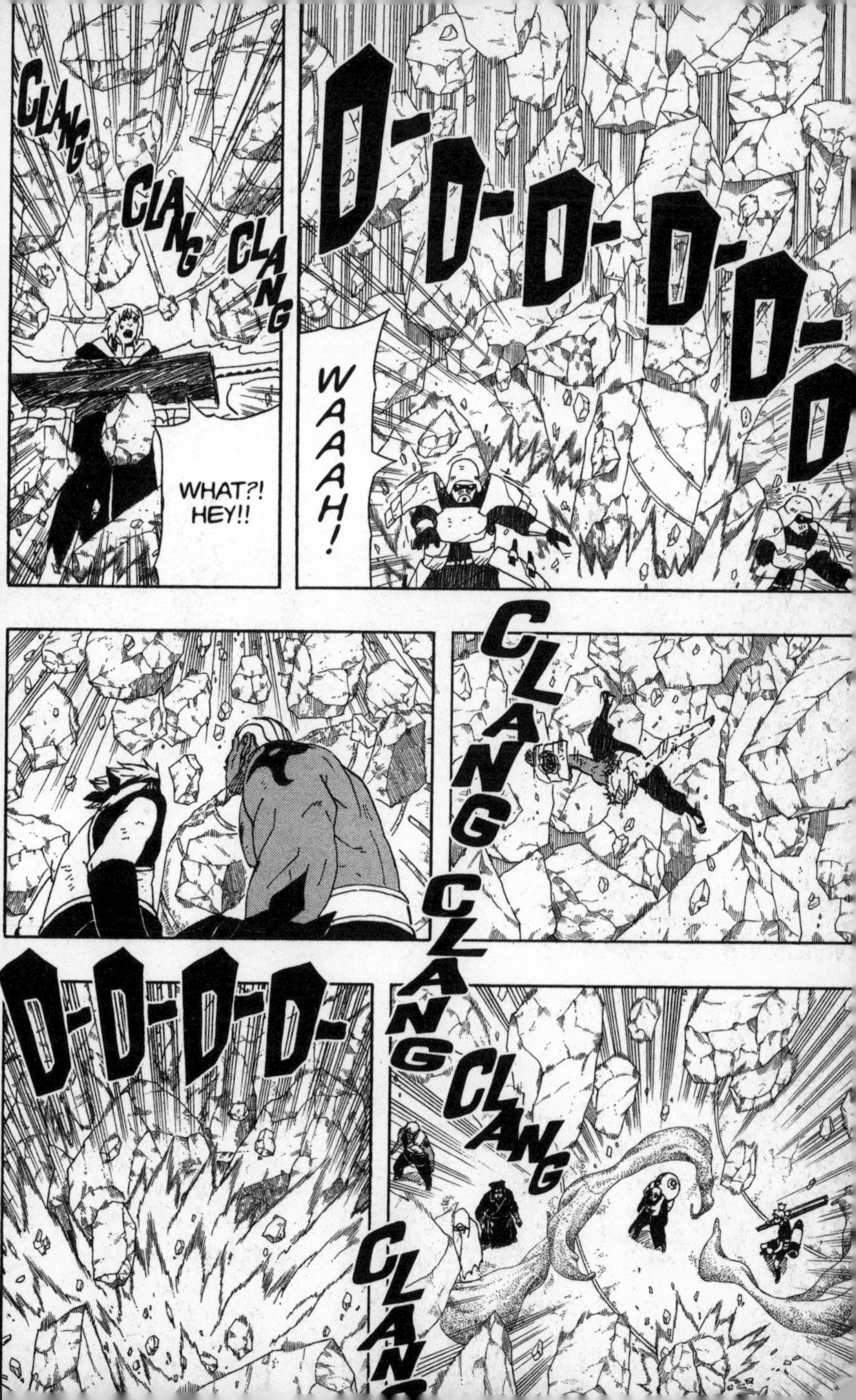
D-D-D-D-D-D-D
WAAAAH!
CLANG
CLANG
CLANG
WHAT?! HEY!!
CLANG
CLANG
CLANG
D-D-D-D-

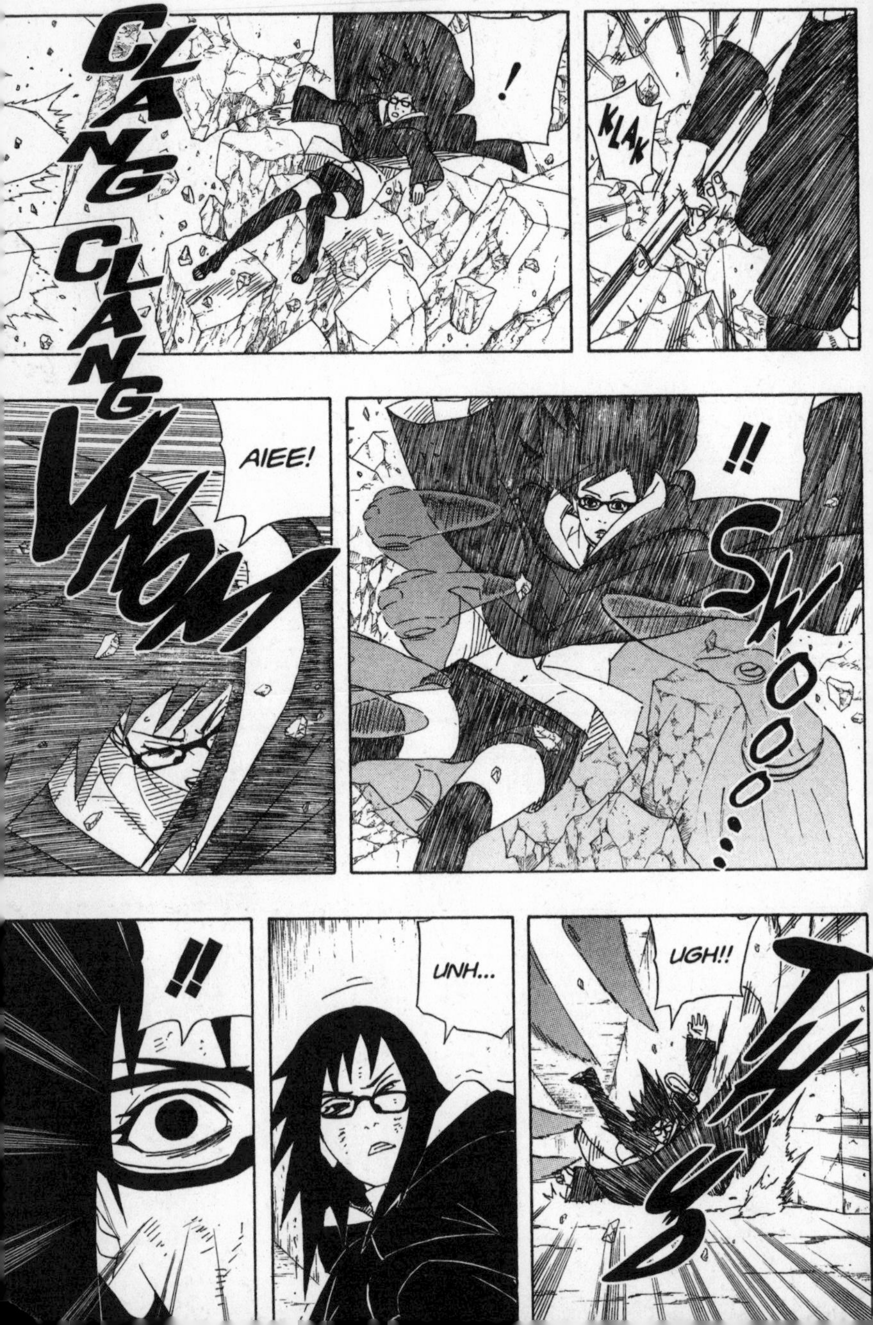
KLAK
!
CLANG
CLANG
CLANG
!!
SWOOO...
AIEE!
VWOM
UGH!!
UNH...
!!

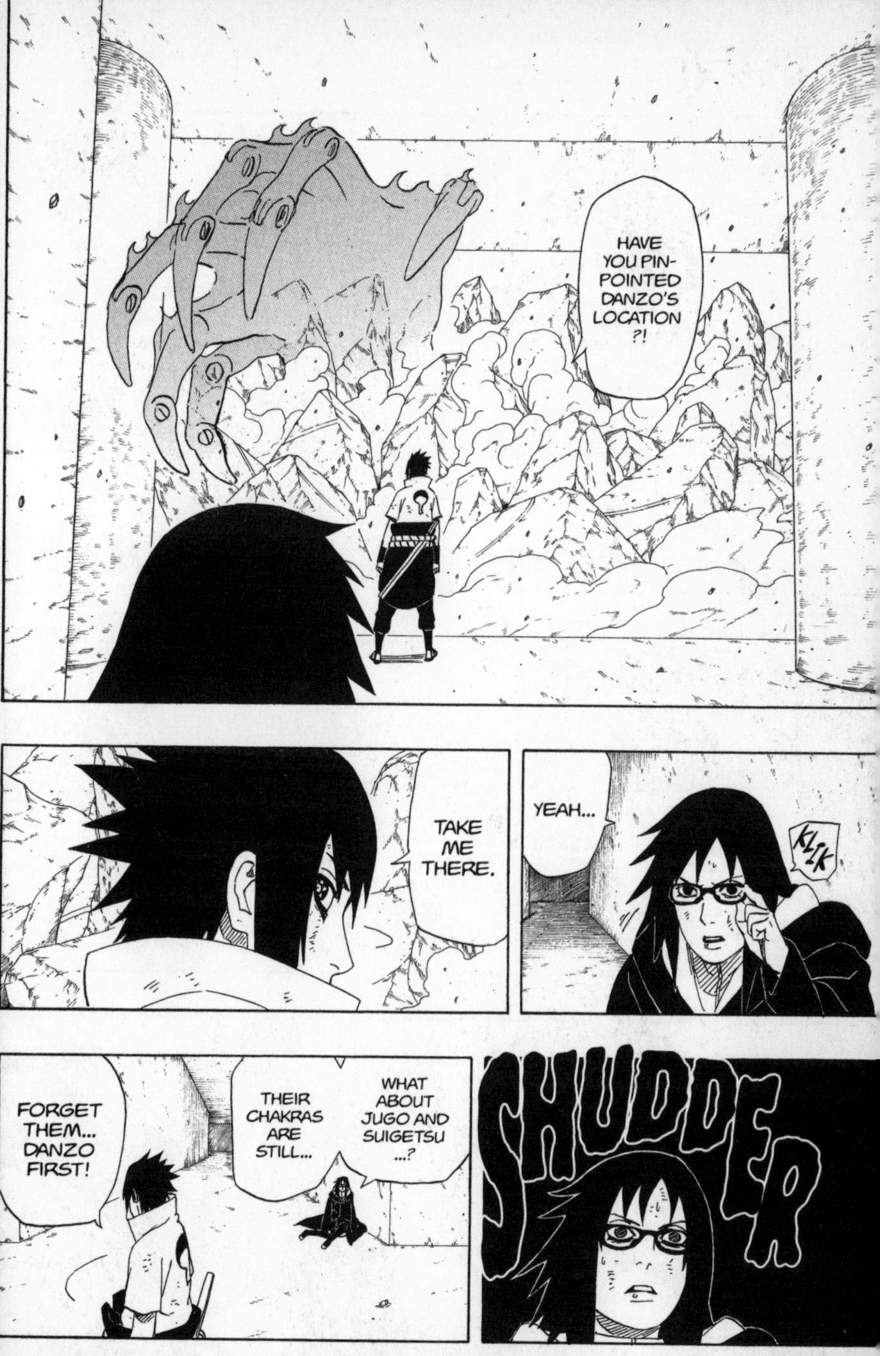
HAVE YOU PIN-POINTED DANZO'S LOCATION ?!
YEAH...
KLIK
TAKE ME THERE.
SHUDDER
WHAT ABOUT JUGO AND SUIGETSU ...?
THEIR CHAKRAS ARE STILL...
FORGET THEM... DANZO FIRST!

READ THIS WAY

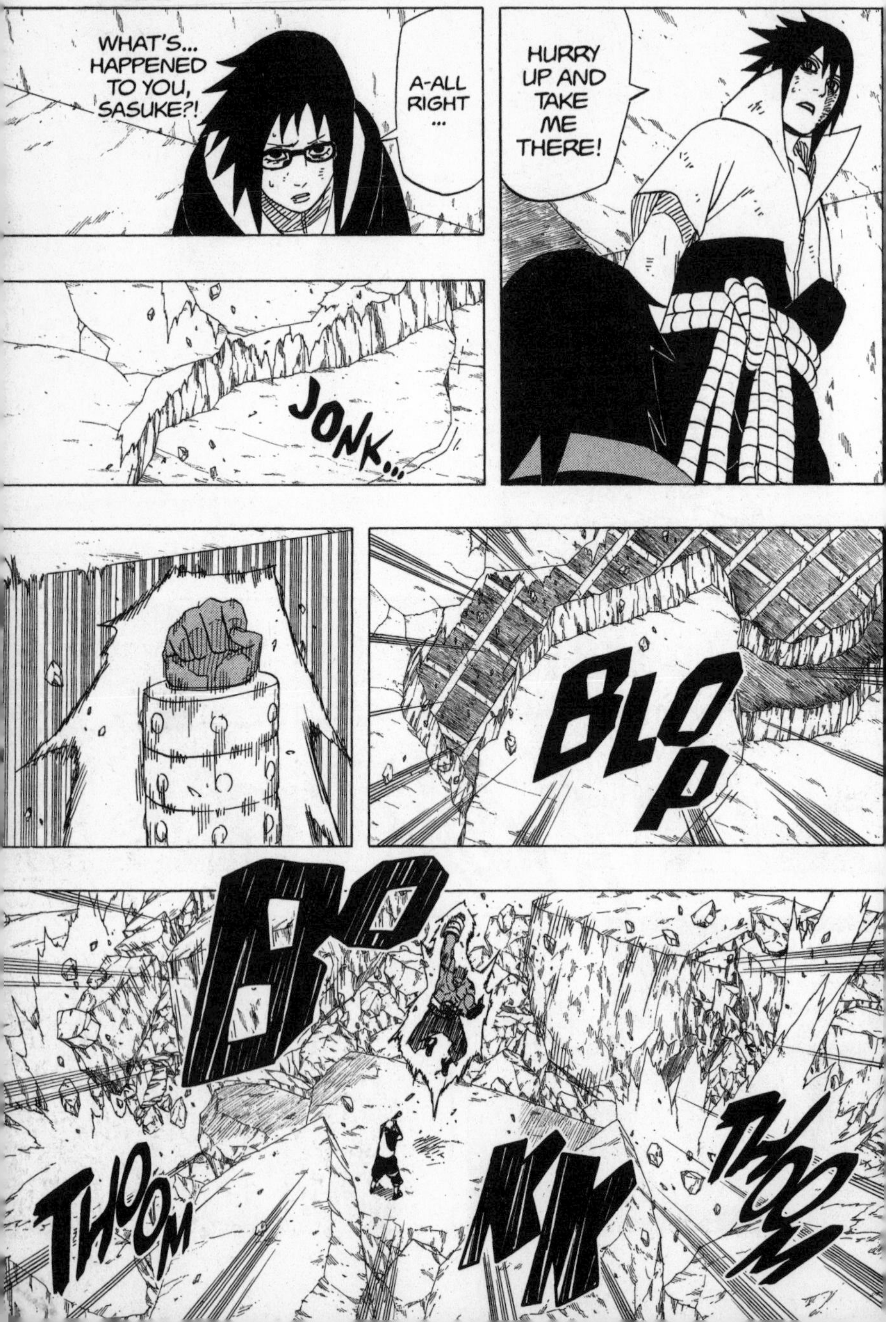
HURRY UP AND TAKE ME THERE!
A-ALL RIGHT ...
WHAT'S... HAPPENED TO YOU, SASUKE?!
JONK...
BLOP
BO
THOOM
KNK
THOOM

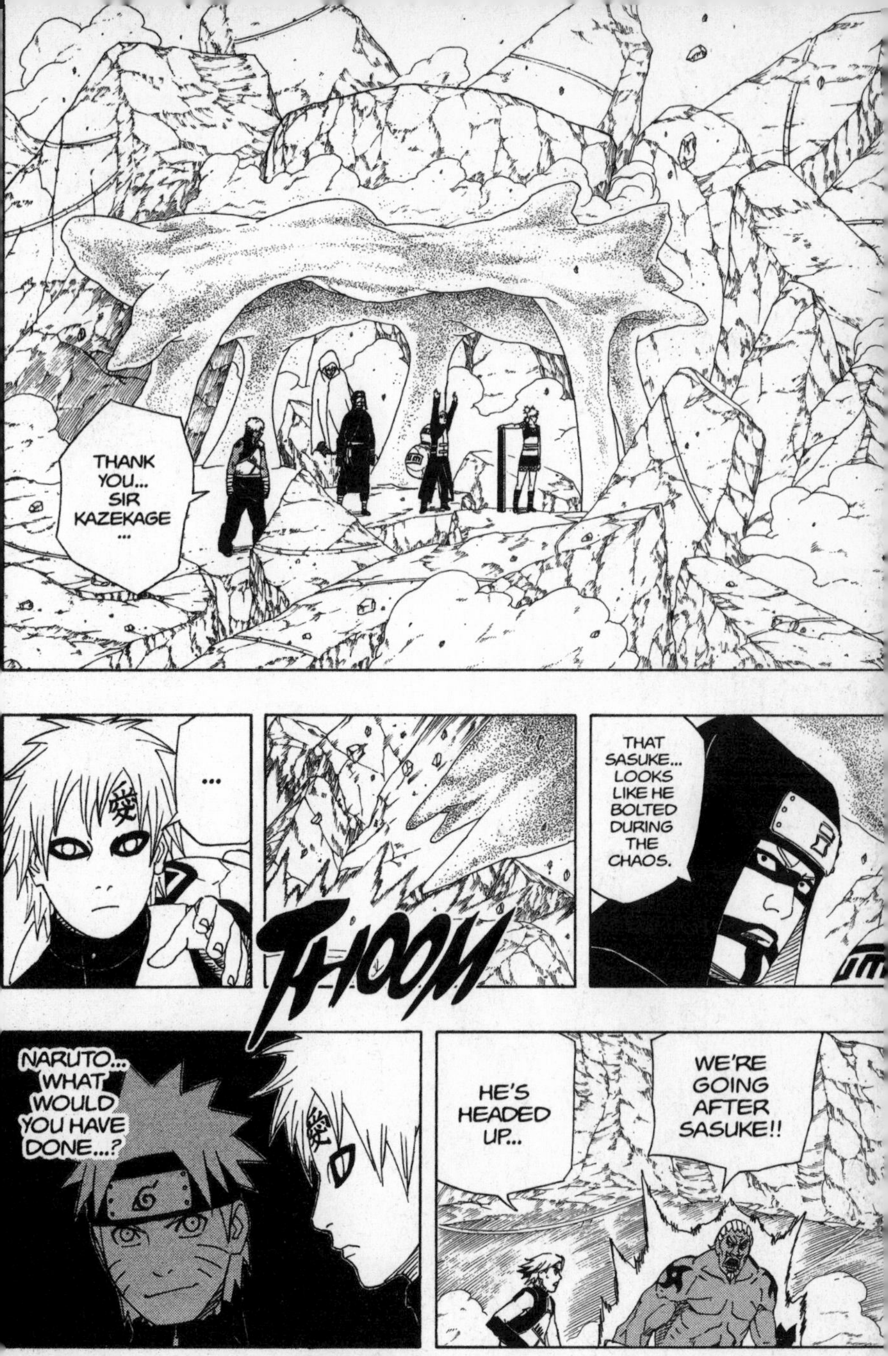
THANK YOU... SIR KAZEKAGE ...
THAT SASUKE... LOOKS LIKE HE BOLTED DURING THE CHAOS.
THOOM
...
WE'RE GOING AFTER SASUKE!!
HE'S HEADED UP...
NARUTO... WHAT WOULD YOU HAVE DONE...?

READ THIS WAY

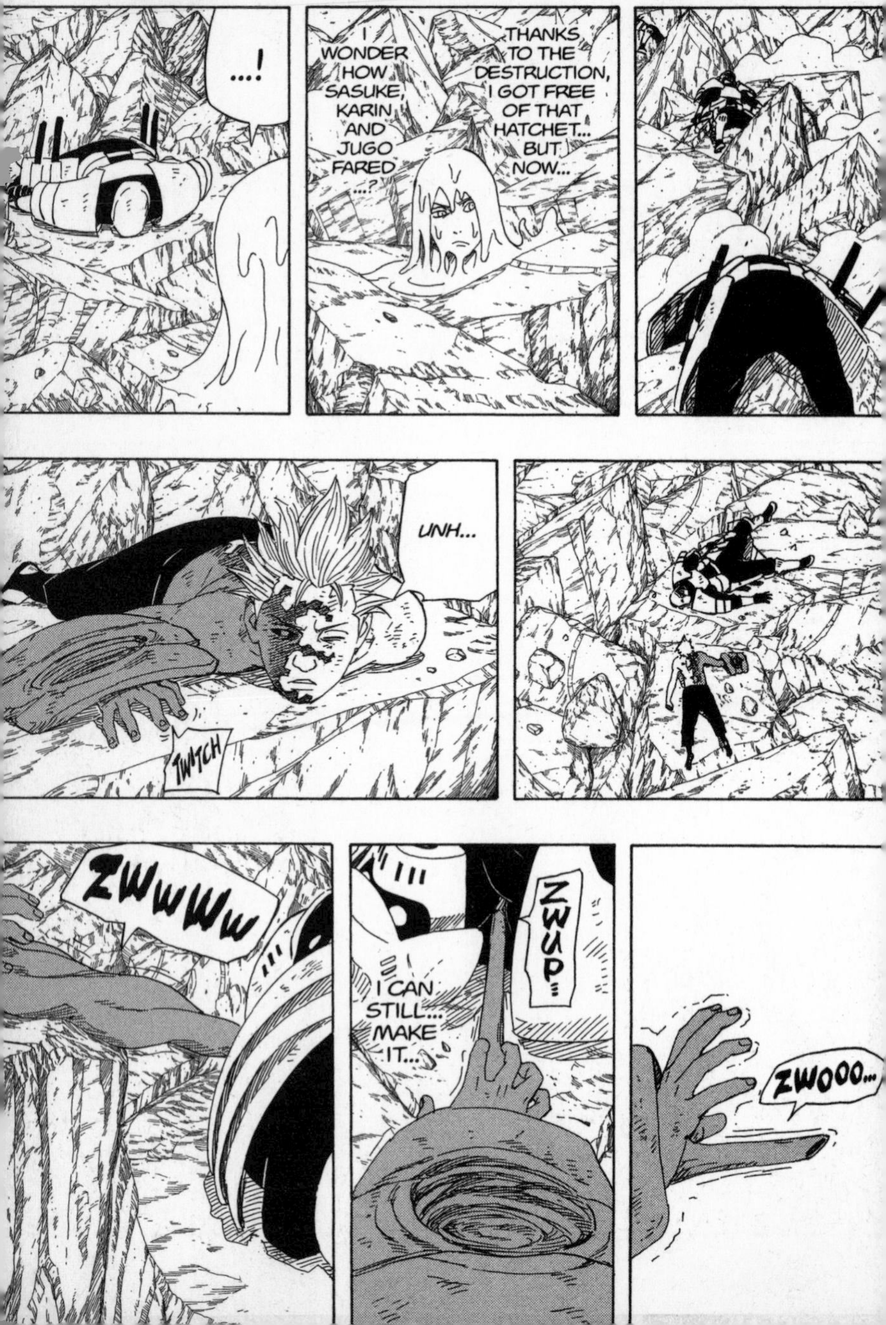
THANKS TO THE DESTRUCTION, I GOT FREE OF THAT HATCHET... BUT NOW...
I WONDER HOW SASUKE, KARIN AND JUGO FARED...?
...!
UNH...
TWITCH
ZWOOO...
ZWUP...
I CAN STILL... MAKE IT...
ZWWWW

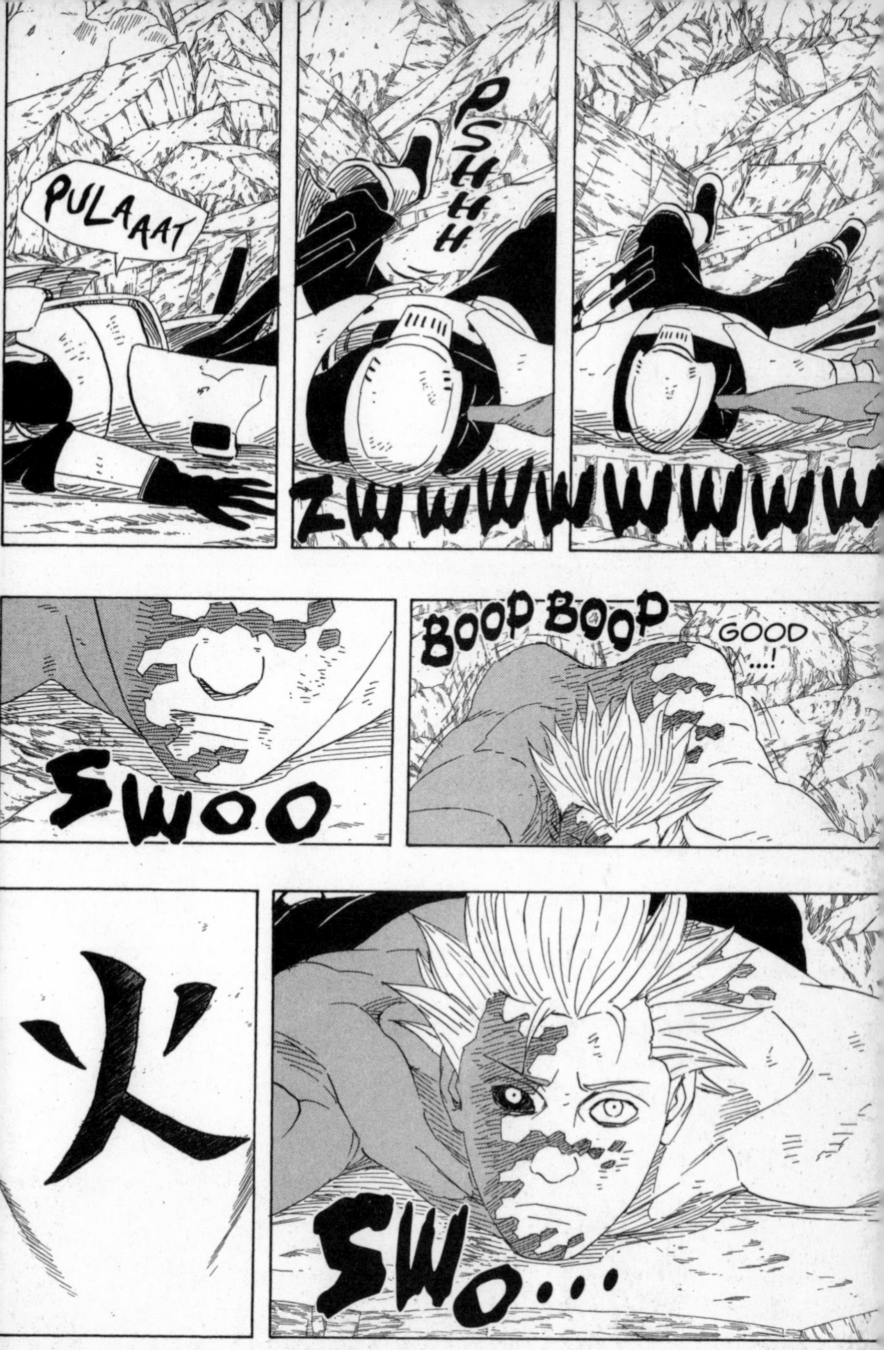
ZWWWWWWWWW
PSHHH
PULAAAT
BOOP BOOP
GOOD ...!
SWOO
SWO...
火

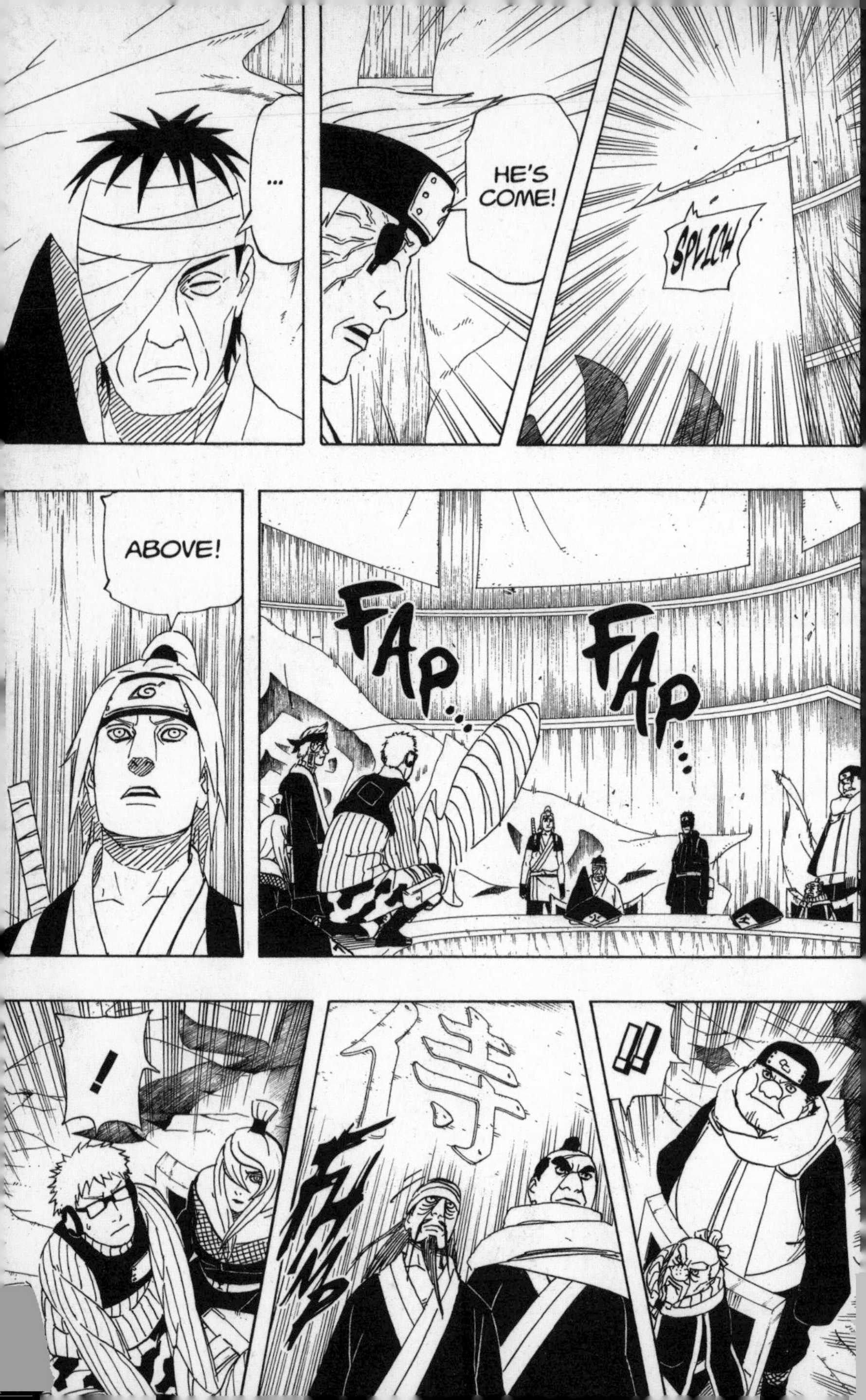
SPLICH
HE'S COME!
...
FAP...
FAP...
ABOVE!
!!
侍
!

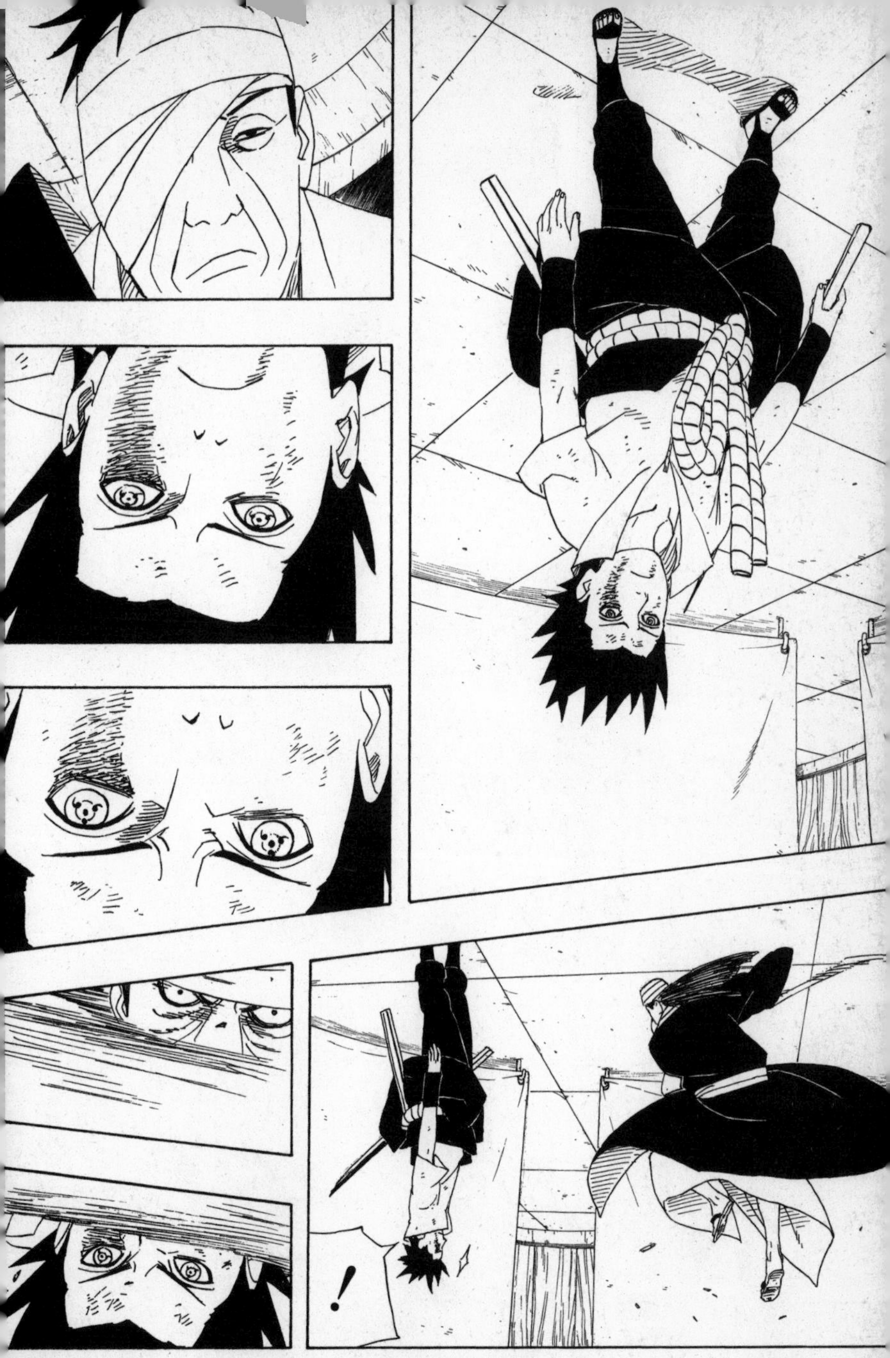
!

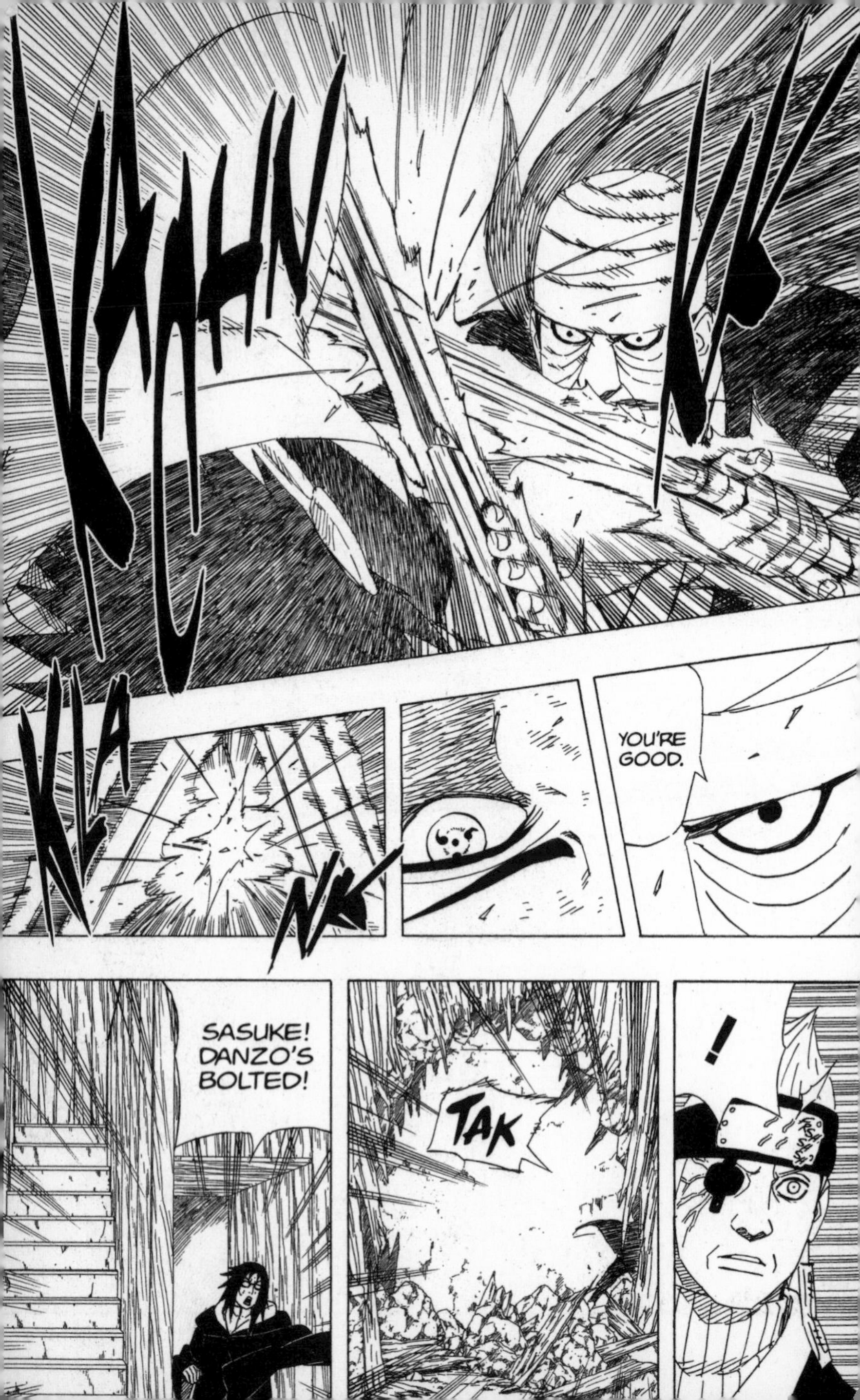
KACHIN
YOU'RE GOOD.
KLANK
!
TAK
SASUKE! DANZO'S BOLTED!

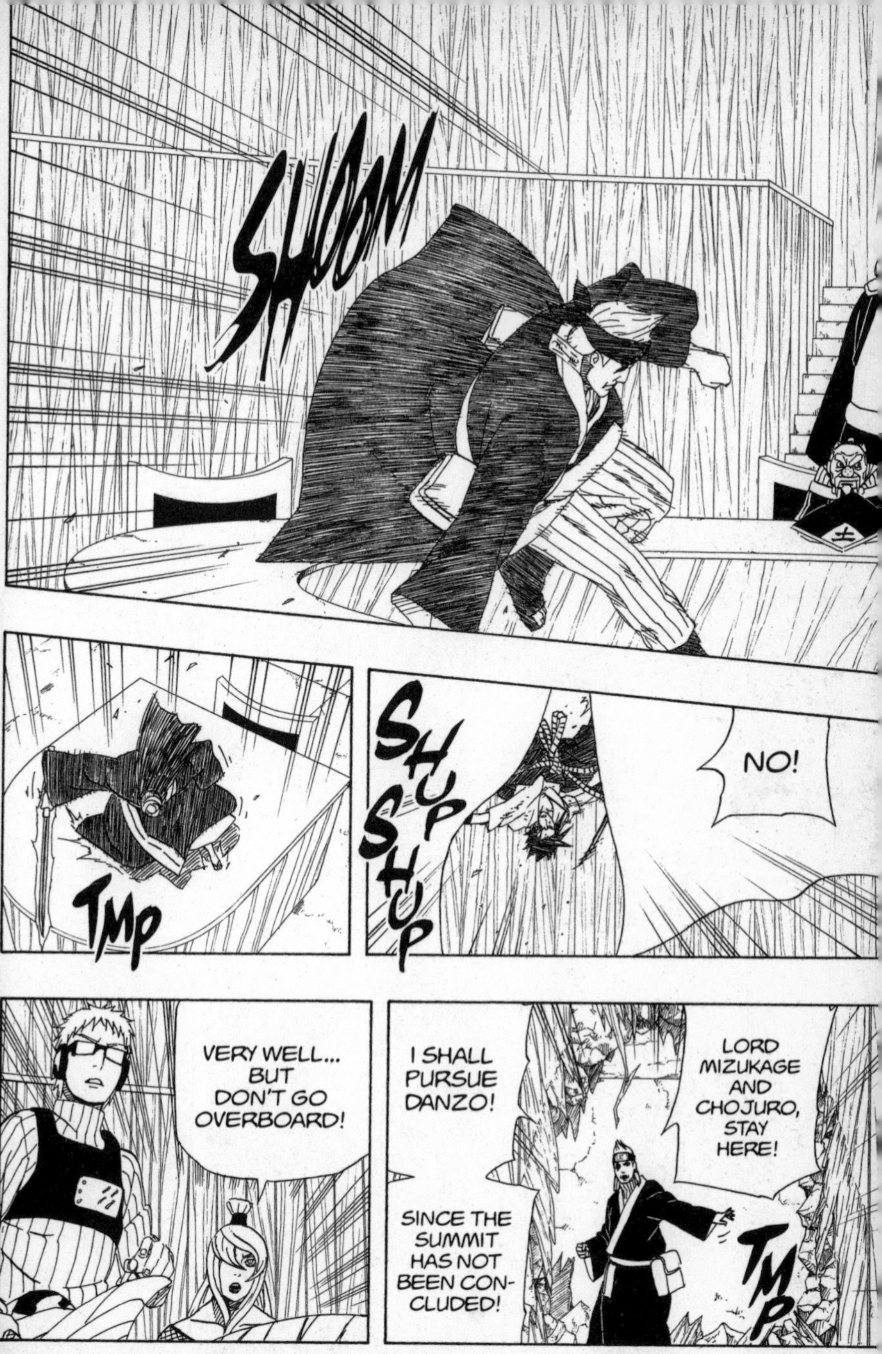
SHOOM
NO!
SHUP SHUP SHUP
TMP
LORD MIZUKAGE AND CHOJURO, STAY HERE!
I SHALL PURSUE DANZO!
SINCE THE SUMMIT HAS NOT BEEN CON-CLUDED!
TMP
VERY WELL... BUT DON'T GO OVERBOARD!

READ THIS WAY

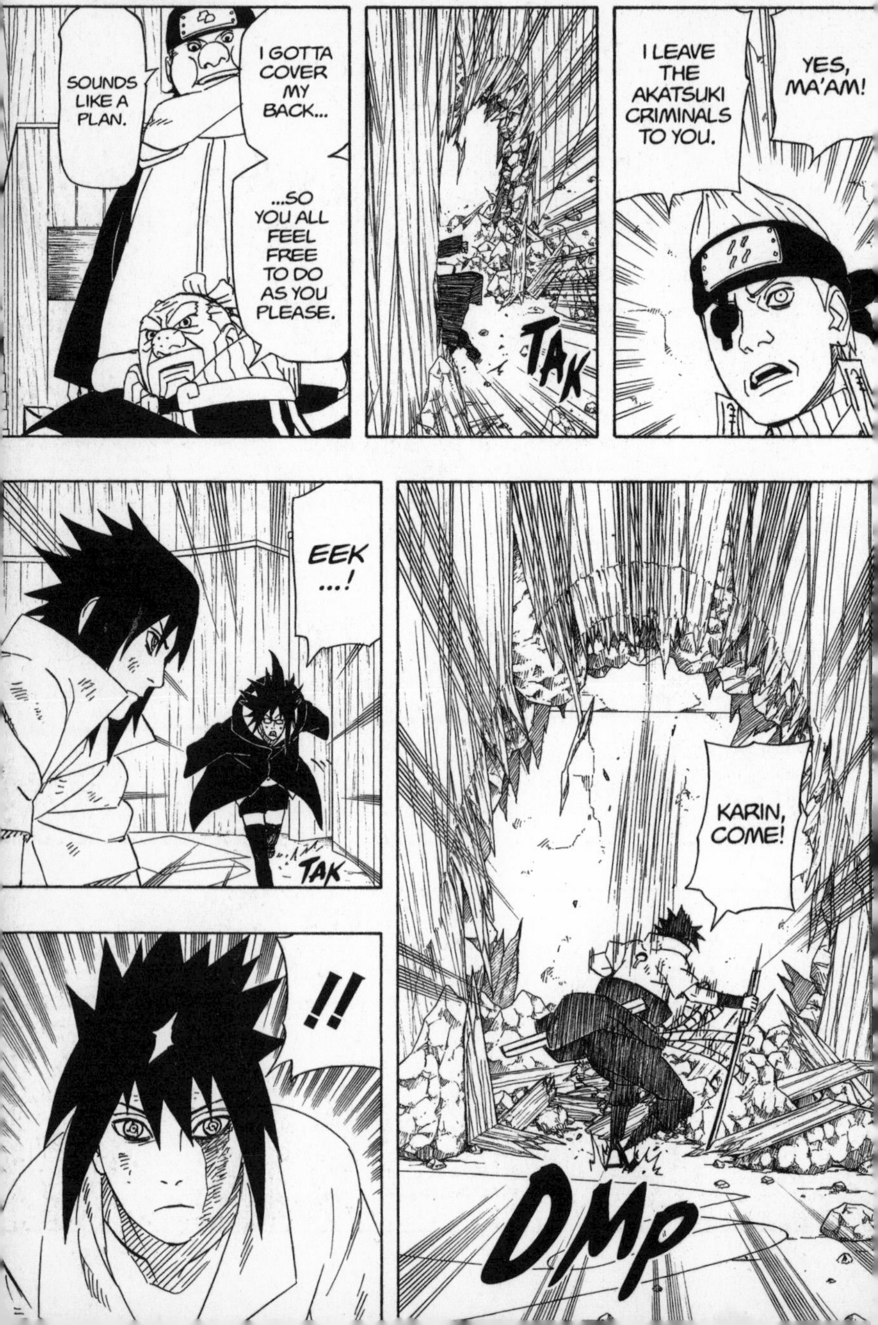
I LEAVE THE AKATSUKI CRIMINALS TO YOU.
YES, MA'AM!
TAK
I GOTTA COVER MY BACK...
...SO YOU ALL FEEL FREE TO DO AS YOU PLEASE.
SOUNDS LIKE A PLAN.
KARIN, COME!
DMP
EEK ...!
TAK
!!

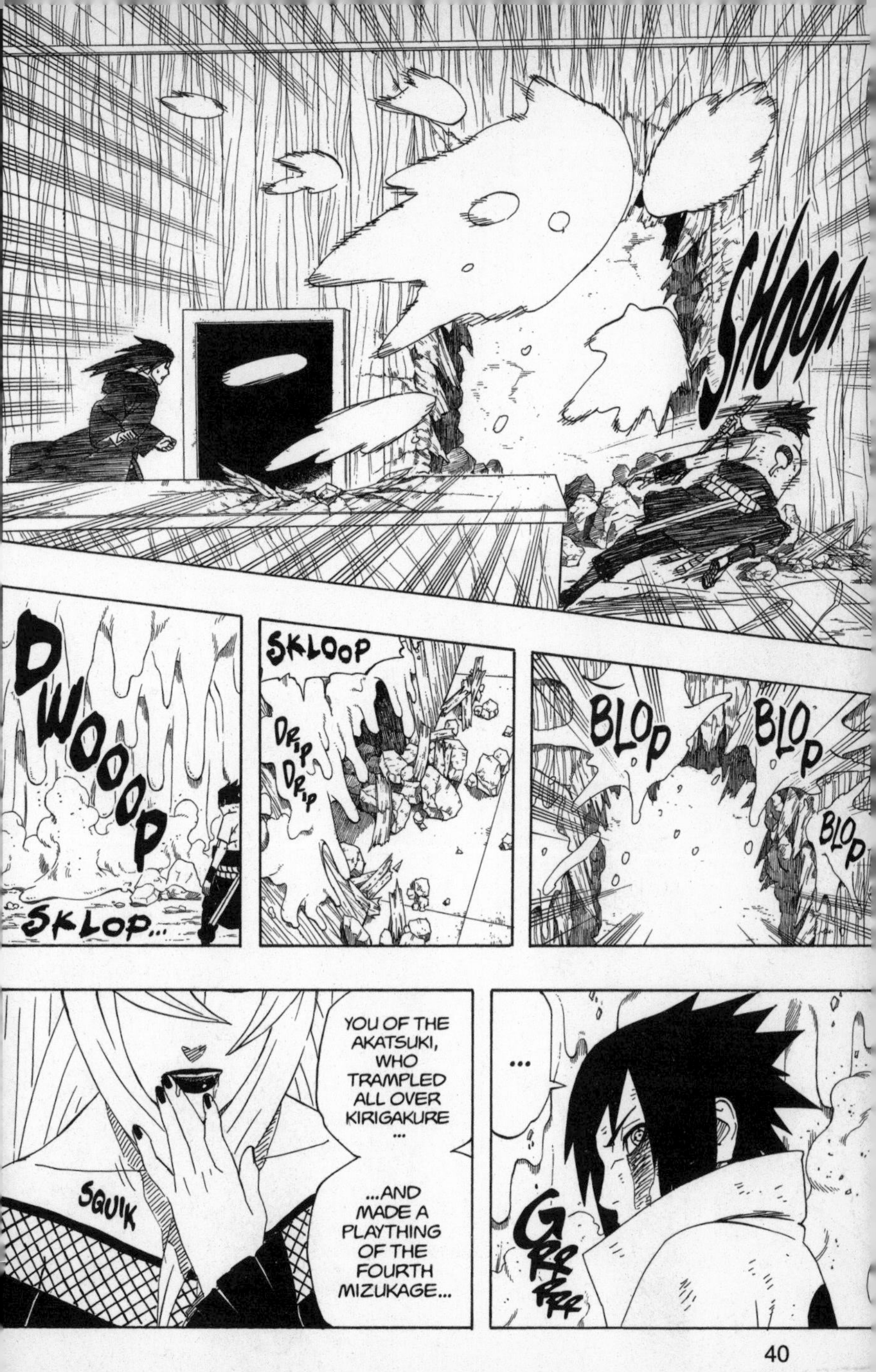
SHOOM
BLOP
BLOP
BLOP
SKLOOP
DRIP DRIP
DWOOOP
SKLOP...
...
GRRRR
YOU OF THE AKATSUKI, WHO TRAMPLED ALL OVER KIRIGAKURE ...
...AND MADE A PLAYTHING OF THE FOURTH MIZUKAGE...
SQUIK

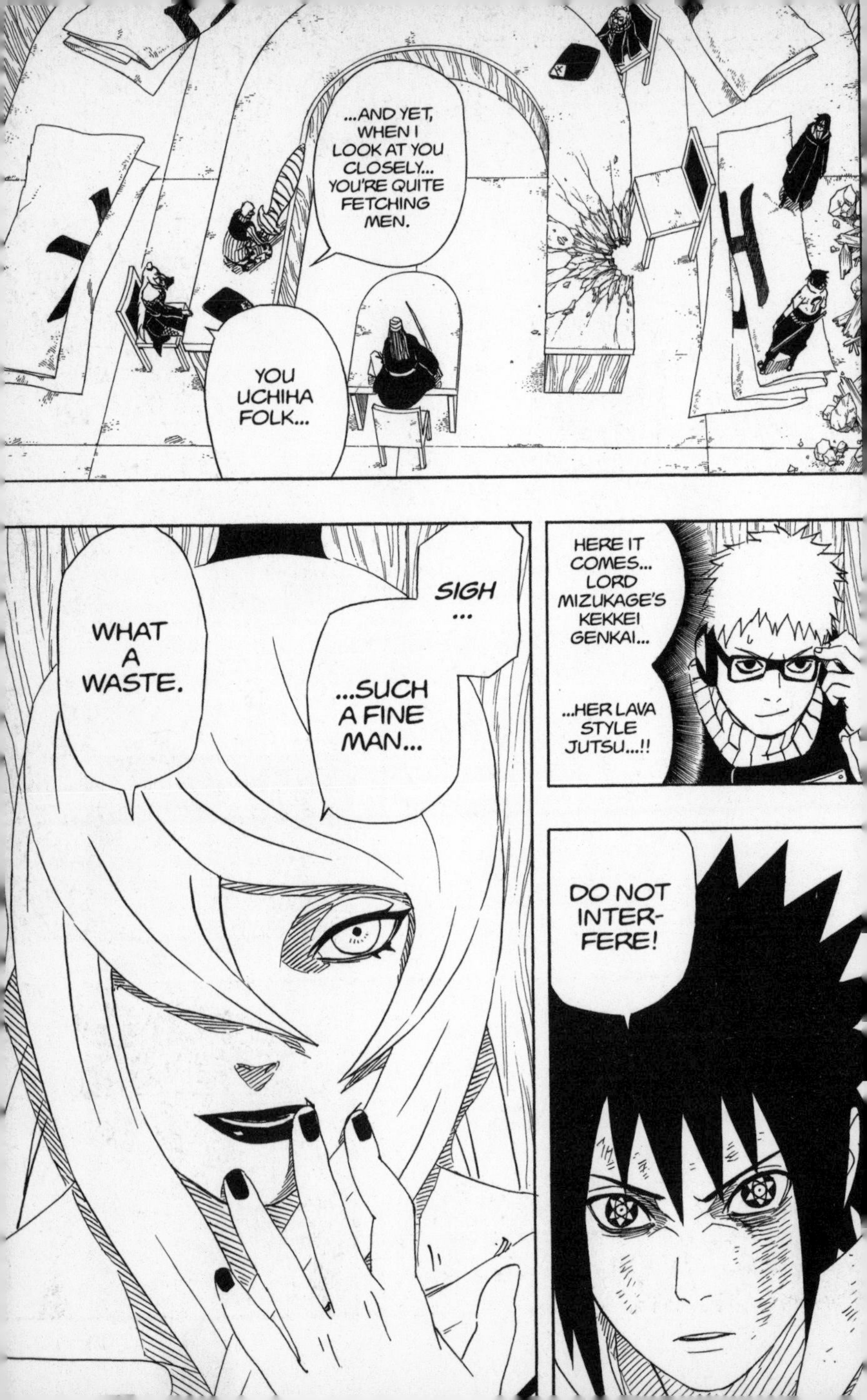
...AND YET, WHEN I LOOK AT YOU CLOSELY... YOU'RE QUITE FETCHING MEN.
YOU UCHIHA FOLK...
HERE IT COMES... LORD MIZUKAGE'S KEKKEI GENKAI...
...HER LAVA STYLE JUTSU...!!
DO NOT INTER-FERE!
SIGH ...
...SUCH A FINE MAN...
WHAT A WASTE.

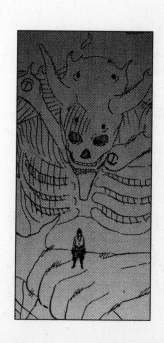

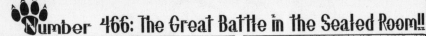

Number 466: The Great Battle in the Sealed Room!!

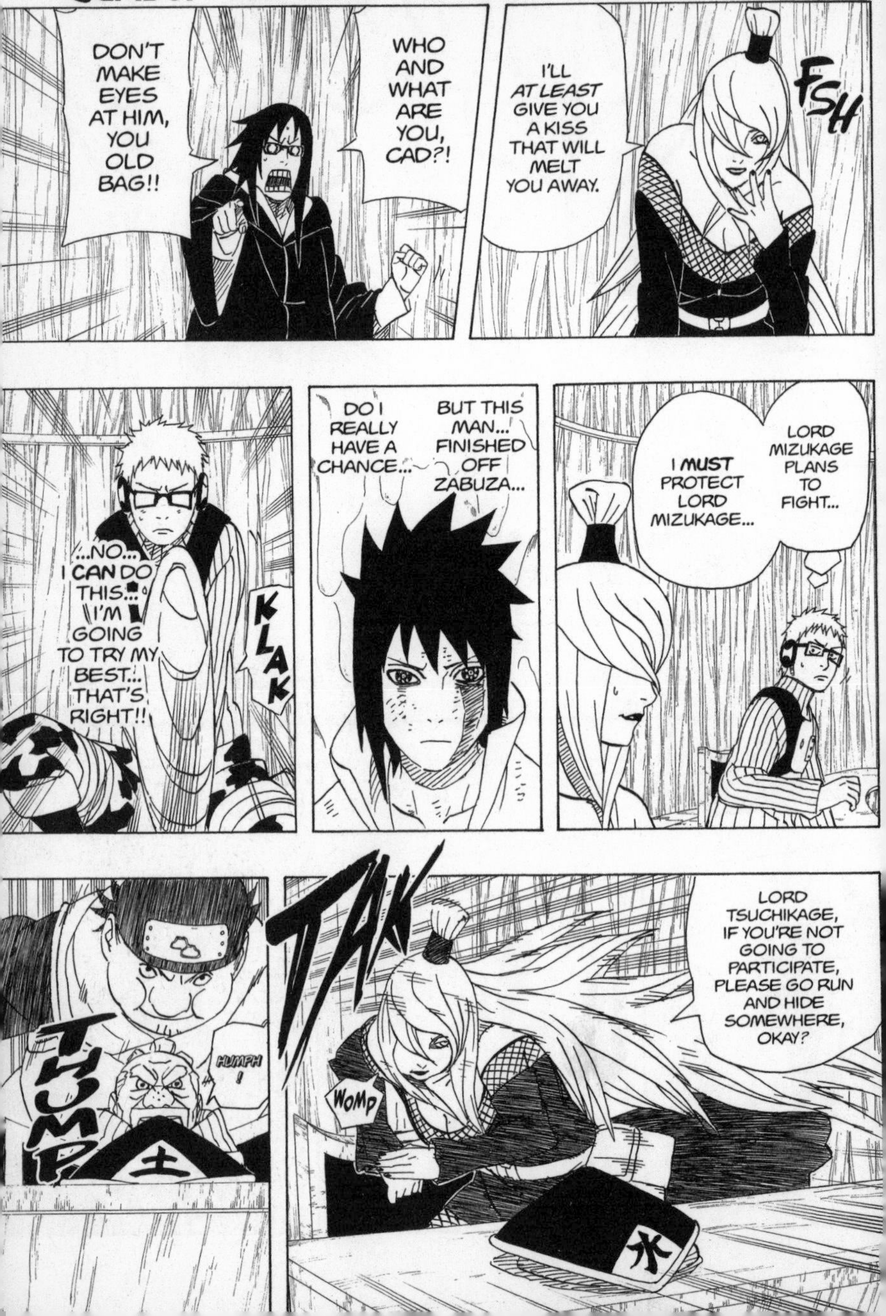
I'LL AT LEAST GIVE YOU A KISS THAT WILL MELT YOU AWAY.
FSH
WHO AND WHAT ARE YOU, CAD?!
DON'T MAKE EYES AT HIM, YOU OLD BAG!!
LORD MIZUKAGE PLANS TO FIGHT...
I MUST PROTECT LORD MIZUKAGE...
BUT THIS MAN... FINISHED OFF ZABUZA...
DO I REALLY HAVE A CHANCE...
...NO... I CAN DO THIS... I'M GOING TO TRY MY BEST... THAT'S RIGHT!!
KLAK
TAK
LORD TSUCHIKAGE, IF YOU'RE NOT GOING TO PARTICIPATE, PLEASE GO RUN AND HIDE SOMEWHERE, OKAY?
WOMP
HUMPH!
THUMP

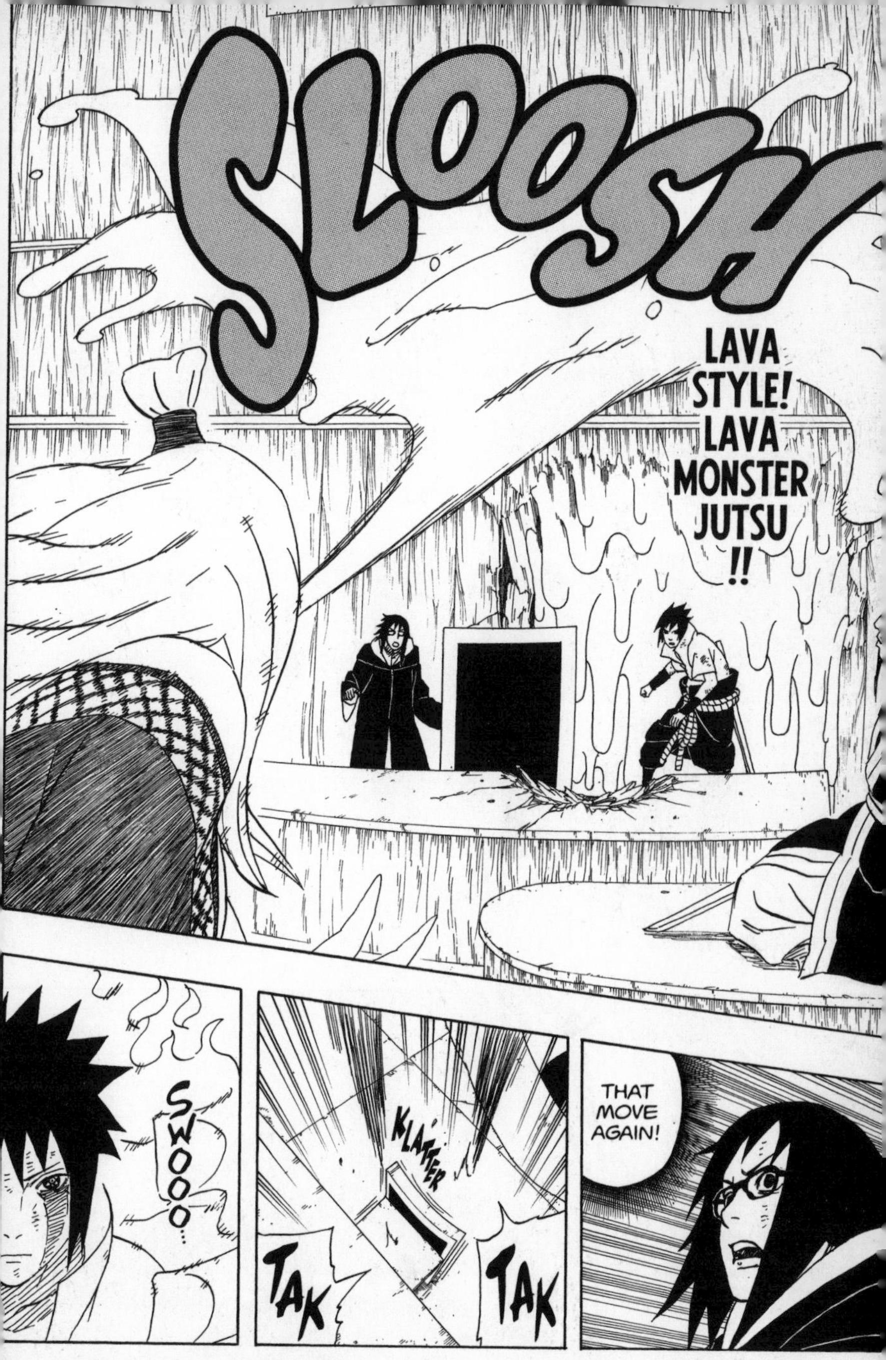
SLOOSH
LAVA STYLE! LAVA MONSTER JUTSU!!
THAT MOVE AGAIN!
KLATTER
TAK
TAK
SWOOOO...

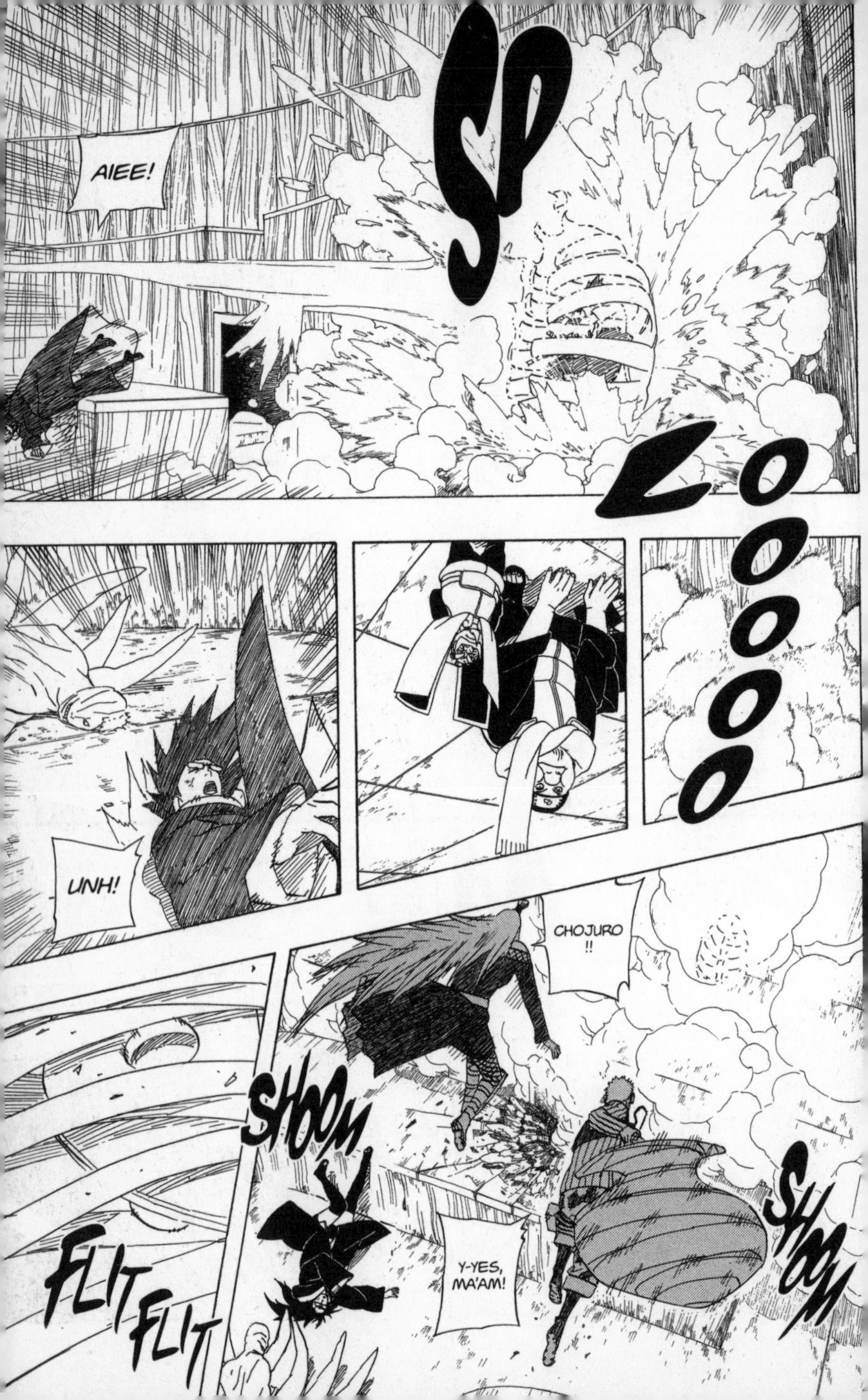
SPLOOOOOO
AIEE!
UNH!
CHOJURO !!
SHOOM
Y-YES, MA'AM!
SHOOM
FLIT FLIT

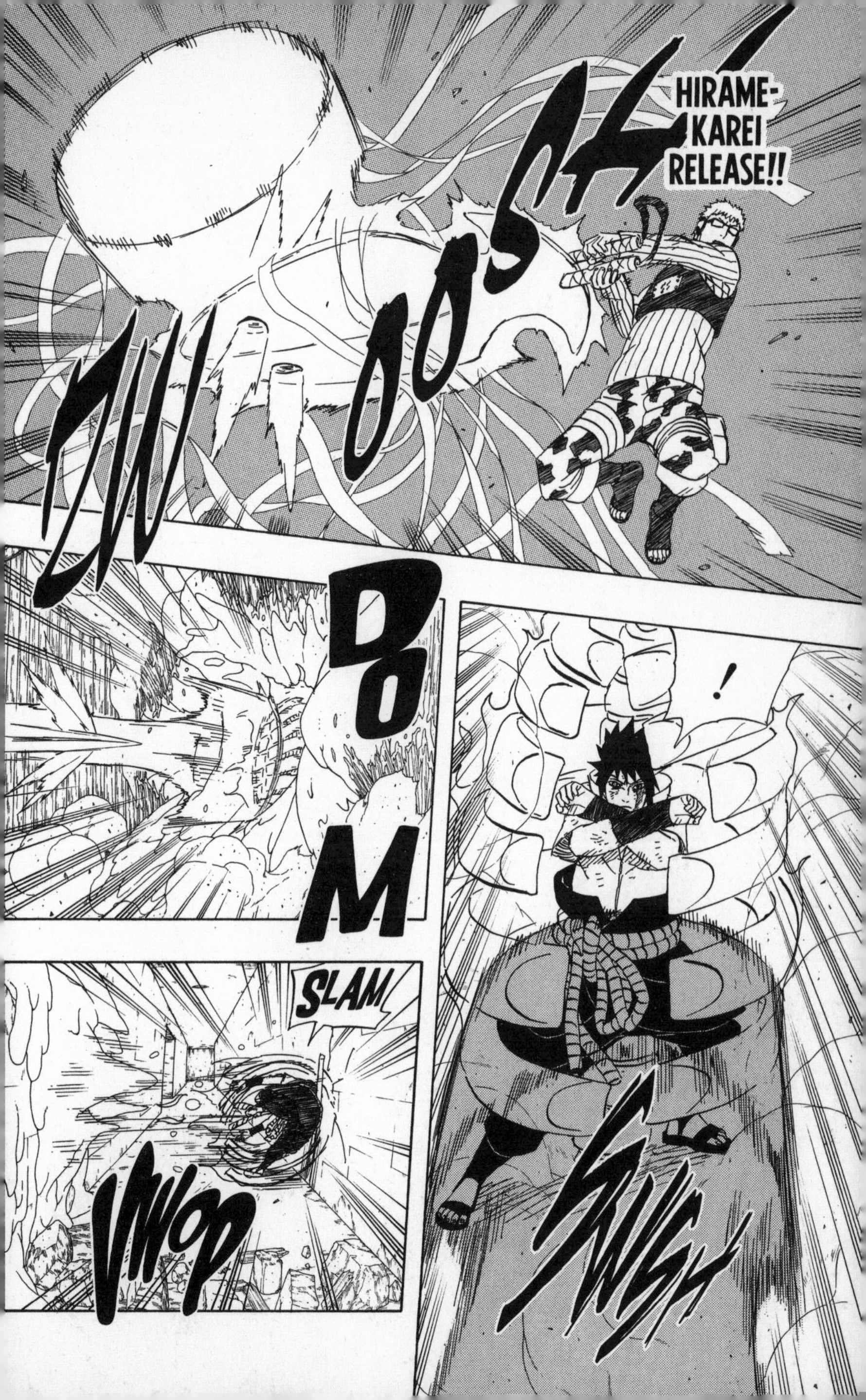
HIRAME-KAREI RELEASE!!
ZWOOOSH
DOOM
!
SLAM
VWOOP
SWISH

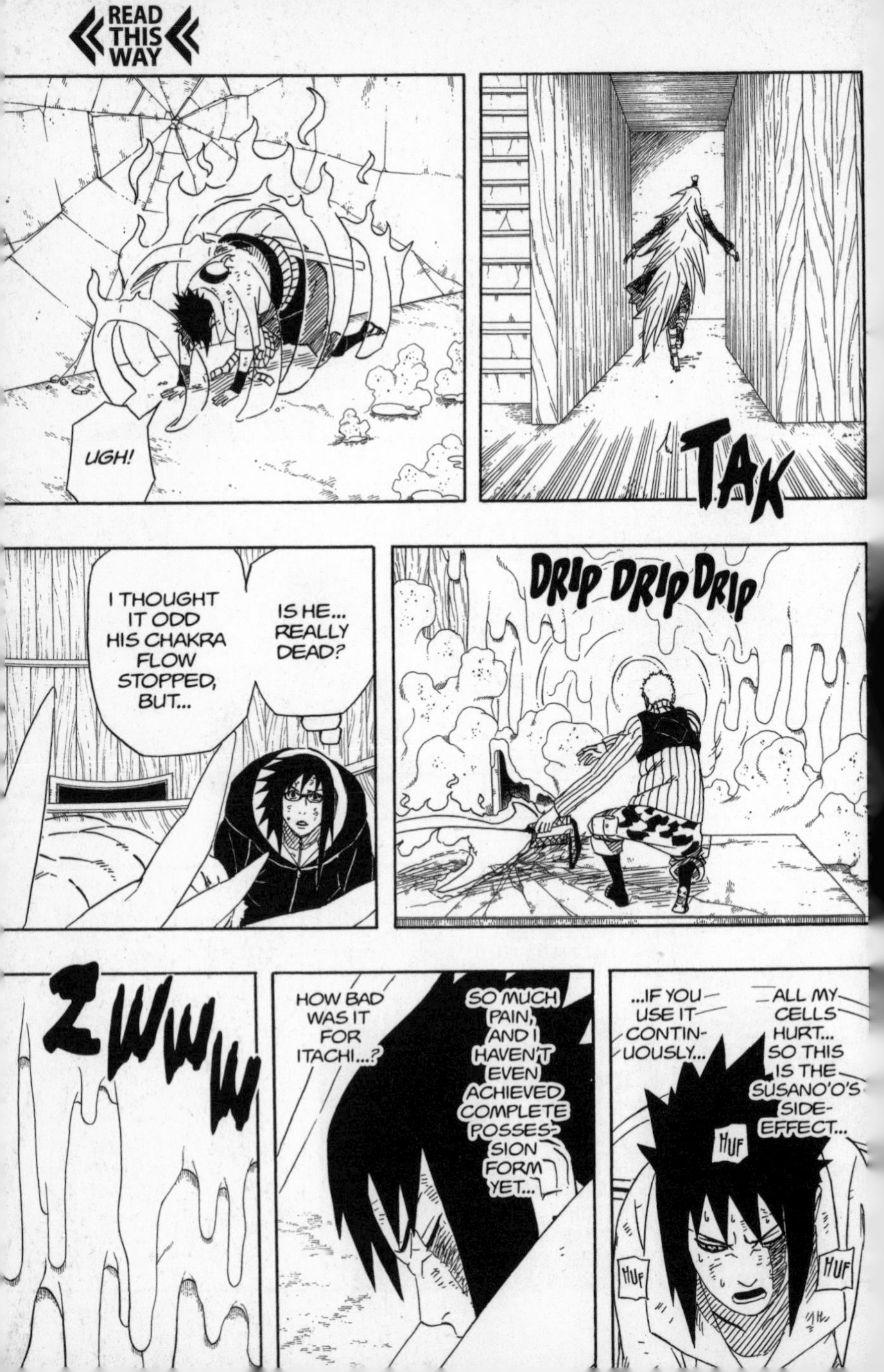
READ THIS WAY
TAK
UGH!
DRIP DRIP DRIP
IS HE... REALLY DEAD?
I THOUGHT IT ODD HIS CHAKRA FLOW STOPPED, BUT...
ALL MY CELLS HURT... SO THIS IS THE SUSANO'O'S SIDE-EFFECT...
...IF YOU USE IT CONTIN-UOUSLY...
HUF
HUF
HUF
SO MUCH PAIN, AND I HAVEN'T EVEN ACHIEVED COMPLETE POSSES-SION FORM YET...
HOW BAD WAS IT FOR ITACHI...?
ZWWW

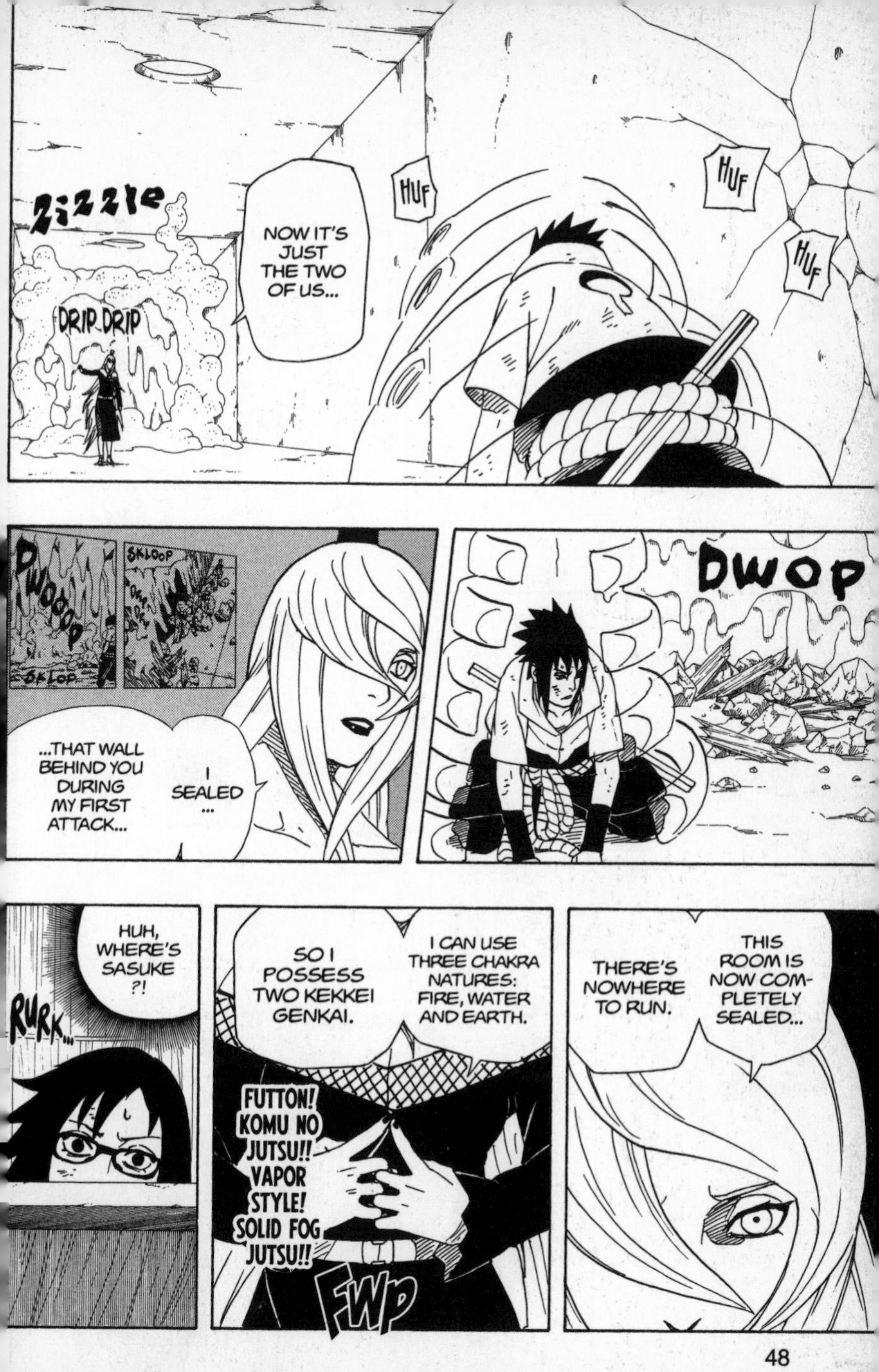
HUF
HUF
HUF
NOW IT'S JUST THE TWO OF US...
ZIZZLE
DRIP DRIP
DWOP
I SEALED...
...THAT WALL BEHIND YOU DURING MY FIRST ATTACK...
THIS ROOM IS NOW COMPLETELY SEALED...
THERE'S NOWHERE TO RUN.
I CAN USE THREE CHAKRA NATURES: FIRE, WATER AND EARTH.
SO I POSSESS TWO KEKKEI GENKAI.
FUTTON! KOMU NO JUTSU!! VAPOR STYLE! SOLID FOG JUTSU!!
FWP
HUH, WHERE'S SASUKE?!
RURK...

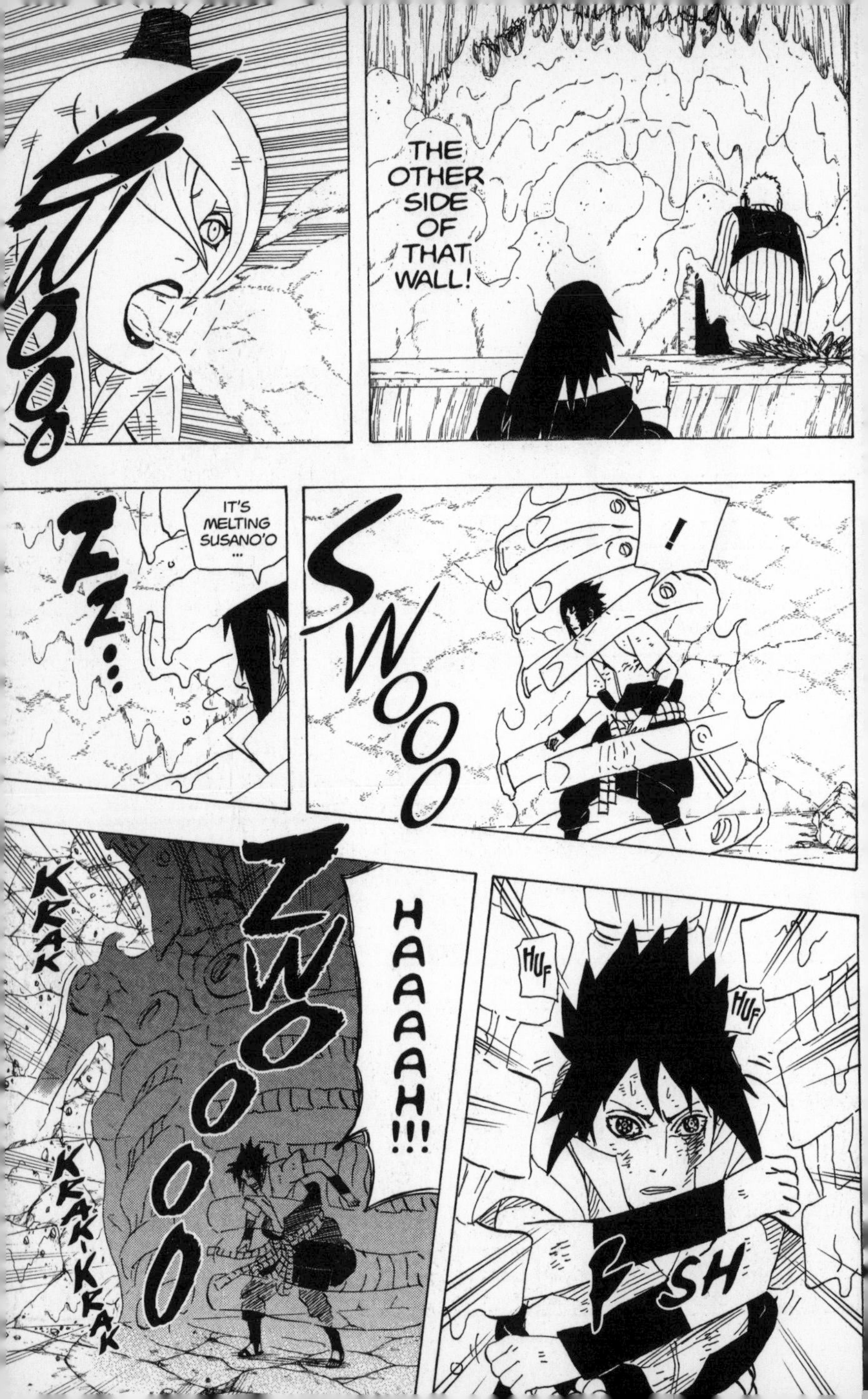
THE OTHER SIDE OF THAT WALL!
SWOOO
!
SWOOO
IT'S MELTING SUSANO'O ...
ZZZ...
HUF
HUF
FSH
HAAAAAH!!!
ZWOOOOO
KRAK
KRAKKRAKKRAK

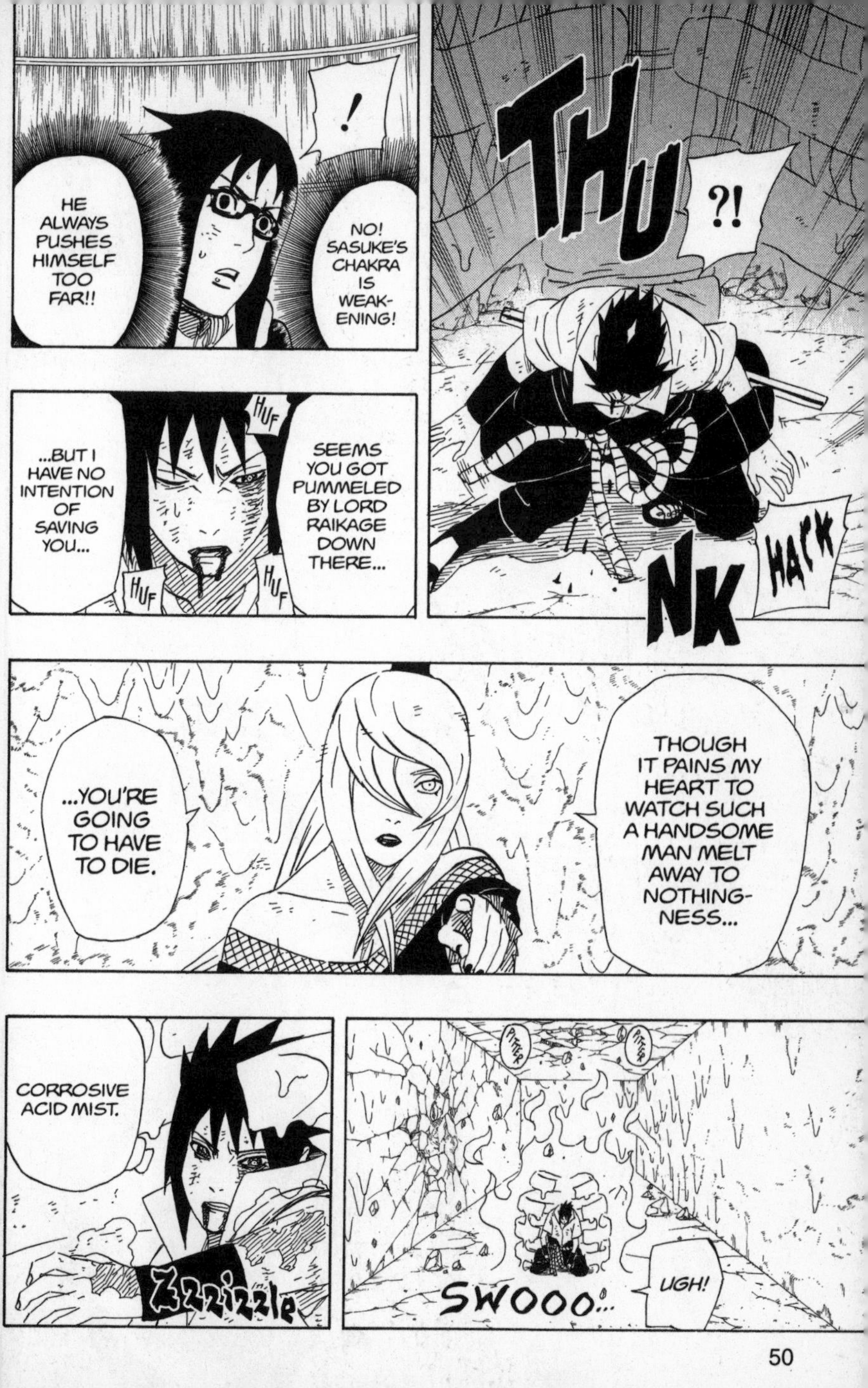
THU
?!
HACK
NK
!
NO! SASUKE'S CHAKRA IS WEAK-ENING!
HE ALWAYS PUSHES HIMSELF TOO FAR!!
HUF
SEEMS YOU GOT PUMMELED BY LORD RAIKAGE DOWN THERE...
...BUT I HAVE NO INTENTION OF SAVING YOU...
HUF
HUF
THOUGH IT PAINS MY HEART TO WATCH SUCH A HANDSOME MAN MELT AWAY TO NOTHING-NESS...
...YOU'RE GOING TO HAVE TO DIE.
PITTER
PITTER
UGH!
SWOOO...
CORROSIVE ACID MIST.
Zzzizzle

READ THIS WAY

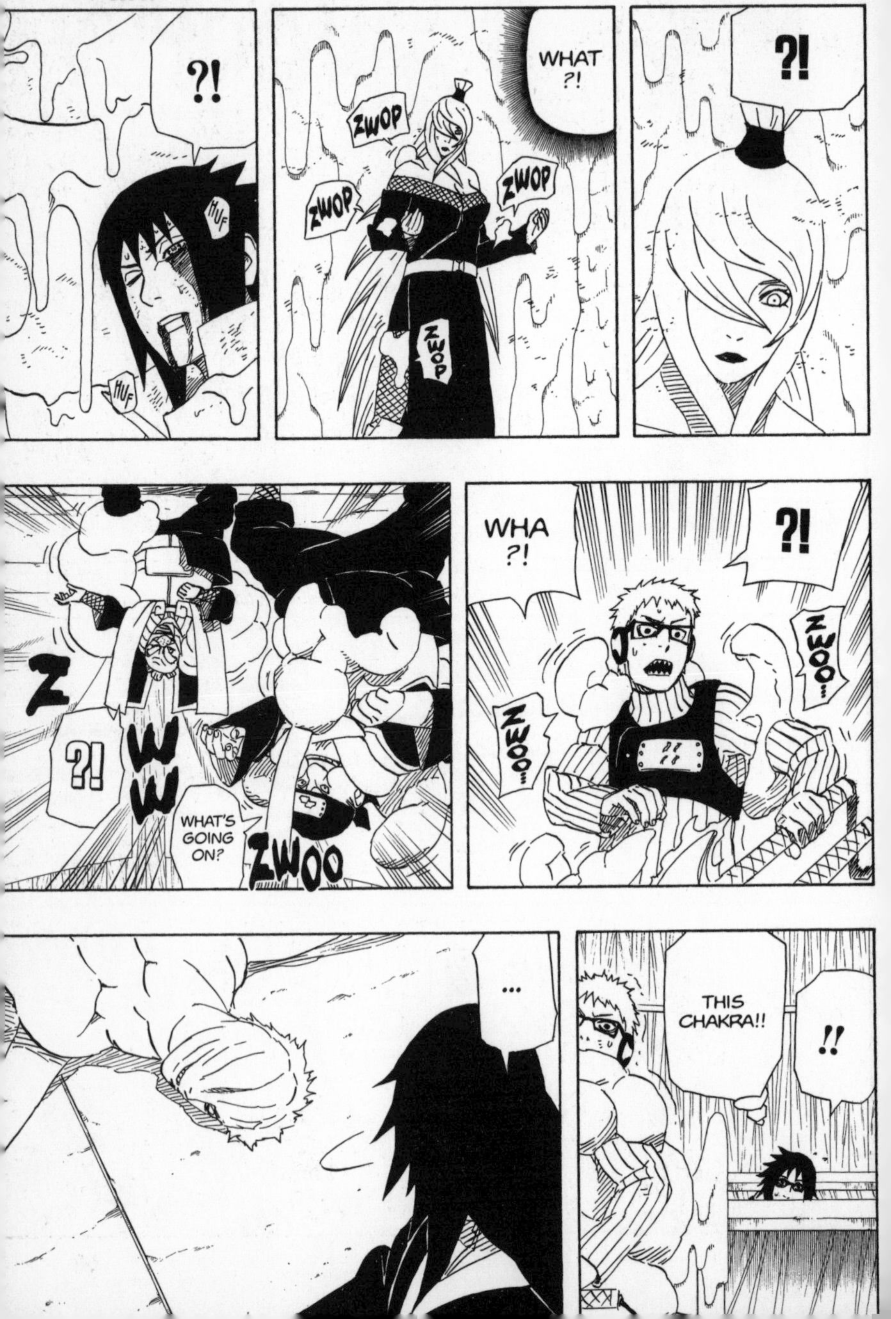
?!
WHAT ?!
ZWOP
ZWOP
ZWOP
ZWOP
?!
HUF
HUF
?!
WHA ?!
ZWOO...
ZWOO...
?!
WHAT'S GOING ON?
ZWOO
THIS CHAKRA!!
!!
...

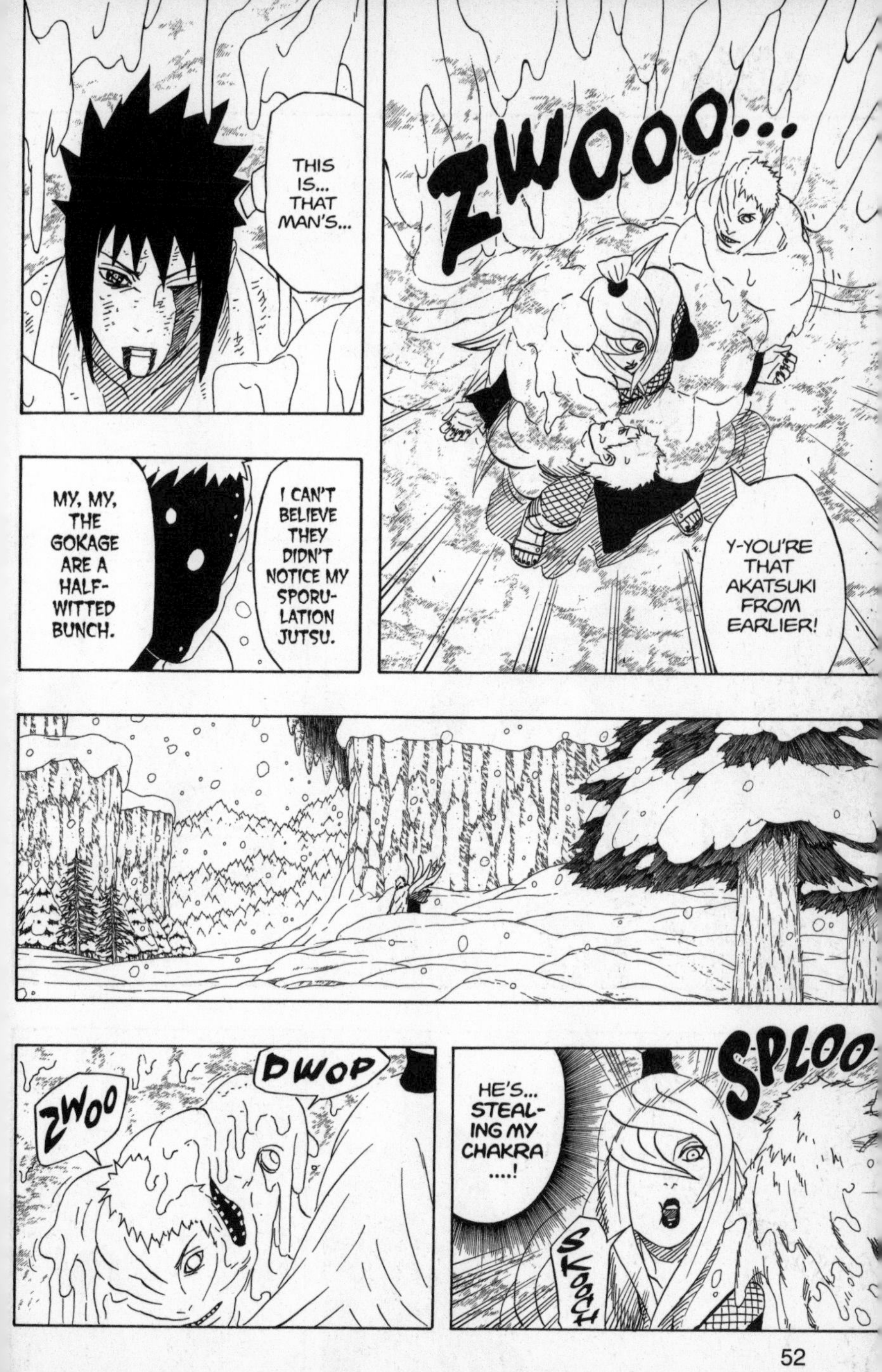

ZWOOO...
Y-YOU'RE THAT AKATSUKI FROM EARLIER!
THIS IS... THAT MAN'S...
I CAN'T BELIEVE THEY DIDN'T NOTICE MY SPORULATION JUTSU.
MY, MY, THE GOKAGE ARE A HALF-WITTED BUNCH.
SPLOO
HE'S... STEALING MY CHAKRA ....!
SKOOCH
DWOP
ZWOO

READ THIS WAY

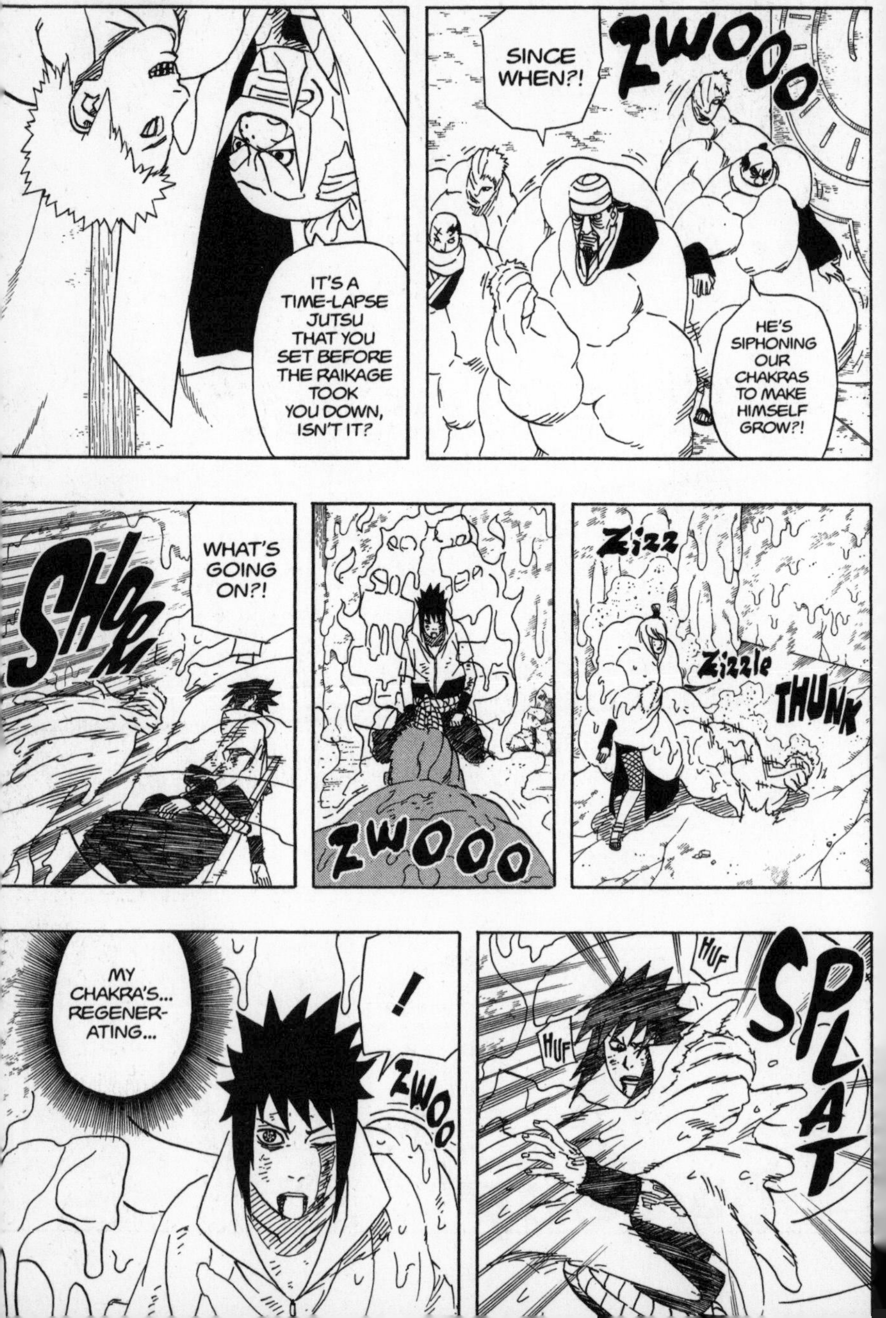
SINCE WHEN?!
ZWOOO
HE'S SIPHONING OUR CHAKRAS TO MAKE HIMSELF GROW?!
IT'S A TIME-LAPSE JUTSU THAT YOU SET BEFORE THE RAIKAGE TOOK YOU DOWN, ISN'T IT?
Zizz
Zizzle
THUNK
ZWOOO
WHAT'S GOING ON?!
SHOOM
HUF
SPLAT
HUF
MY CHAKRA'S... REGENER-ATING...
!
ZWOO

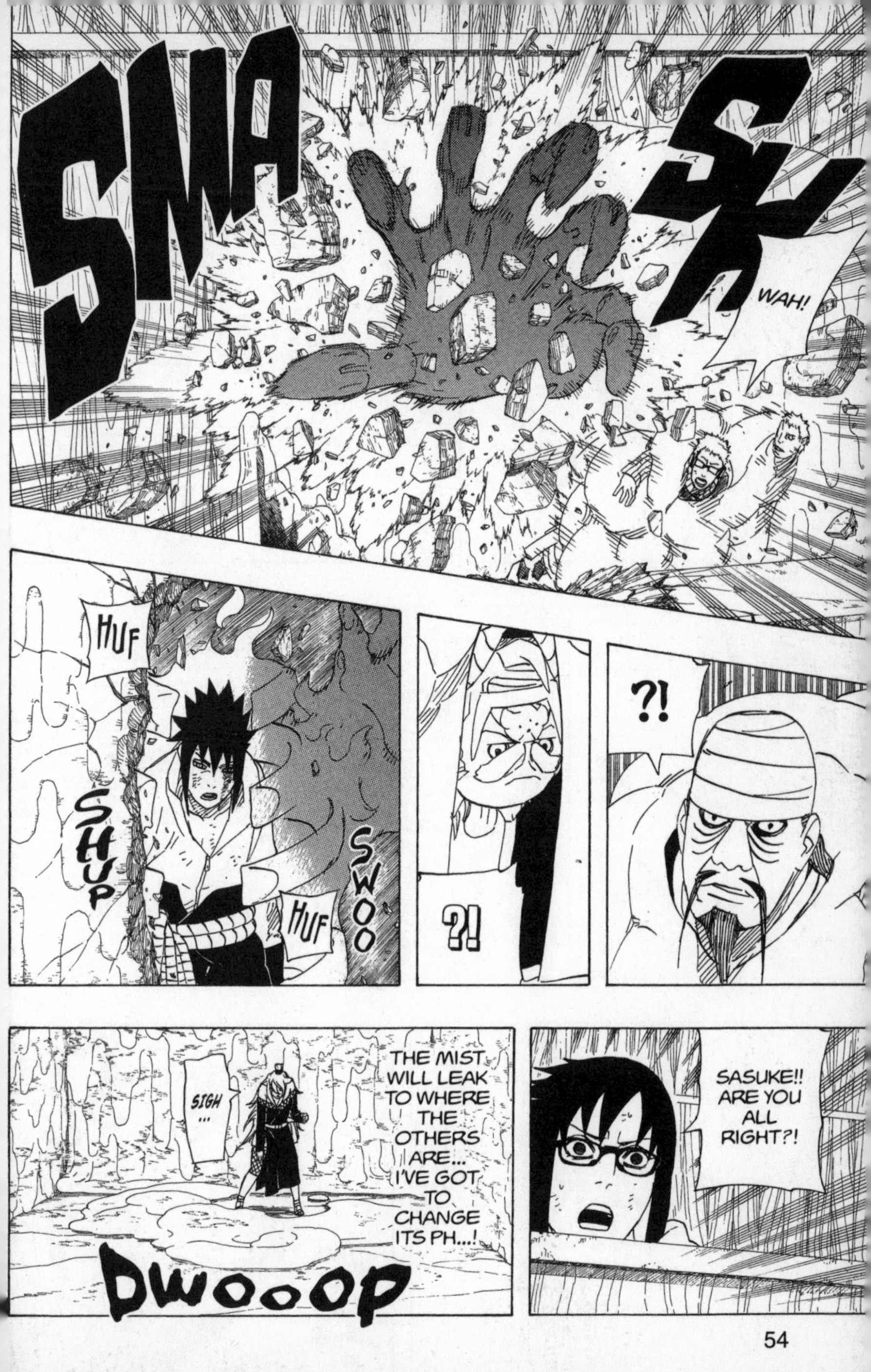
SMASH
WAH!
?!
?!
HUF
SHUP
HUF
SWOO
SASUKE!! ARE YOU ALL RIGHT?!
THE MIST WILL LEAK TO WHERE THE OTHERS ARE... I'VE GOT TO CHANGE ITS PH...!
SIGH ...
DWOOOP

READ THIS WAY

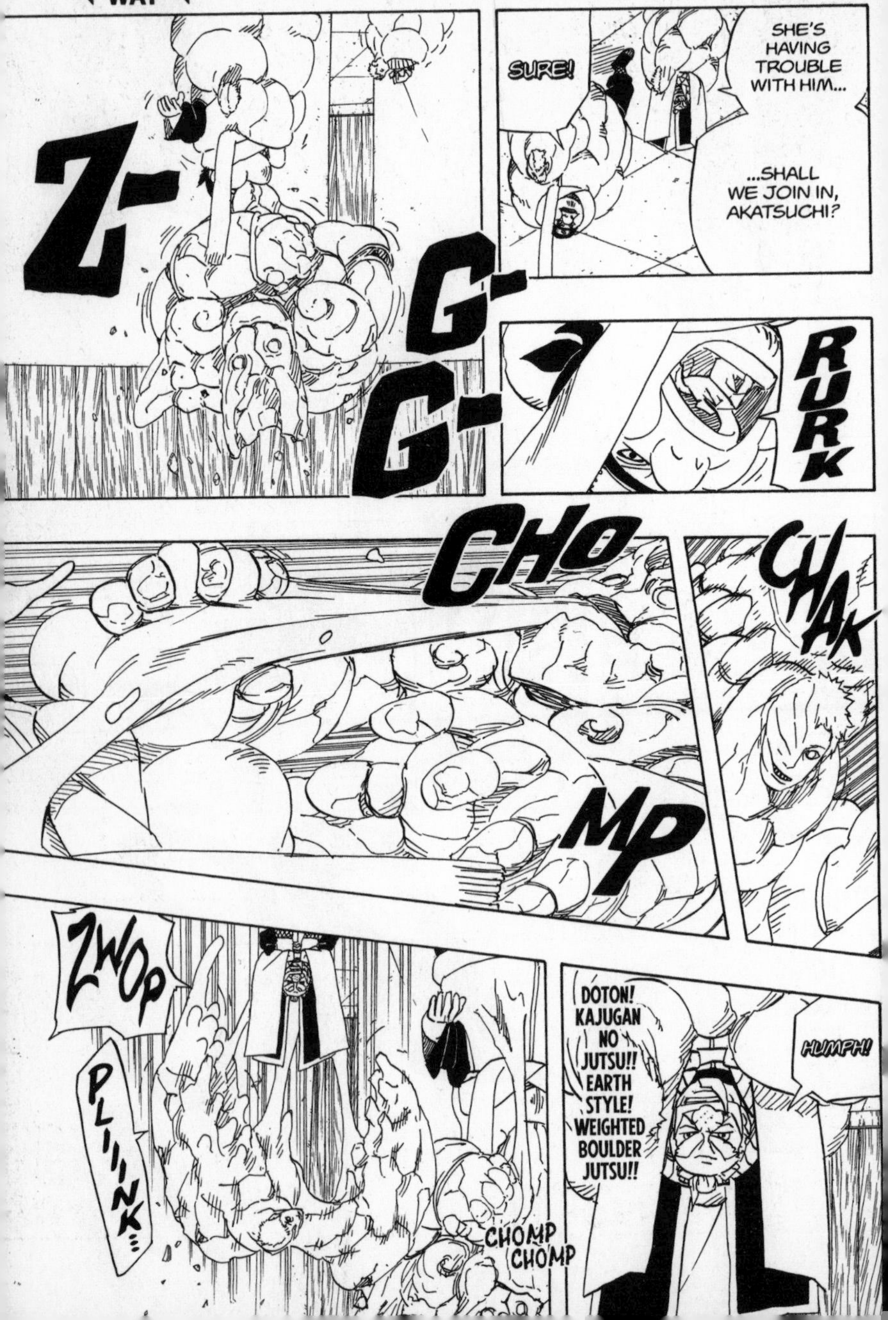
SHE'S HAVING TROUBLE WITH HIM...
...SHALL WE JOIN IN, AKATSUCHI?
SURE!
RURK
Z-
G-
G-
CHAK
CHO
MP
DOTON! KAJUGAN NO JUTSU!! EARTH STYLE! WEIGHTED BOULDER JUTSU!!
HUMPH!
ZWOP
PLIIINK...
CHOMP CHOMP

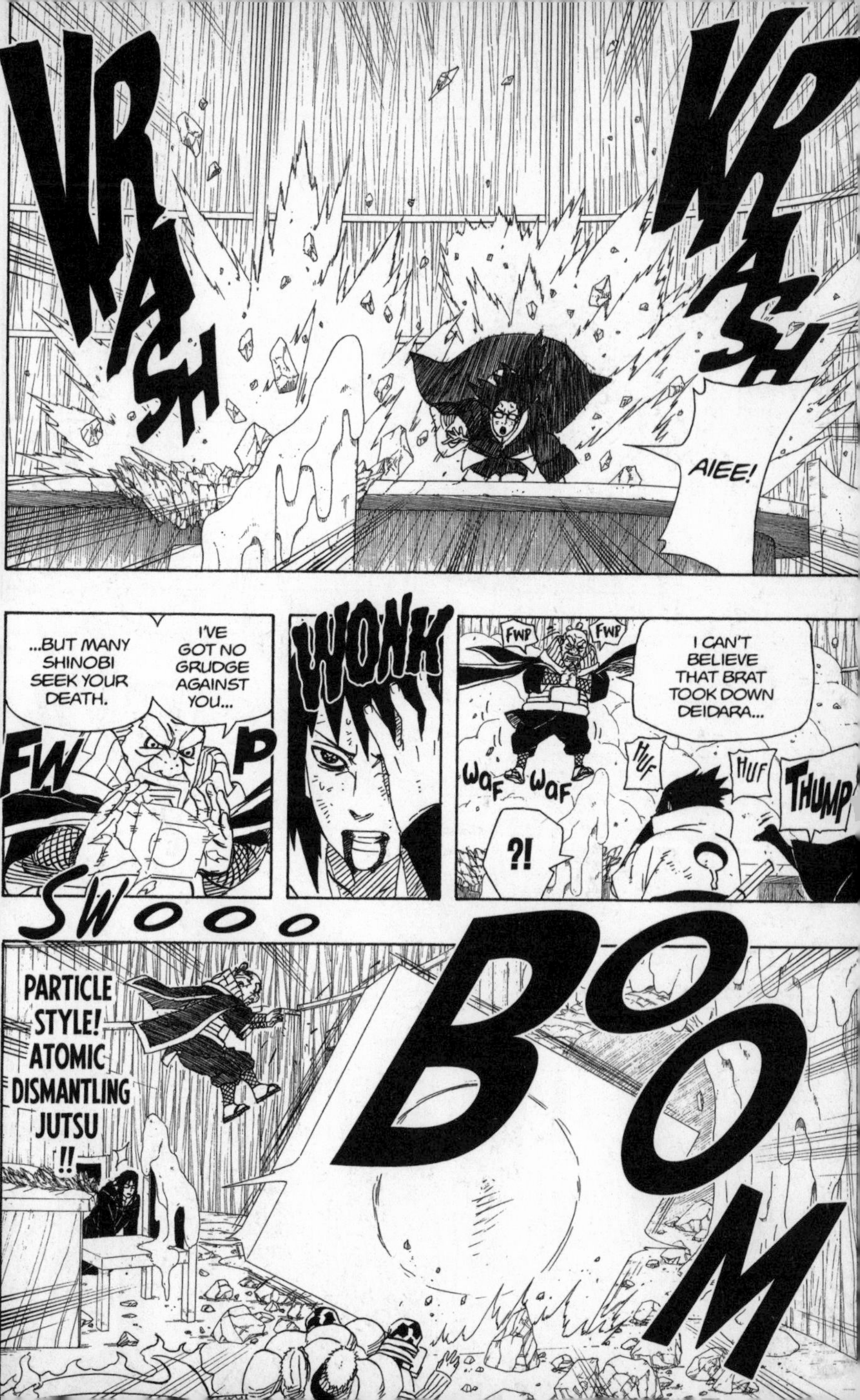
VRASH
AIEE!
VRASH
FWP
FWP
I CAN'T BELIEVE THAT BRAT TOOK DOWN DEIDARA...
HUF
HUF
THUMP
WAF WAF
?!
WONK
I'VE GOT NO GRUDGE AGAINST YOU...
...BUT MANY SHINOBI SEEK YOUR DEATH.
FWP
SWOOO
BOOM
PARTICLE STYLE! ATOMIC DISMANTLING JUTSU!!

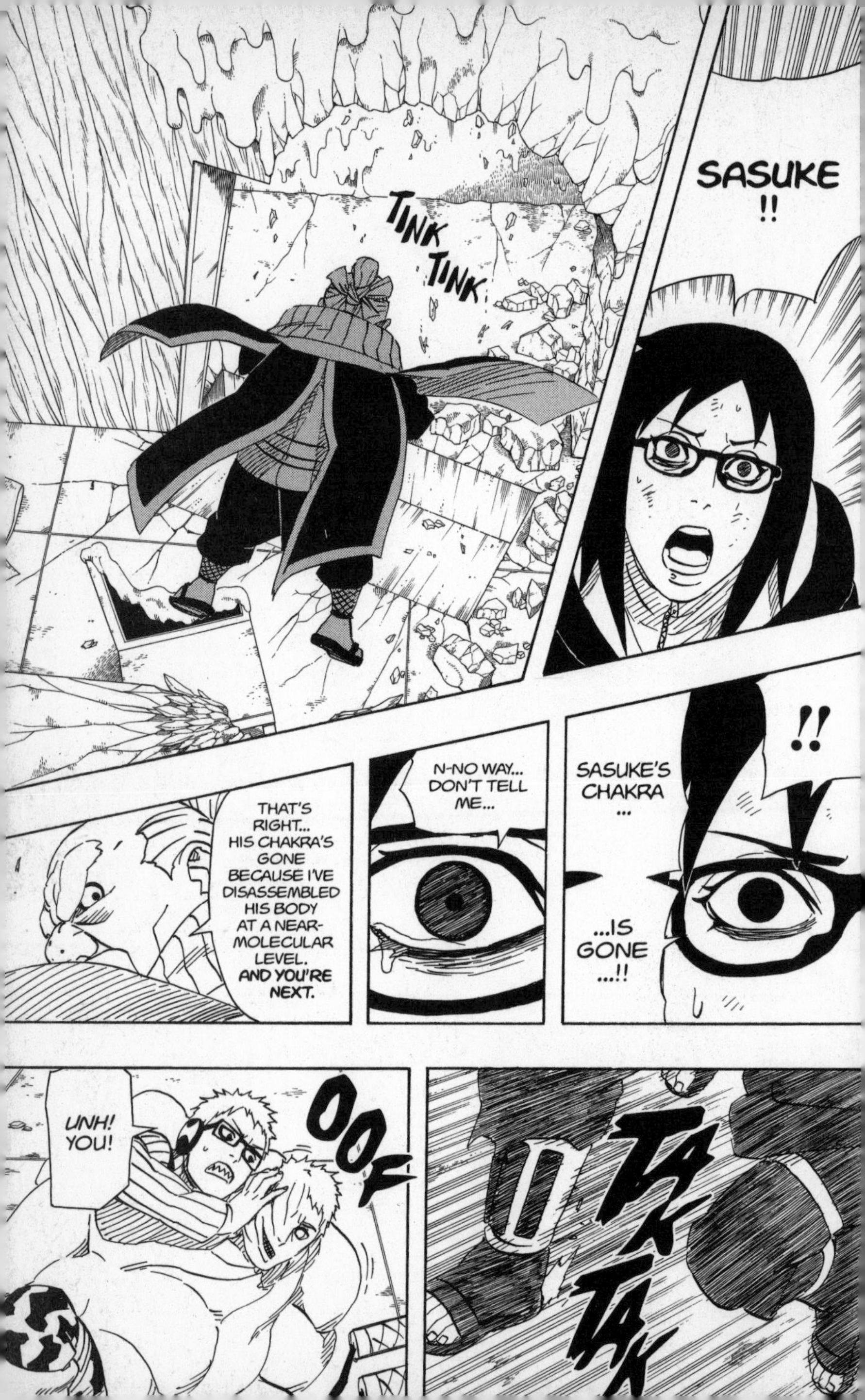
SASUKE !!
TINK TINK
!!
SASUKE'S CHAKRA ...
...IS GONE ...!!
N-NO WAY... DON'T TELL ME...
THAT'S RIGHT... HIS CHAKRA'S GONE BECAUSE I'VE DISASSEMBLED HIS BODY AT A NEAR-MOLECULAR LEVEL. **AND YOU'RE NEXT.**
TAK TAK
OOF
UNH! YOU!

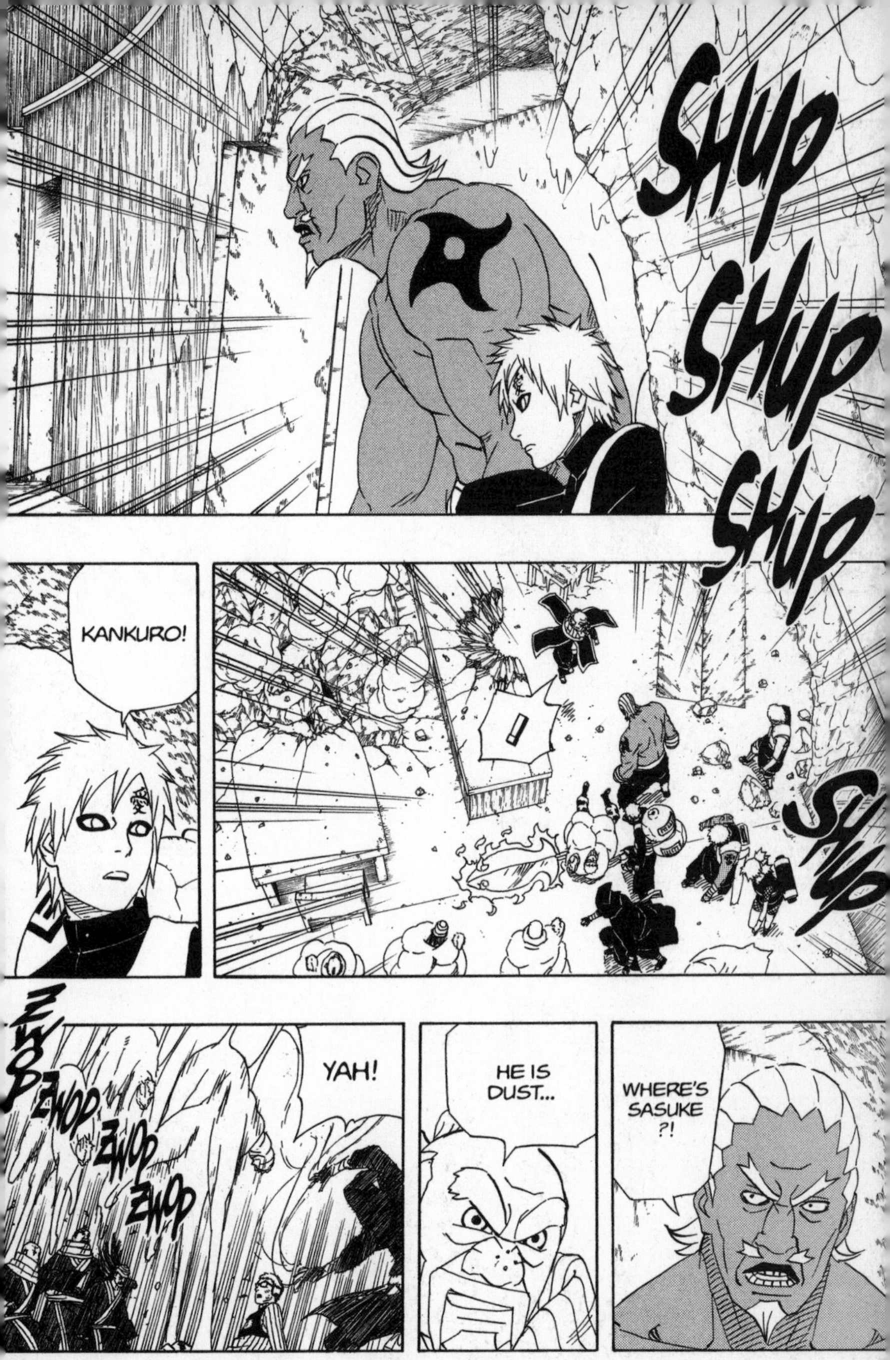
SHUP
SHUP
SHUP
SHUP
!
SHUP
SHUP
KANKURO!
WHERE'S SASUKE ?!
HE IS DUST...
YAH!
ZWOP ZWOP ZWOP ZWOP

READ THIS WAY

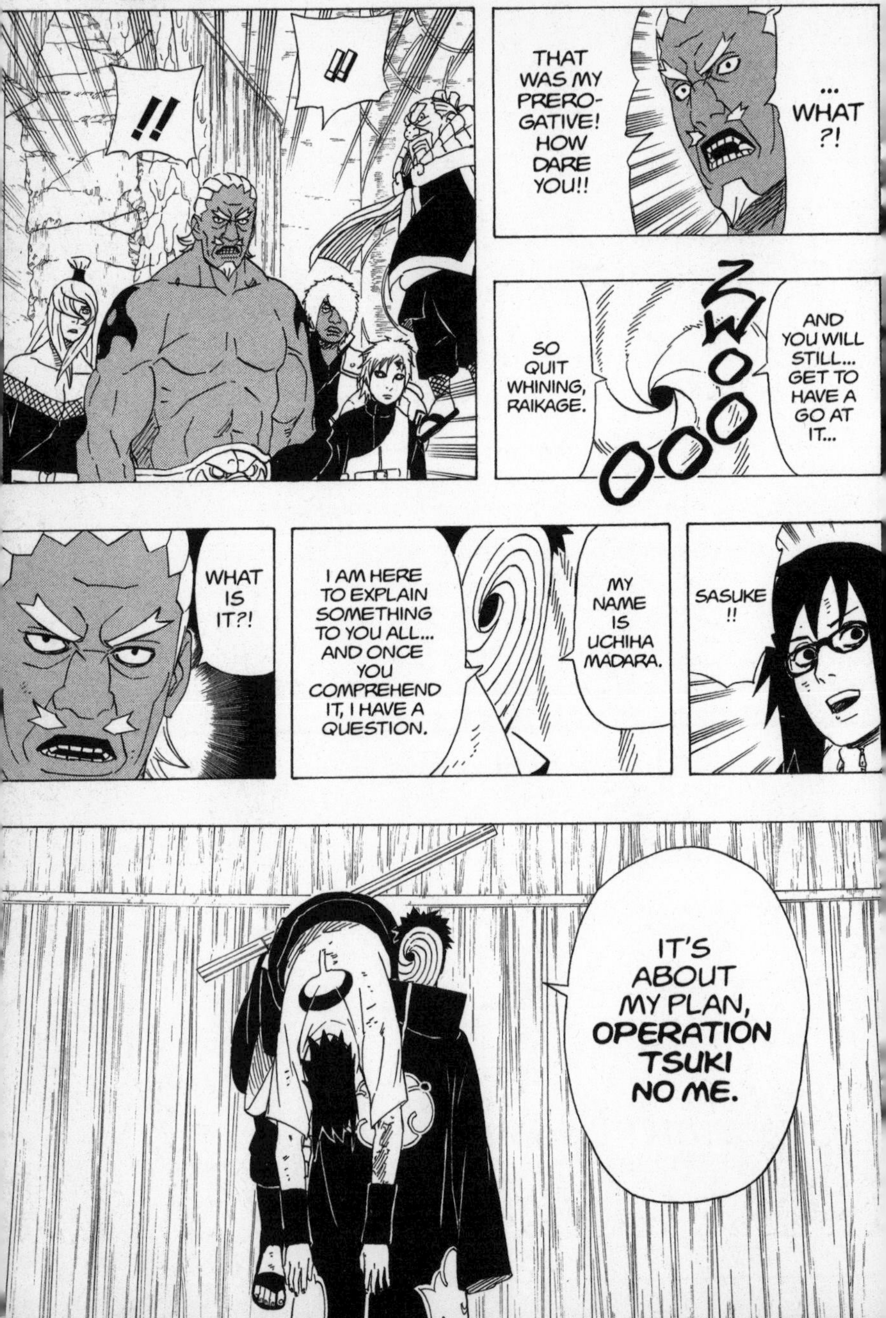

... WHAT ?!
THAT WAS MY PREROGATIVE! HOW DARE YOU!!
AND YOU WILL STILL... GET TO HAVE A GO AT IT...
ZWOOOOO
SO QUIT WHINING, RAIKAGE.
!!
!!
SASUKE !!
MY NAME IS UCHIHA MADARA.
I AM HERE TO EXPLAIN SOMETHING TO YOU ALL... AND ONCE YOU COMPREHEND IT, I HAVE A QUESTION.
WHAT IS IT?!
IT'S ABOUT MY PLAN, OPERATION TSUKI NO ME.

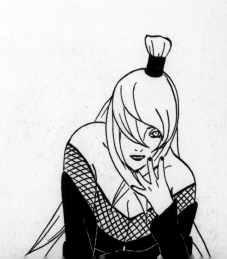

Number 467: Declaration of War

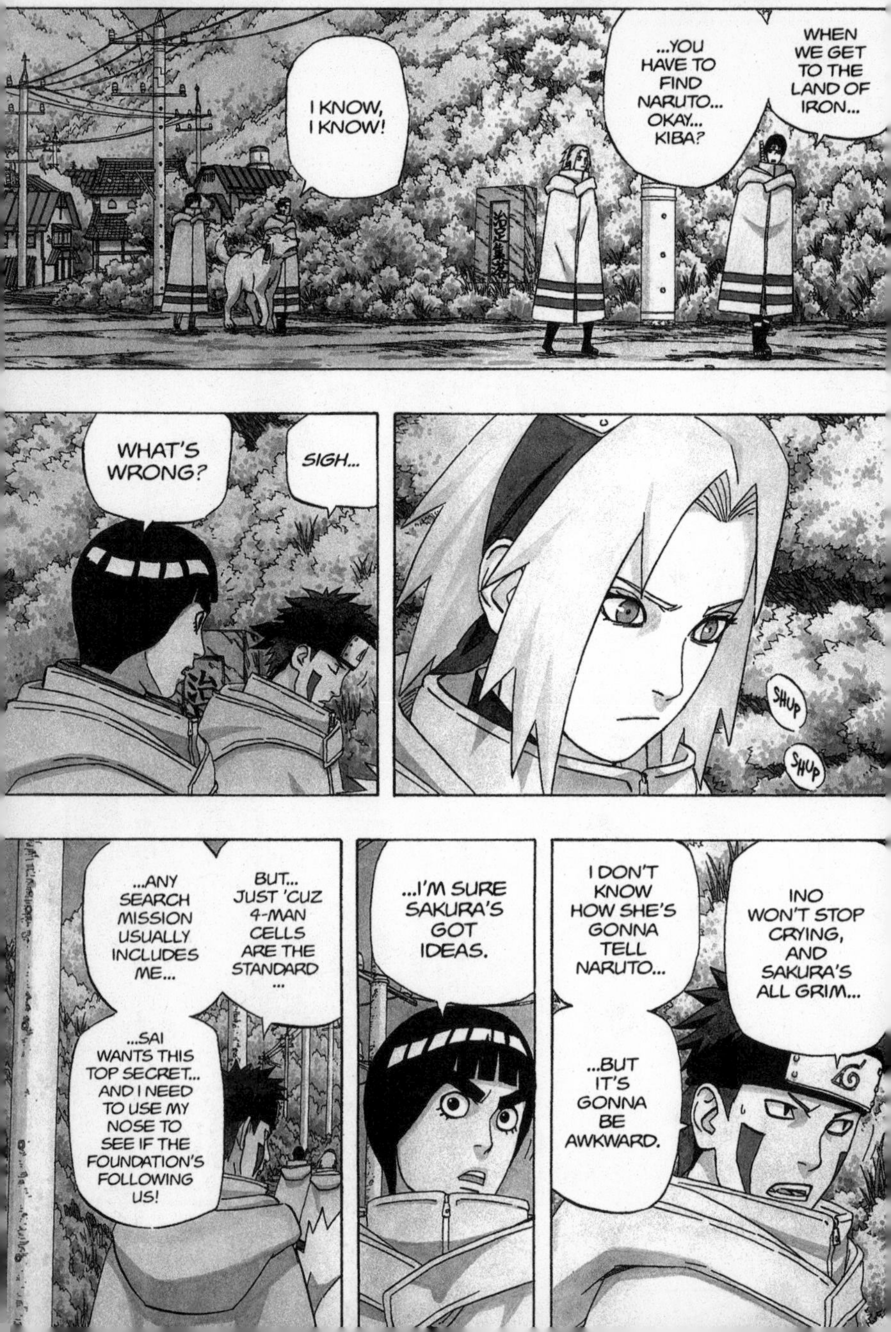
WHEN WE GET TO THE LAND OF IRON...
...YOU HAVE TO FIND NARUTO... OKAY... KIBA?
I KNOW, I KNOW!
SHUP
SHUP
SIGH...
WHAT'S WRONG?
INO WON'T STOP CRYING, AND SAKURA'S ALL GRIM...
I DON'T KNOW HOW SHE'S GONNA TELL NARUTO...
...BUT IT'S GONNA BE AWKWARD.
...I'M SURE SAKURA'S GOT IDEAS.
BUT... JUST 'CUZ 4-MAN CELLS ARE THE STANDARD...
...ANY SEARCH MISSION USUALLY INCLUDES ME...
...SAI WANTS THIS TOP SECRET... AND I NEED TO USE MY NOSE TO SEE IF THE FOUNDATION'S FOLLOWING US!

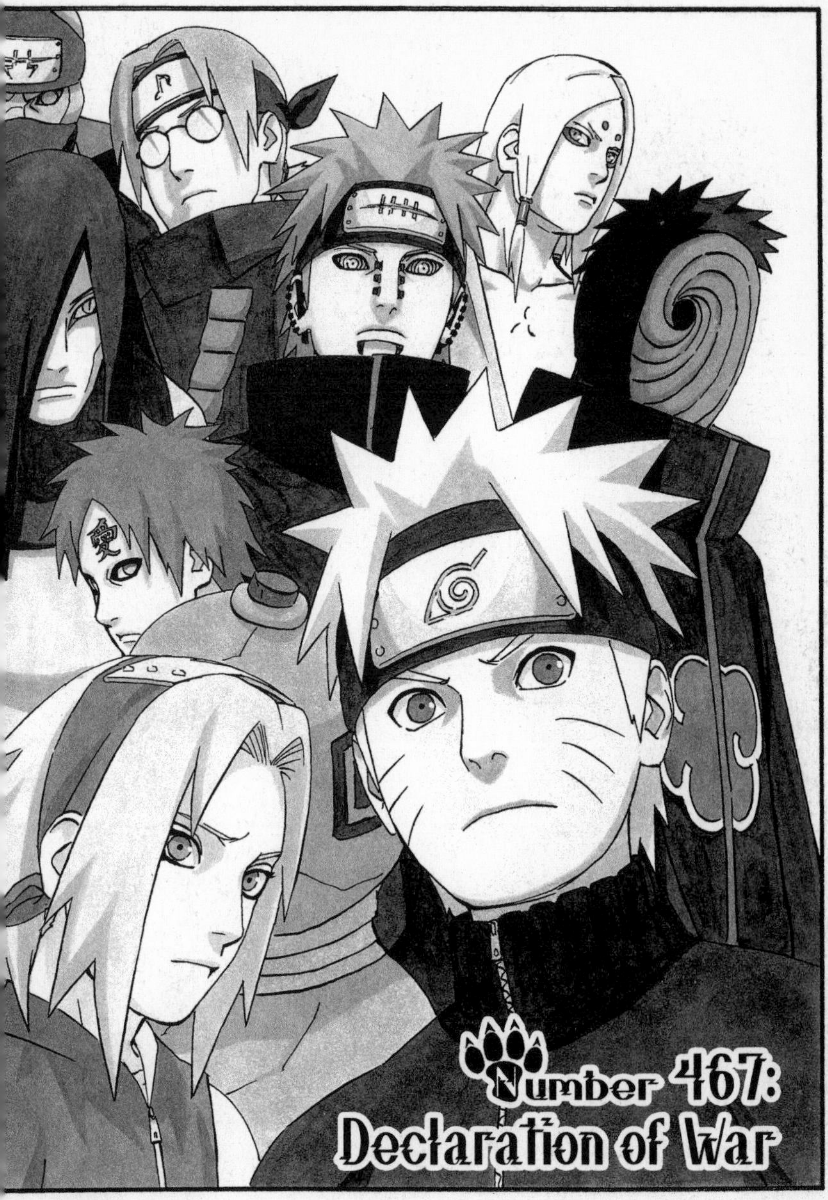
Number 467:
Declaration of War

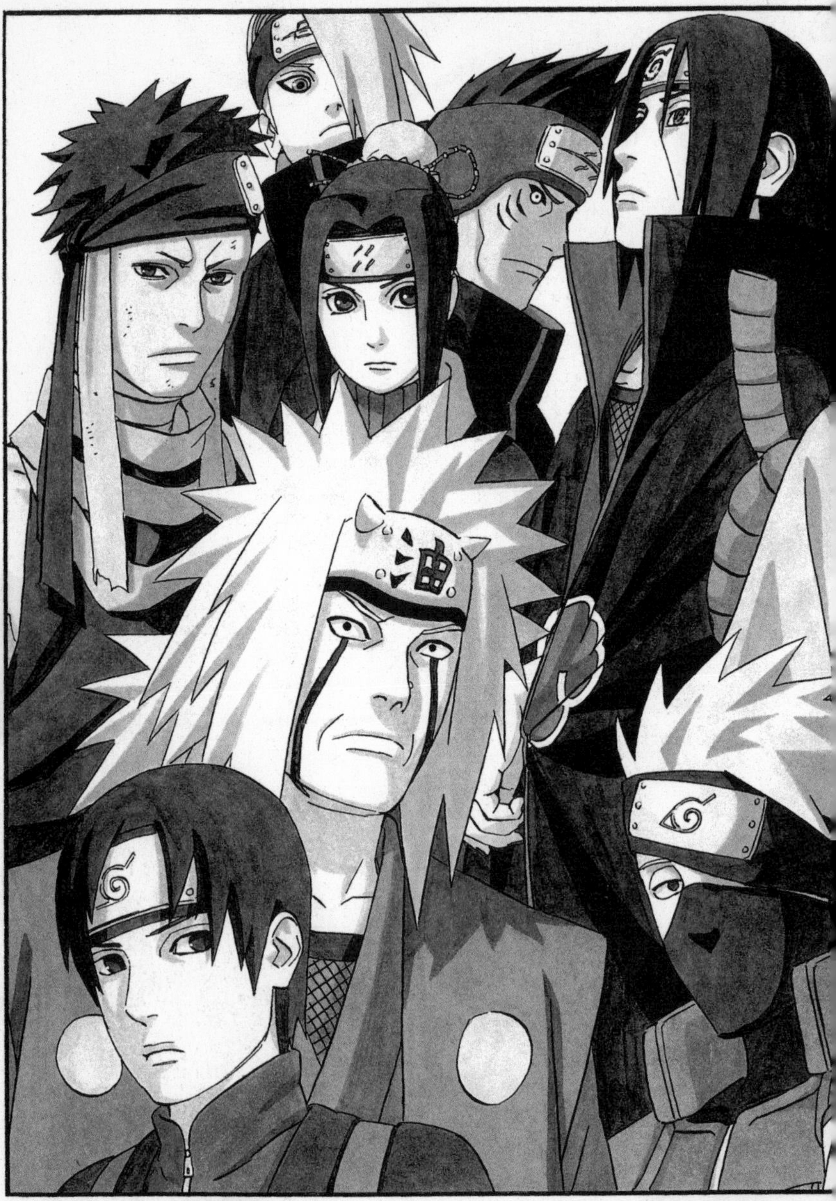

NARUTO

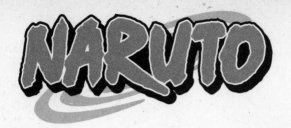

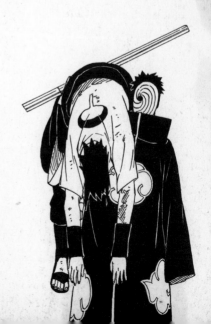

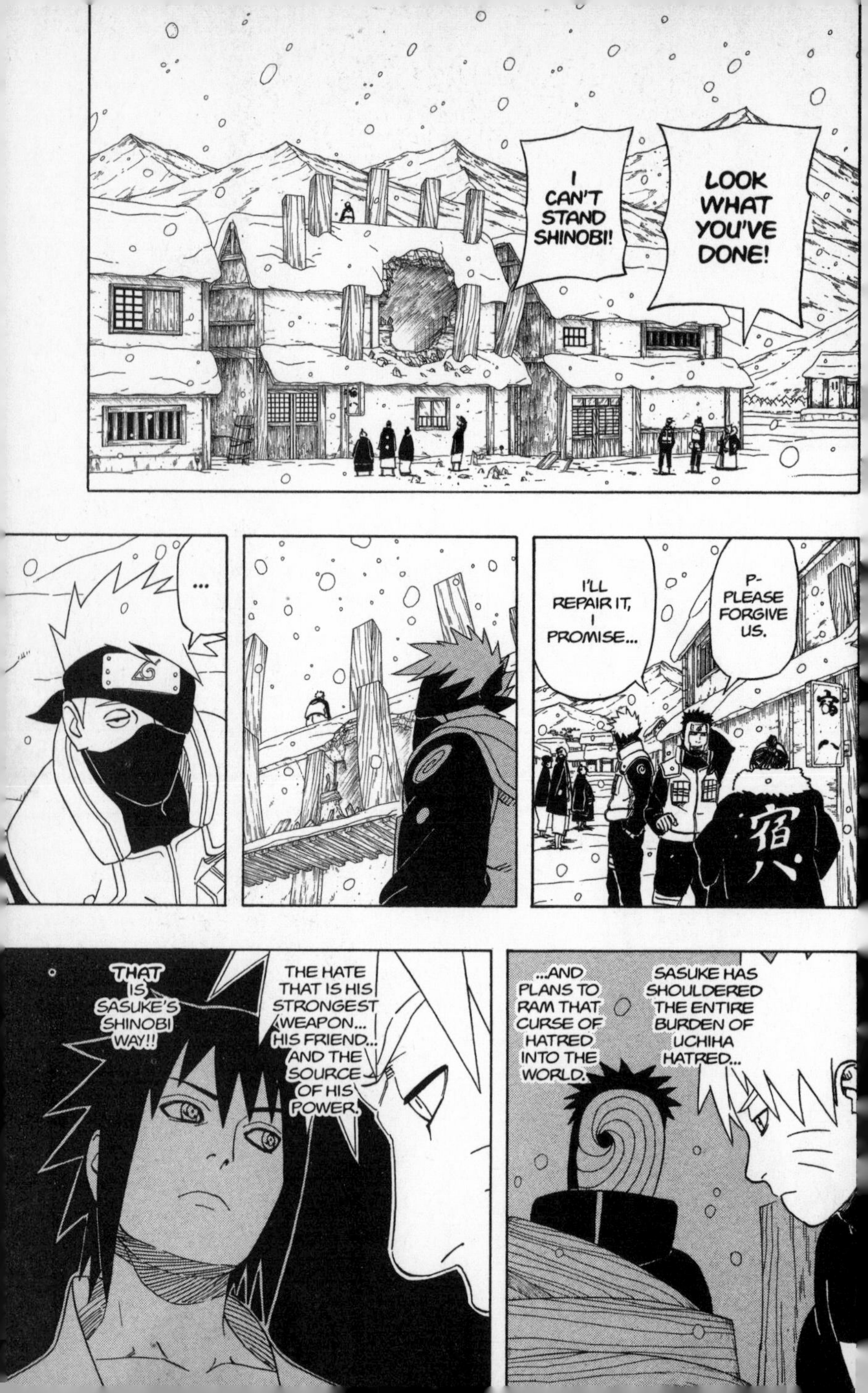
LOOK WHAT YOU'VE DONE!
I CAN'T STAND SHINOBI!
P-PLEASE FORGIVE US.
I'LL REPAIR IT, I PROMISE...
...
SASUKE HAS SHOULDERED THE ENTIRE BURDEN OF UCHIHA HATRED...
...AND PLANS TO RAM THAT CURSE OF HATRED INTO THE WORLD.
THE HATE THAT IS HIS STRONGEST WEAPON... HIS FRIEND... AND THE SOURCE OF HIS POWER.
THAT IS SASUKE'S SHINOBI WAY!!

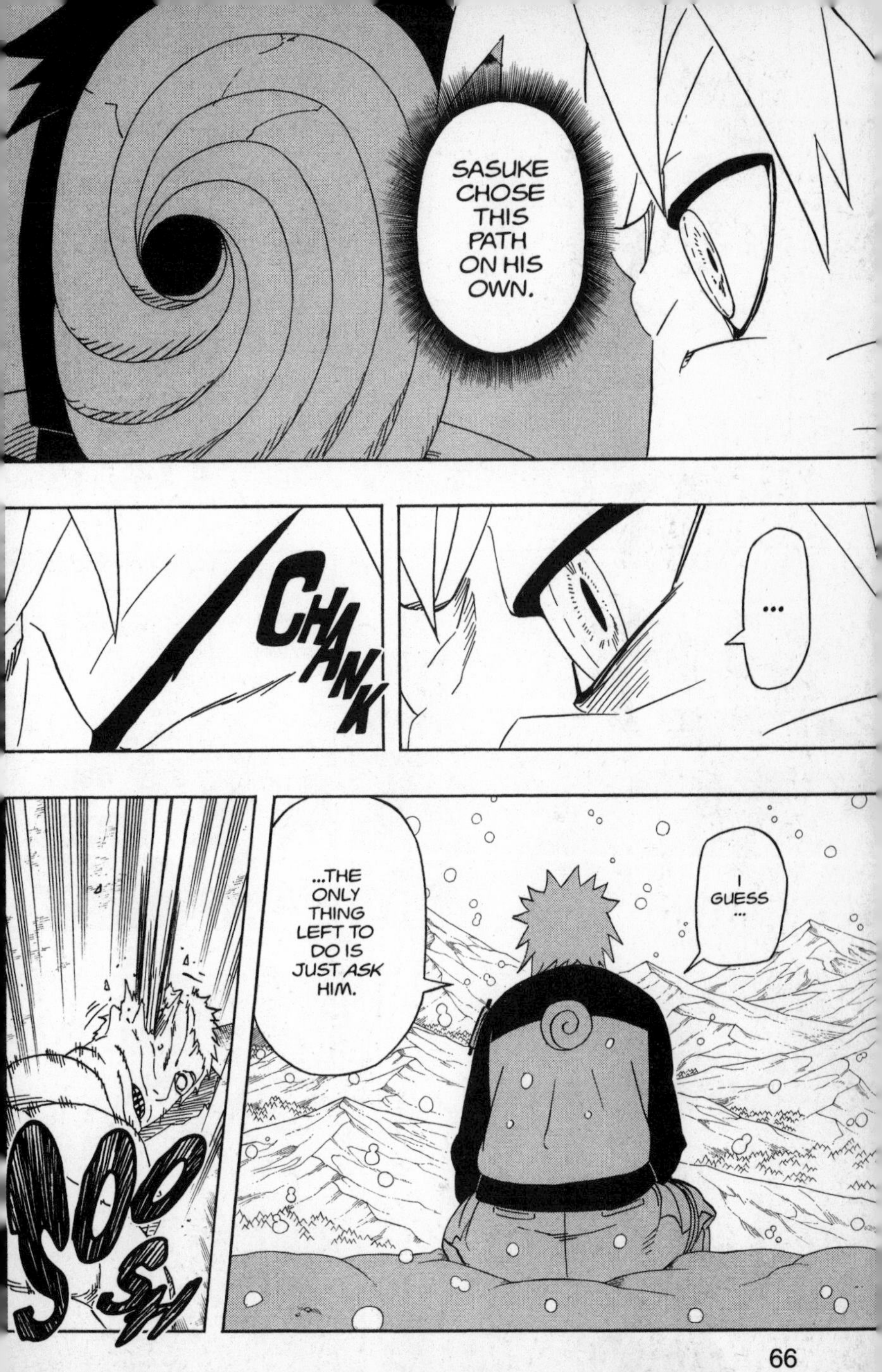
SASUKE CHOSE THIS PATH ON HIS OWN.
...
CHANK
I GUESS ...
...THE ONLY THING LEFT TO DO IS JUST *ASK* HIM.
SOOSH

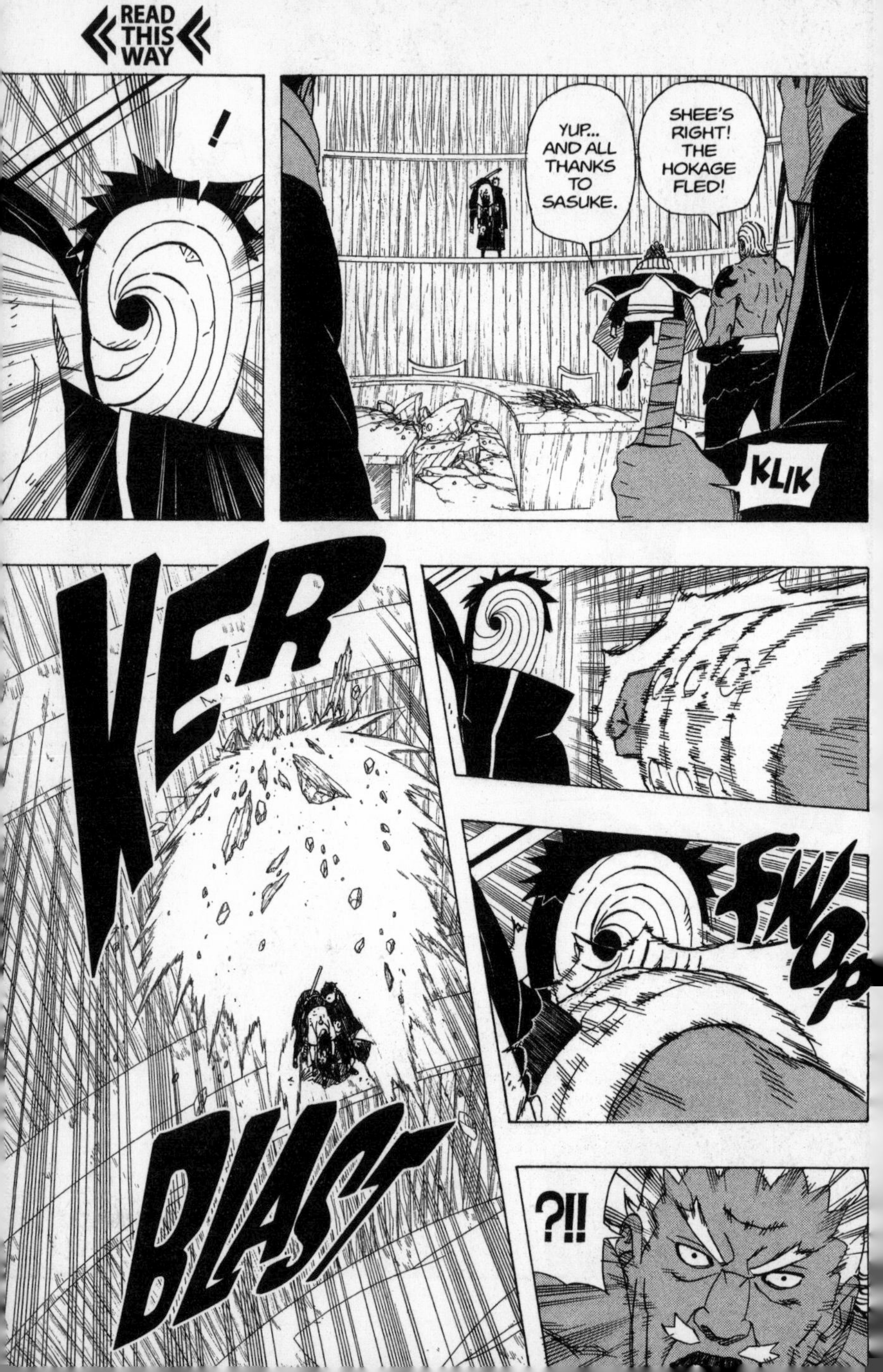
READ THIS WAY
SHEE'S RIGHT! THE HOKAGE FLED!
YUP... AND ALL THANKS TO SASUKE.
KLIK
!
FWOP
VER
BLAST
?!!

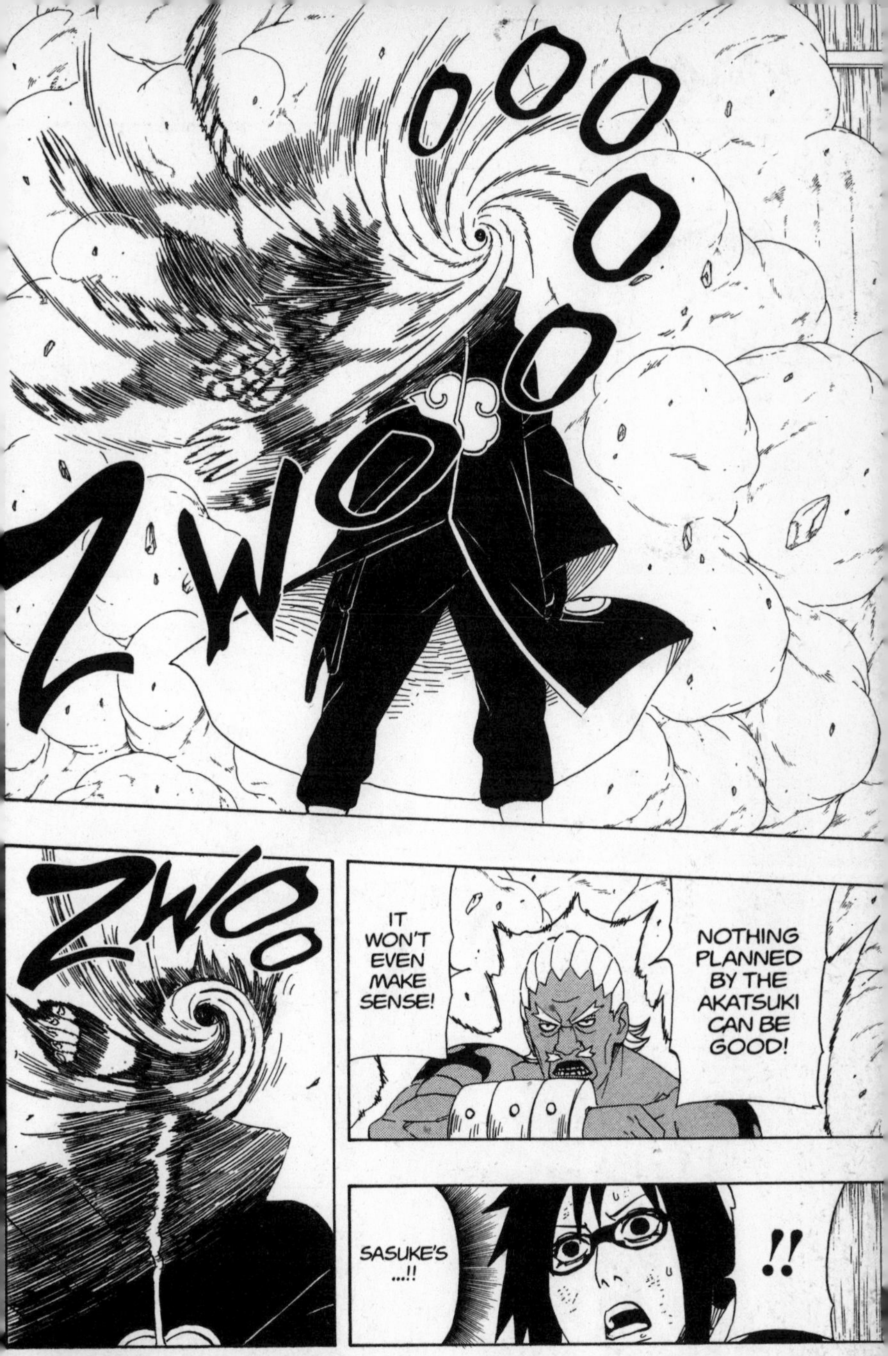
ZWOOOOOOO
NOTHING PLANNED BY THE AKATSUKI CAN BE GOOD!
IT WON'T EVEN MAKE SENSE!
!!
SASUKE'S ...!!
ZWOO

READ THIS WAY

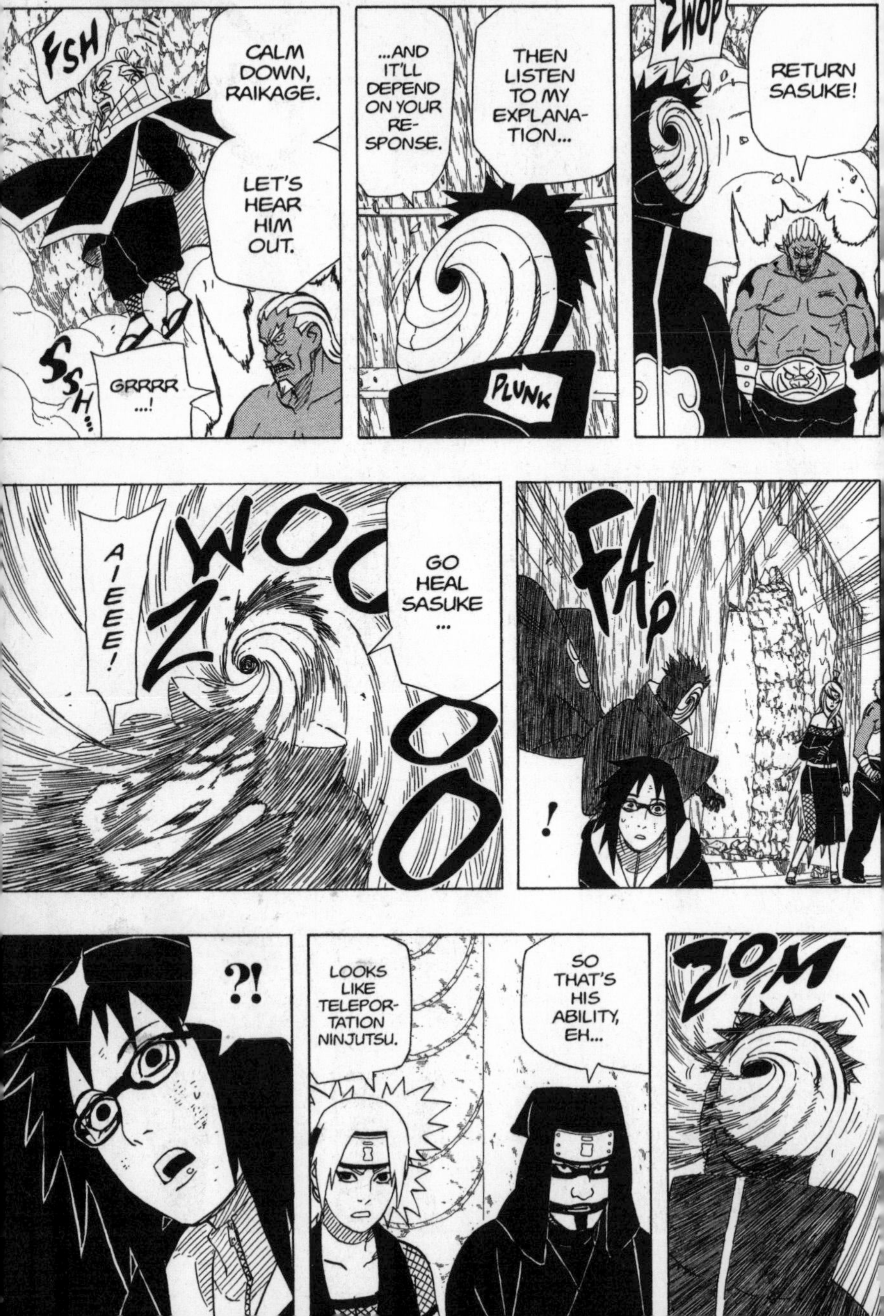
ZWOP
RETURN SASUKE!
THEN LISTEN TO MY EXPLANATION...
...AND IT'LL DEPEND ON YOUR RESPONSE.
PLUNK
FSH
CALM DOWN, RAIKAGE.
LET'S HEAR HIM OUT.
GRRRR ...!
SSH...
FAP
!
GO HEAL SASUKE ...
WOOOOZ
AIEEE!
ZOM
SO THAT'S HIS ABILITY, EH...
LOOKS LIKE TELEPORTATION NINJUTSU.
?!

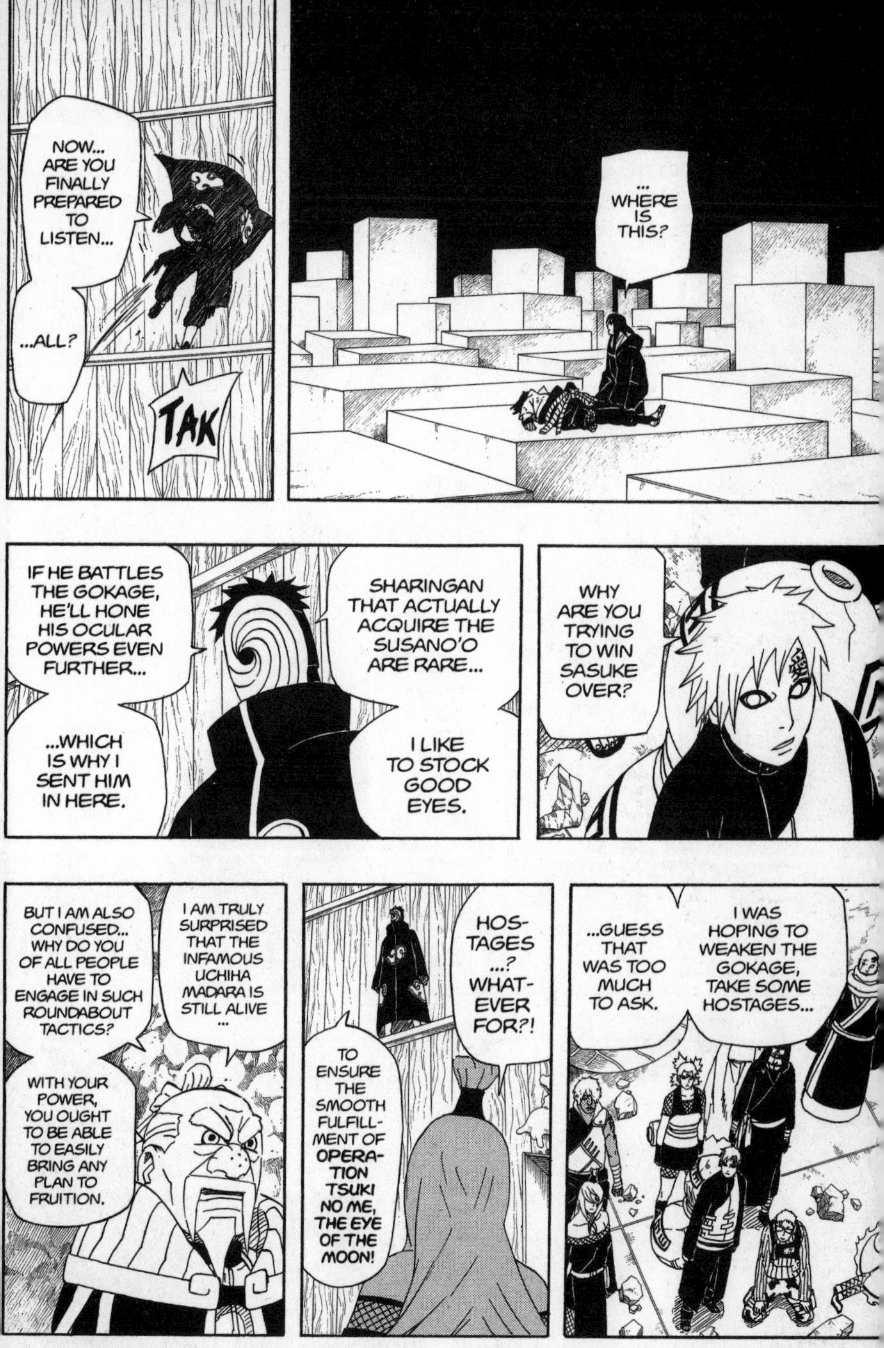
... WHERE IS THIS?
NOW... ARE YOU FINALLY PREPARED TO LISTEN...
...ALL?
TAK
WHY ARE YOU TRYING TO WIN SASUKE OVER?
SHARINGAN THAT ACTUALLY ACQUIRE THE SUSANO'O ARE RARE...
I LIKE TO STOCK GOOD EYES.
IF HE BATTLES THE GOKAGE, HE'LL HONE HIS OCULAR POWERS EVEN FURTHER...
...WHICH IS WHY I SENT HIM IN HERE.
I WAS HOPING TO WEAKEN THE GOKAGE, TAKE SOME HOSTAGES...
...GUESS THAT WAS TOO MUCH TO ASK.
HOS-TAGES ...? WHAT-EVER FOR?!
TO ENSURE THE SMOOTH FULFILL-MENT OF OPERA-TION TSUKI NO ME, THE EYE OF THE MOON!
I AM TRULY SURPRISED THAT THE INFAMOUS UCHIHA MADARA IS STILL ALIVE ...
BUT I AM ALSO CONFUSED... WHY DO YOU OF ALL PEOPLE HAVE TO ENGAGE IN SUCH ROUNDABOUT TACTICS?
WITH YOUR POWER, YOU OUGHT TO BE ABLE TO EASILY BRING ANY PLAN TO FRUITION.

READ THIS WAY

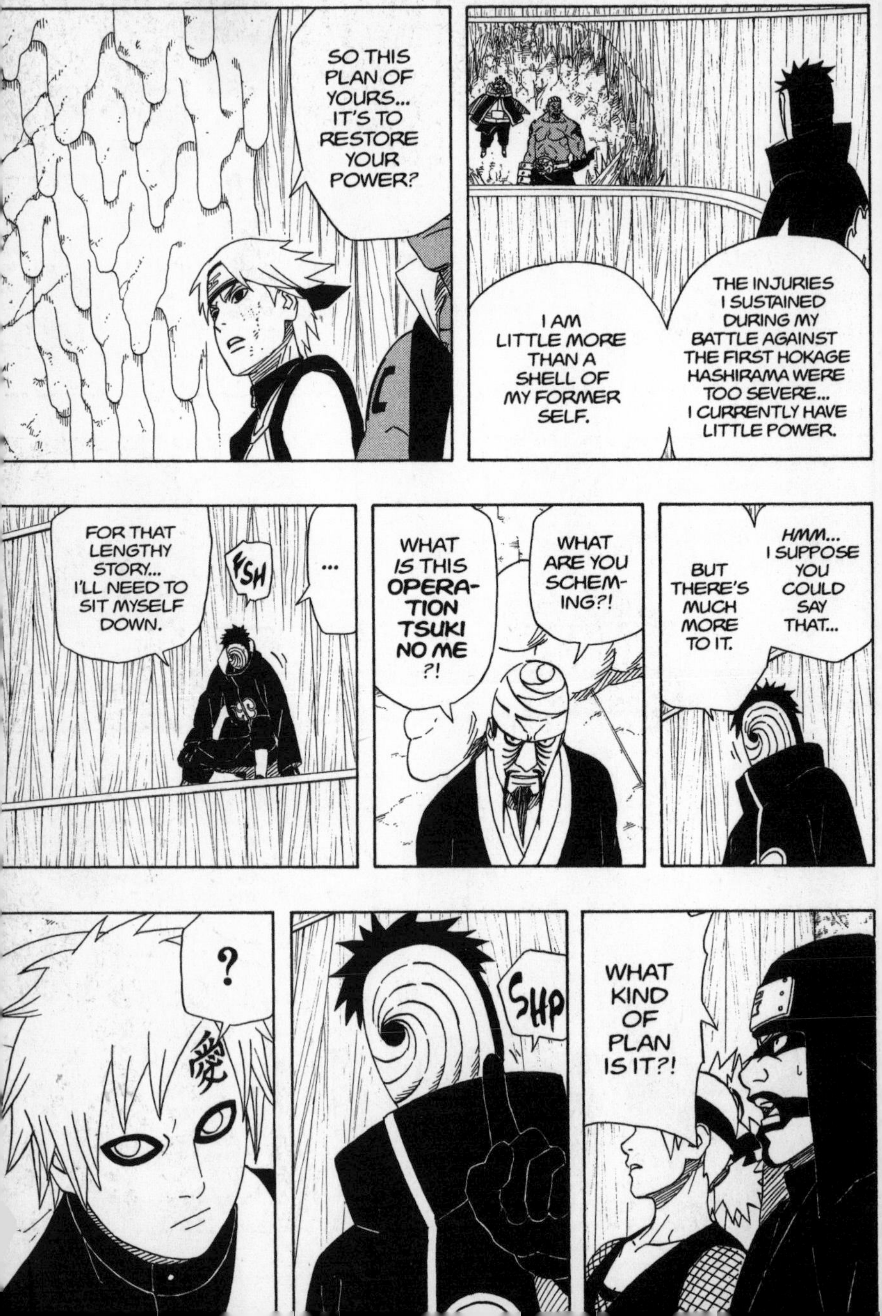
THE INJURIES I SUSTAINED DURING MY BATTLE AGAINST THE FIRST HOKAGE HASHIRAMA WERE TOO SEVERE... I CURRENTLY HAVE LITTLE POWER.
I AM LITTLE MORE THAN A SHELL OF MY FORMER SELF.
SO THIS PLAN OF YOURS... IT'S TO RESTORE YOUR POWER?
HMM... I SUPPOSE YOU COULD SAY THAT...
BUT THERE'S MUCH MORE TO IT.
WHAT ARE YOU SCHEMING?!
WHAT IS THIS OPERATION TSUKI NO ME?!
...
YSH
FOR THAT LENGTHY STORY... I'LL NEED TO SIT MYSELF DOWN.
WHAT KIND OF PLAN IS IT?!
SHP
?

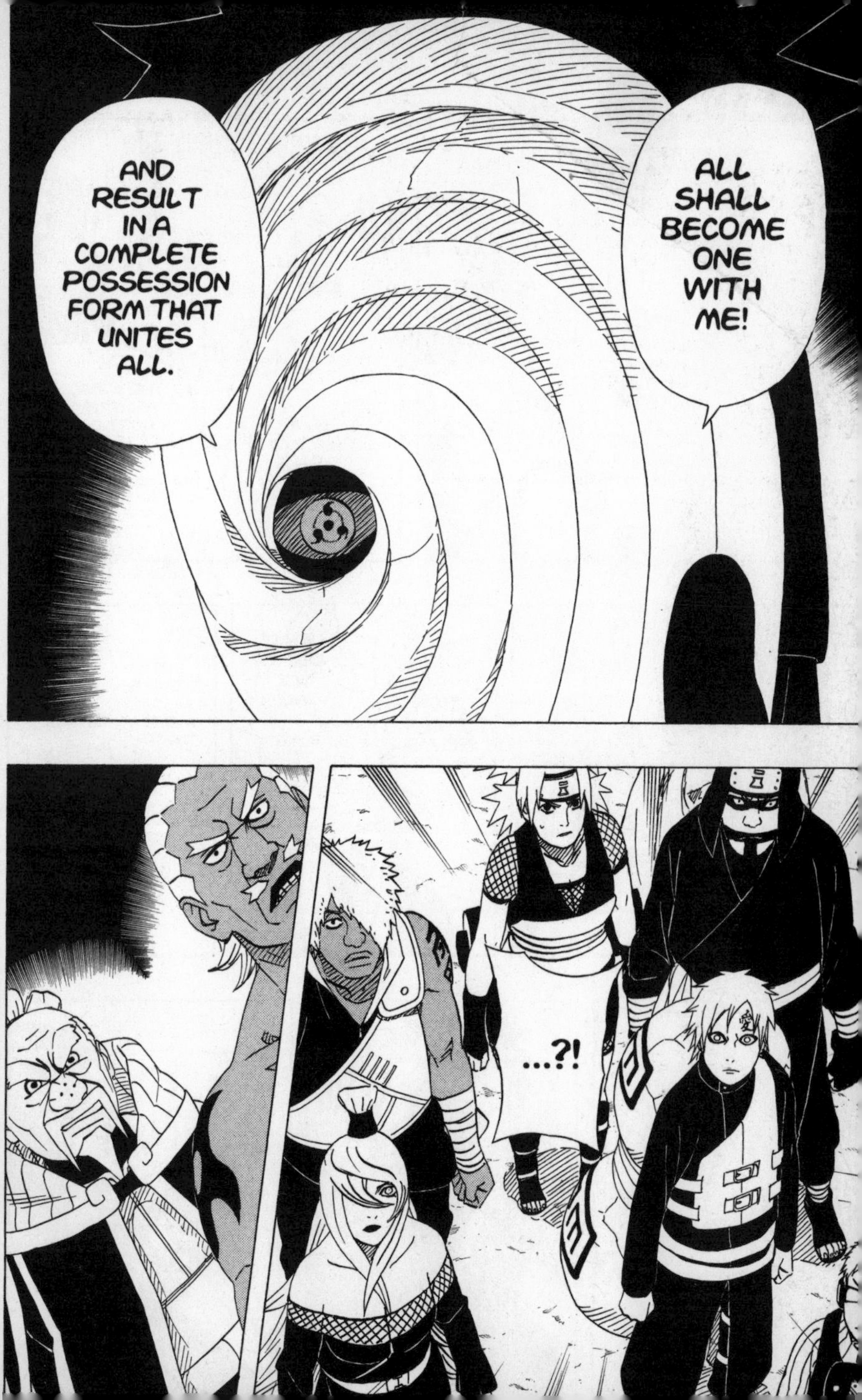
ALL SHALL BECOME ONE WITH ME!
AND RESULT IN A COMPLETE POSSESSION FORM THAT UNITES ALL.
...?!

READ THIS WAY

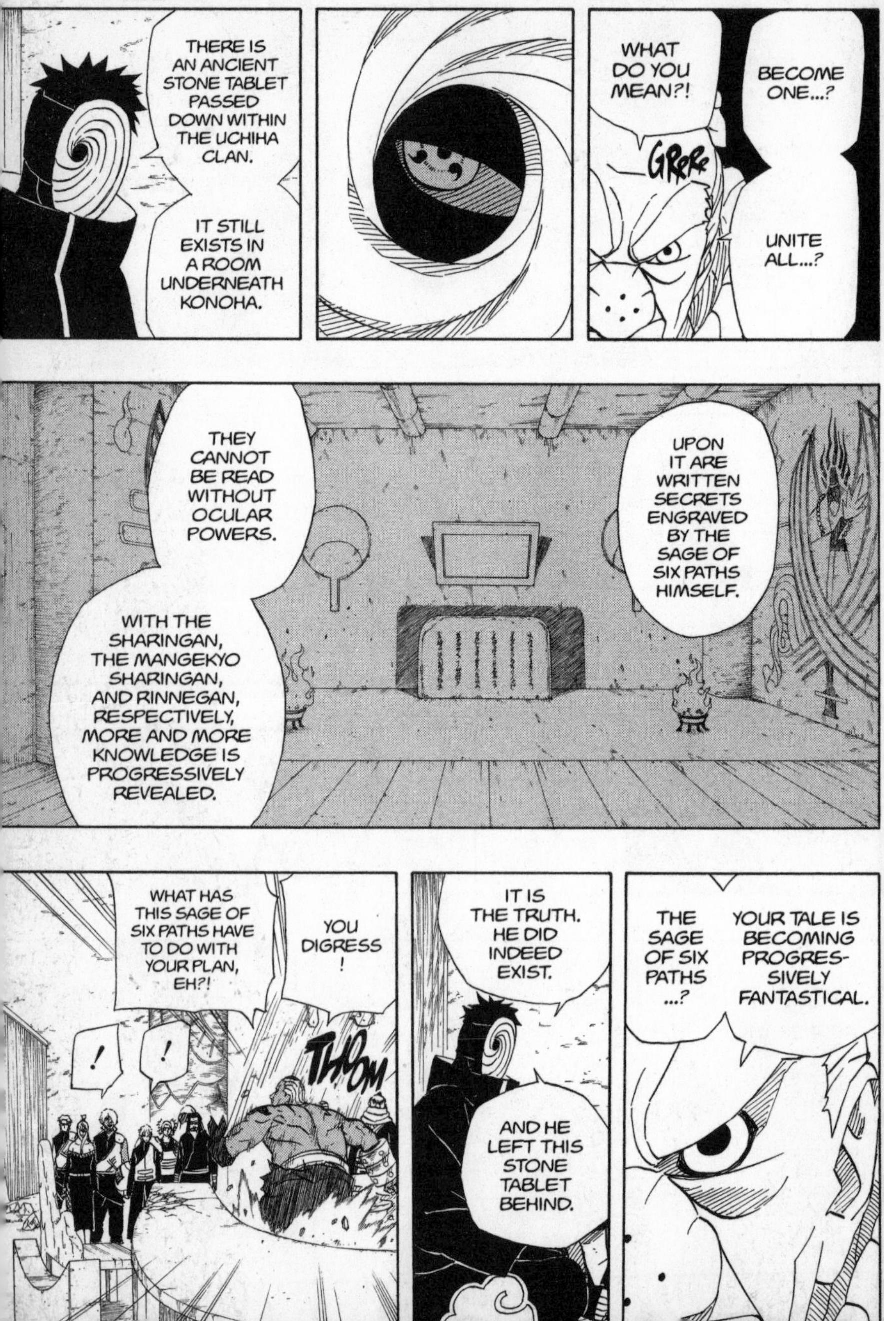
BECOME ONE...?
UNITE ALL...?
WHAT DO YOU MEAN?!
GRRRR
THERE IS AN ANCIENT STONE TABLET PASSED DOWN WITHIN THE UCHIHA CLAN.
IT STILL EXISTS IN A ROOM UNDERNEATH KONOHA.
UPON IT ARE WRITTEN SECRETS ENGRAVED BY THE SAGE OF SIX PATHS HIMSELF.
THEY CANNOT BE READ WITHOUT OCULAR POWERS.
WITH THE SHARINGAN, THE MANGEKYO SHARINGAN, AND RINNEGAN, RESPECTIVELY, MORE AND MORE KNOWLEDGE IS PROGRESSIVELY REVEALED.
YOUR TALE IS BECOMING PROGRES-SIVELY FANTASTICAL.
THE SAGE OF SIX PATHS ...?
IT IS THE TRUTH. HE DID INDEED EXIST.
AND HE LEFT THIS STONE TABLET BEHIND.
YOU DIGRESS!
WHAT HAS THIS SAGE OF SIX PATHS HAVE TO DO WITH YOUR PLAN, EH?!
THOOM
!
!

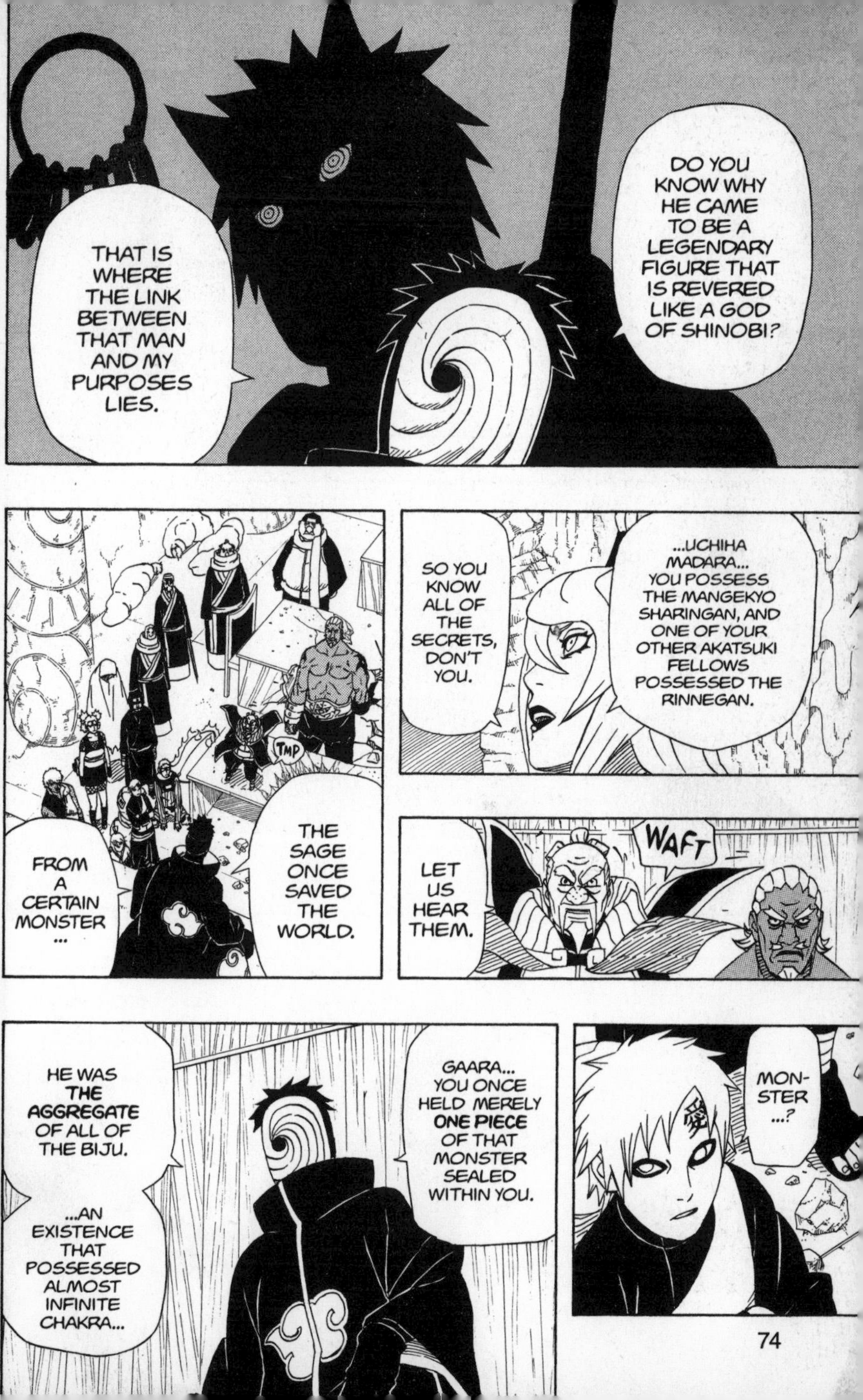
DO YOU KNOW WHY HE CAME TO BE A LEGENDARY FIGURE THAT IS REVERED LIKE A GOD OF SHINOBI?
THAT IS WHERE THE LINK BETWEEN THAT MAN AND MY PURPOSES LIES.
...UCHIHA MADARA... YOU POSSESS THE MANGEKYO SHARINGAN, AND ONE OF YOUR OTHER AKATSUKI FELLOWS POSSESSED THE RINNEGAN.
SO YOU KNOW ALL OF THE SECRETS, DON'T YOU.
WAFT
LET US HEAR THEM.
TMP
THE SAGE ONCE SAVED THE WORLD.
FROM A CERTAIN MONSTER...
MON-STER...?
GAARA... YOU ONCE HELD MERELY **ONE PIECE** OF THAT MONSTER SEALED WITHIN YOU.
HE WAS **THE AGGREGATE** OF ALL OF THE BIJU.
...AN EXISTENCE THAT POSSESSED ALMOST INFINITE CHAKRA...

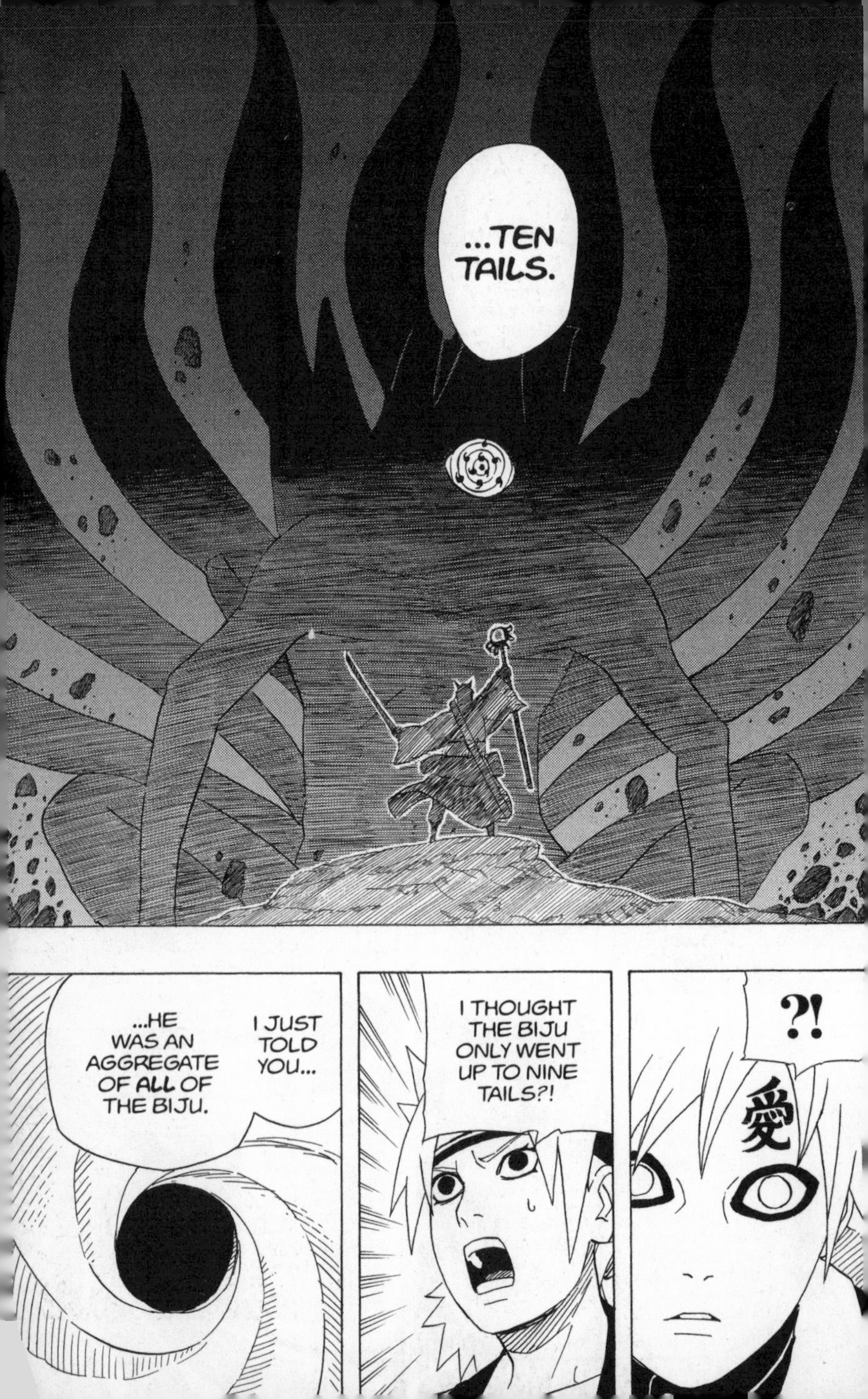
...TEN TAILS.
?!
I THOUGHT THE BIJU ONLY WENT UP TO NINE TAILS?!
I JUST TOLD YOU...
...HE WAS AN AGGREGATE OF **ALL** OF THE BIJU.
愛

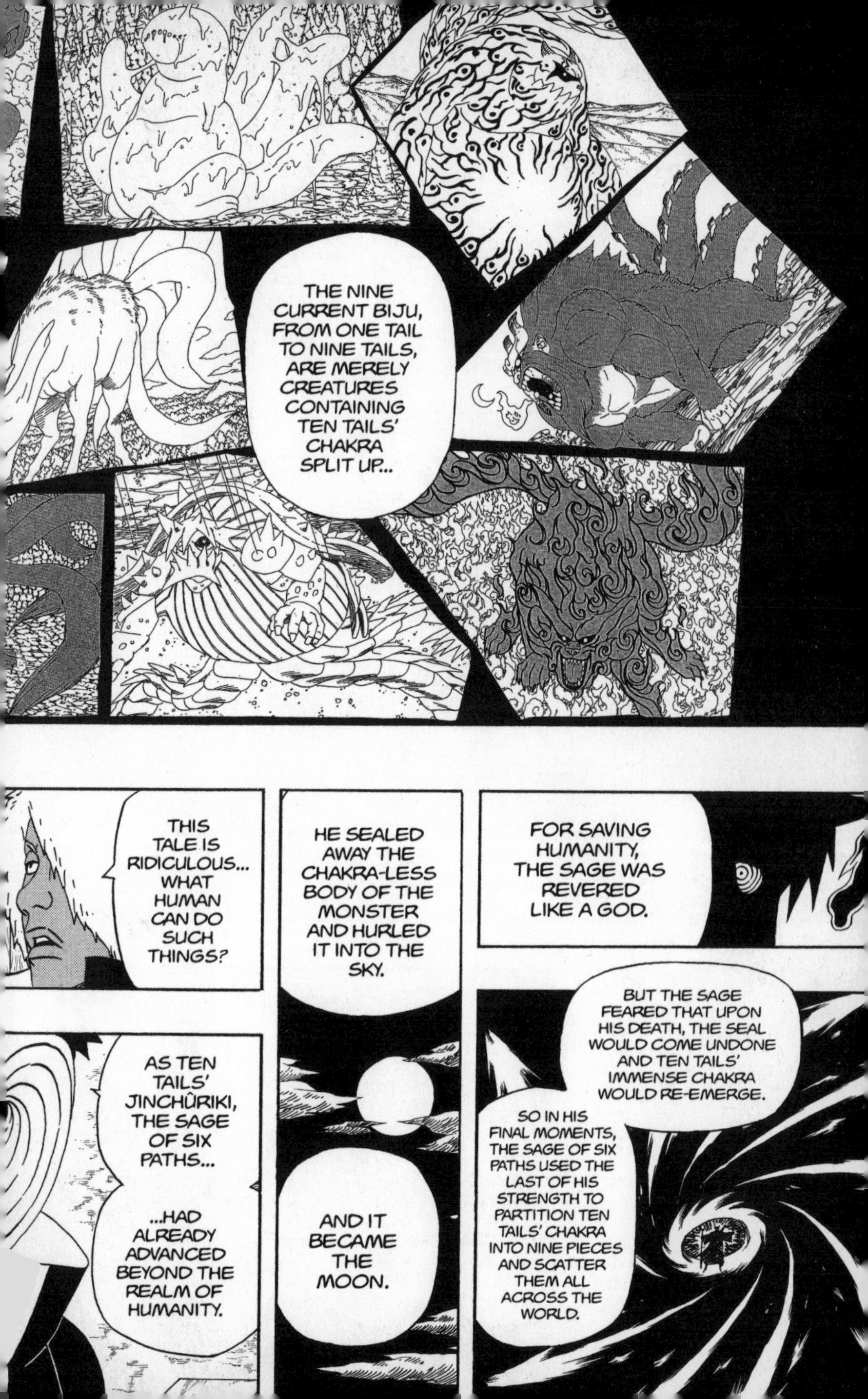
THE NINE CURRENT BIJU, FROM ONE TAIL TO NINE TAILS, ARE MERELY CREATURES CONTAINING TEN TAILS' CHAKRA SPLIT UP...
FOR SAVING HUMANITY, THE SAGE WAS REVERED LIKE A GOD.
BUT THE SAGE FEARED THAT UPON HIS DEATH, THE SEAL WOULD COME UNDONE AND TEN TAILS' IMMENSE CHAKRA WOULD RE-EMERGE.
SO IN HIS FINAL MOMENTS, THE SAGE OF SIX PATHS USED THE LAST OF HIS STRENGTH TO PARTITION TEN TAILS' CHAKRA INTO NINE PIECES AND SCATTER THEM ALL ACROSS THE WORLD.
HE SEALED AWAY THE CHAKRA-LESS BODY OF THE MONSTER AND HURLED IT INTO THE SKY.
AND IT BECAME THE MOON.
THIS TALE IS RIDICULOUS... WHAT HUMAN CAN DO SUCH THINGS?
AS TEN TAILS' JINCHÛRIKI, THE SAGE OF SIX PATHS...
...HAD ALREADY ADVANCED BEYOND THE REALM OF HUMANITY.

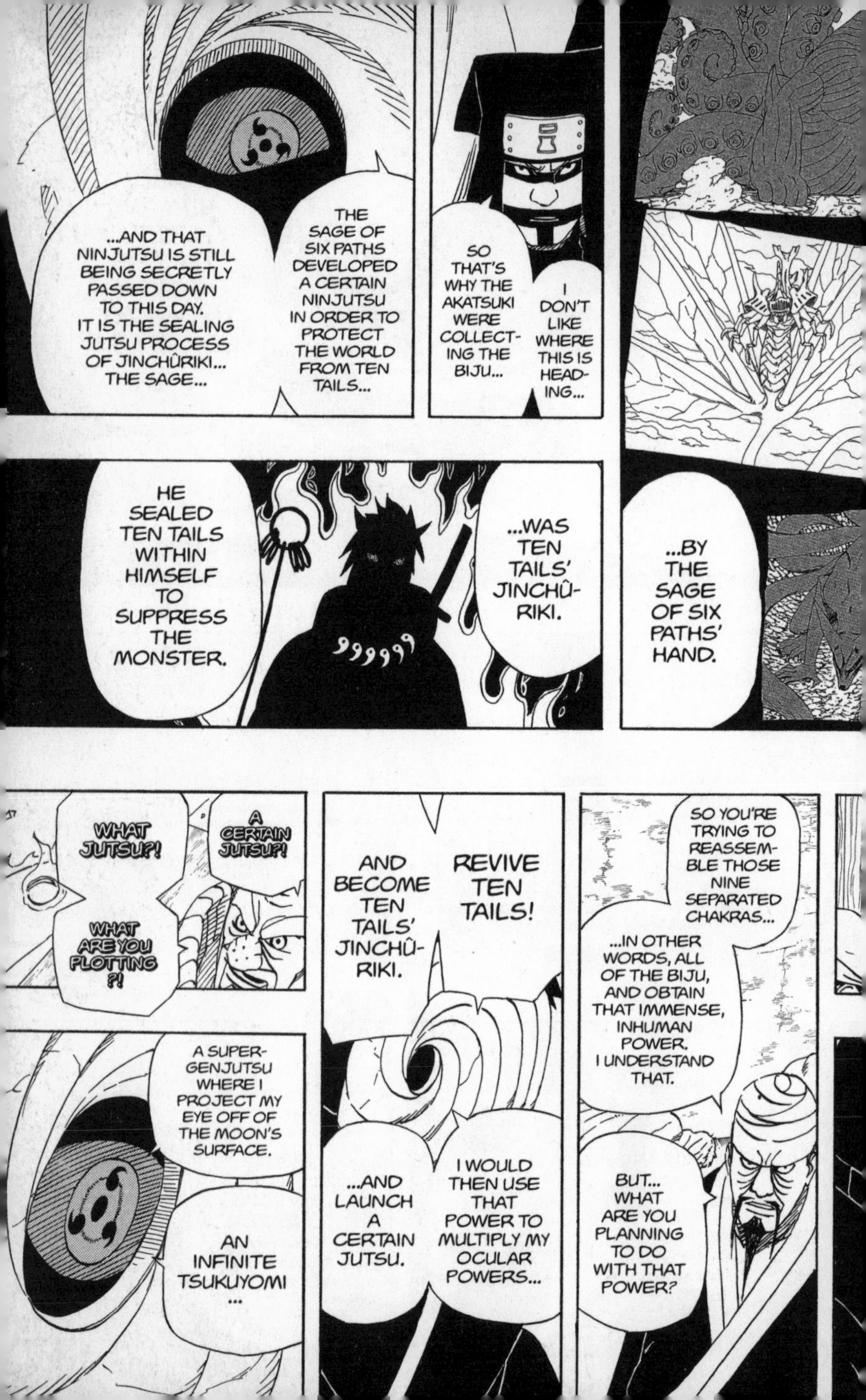
SO THAT'S WHY THE AKATSUKI WERE COLLECT-ING THE BIJU...
I DON'T LIKE WHERE THIS IS HEAD-ING...
THE SAGE OF SIX PATHS DEVELOPED A CERTAIN NINJUTSU IN ORDER TO PROTECT THE WORLD FROM TEN TAILS...
...AND THAT NINJUTSU IS STILL BEING SECRETLY PASSED DOWN TO THIS DAY. IT IS THE SEALING JUTSU PROCESS OF JINCHÛRIKI... THE SAGE...
...BY THE SAGE OF SIX PATHS' HAND.
...WAS TEN TAILS' JINCHÛ-RIKI.
HE SEALED TEN TAILS WITHIN HIMSELF TO SUPPRESS THE MONSTER.
SO YOU'RE TRYING TO REASSEM-BLE THOSE NINE SEPARATED CHAKRAS...
...IN OTHER WORDS, ALL OF THE BIJU, AND OBTAIN THAT IMMENSE, INHUMAN POWER. I UNDERSTAND THAT.
BUT... WHAT ARE YOU PLANNING TO DO WITH THAT POWER?
REVIVE TEN TAILS!
AND BECOME TEN TAILS' JINCHÛ-RIKI.
I WOULD THEN USE THAT POWER TO MULTIPLY MY OCULAR POWERS...
...AND LAUNCH A CERTAIN JUTSU.
A CERTAIN JUTSU?!
WHAT JUTSU?!
WHAT ARE YOU PLOTTING?!
A SUPER-GENJUTSU WHERE I PROJECT MY EYE OFF OF THE MOON'S SURFACE.
AN INFINITE TSUKUYOMI...

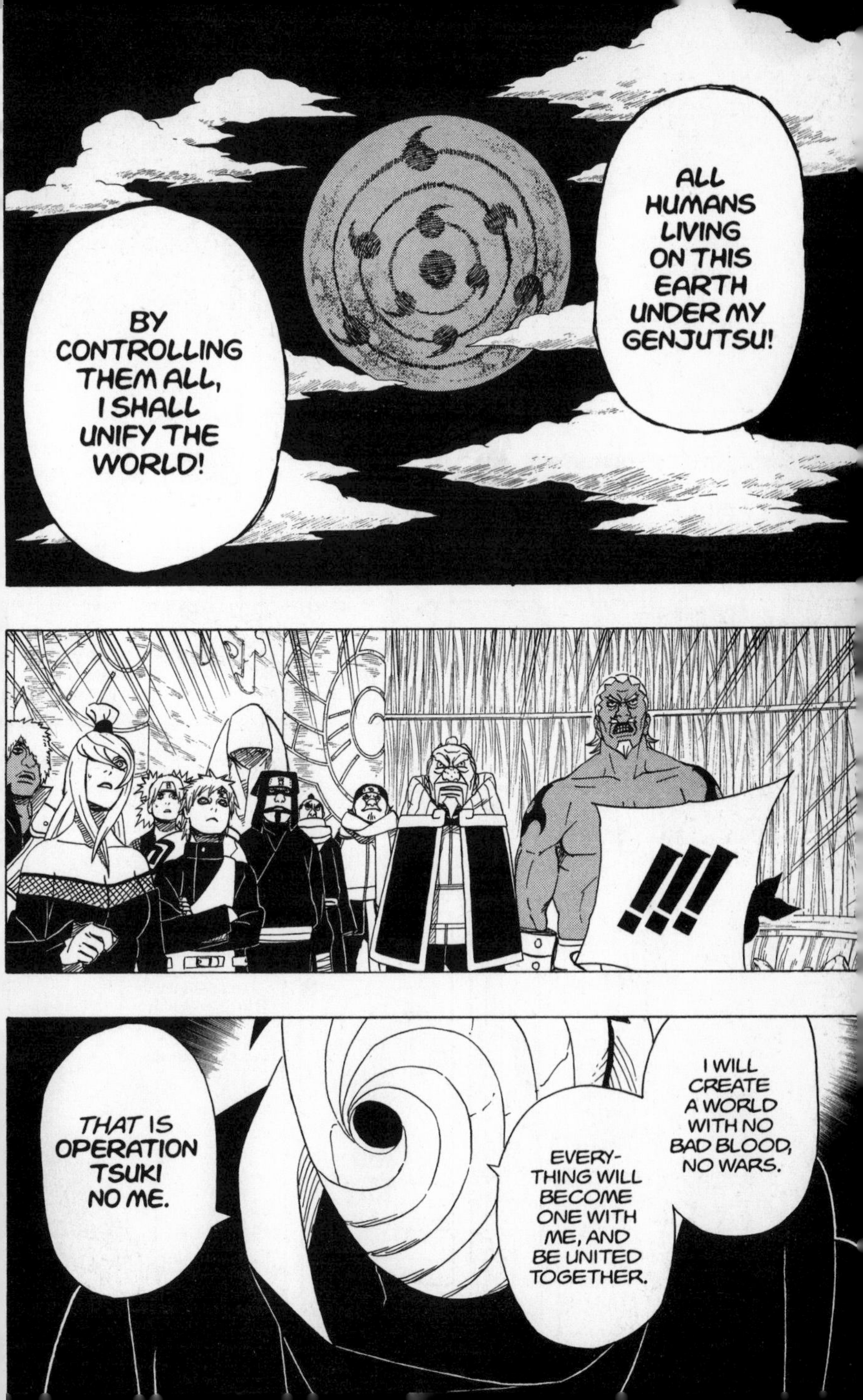
ALL HUMANS LIVING ON THIS EARTH UNDER MY GENJUTSU!
BY CONTROLLING THEM ALL, I SHALL UNIFY THE WORLD!
!!!
I WILL CREATE A WORLD WITH NO BAD BLOOD, NO WARS.
EVERY-THING WILL BECOME ONE WITH ME, AND BE UNITED TOGETHER.
THAT IS OPERATION TSUKI NO ME.

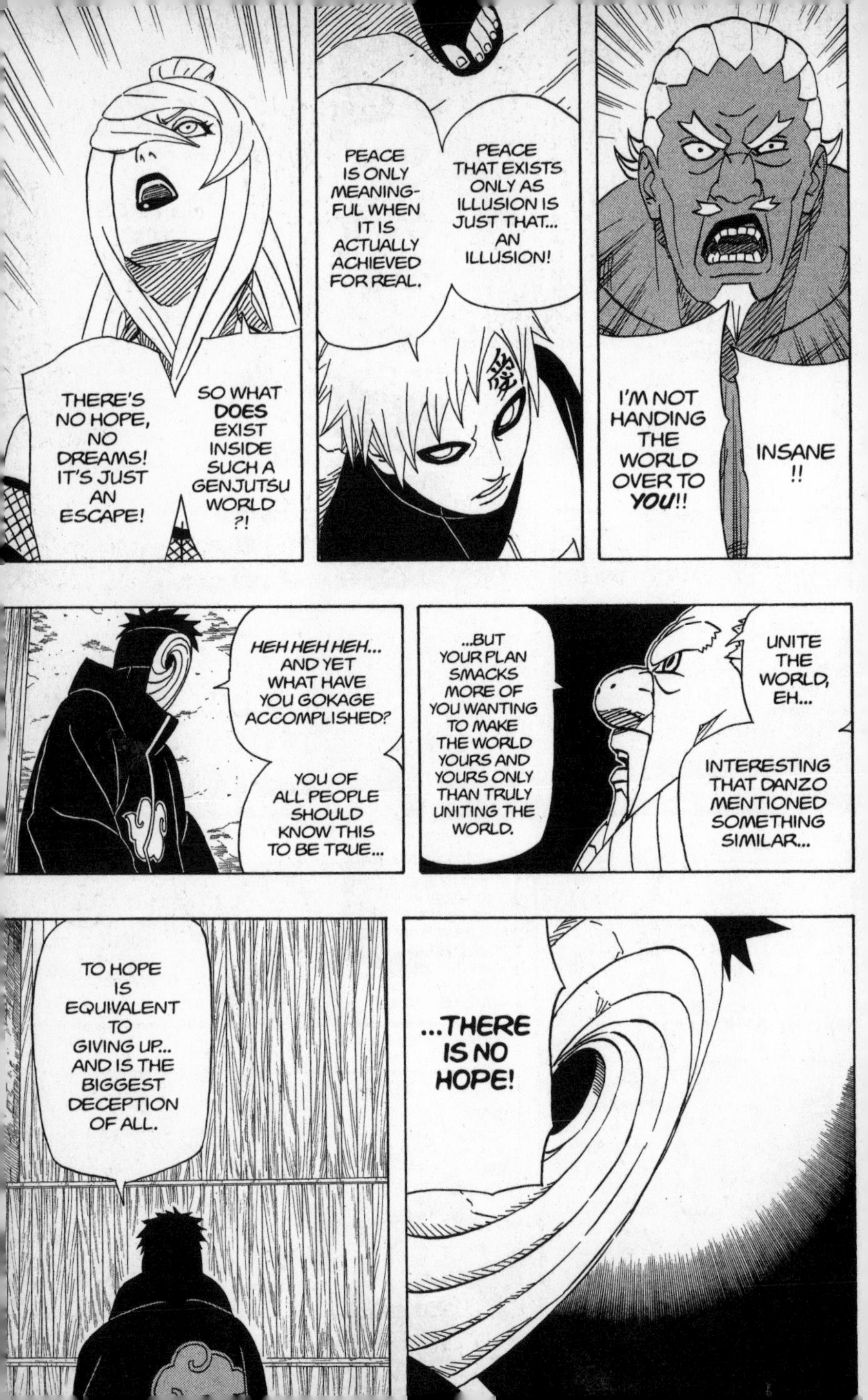
INSANE !!
I'M NOT HANDING THE WORLD OVER TO YOU!!
PEACE THAT EXISTS ONLY AS ILLUSION IS JUST THAT... AN ILLUSION!
PEACE IS ONLY MEANINGFUL WHEN IT IS ACTUALLY ACHIEVED FOR REAL.
SO WHAT DOES EXIST INSIDE SUCH A GENJUTSU WORLD ?!
THERE'S NO HOPE, NO DREAMS! IT'S JUST AN ESCAPE!
UNITE THE WORLD, EH...
INTERESTING THAT DANZO MENTIONED SOMETHING SIMILAR...
...BUT YOUR PLAN SMACKS MORE OF YOU WANTING TO MAKE THE WORLD YOURS AND YOURS ONLY THAN TRULY UNITING THE WORLD.
HEH HEH HEH... AND YET WHAT HAVE YOU GOKAGE ACCOMPLISHED?
YOU OF ALL PEOPLE SHOULD KNOW THIS TO BE TRUE...
...THERE IS NO HOPE!
TO HOPE IS EQUIVALENT TO GIVING UP... AND IS THE BIGGEST DECEPTION OF ALL.

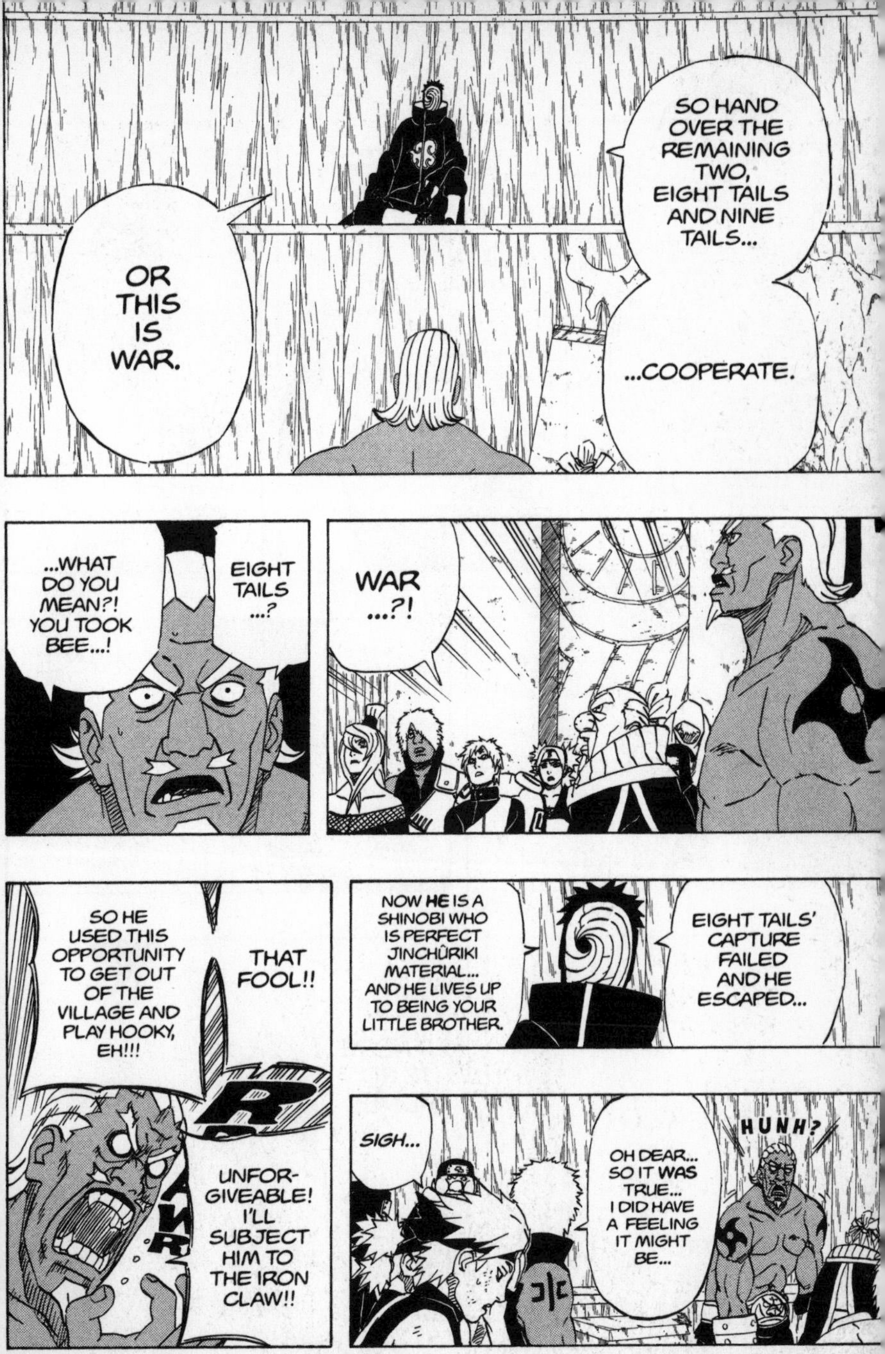
SO HAND OVER THE REMAINING TWO, EIGHT TAILS AND NINE TAILS... ...COOPERATE.
OR THIS IS WAR.
WAR ...?!
EIGHT TAILS ...?
...WHAT DO YOU MEAN?! YOU TOOK BEE...!
EIGHT TAILS' CAPTURE FAILED AND HE ESCAPED...
NOW **HE** IS A SHINOBI WHO IS PERFECT JINCHŪRIKI MATERIAL... AND HE LIVES UP TO BEING YOUR LITTLE BROTHER.
HUNH?
OH DEAR... SO IT **WAS** TRUE... I DID HAVE A FEELING IT MIGHT BE...
SIGH...
THAT FOOL!!
SO HE USED THIS OPPORTUNITY TO GET OUT OF THE VILLAGE AND PLAY HOOKY, EH!!!
RAWR
UNFOR-GIVEABLE! I'LL SUBJECT HIM TO THE IRON CLAW!!

READ THIS WAY

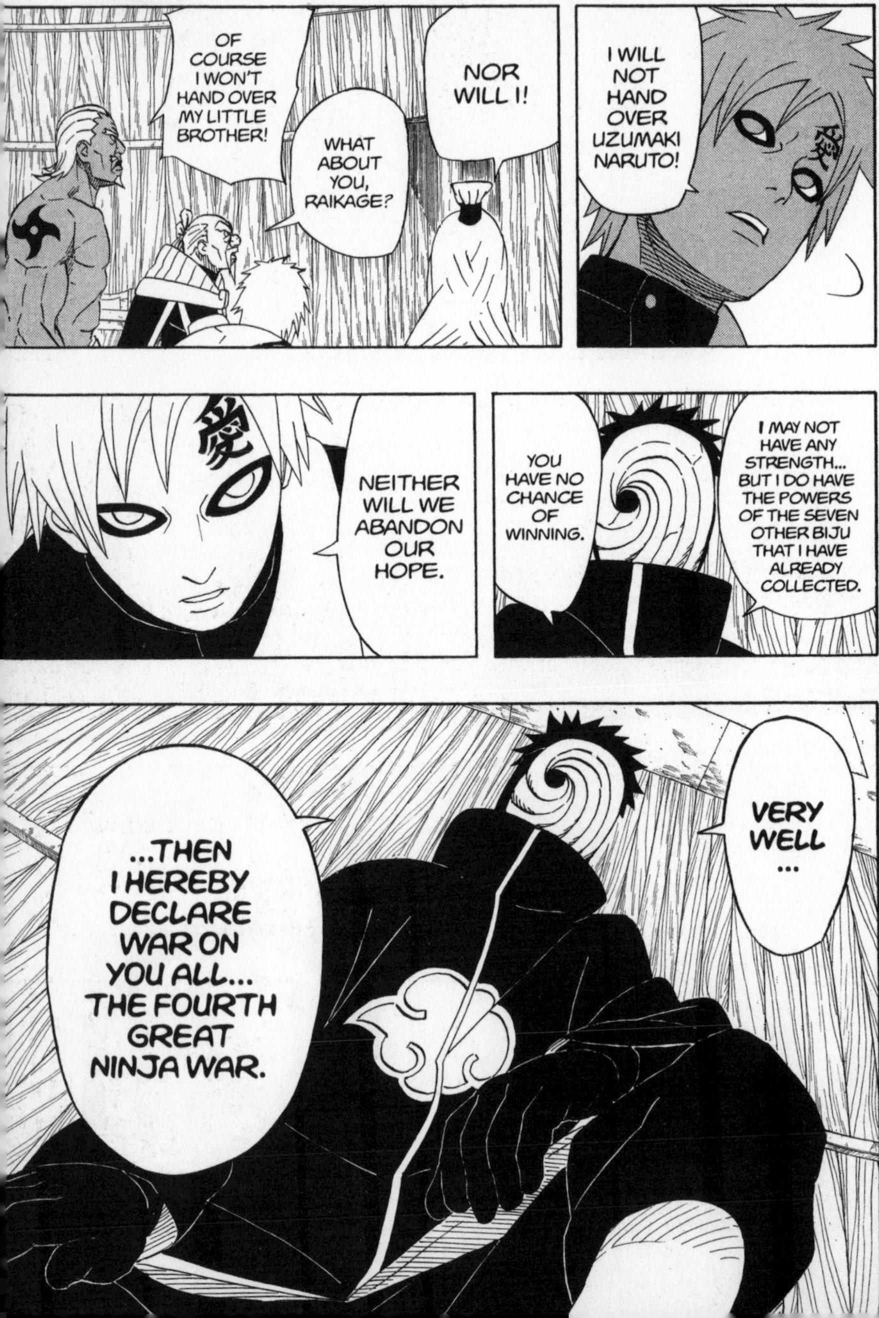
I WILL NOT HAND OVER UZUMAKI NARUTO!
NOR WILL I!
WHAT ABOUT YOU, RAIKAGE?
OF COURSE I WON'T HAND OVER MY LITTLE BROTHER!
I MAY NOT HAVE ANY STRENGTH... BUT I DO HAVE THE POWERS OF THE SEVEN OTHER BIJU THAT I HAVE ALREADY COLLECTED.
YOU HAVE NO CHANCE OF WINNING.
NEITHER WILL WE ABANDON OUR HOPE.
VERY WELL...
...THEN I HEREBY DECLARE WAR ON YOU ALL... THE FOURTH GREAT NINJA WAR.

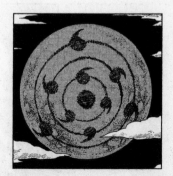

Number 468: Eight Tails and Nine Tails

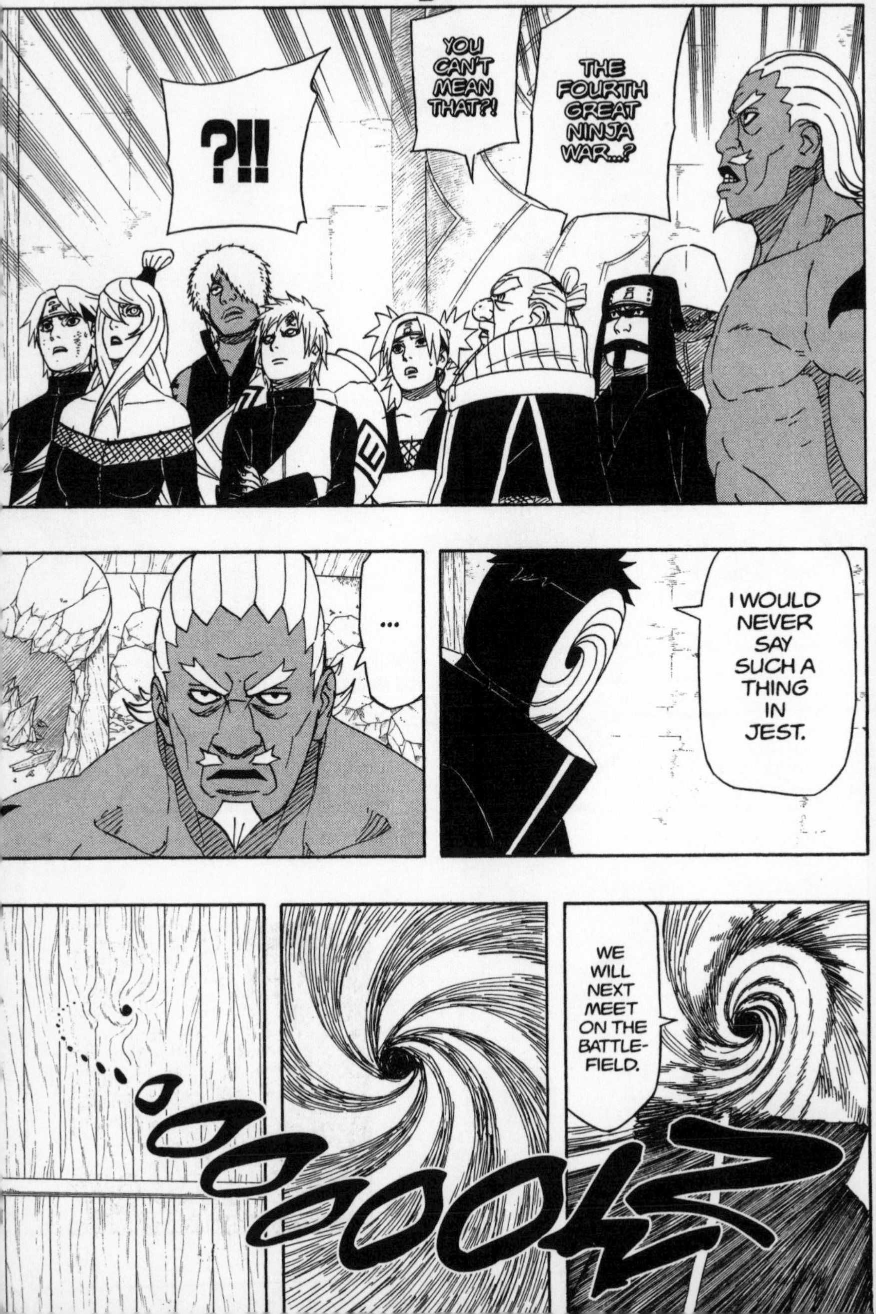
THE FOURTH GREAT NINJA WAR...?
YOU CAN'T MEAN THAT?!
?!!
I WOULD NEVER SAY SUCH A THING IN JEST.
...
WE WILL NEXT MEET ON THE BATTLE-FIELD.

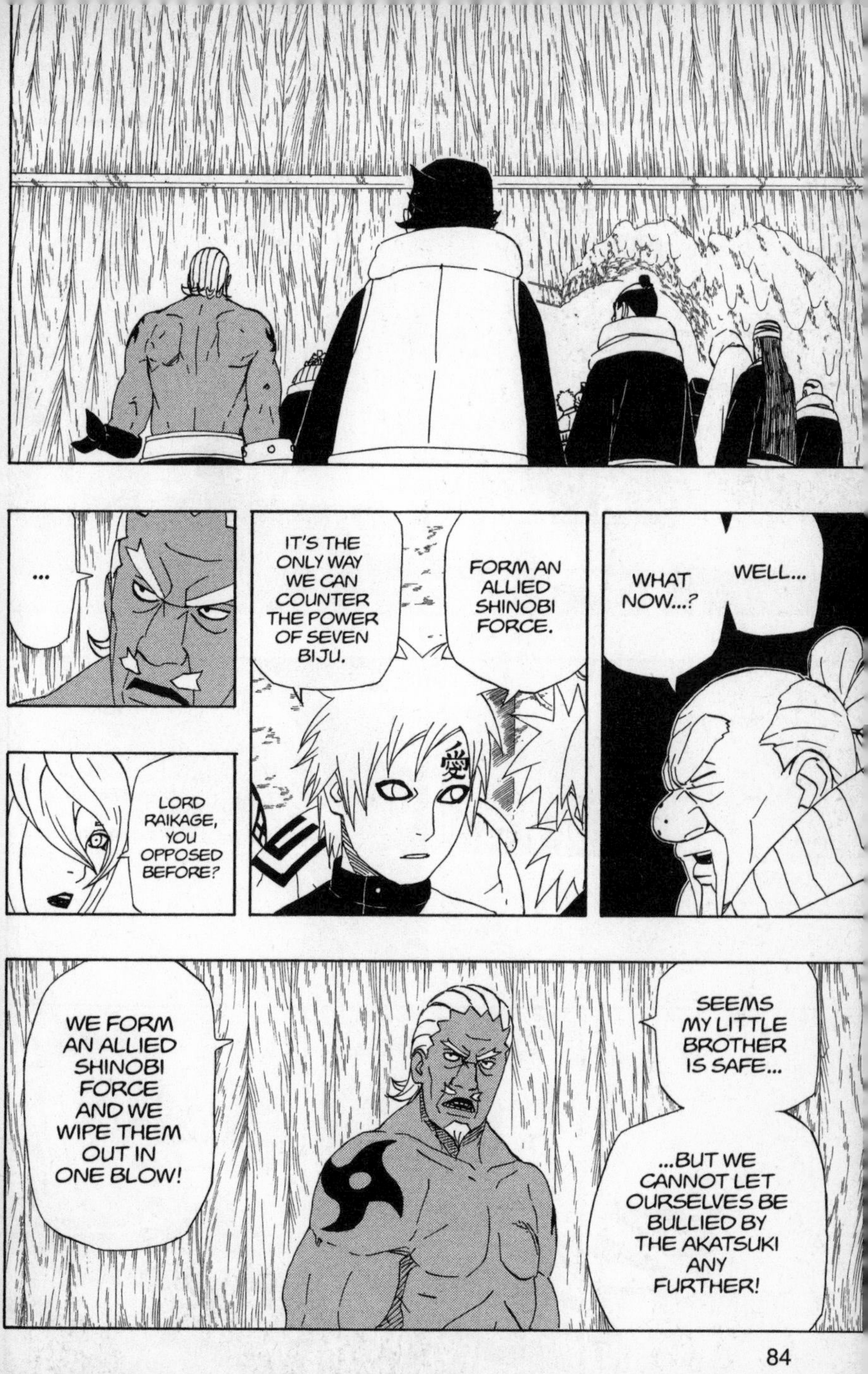
WELL...
WHAT NOW...?
FORM AN ALLIED SHINOBI FORCE.
IT'S THE ONLY WAY WE CAN COUNTER THE POWER OF SEVEN BIJU.
...
LORD RAIKAGE, YOU OPPOSED BEFORE?
SEEMS MY LITTLE BROTHER IS SAFE...
...BUT WE CANNOT LET OURSELVES BE BULLIED BY THE AKATSUKI ANY FURTHER!
WE FORM AN ALLIED SHINOBI FORCE AND WE WIPE THEM OUT IN ONE BLOW!

READ THIS WAY

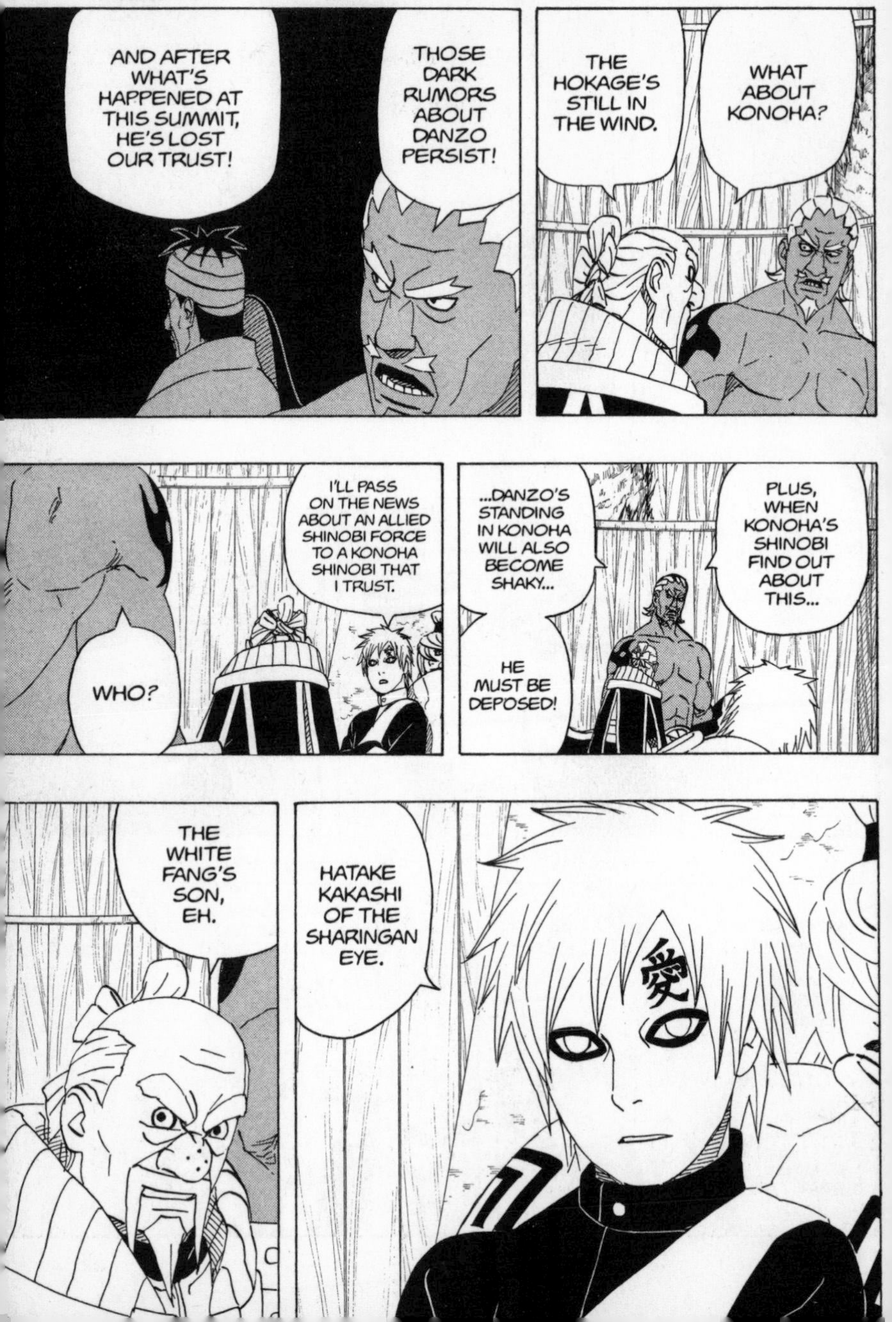
WHAT ABOUT KONOHA?
THE HOKAGE'S STILL IN THE WIND.
THOSE DARK RUMORS ABOUT DANZO PERSIST!
AND AFTER WHAT'S HAPPENED AT THIS SUMMIT, HE'S LOST OUR TRUST!
PLUS, WHEN KONOHA'S SHINOBI FIND OUT ABOUT THIS...
...DANZO'S STANDING IN KONOHA WILL ALSO BECOME SHAKY...
HE MUST BE DEPOSED!
I'LL PASS ON THE NEWS ABOUT AN ALLIED SHINOBI FORCE TO A KONOHA SHINOBI THAT I TRUST.
WHO?
HATAKE KAKASHI OF THE SHARINGAN EYE.
THE WHITE FANG'S SON, EH.

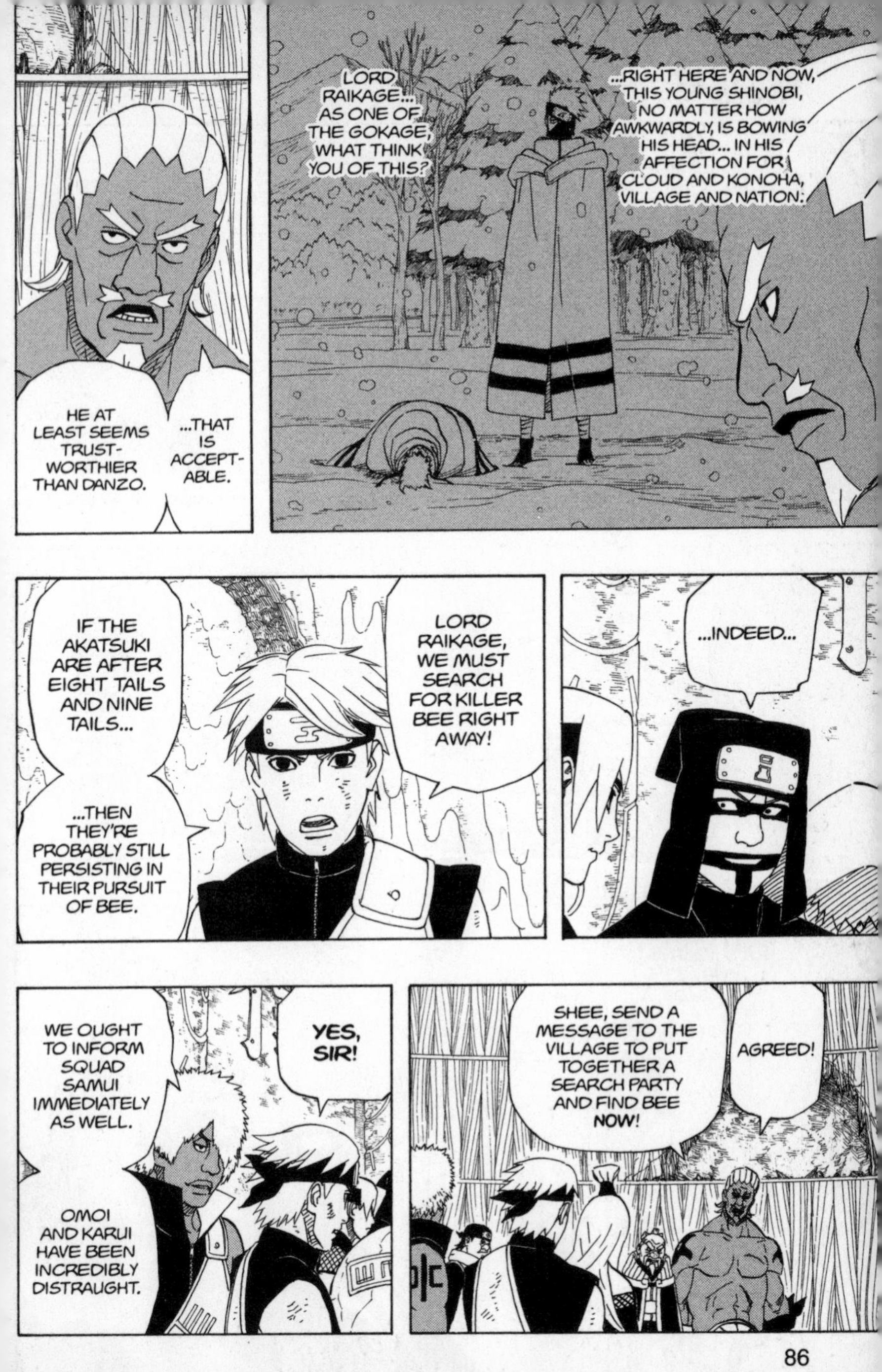
...RIGHT HERE AND NOW, THIS YOUNG SHINOBI, NO MATTER HOW AWKWARDLY, IS BOWING HIS HEAD... IN HIS AFFECTION FOR CLOUD AND KONOHA, VILLAGE AND NATION.
LORD RAIKAGE... AS ONE OF THE GOKAGE, WHAT THINK YOU OF THIS?
...THAT IS ACCEPTABLE.
HE AT LEAST SEEMS TRUSTWORTHIER THAN DANZO.
...INDEED...
LORD RAIKAGE, WE MUST SEARCH FOR KILLER BEE RIGHT AWAY!
IF THE AKATSUKI ARE AFTER EIGHT TAILS AND NINE TAILS...
...THEN THEY'RE PROBABLY STILL PERSISTING IN THEIR PURSUIT OF BEE.
AGREED!
SHEE, SEND A MESSAGE TO THE VILLAGE TO PUT TOGETHER A SEARCH PARTY AND FIND BEE NOW!
YES, SIR!
WE OUGHT TO INFORM SQUAD SAMUI IMMEDIATELY AS WELL.
OMOI AND KARUI HAVE BEEN INCREDIBLY DISTRAUGHT.

READ THIS WAY

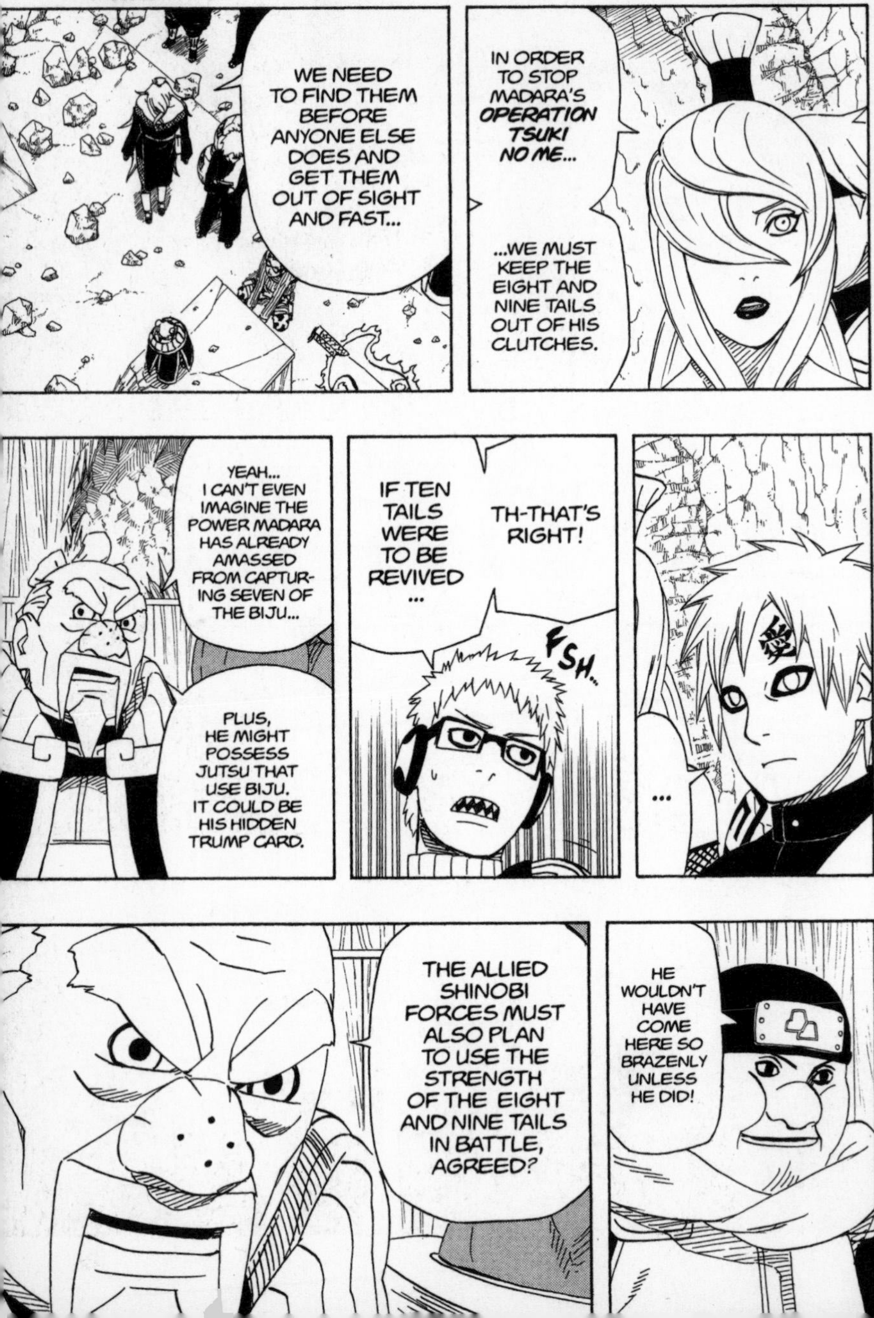
IN ORDER TO STOP MADARA'S *OPERATION TSUKI NO ME*...
...WE MUST KEEP THE EIGHT AND NINE TAILS OUT OF HIS CLUTCHES.
WE NEED TO FIND THEM BEFORE ANYONE ELSE DOES AND GET THEM OUT OF SIGHT AND FAST...
...
TH-THAT'S RIGHT!
IF TEN TAILS WERE TO BE REVIVED ...
FSH..
YEAH... I CAN'T EVEN IMAGINE THE POWER MADARA HAS ALREADY AMASSED FROM CAPTURING SEVEN OF THE BIJU...
PLUS, HE MIGHT POSSESS JUTSU THAT USE BIJU. IT COULD BE HIS HIDDEN TRUMP CARD.
HE WOULDN'T HAVE COME HERE SO BRAZENLY UNLESS HE DID!
THE ALLIED SHINOBI FORCES MUST ALSO PLAN TO USE THE STRENGTH OF THE EIGHT AND NINE TAILS IN BATTLE, AGREED?

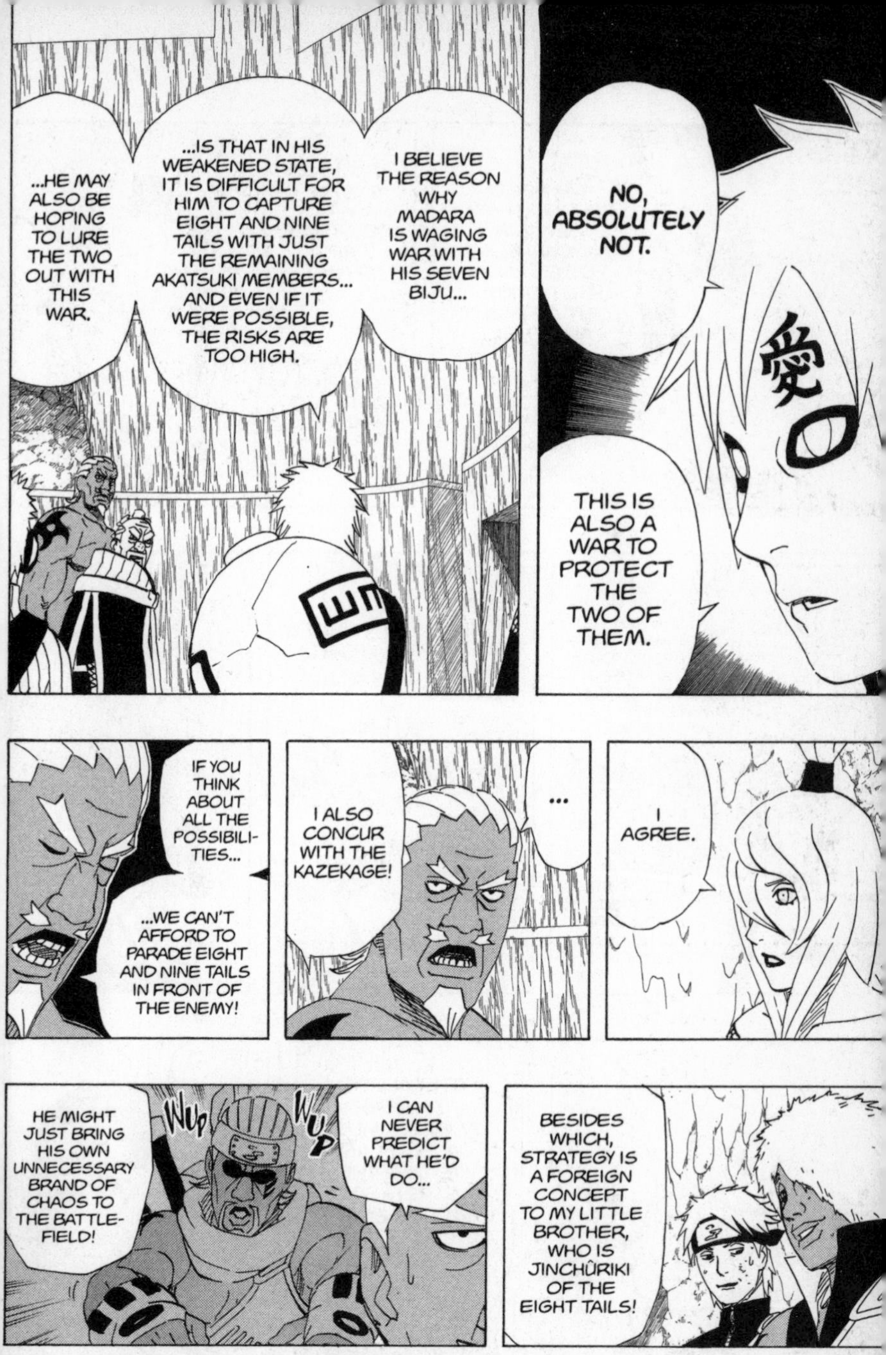
NO, ABSOLUTELY NOT.
THIS IS ALSO A WAR TO PROTECT THE TWO OF THEM.
I BELIEVE THE REASON WHY MADARA IS WAGING WAR WITH HIS SEVEN BIJU...
...IS THAT IN HIS WEAKENED STATE, IT IS DIFFICULT FOR HIM TO CAPTURE EIGHT AND NINE TAILS WITH JUST THE REMAINING AKATSUKI MEMBERS... AND EVEN IF IT WERE POSSIBLE, THE RISKS ARE TOO HIGH.
...HE MAY ALSO BE HOPING TO LURE THE TWO OUT WITH THIS WAR.
I AGREE.
...
I ALSO CONCUR WITH THE KAZEKAGE!
IF YOU THINK ABOUT ALL THE POSSIBILITIES...
...WE CAN'T AFFORD TO PARADE EIGHT AND NINE TAILS IN FRONT OF THE ENEMY!
BESIDES WHICH, STRATEGY IS A FOREIGN CONCEPT TO MY LITTLE BROTHER, WHO IS JINCHÛRIKI OF THE EIGHT TAILS!
I CAN NEVER PREDICT WHAT HE'D DO...
WUP
WUP
HE MIGHT JUST BRING HIS OWN UNNECESSARY BRAND OF CHAOS TO THE BATTLEFIELD!

READ THIS WAY

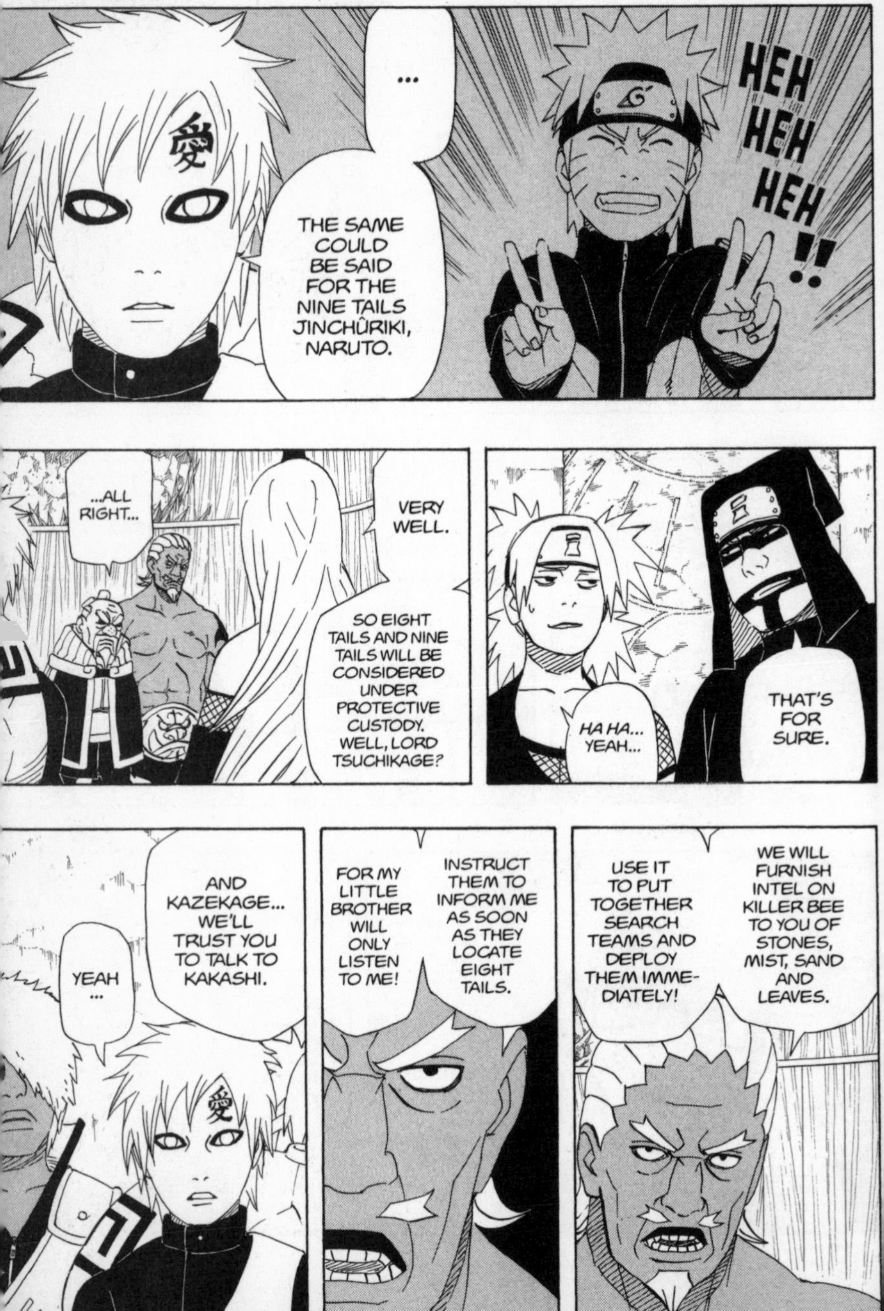

HEH HEH HEH!!
...
THE SAME COULD BE SAID FOR THE NINE TAILS JINCHÛRIKI, NARUTO.
THAT'S FOR SURE.
HA HA... YEAH...
VERY WELL.
SO EIGHT TAILS AND NINE TAILS WILL BE CONSIDERED UNDER PROTECTIVE CUSTODY. WELL, LORD TSUCHIKAGE?
...ALL RIGHT...
WE WILL FURNISH INTEL ON KILLER BEE TO YOU OF STONES, MIST, SAND AND LEAVES.
USE IT TO PUT TOGETHER SEARCH TEAMS AND DEPLOY THEM IMME-DIATELY!
INSTRUCT THEM TO INFORM ME AS SOON AS THEY LOCATE EIGHT TAILS.
FOR MY LITTLE BROTHER WILL ONLY LISTEN TO ME!
AND KAZEKAGE... WE'LL TRUST YOU TO TALK TO KAKASHI.
YEAH ...

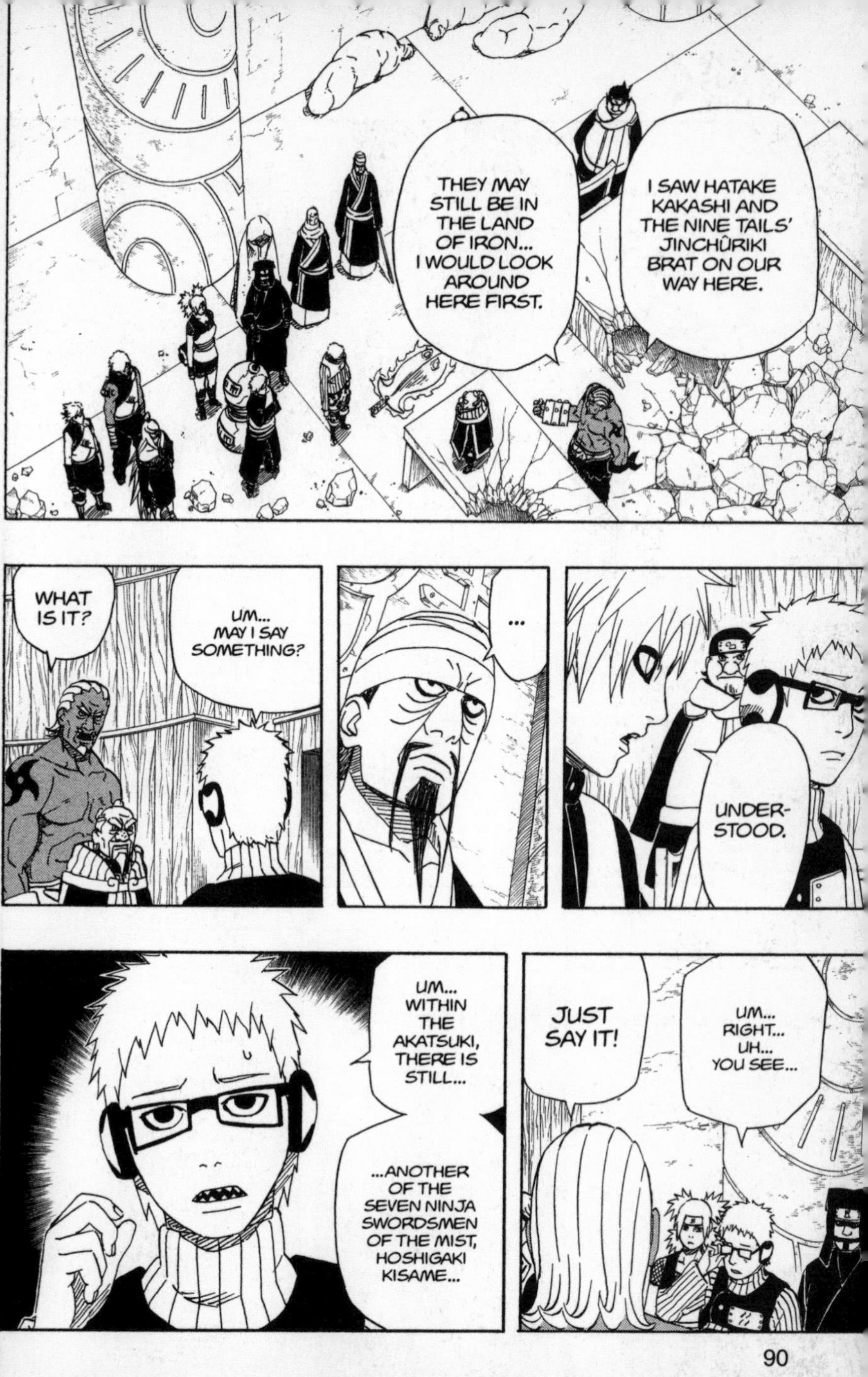
I SAW HATAKE KAKASHI AND THE NINE TAILS' JINCHÛRIKI BRAT ON OUR WAY HERE.
THEY MAY STILL BE IN THE LAND OF IRON... I WOULD LOOK AROUND HERE FIRST.
UNDER-STOOD.
...
UM... MAY I SAY SOMETHING?
WHAT IS IT?
UM... RIGHT... UH... YOU SEE...
JUST SAY IT!
UM... WITHIN THE AKATSUKI, THERE IS STILL...
...ANOTHER OF THE SEVEN NINJA SWORDSMEN OF THE MIST, HOSHIGAKI KISAME...

READ THIS WAY

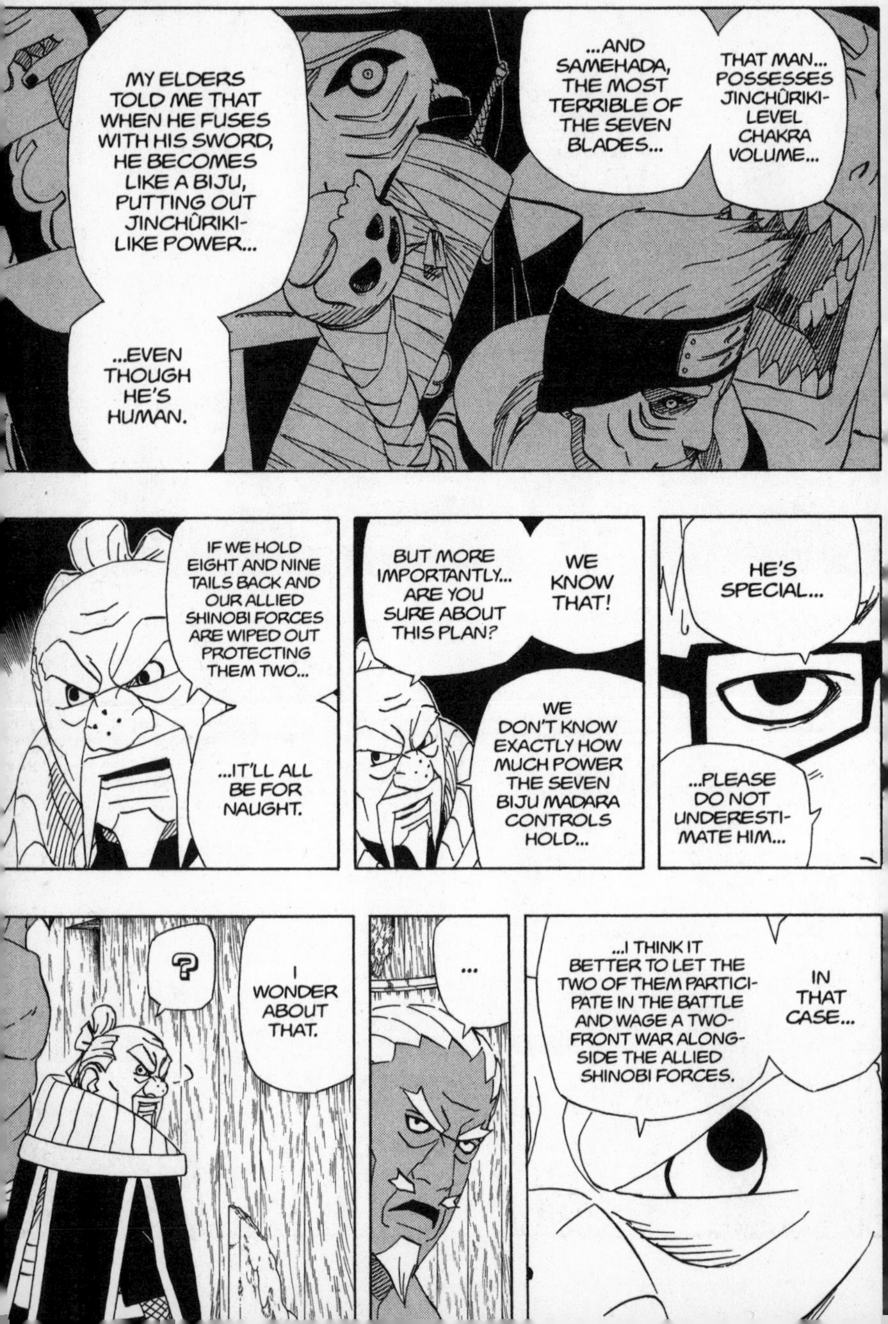
THAT MAN... POSSESSES JINCHÛRIKI-LEVEL CHAKRA VOLUME...
...AND SAMEHADA, THE MOST TERRIBLE OF THE SEVEN BLADES...
MY ELDERS TOLD ME THAT WHEN HE FUSES WITH HIS SWORD, HE BECOMES LIKE A BIJU, PUTTING OUT JINCHÛRIKI-LIKE POWER...
...EVEN THOUGH HE'S HUMAN.
HE'S SPECIAL...
...PLEASE DO NOT UNDERESTI-MATE HIM...
WE KNOW THAT!
BUT MORE IMPORTANTLY... ARE YOU SURE ABOUT THIS PLAN?
WE DON'T KNOW EXACTLY HOW MUCH POWER THE SEVEN BIJU MADARA CONTROLS HOLD...
IF WE HOLD EIGHT AND NINE TAILS BACK AND OUR ALLIED SHINOBI FORCES ARE WIPED OUT PROTECTING THEM TWO...
...IT'LL ALL BE FOR NAUGHT.
IN THAT CASE...
...I THINK IT BETTER TO LET THE TWO OF THEM PARTICI-PATE IN THE BATTLE AND WAGE A TWO-FRONT WAR ALONG-SIDE THE ALLIED SHINOBI FORCES.
...
I WONDER ABOUT THAT.
?

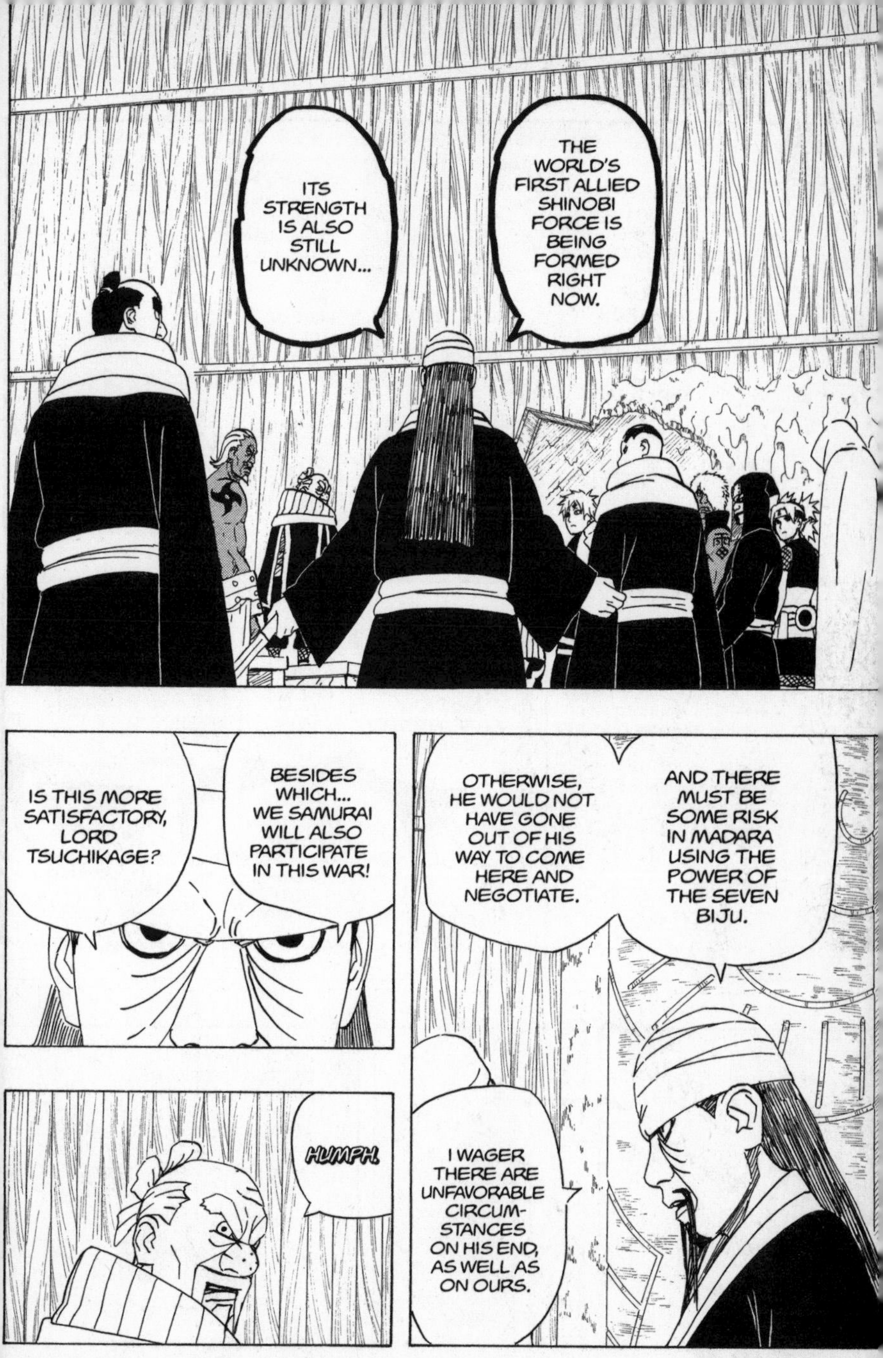
THE WORLD'S FIRST ALLIED SHINOBI FORCE IS BEING FORMED RIGHT NOW.
ITS STRENGTH IS ALSO STILL UNKNOWN...
AND THERE MUST BE SOME RISK IN MADARA USING THE POWER OF THE SEVEN BIJU.
OTHERWISE, HE WOULD NOT HAVE GONE OUT OF HIS WAY TO COME HERE AND NEGOTIATE.
I WAGER THERE ARE UNFAVORABLE CIRCUM-STANCES ON HIS END, AS WELL AS ON OURS.
BESIDES WHICH... WE SAMURAI WILL ALSO PARTICIPATE IN THIS WAR!
IS THIS MORE SATISFACTORY, LORD TSUCHIKAGE?
HUMPH.

READ THIS WAY

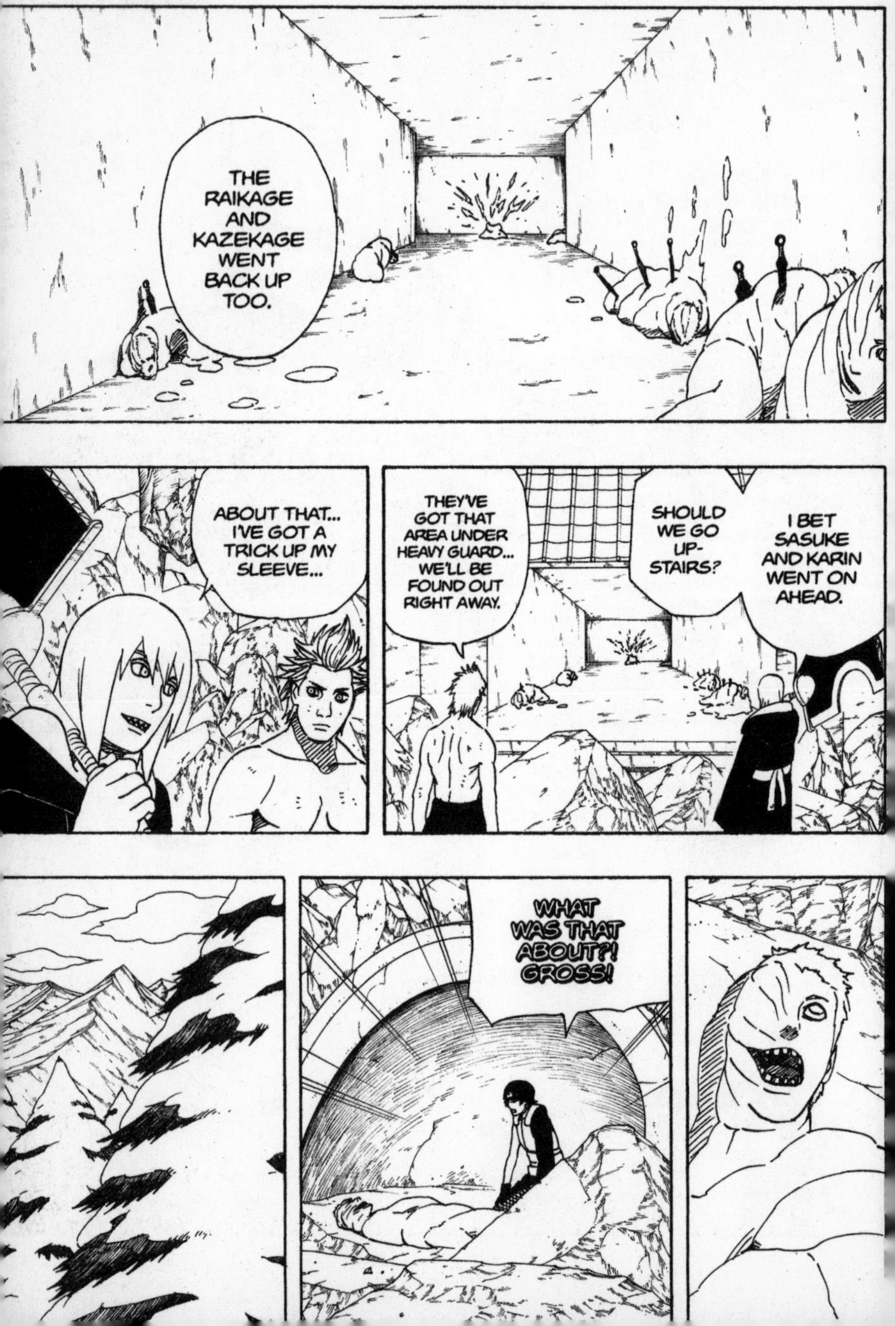
THE RAIKAGE AND KAZEKAGE WENT BACK UP TOO.
I BET SASUKE AND KARIN WENT ON AHEAD.
SHOULD WE GO UP-STAIRS?
THEY'VE GOT THAT AREA UNDER HEAVY GUARD... WE'LL BE FOUND OUT RIGHT AWAY.
ABOUT THAT... I'VE GOT A TRICK UP MY SLEEVE...
WHAT WAS THAT ABOUT?! GROSS!

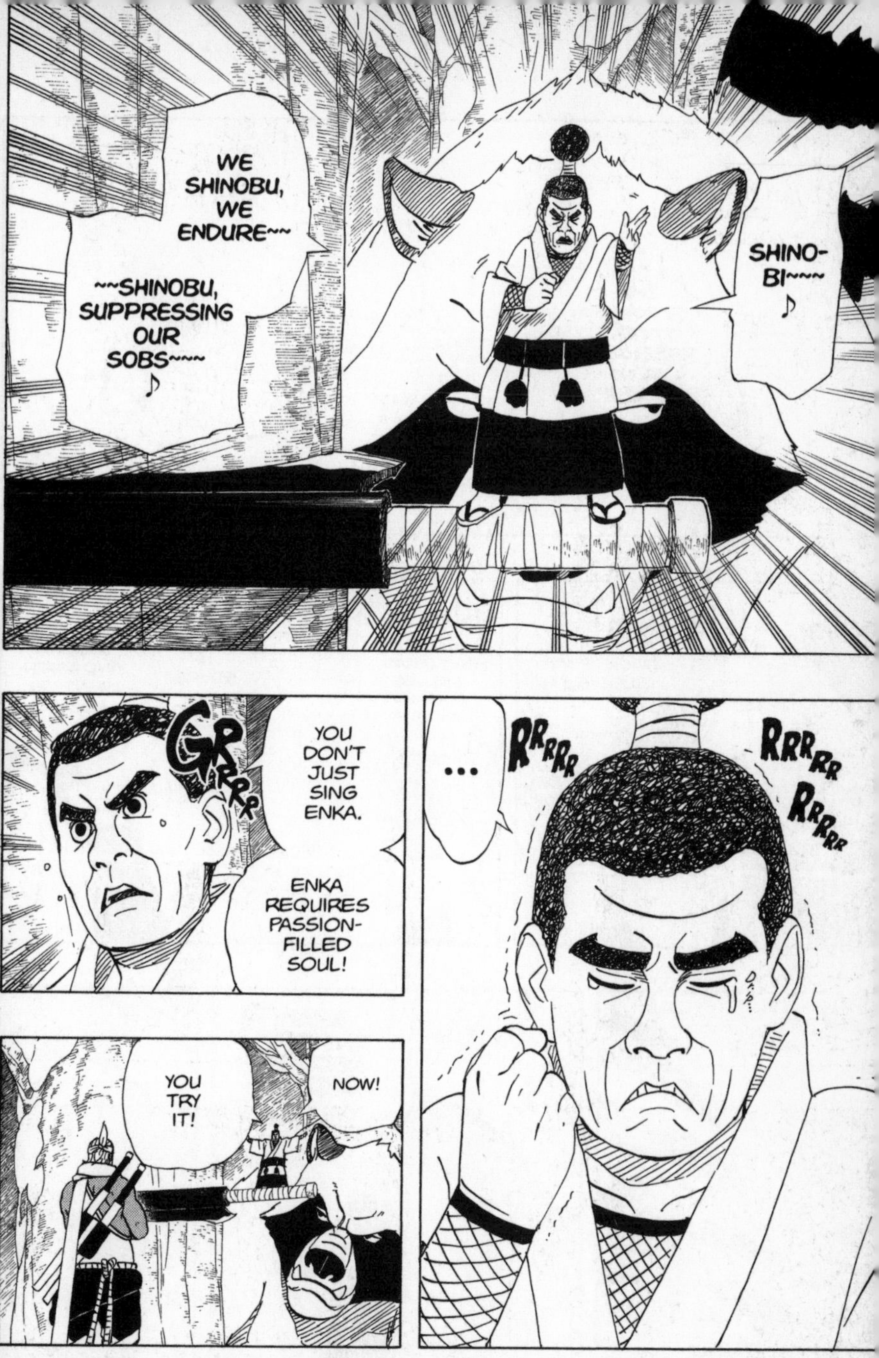
SHINO-BI~~~ ♪
WE SHINOBU, WE ENDURE~~
~~SHINOBU, SUPPRESSING OUR SOBS~~~ ♪
...
RRRRR
RRRRR
RRRRR
GRRRR
YOU DON'T JUST SING ENKA.
ENKA REQUIRES PASSION-FILLED SOUL!
NOW!
YOU TRY IT!

READ THIS WAY

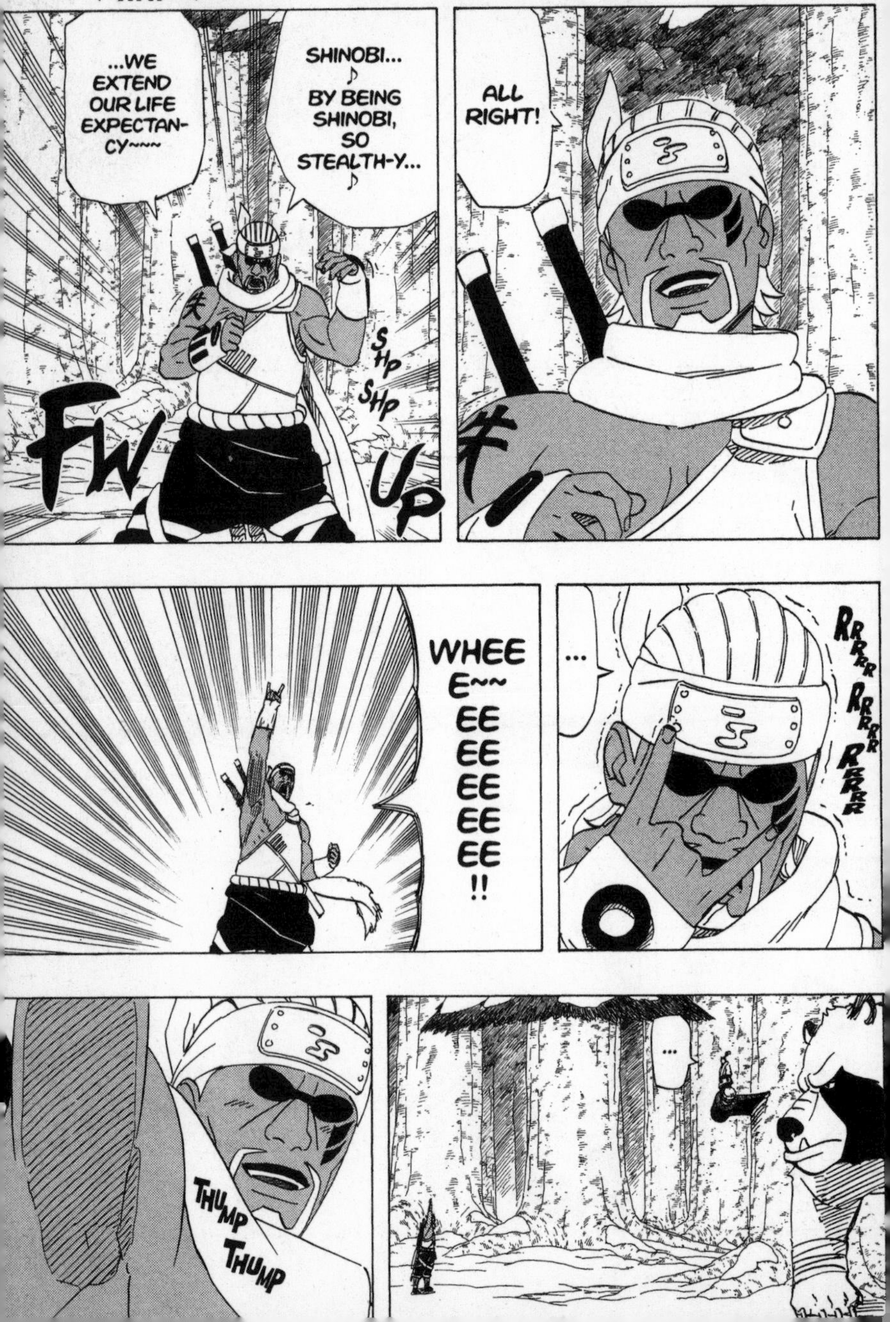
ALL RIGHT!
SHINOBI... ♪ BY BEING SHINOBI, SO STEALTH-Y... ♪
...WE EXTEND OUR LIFE EXPECTANCY~~~
SHP SHP
FW UP
...
RRRR RRRR RRRR
WHEEE~~EEEEEEEEEE!!
...
THUMP THUMP

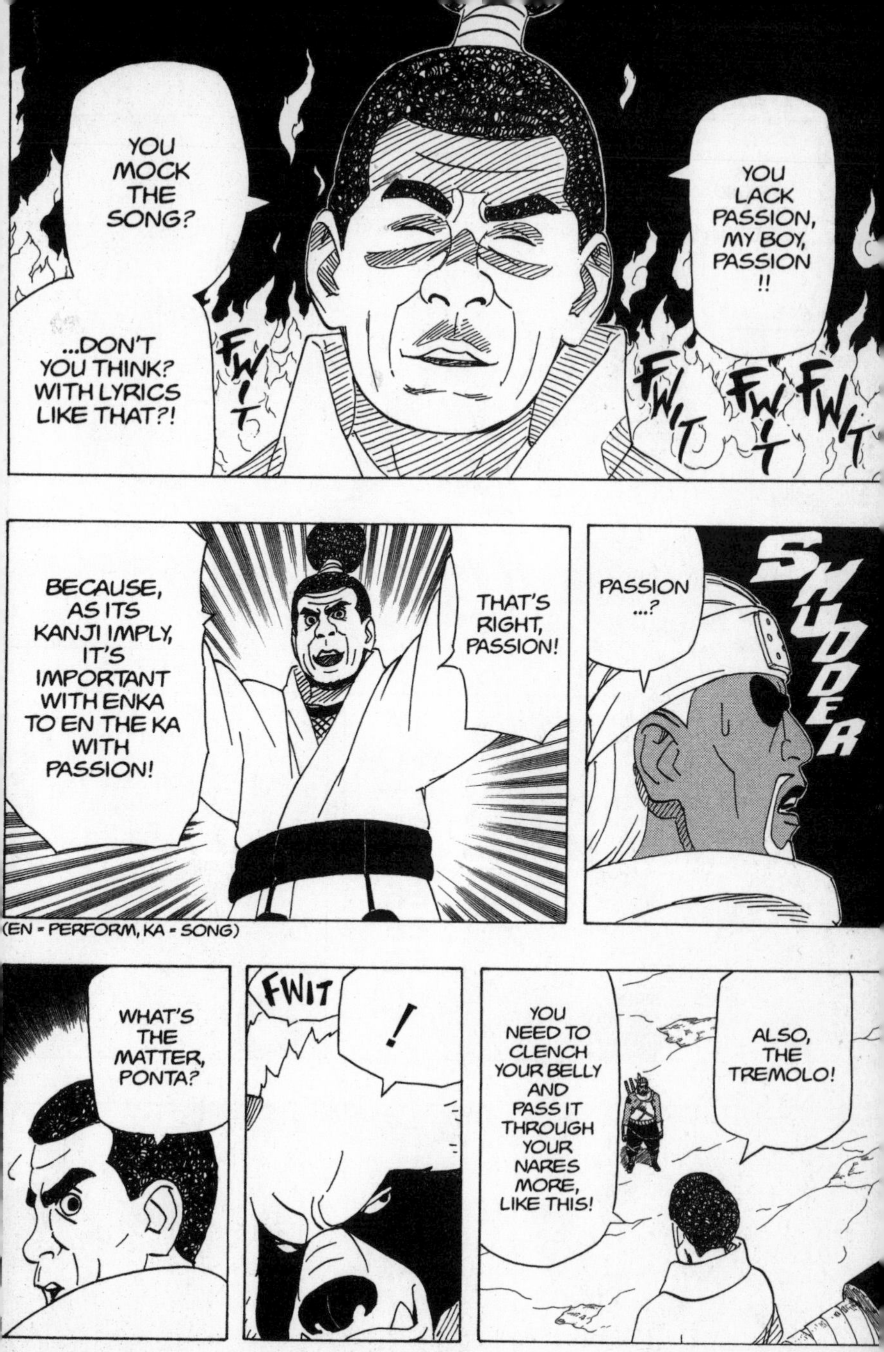
YOU LACK PASSION, MY BOY, PASSION !!
FWIT FWIT FWIT
YOU MOCK THE SONG?
...DON'T YOU THINK? WITH LYRICS LIKE THAT?!
FWIT
SHUDDER
PASSION ...?
THAT'S RIGHT, PASSION!
BECAUSE, AS ITS KANJI IMPLY, IT'S IMPORTANT WITH ENKA TO EN THE KA WITH PASSION!
(EN = PERFORM, KA = SONG)
ALSO, THE TREMOLO!
YOU NEED TO CLENCH YOUR BELLY AND PASS IT THROUGH YOUR NARES MORE, LIKE THIS!
FWIT
!
WHAT'S THE MATTER, PONTA?

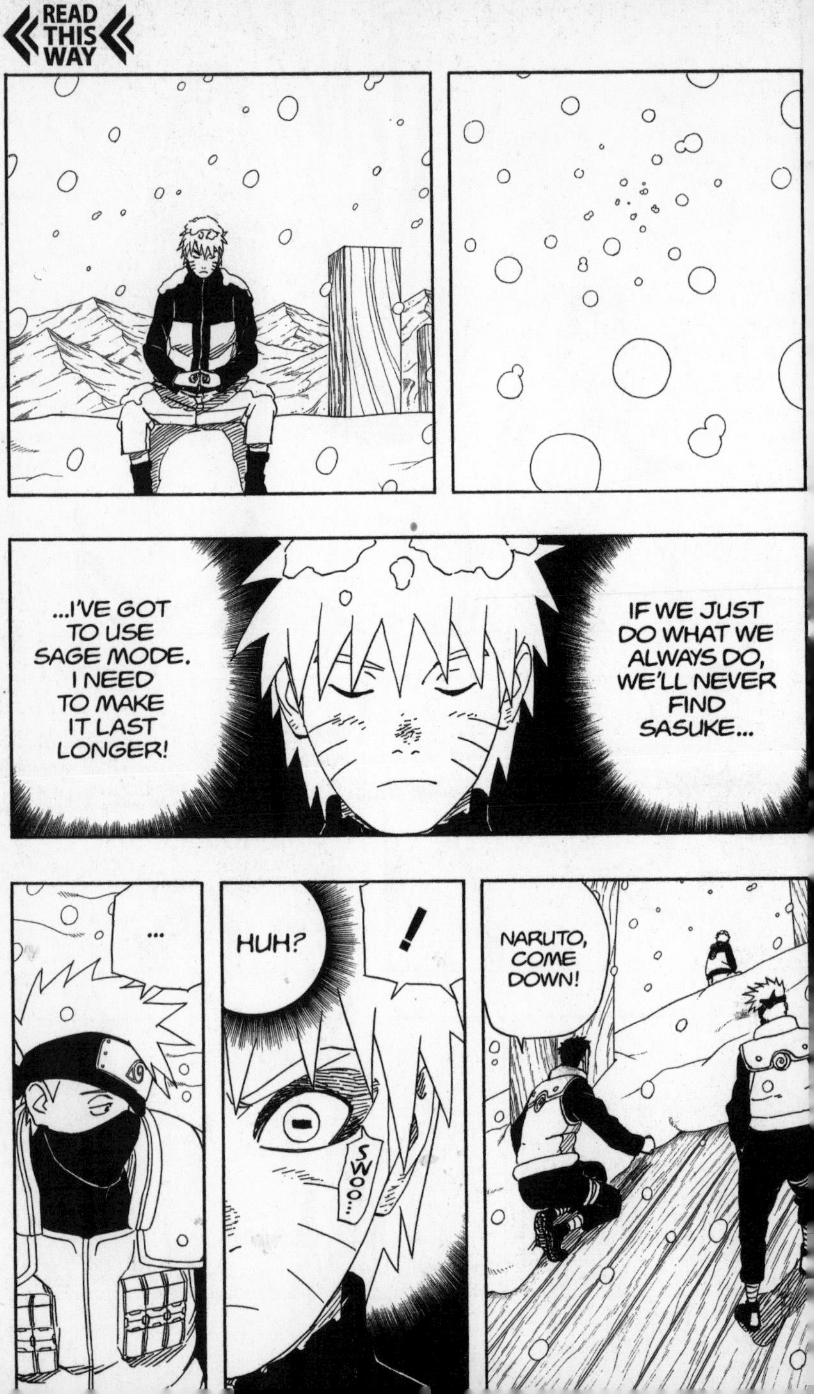
READ THIS WAY
IF WE JUST DO WHAT WE ALWAYS DO, WE'LL NEVER FIND SASUKE...
...I'VE GOT TO USE SAGE MODE. I NEED TO MAKE IT LAST LONGER!
NARUTO, COME DOWN!
!
HUH?
SWOO...
...

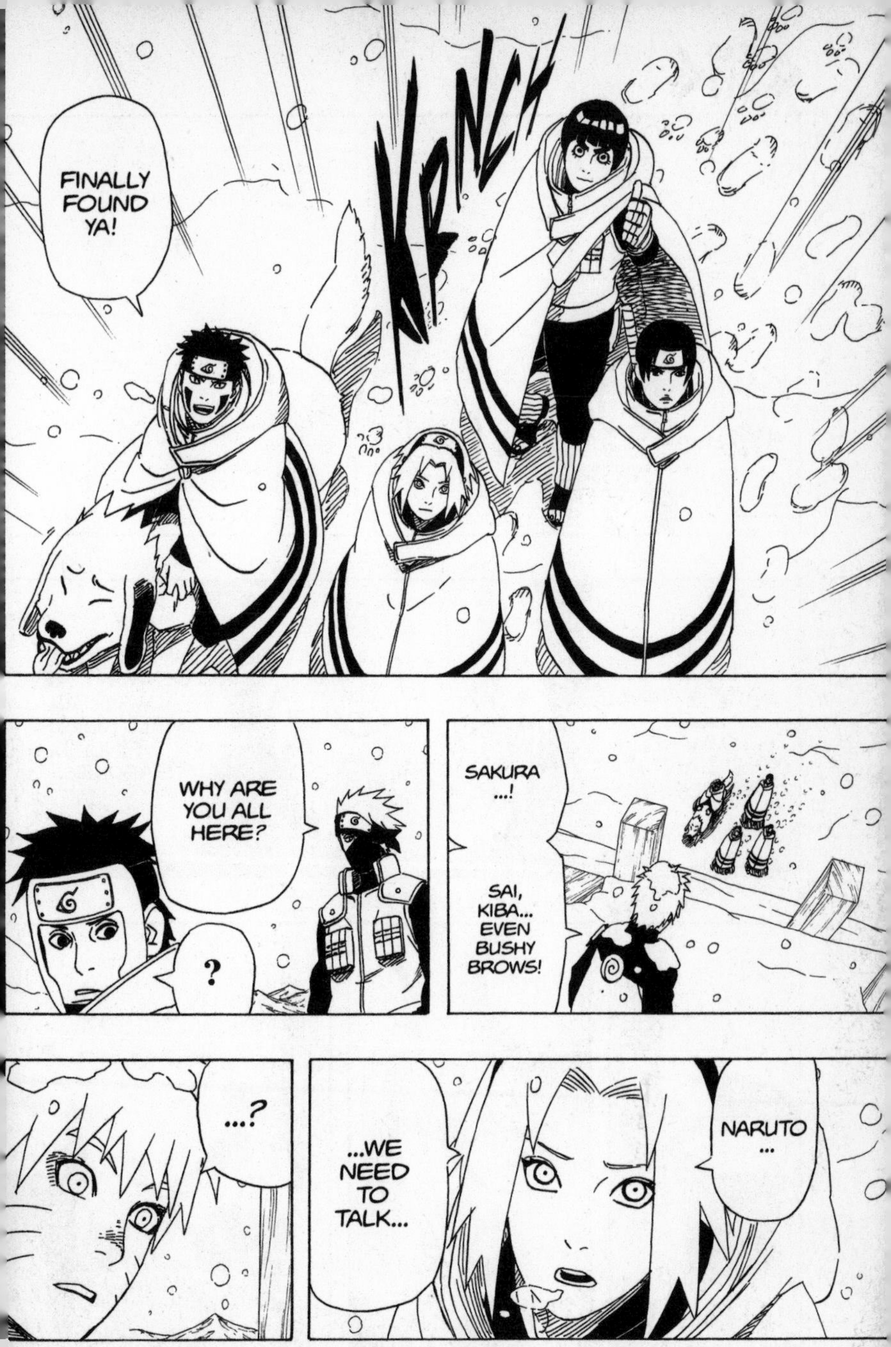
KRNCH
FINALLY FOUND YA!
SAKURA ...!
SAI, KIBA... EVEN BUSHY BROWS!
WHY ARE YOU ALL HERE?
?
NARUTO ...
...WE NEED TO TALK...
...?

READ THIS WAY

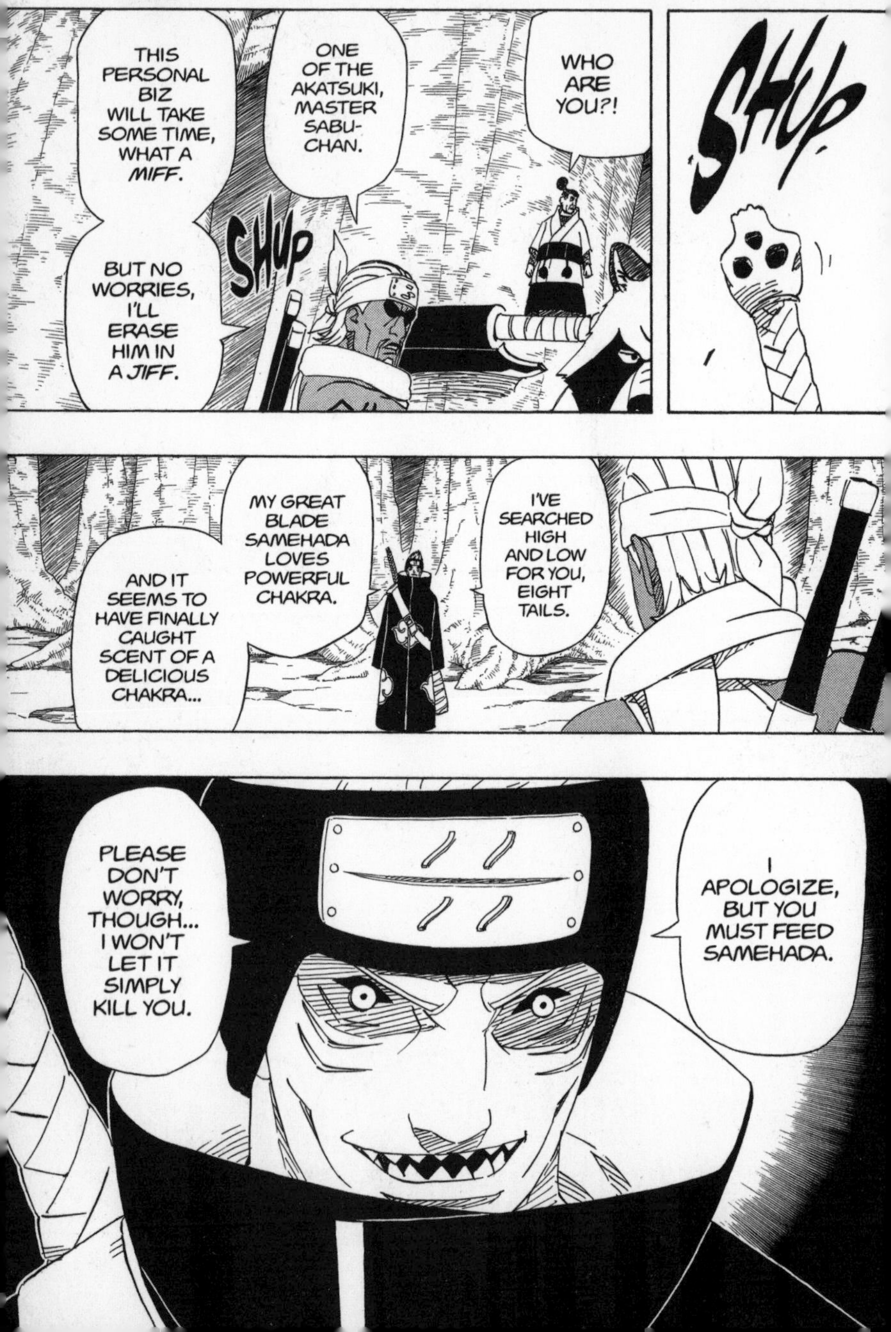
SHUP
WHO ARE YOU?!
ONE OF THE AKATSUKI, MASTER SABU-CHAN.
THIS PERSONAL BIZ WILL TAKE SOME TIME, WHAT A *MIFF*.
SHUP
BUT NO WORRIES, I'LL ERASE HIM IN A *JIFF*.
I'VE SEARCHED HIGH AND LOW FOR YOU, EIGHT TAILS.
MY GREAT BLADE SAMEHADA LOVES POWERFUL CHAKRA.
AND IT SEEMS TO HAVE FINALLY CAUGHT SCENT OF A DELICIOUS CHAKRA...
I APOLOGIZE, BUT YOU MUST FEED SAMEHADA.
PLEASE DON'T WORRY, THOUGH... I WON'T LET IT SIMPLY KILL YOU.

NARUTO

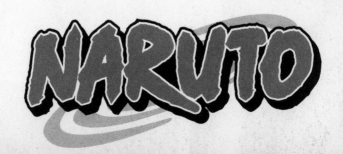

Number 469: Sakura's Confession!!

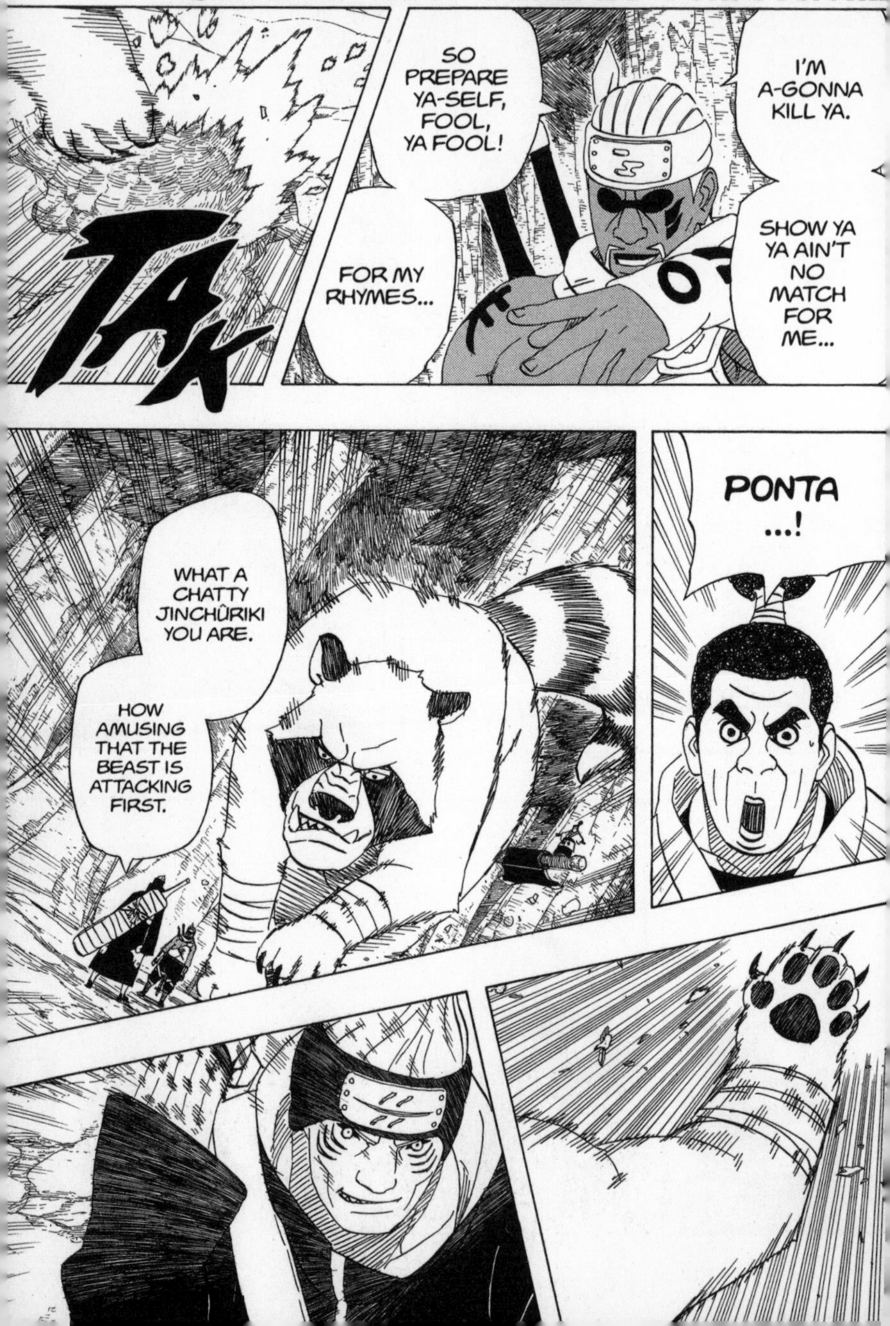
I'M A-GONNA KILL YA.
SHOW YA YA AIN'T NO MATCH FOR ME...
SO PREPARE YA-SELF, FOOL, YA FOOL!
FOR MY RHYMES...
TAK
PONTA ...!
WHAT A CHATTY JINCHÛRIKI YOU ARE.
HOW AMUSING THAT THE BEAST IS ATTACKING FIRST.

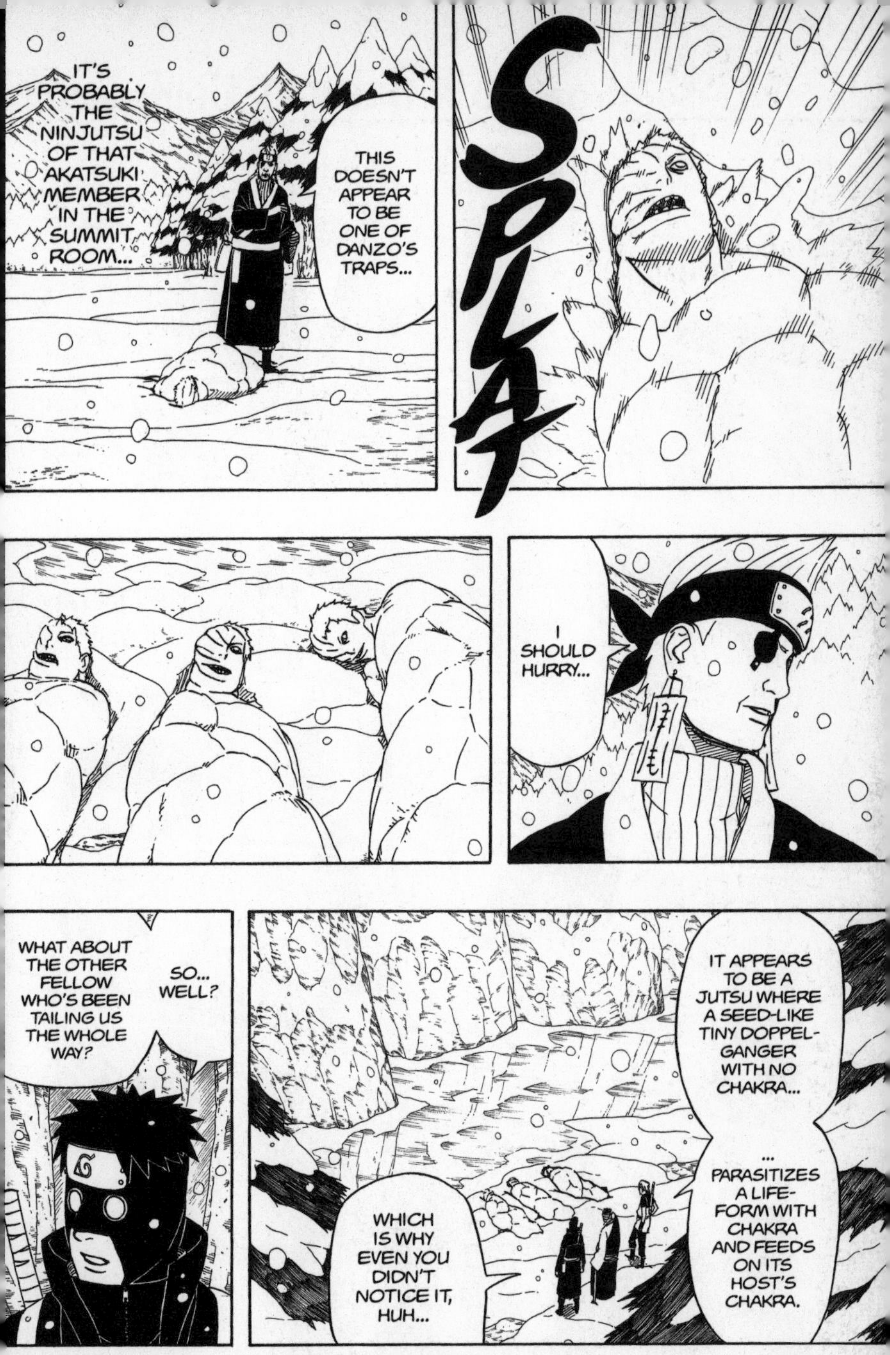
SPLAT
THIS DOESN'T APPEAR TO BE ONE OF DANZO'S TRAPS...
IT'S PROBABLY THE NINJUTSU OF THAT AKATSUKI MEMBER IN THE SUMMIT ROOM...
I SHOULD HURRY...
IT APPEARS TO BE A JUTSU WHERE A SEED-LIKE TINY DOPPEL-GANGER WITH NO CHAKRA...
...PARASITIZES A LIFE-FORM WITH CHAKRA AND FEEDS ON ITS HOST'S CHAKRA.
WHICH IS WHY EVEN YOU DIDN'T NOTICE IT, HUH...
SO... WELL?
WHAT ABOUT THE OTHER FELLOW WHO'S BEEN TAILING US THE WHOLE WAY?

READ THIS WAY

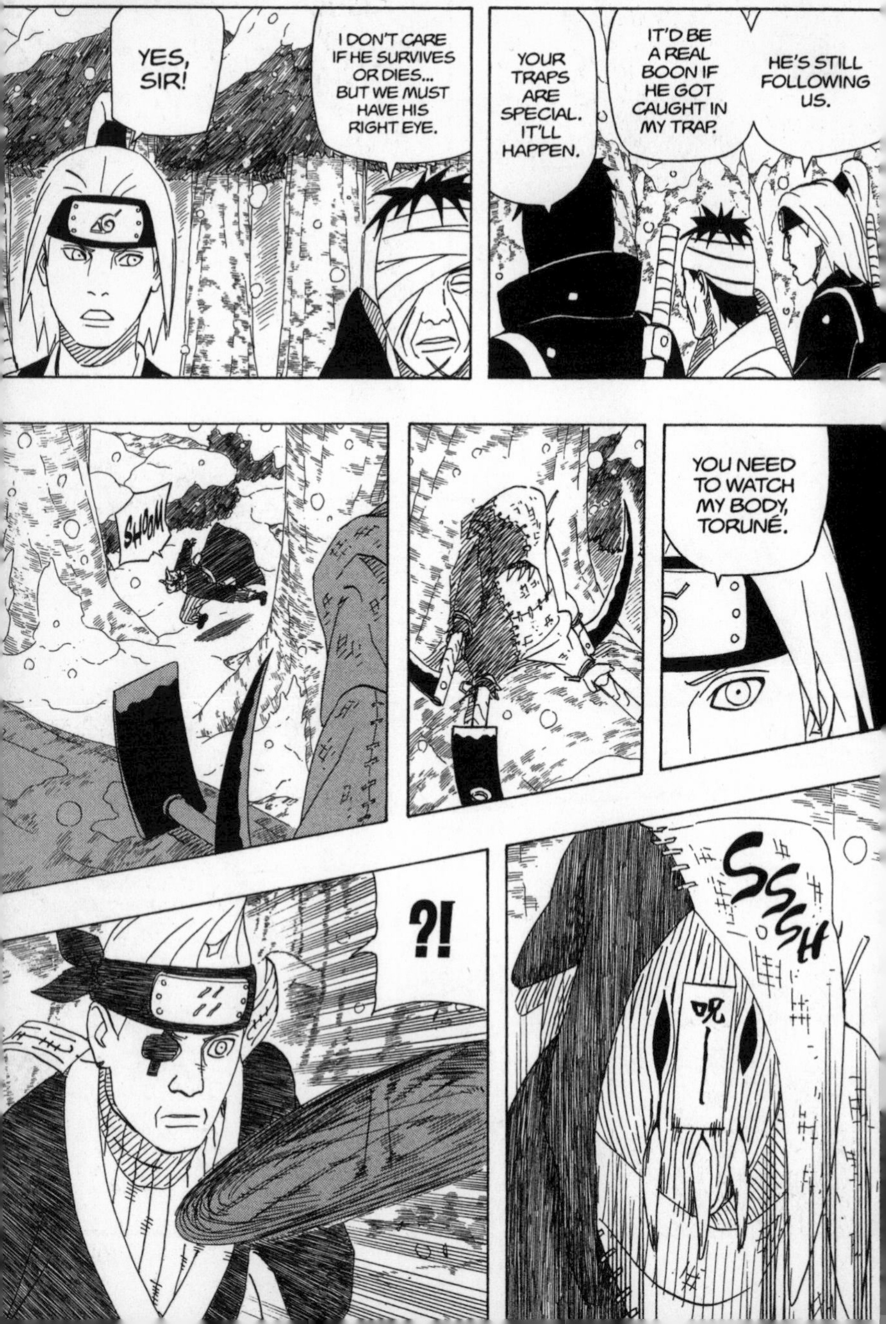
HE'S STILL FOLLOWING US.
IT'D BE A REAL BOON IF HE GOT CAUGHT IN MY TRAP.
YOUR TRAPS ARE SPECIAL. IT'LL HAPPEN.
I DON'T CARE IF HE SURVIVES OR DIES... BUT WE MUST HAVE HIS RIGHT EYE.
YES, SIR!
YOU NEED TO WATCH MY BODY, TORUNÉ.
SHOOM
SSSH
呪
?!

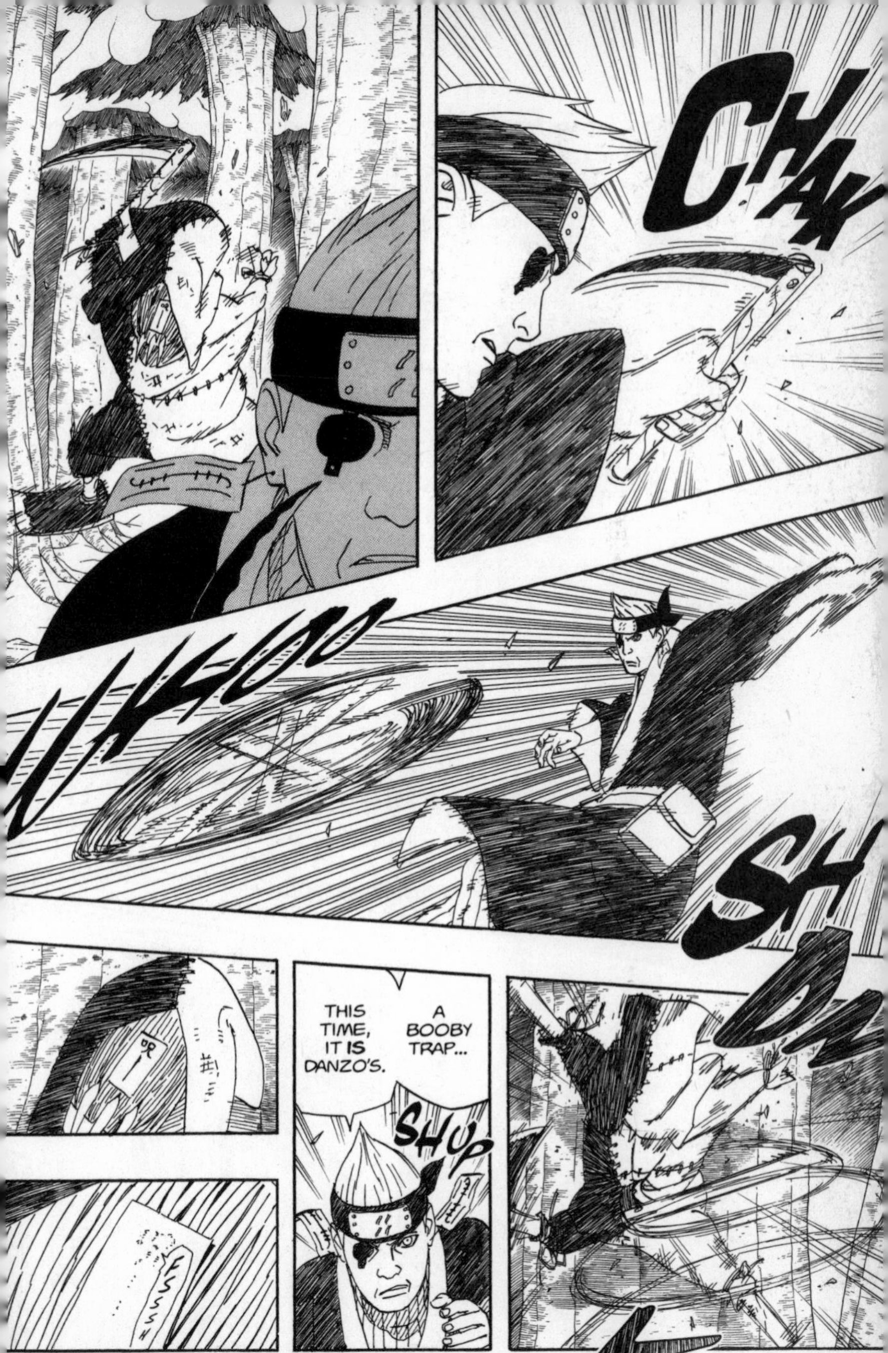
CHAK
WHOOO
A BOOBY TRAP...
THIS TIME, IT IS DANZO'S.
SHUP

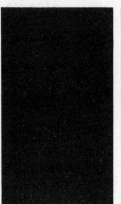

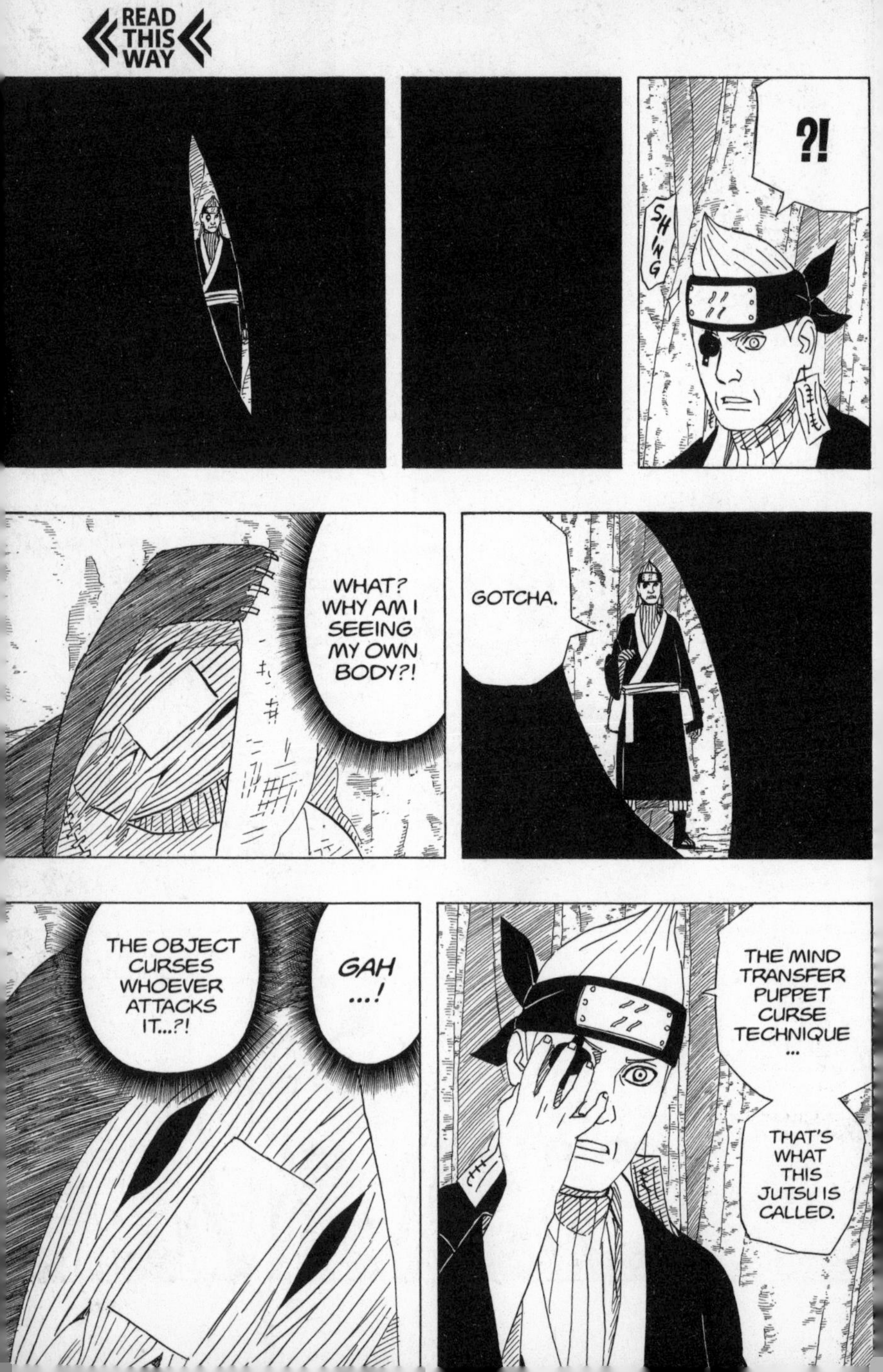
READ THIS WAY
?!
SHING
GOTCHA.
WHAT? WHY AM I SEEING MY OWN BODY?!
THE MIND TRANSFER PUPPET CURSE TECHNIQUE...
THAT'S WHAT THIS JUTSU IS CALLED.
GAH...!
THE OBJECT CURSES WHOEVER ATTACKS IT...?!

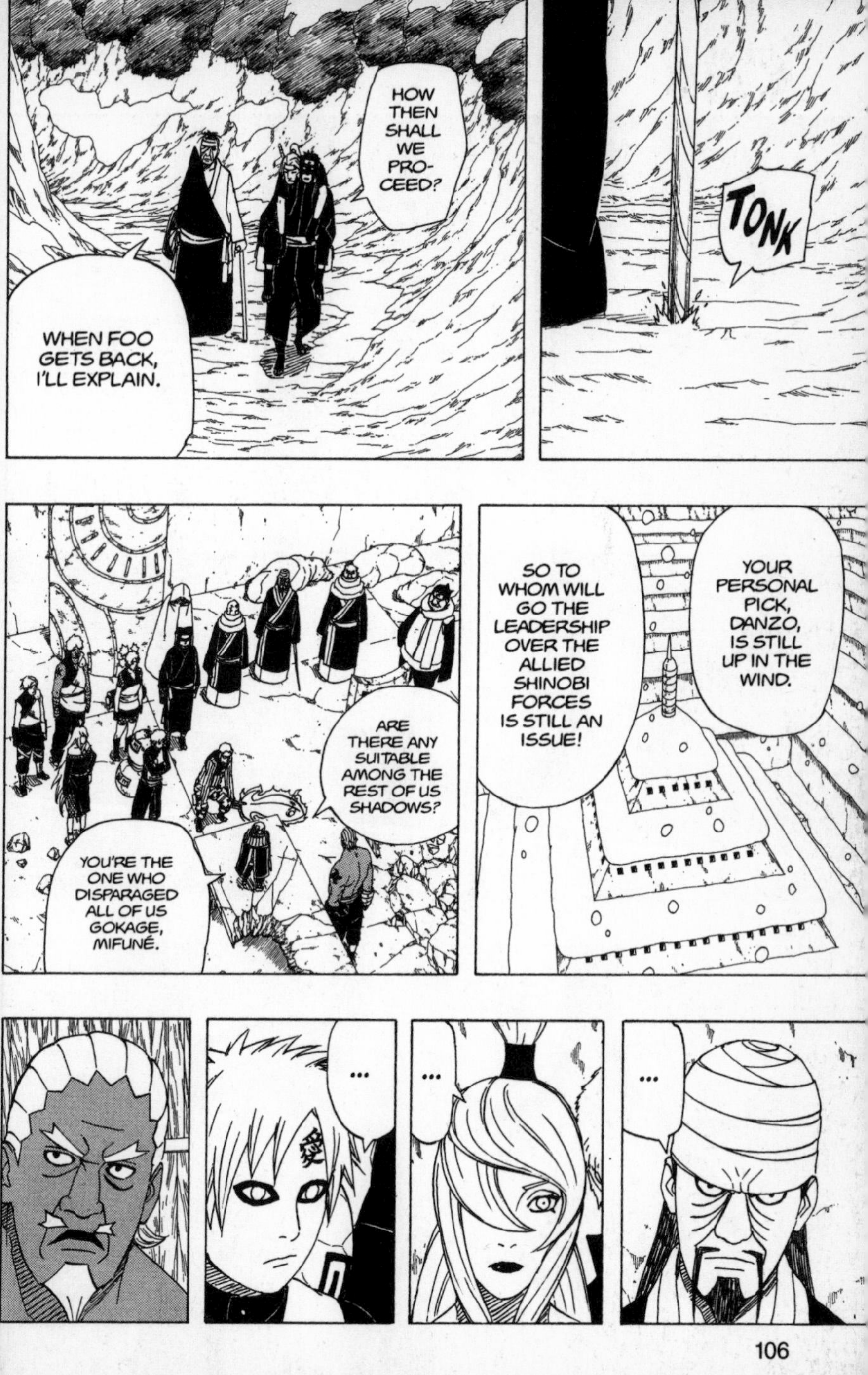
TONK
HOW THEN SHALL WE PRO-CEED?
WHEN FOO GETS BACK, I'LL EXPLAIN.
YOUR PERSONAL PICK, DANZO, IS STILL UP IN THE WIND.
SO TO WHOM WILL GO THE LEADERSHIP OVER THE ALLIED SHINOBI FORCES IS STILL AN ISSUE!
ARE THERE ANY SUITABLE AMONG THE REST OF US SHADOWS?
YOU'RE THE ONE WHO DISPARAGED ALL OF US GOKAGE, MIFUNÉ.
...
...
...

READ THIS WAY

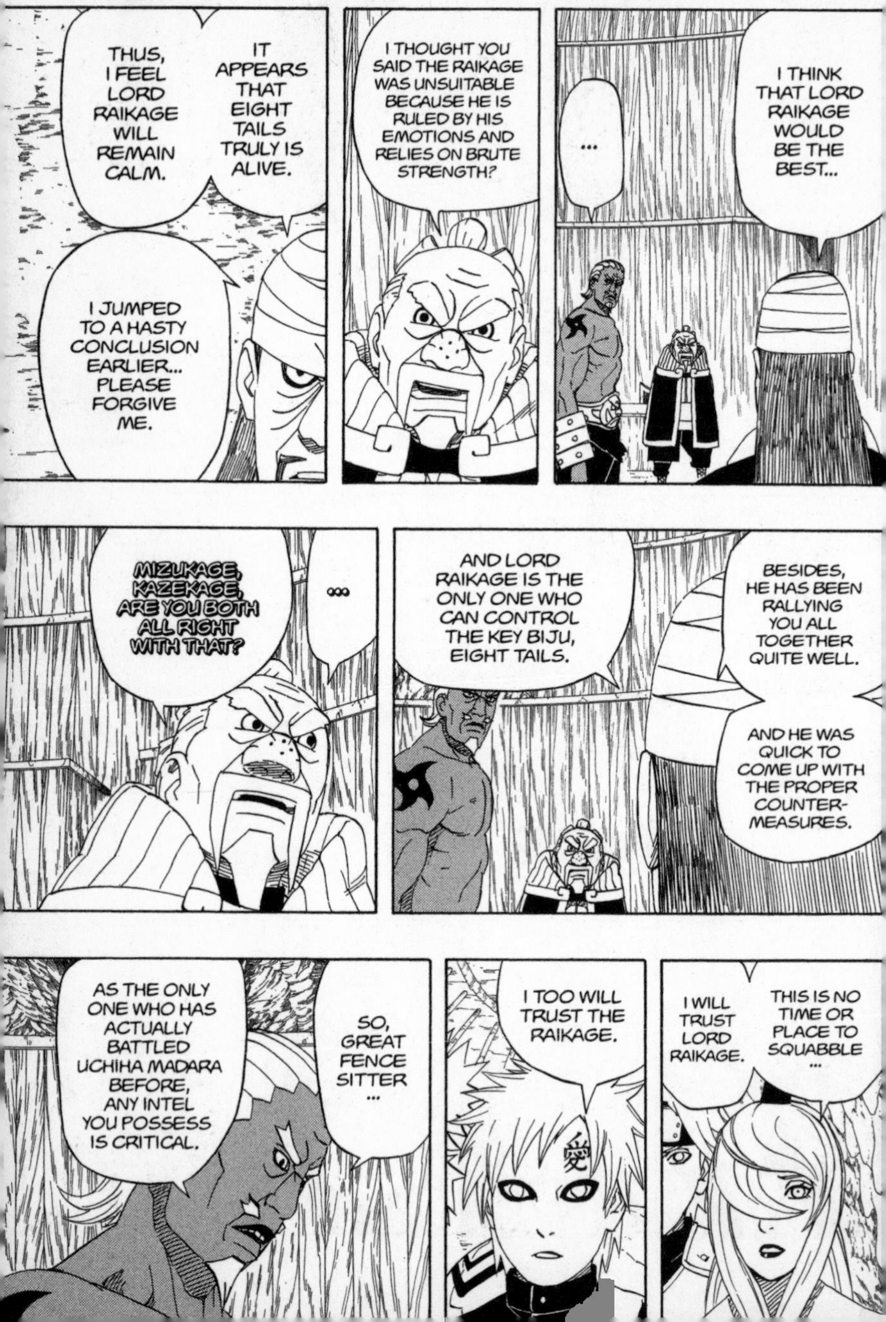
I THINK THAT LORD RAIKAGE WOULD BE THE BEST...
...
I THOUGHT YOU SAID THE RAIKAGE WAS UNSUITABLE BECAUSE HE IS RULED BY HIS EMOTIONS AND RELIES ON BRUTE STRENGTH?
IT APPEARS THAT EIGHT TAILS TRULY IS ALIVE.
THUS, I FEEL LORD RAIKAGE WILL REMAIN CALM.
I JUMPED TO A HASTY CONCLUSION EARLIER... PLEASE FORGIVE ME.
BESIDES, HE HAS BEEN RALLYING YOU ALL TOGETHER QUITE WELL.
AND HE WAS QUICK TO COME UP WITH THE PROPER COUNTER-MEASURES.
AND LORD RAIKAGE IS THE ONLY ONE WHO CAN CONTROL THE KEY BIJU, EIGHT TAILS.
...
MIZUKAGE, KAZEKAGE, ARE YOU BOTH ALL RIGHT WITH THAT?
THIS IS NO TIME OR PLACE TO SQUABBLE...
I WILL TRUST LORD RAIKAGE.
I TOO WILL TRUST THE RAIKAGE.
SO, GREAT FENCE SITTER...
AS THE ONLY ONE WHO HAS ACTUALLY BATTLED UCHIHA MADARA BEFORE, ANY INTEL YOU POSSESS IS CRITICAL.

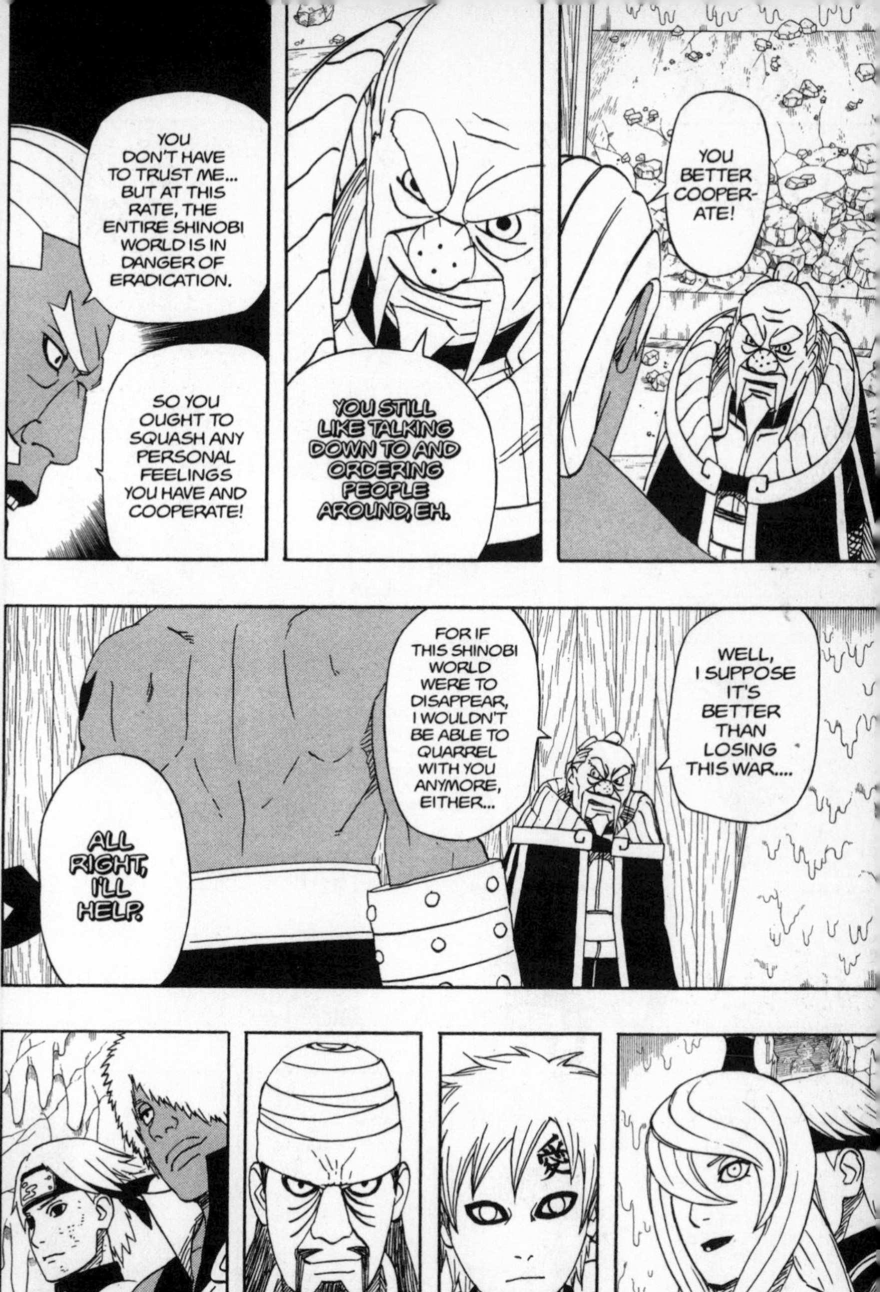
YOU BETTER COOPERATE!
YOU STILL LIKE TALKING DOWN TO AND ORDERING PEOPLE AROUND, EH.
YOU DON'T HAVE TO TRUST ME... BUT AT THIS RATE, THE ENTIRE SHINOBI WORLD IS IN DANGER OF ERADICATION.
SO YOU OUGHT TO SQUASH ANY PERSONAL FEELINGS YOU HAVE AND COOPERATE!
WELL, I SUPPOSE IT'S BETTER THAN LOSING THIS WAR....
FOR IF THIS SHINOBI WORLD WERE TO DISAPPEAR, I WOULDN'T BE ABLE TO QUARREL WITH YOU ANYMORE, EITHER...
ALL RIGHT, I'LL HELP.

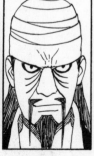

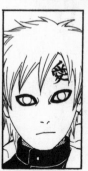

READ THIS WAY

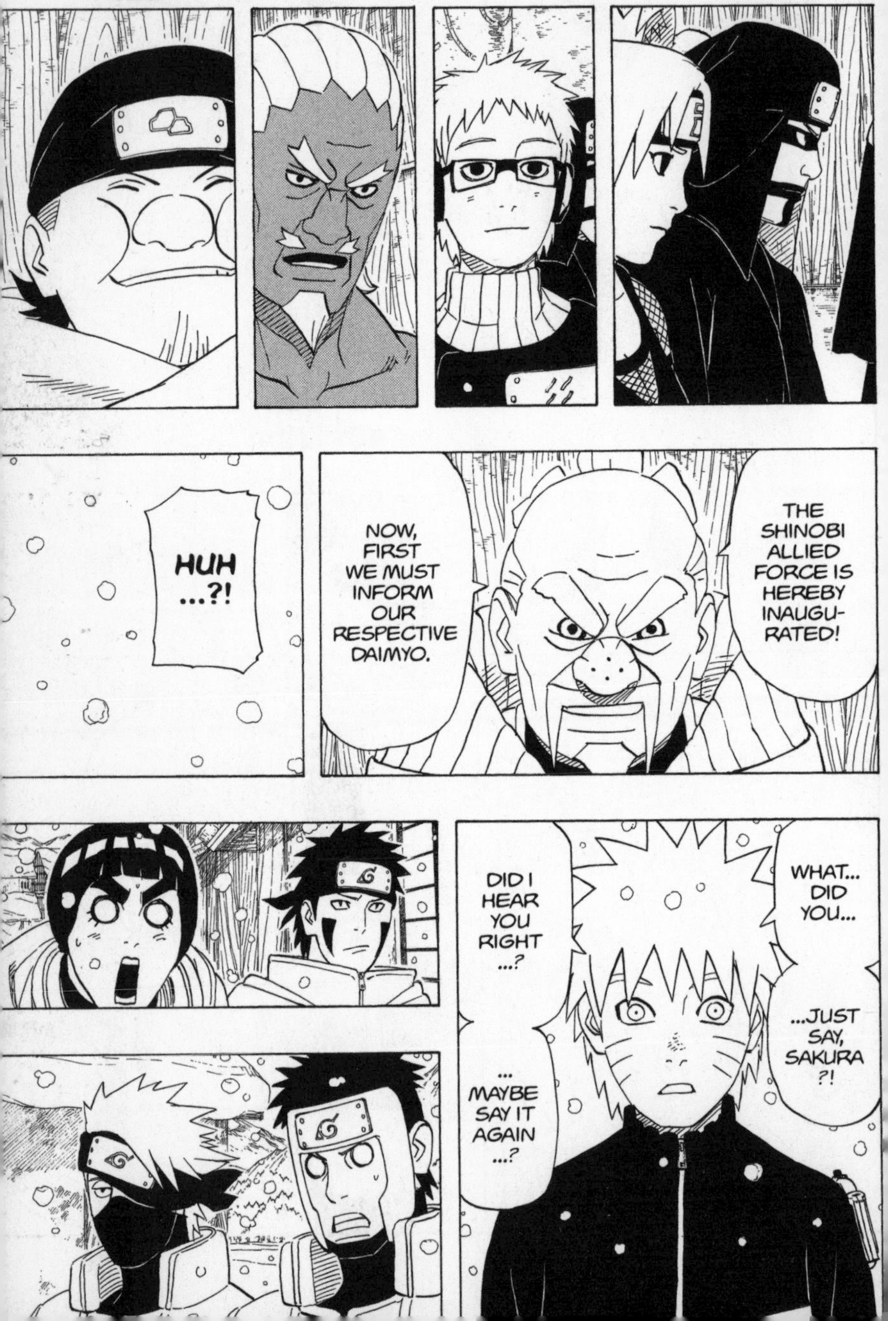
THE SHINOBI ALLIED FORCE IS HEREBY INAUGURATED!
NOW, FIRST WE MUST INFORM OUR RESPECTIVE DAIMYO.
HUH ...?!
WHAT... DID YOU...
...JUST SAY, SAKURA ?!
DID I HEAR YOU RIGHT ...?
... MAYBE SAY IT AGAIN ...?

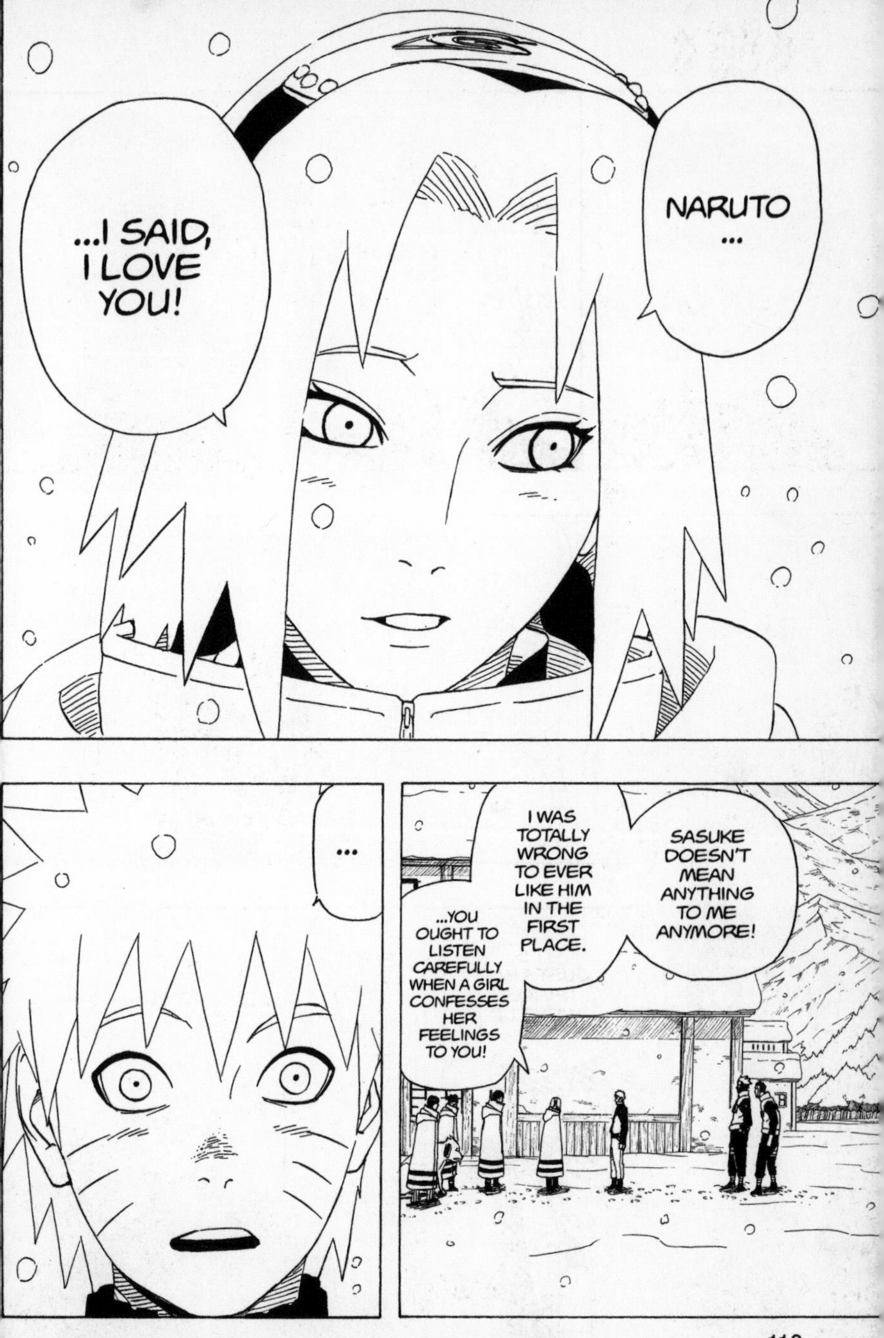
NARUTO ...
...I SAID, I LOVE YOU!
SASUKE DOESN'T MEAN ANYTHING TO ME ANYMORE!
I WAS TOTALLY WRONG TO EVER LIKE HIM IN THE FIRST PLACE.
...YOU OUGHT TO LISTEN CAREFULLY WHEN A GIRL CONFESSES HER FEELINGS TO YOU!
...

READ THIS WAY

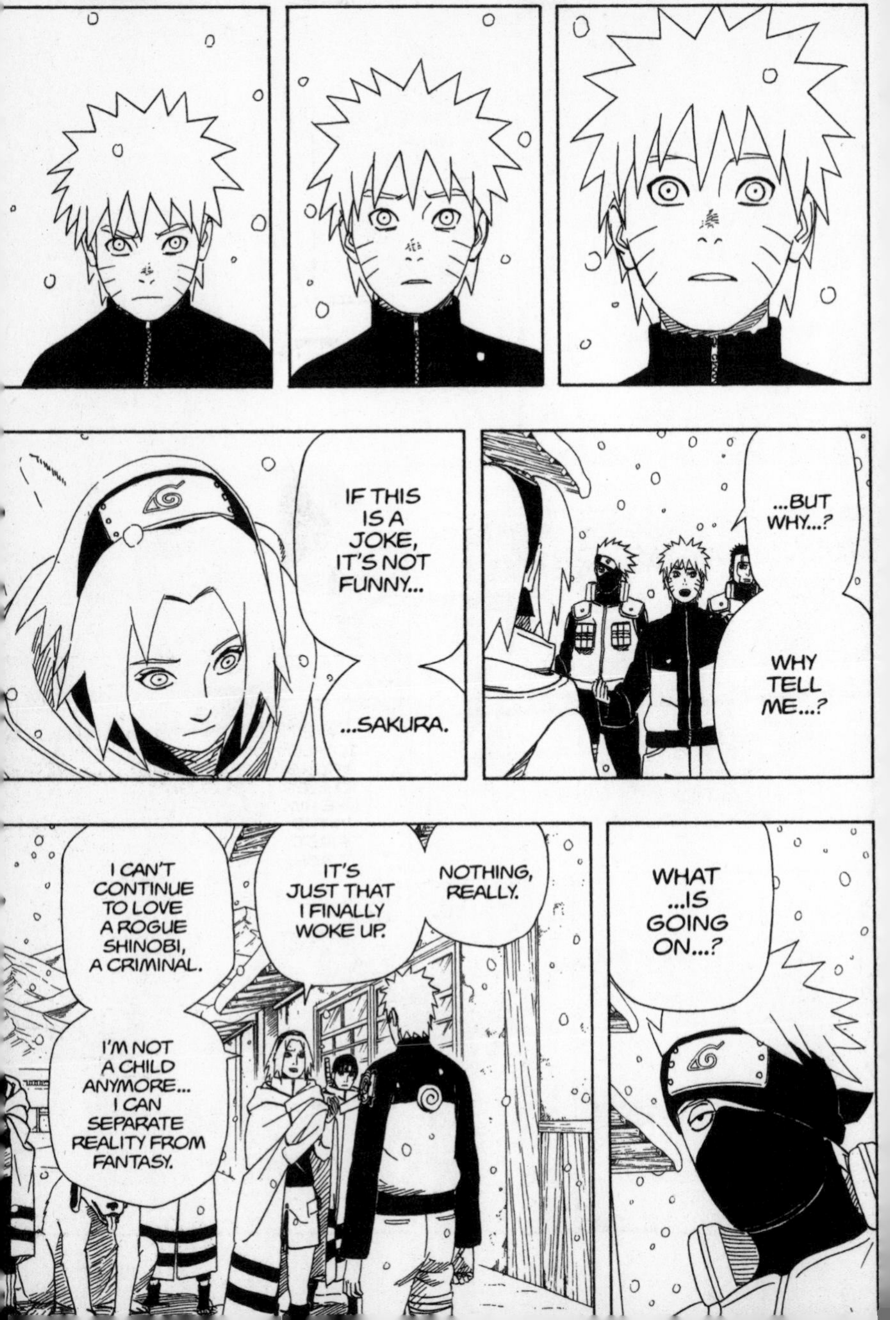
...BUT WHY...?
WHY TELL ME...?
IF THIS IS A JOKE, IT'S NOT FUNNY...
...SAKURA.
WHAT ...IS GOING ON...?
NOTHING, REALLY.
IT'S JUST THAT I FINALLY WOKE UP.
I CAN'T CONTINUE TO LOVE A ROGUE SHINOBI, A CRIMINAL.
I'M NOT A CHILD ANYMORE... I CAN SEPARATE REALITY FROM FANTASY.

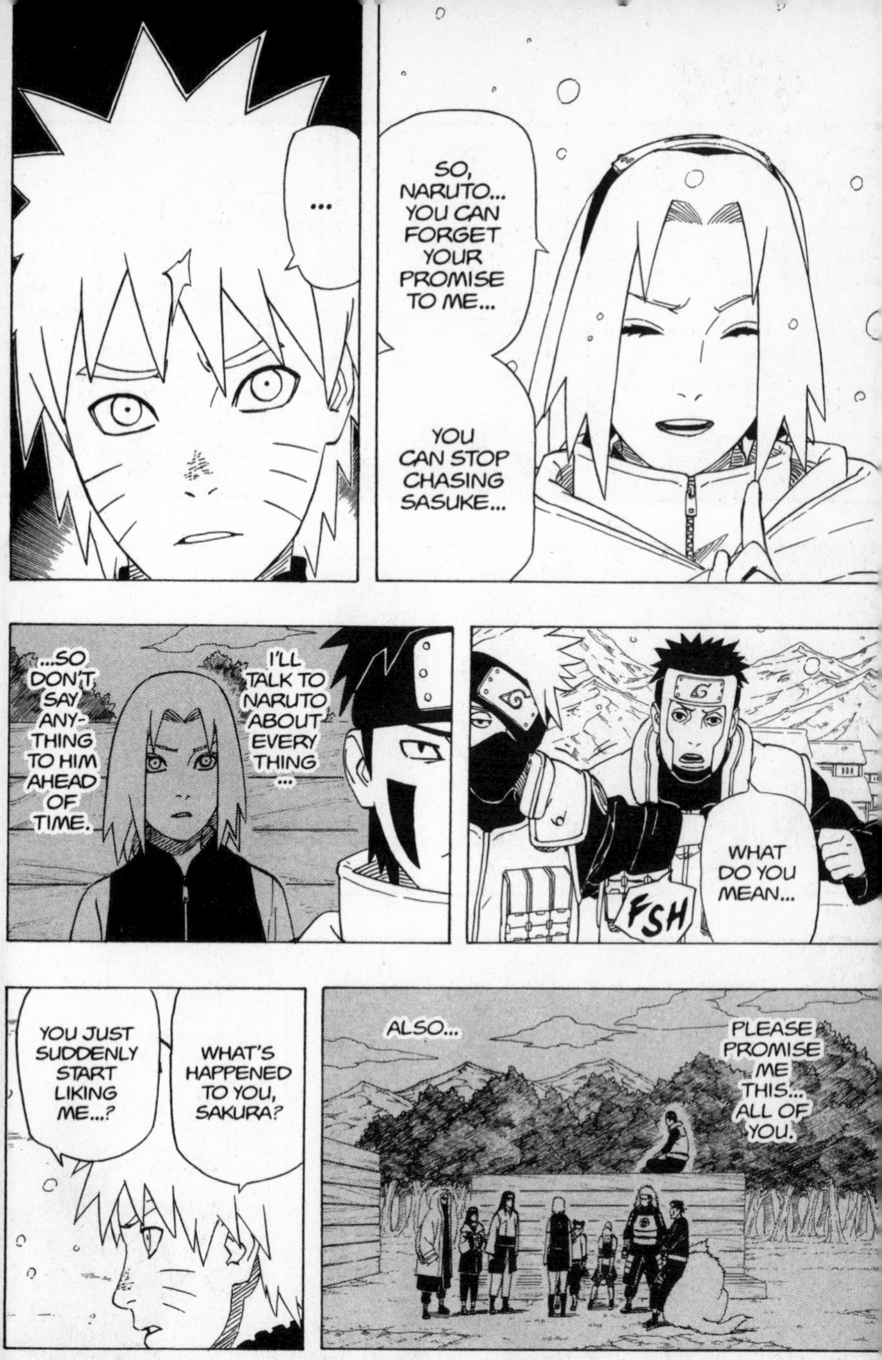

SO, NARUTO... YOU CAN FORGET YOUR PROMISE TO ME...
YOU CAN STOP CHASING SASUKE...
...
WHAT DO YOU MEAN...
FSH
I'LL TALK TO NARUTO ABOUT EVERY THING...
...SO DON'T SAY ANY-THING TO HIM AHEAD OF TIME.
PLEASE PROMISE ME THIS... ALL OF YOU.
ALSO...
WHAT'S HAPPENED TO YOU, SAKURA?
YOU JUST SUDDENLY START LIKING ME...?

READ THIS WAY

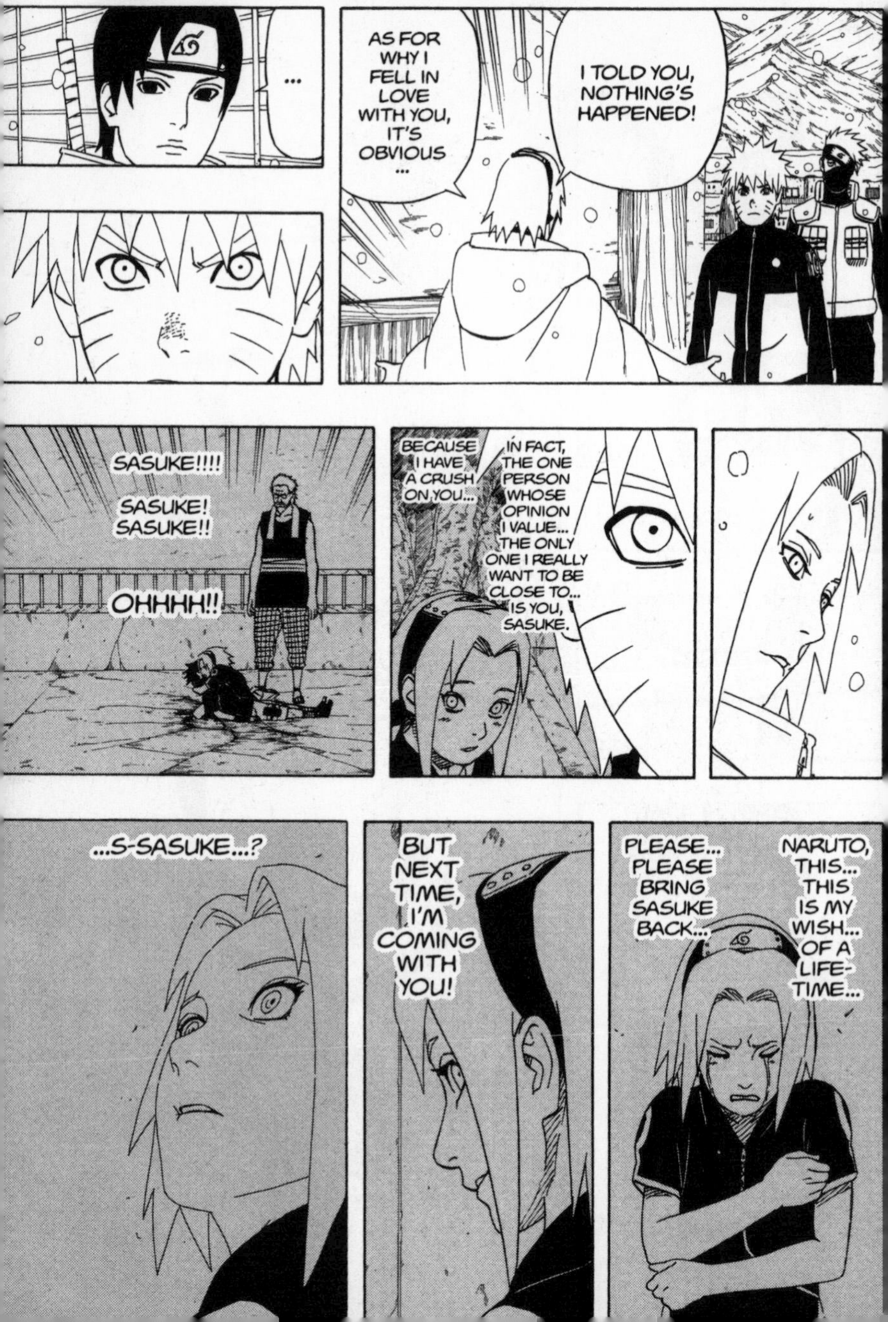
I TOLD YOU, NOTHING'S HAPPENED!
AS FOR WHY I FELL IN LOVE WITH YOU, IT'S OBVIOUS ...
...
IN FACT, THE ONE PERSON WHOSE OPINION I VALUE... THE ONLY ONE I REALLY WANT TO BE CLOSE TO... IS YOU, SASUKE.
BECAUSE I HAVE A CRUSH ON YOU...
SASUKE!!!!
SASUKE! SASUKE!!
OHHHH!!
NARUTO, THIS... THIS IS MY WISH... OF A LIFE-TIME...
PLEASE... PLEASE BRING SASUKE BACK...
BUT NEXT TIME, I'M COMING WITH YOU!
...S-SASUKE...?

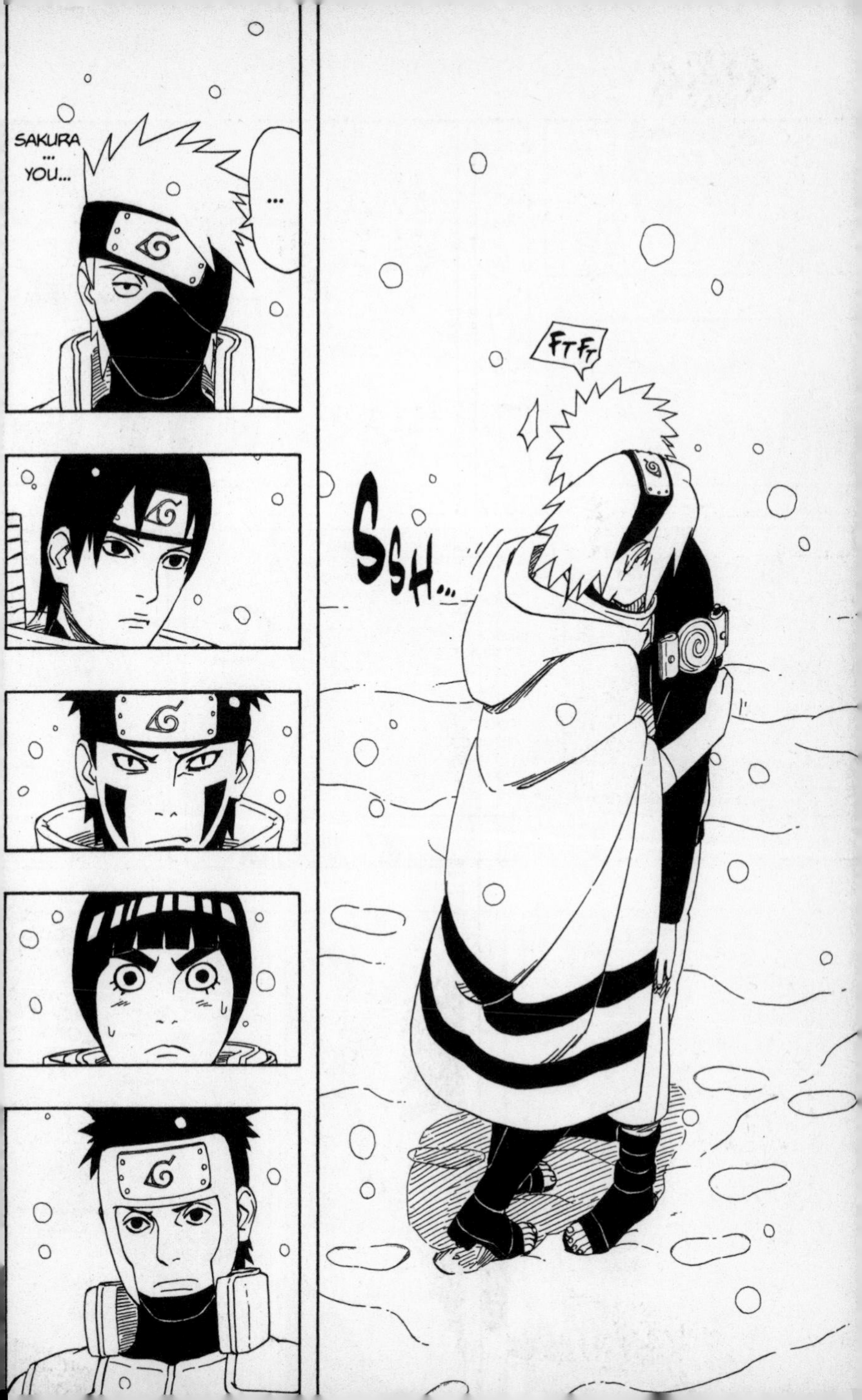
FTFT
SSH...
...
SAKURA ... YOU...

READ THIS WAY

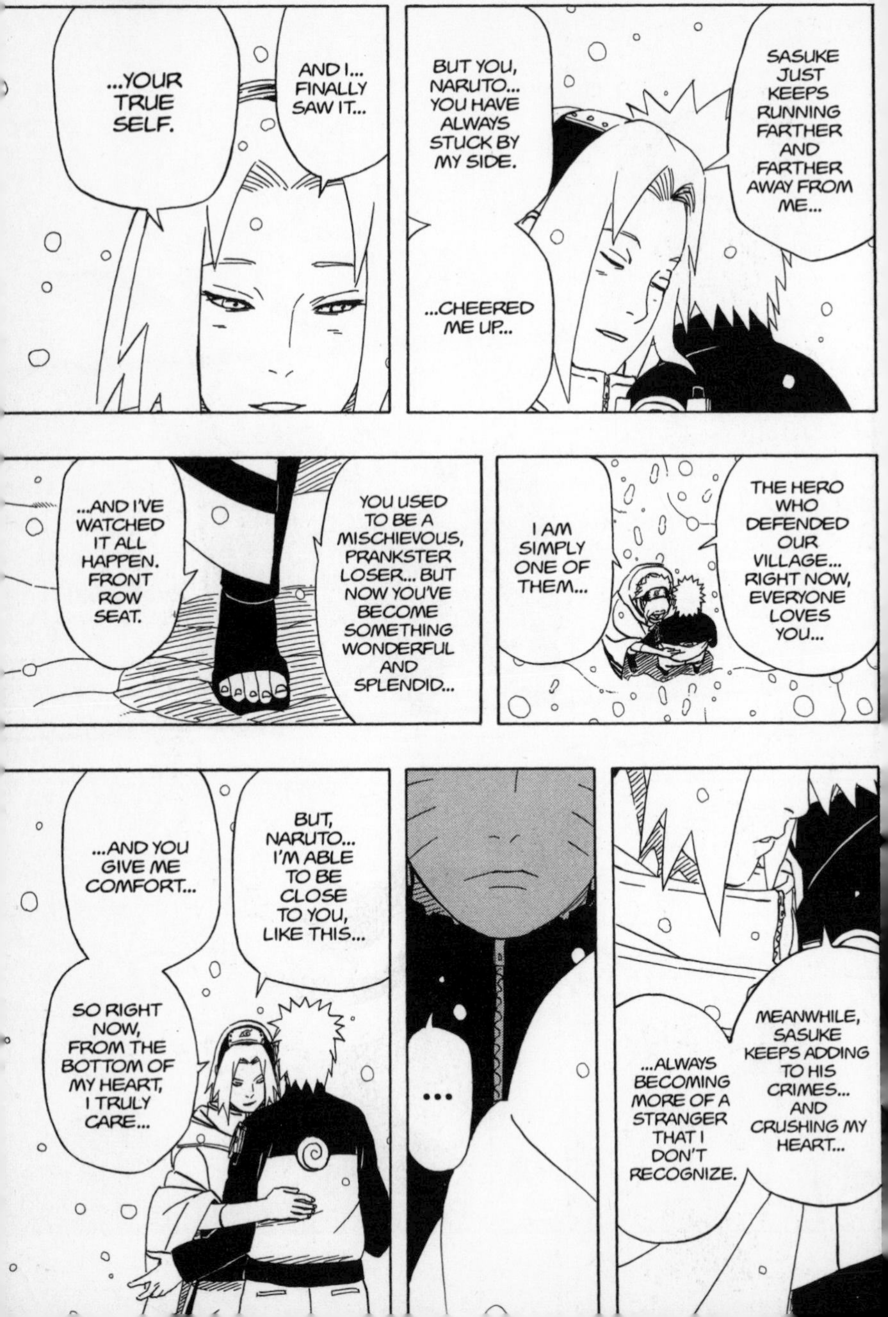
SASUKE JUST KEEPS RUNNING FARTHER AND FARTHER AWAY FROM ME...
BUT YOU, NARUTO... YOU HAVE ALWAYS STUCK BY MY SIDE.
...CHEERED ME UP...
AND I... FINALLY SAW IT...
...YOUR TRUE SELF.
THE HERO WHO DEFENDED OUR VILLAGE... RIGHT NOW, EVERYONE LOVES YOU...
I AM SIMPLY ONE OF THEM...
YOU USED TO BE A MISCHIEVOUS, PRANKSTER LOSER... BUT NOW YOU'VE BECOME SOMETHING WONDERFUL AND SPLENDID...
...AND I'VE WATCHED IT ALL HAPPEN. FRONT ROW SEAT.
MEANWHILE, SASUKE KEEPS ADDING TO HIS CRIMES... AND CRUSHING MY HEART...
...ALWAYS BECOMING MORE OF A STRANGER THAT I DON'T RECOGNIZE.
...
BUT, NARUTO... I'M ABLE TO BE CLOSE TO YOU, LIKE THIS...
...AND YOU GIVE ME COMFORT...
SO RIGHT NOW, FROM THE BOTTOM OF MY HEART, I TRULY CARE...

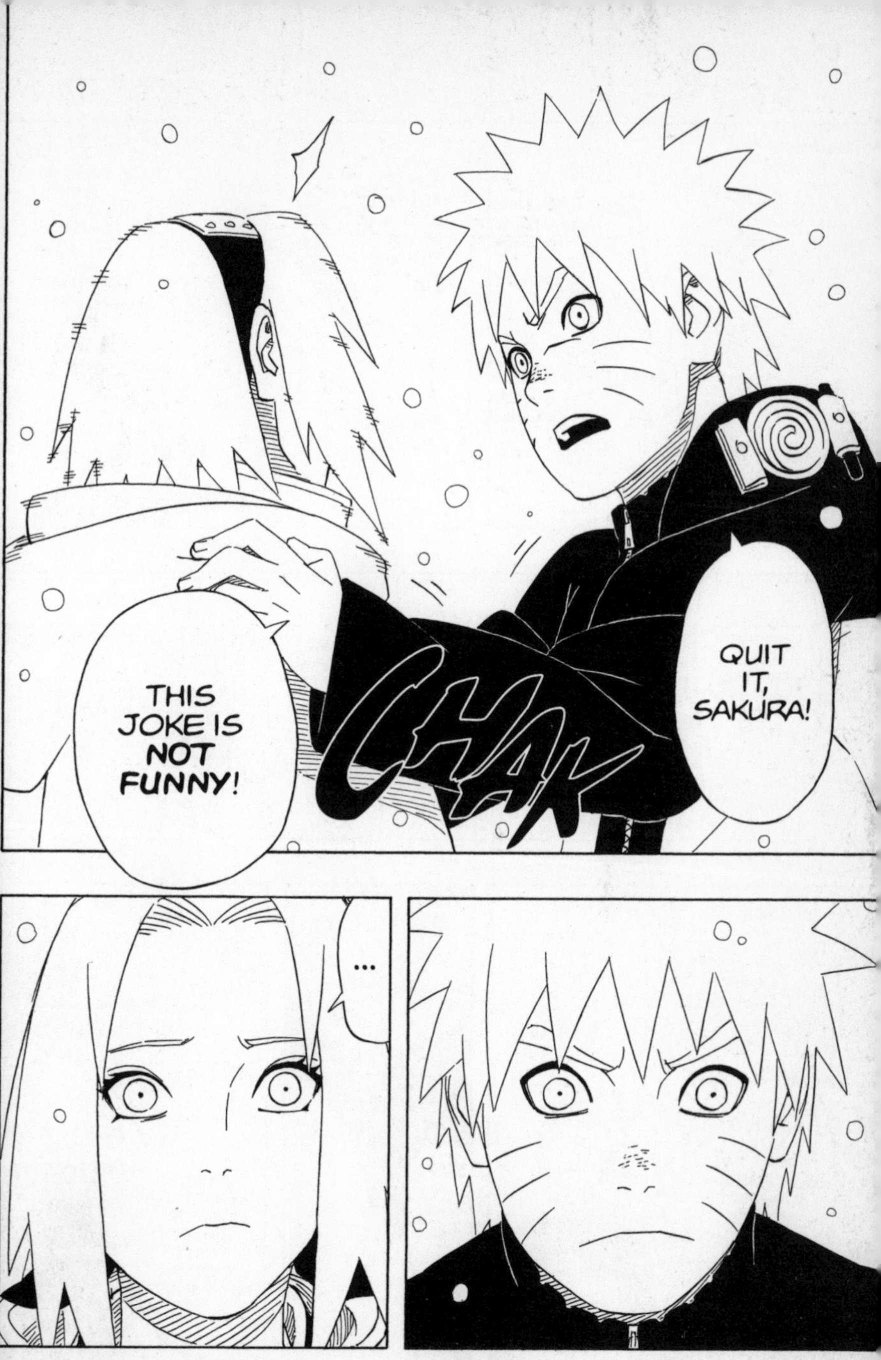
QUIT IT, SAKURA!
CHAK
THIS JOKE IS NOT FUNNY!
...

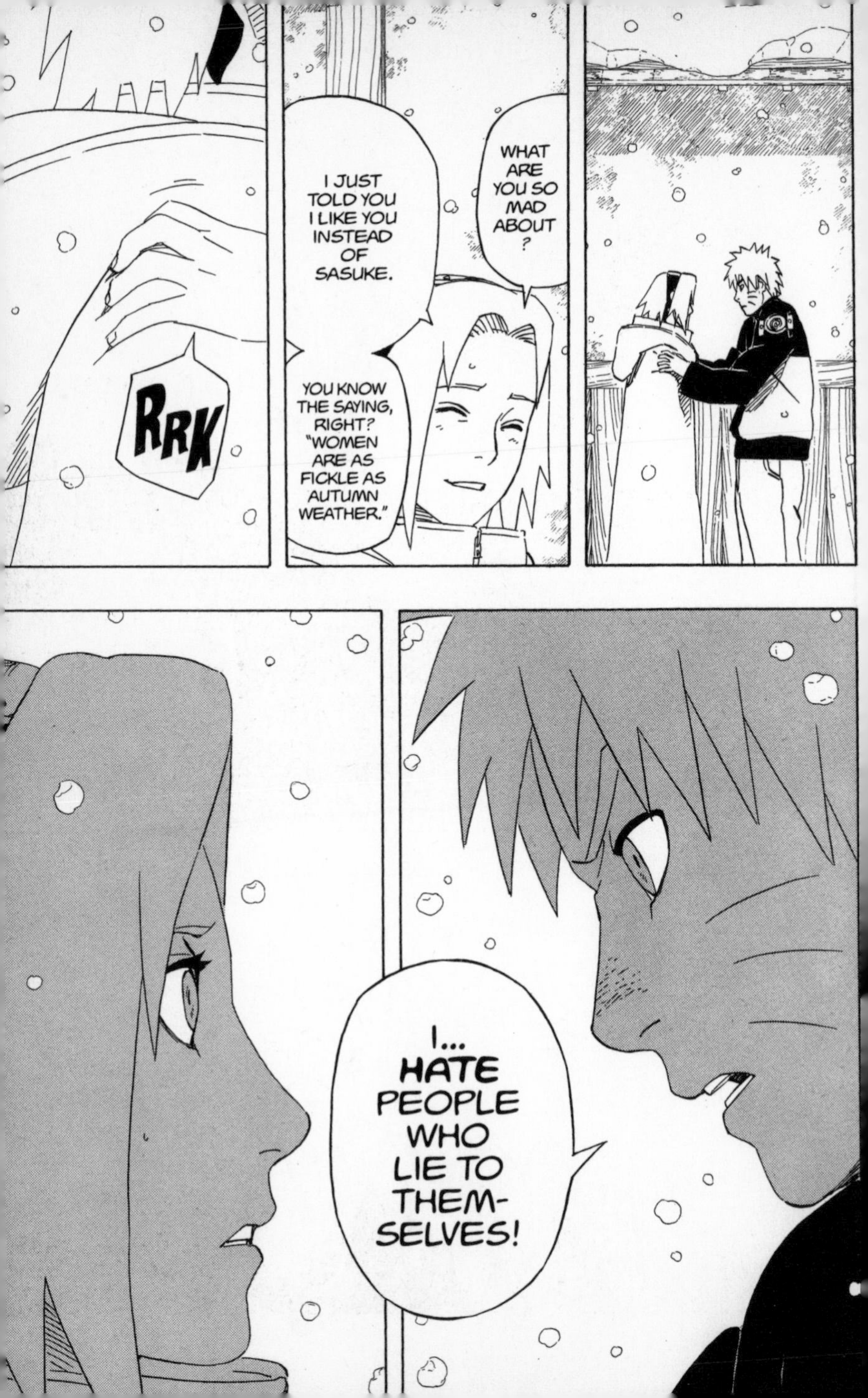
WHAT ARE YOU SO MAD ABOUT?
I JUST TOLD YOU I LIKE YOU INSTEAD OF SASUKE.
YOU KNOW THE SAYING, RIGHT? "WOMEN ARE AS FICKLE AS AUTUMN WEATHER."
RRK
I... HATE PEOPLE WHO LIE TO THEM-SELVES!

NARUTO

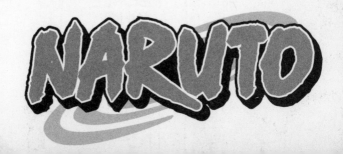

Number 470: Killer Bee vs. Kisame!!

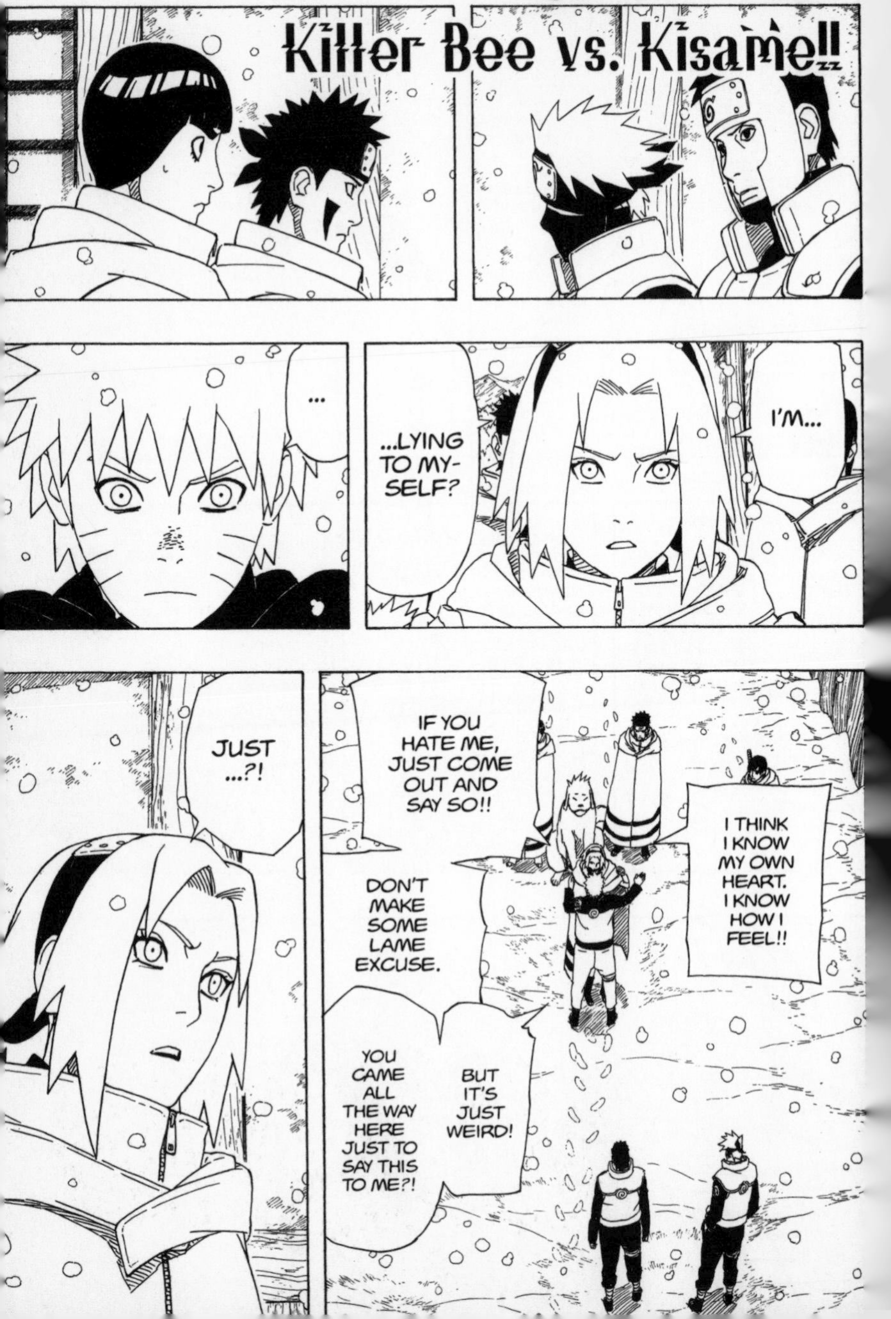
I'M...
...LYING TO MY-SELF?
...
I THINK I KNOW MY OWN HEART. I KNOW HOW I FEEL!!
IF YOU HATE ME, JUST COME OUT AND SAY SO!!
DON'T MAKE SOME LAME EXCUSE.
BUT IT'S JUST WEIRD!
YOU CAME ALL THE WAY HERE JUST TO SAY THIS TO ME?!
JUST ...?!

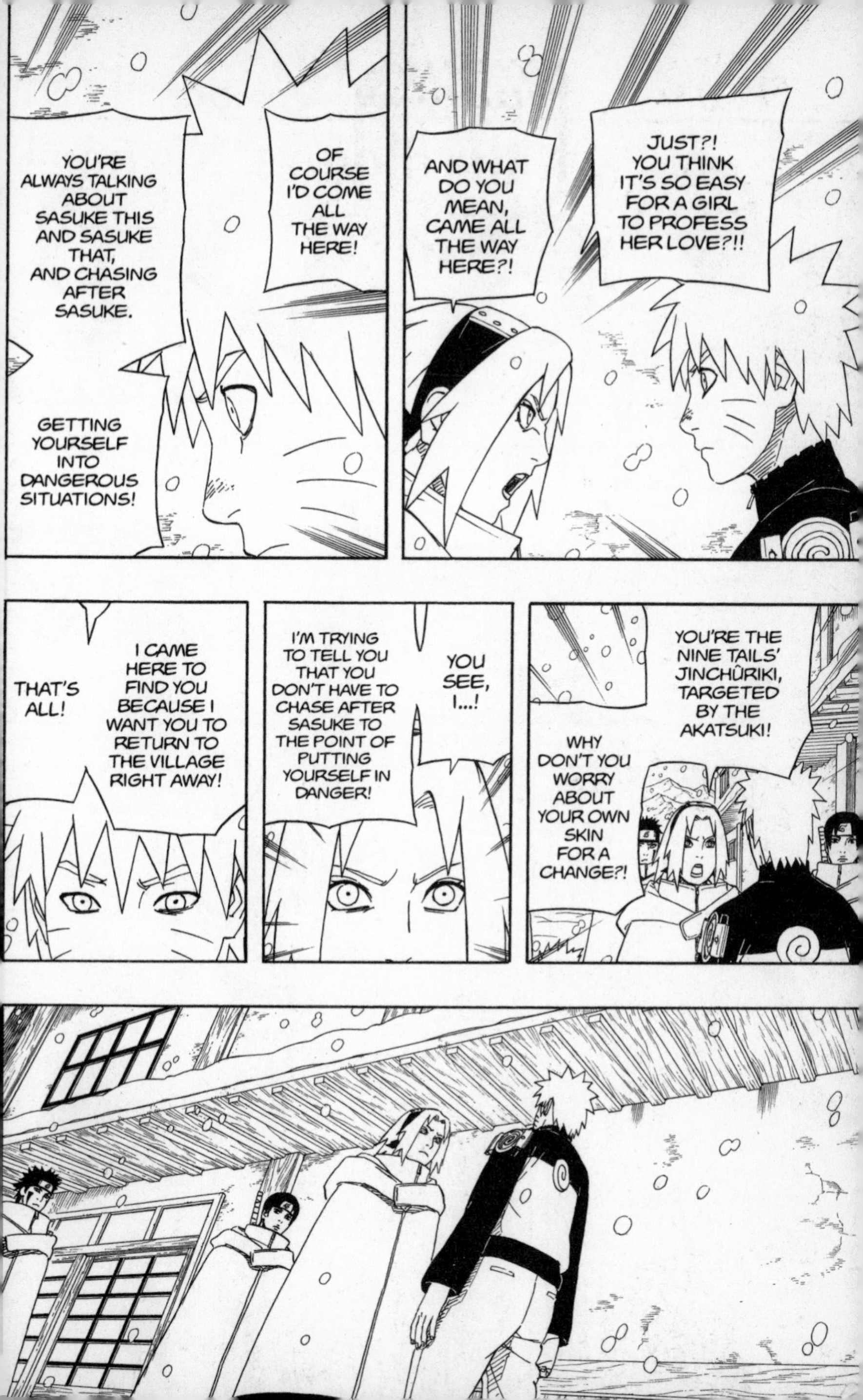
JUST?! YOU THINK IT'S SO EASY FOR A GIRL TO PROFESS HER LOVE?!!
AND WHAT DO YOU MEAN, CAME ALL THE WAY HERE?!
OF COURSE I'D COME ALL THE WAY HERE!
YOU'RE ALWAYS TALKING ABOUT SASUKE THIS AND SASUKE THAT, AND CHASING AFTER SASUKE.
GETTING YOURSELF INTO DANGEROUS SITUATIONS!
YOU'RE THE NINE TAILS' JINCHÛRIKI, TARGETED BY THE AKATSUKI!
WHY DON'T YOU WORRY ABOUT YOUR OWN SKIN FOR A CHANGE?!
YOU SEE, I...!
I'M TRYING TO TELL YOU THAT YOU DON'T HAVE TO CHASE AFTER SASUKE TO THE POINT OF PUTTING YOURSELF IN DANGER!
I CAME HERE TO FIND YOU BECAUSE I WANT YOU TO RETURN TO THE VILLAGE RIGHT AWAY!
THAT'S ALL!

READ THIS WAY

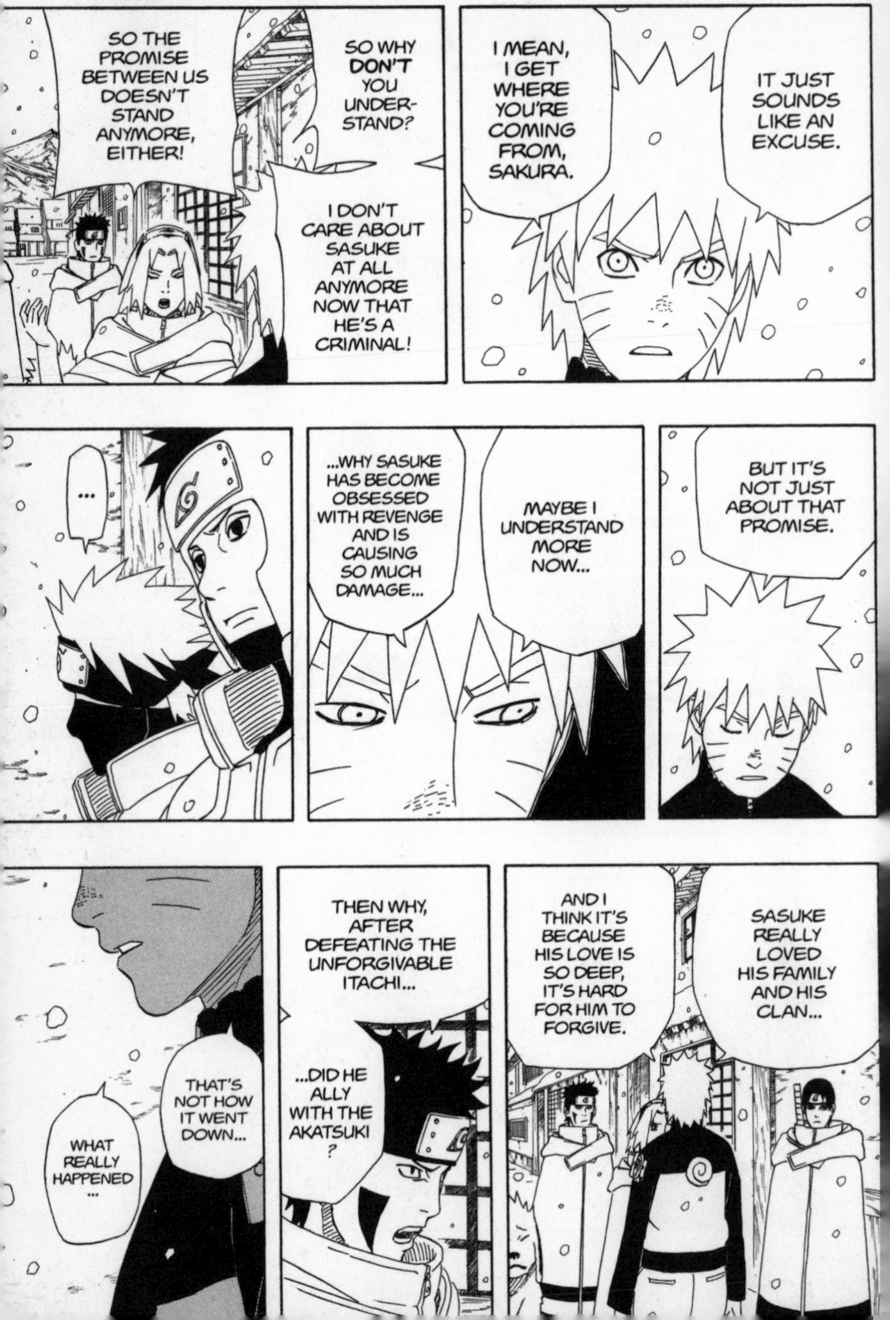
I MEAN, I GET WHERE YOU'RE COMING FROM, SAKURA.
IT JUST SOUNDS LIKE AN EXCUSE.
SO WHY DON'T YOU UNDERSTAND?
I DON'T CARE ABOUT SASUKE AT ALL ANYMORE NOW THAT HE'S A CRIMINAL!
SO THE PROMISE BETWEEN US DOESN'T STAND ANYMORE, EITHER!
BUT IT'S NOT JUST ABOUT THAT PROMISE.
MAYBE I UNDERSTAND MORE NOW...
...WHY SASUKE HAS BECOME OBSESSED WITH REVENGE AND IS CAUSING SO MUCH DAMAGE...
...
SASUKE REALLY LOVED HIS FAMILY AND HIS CLAN...
AND I THINK IT'S BECAUSE HIS LOVE IS SO DEEP, IT'S HARD FOR HIM TO FORGIVE.
THEN WHY, AFTER DEFEATING THE UNFORGIVABLE ITACHI...
...DID HE ALLY WITH THE AKATSUKI?
THAT'S NOT HOW IT WENT DOWN...
WHAT REALLY HAPPENED...

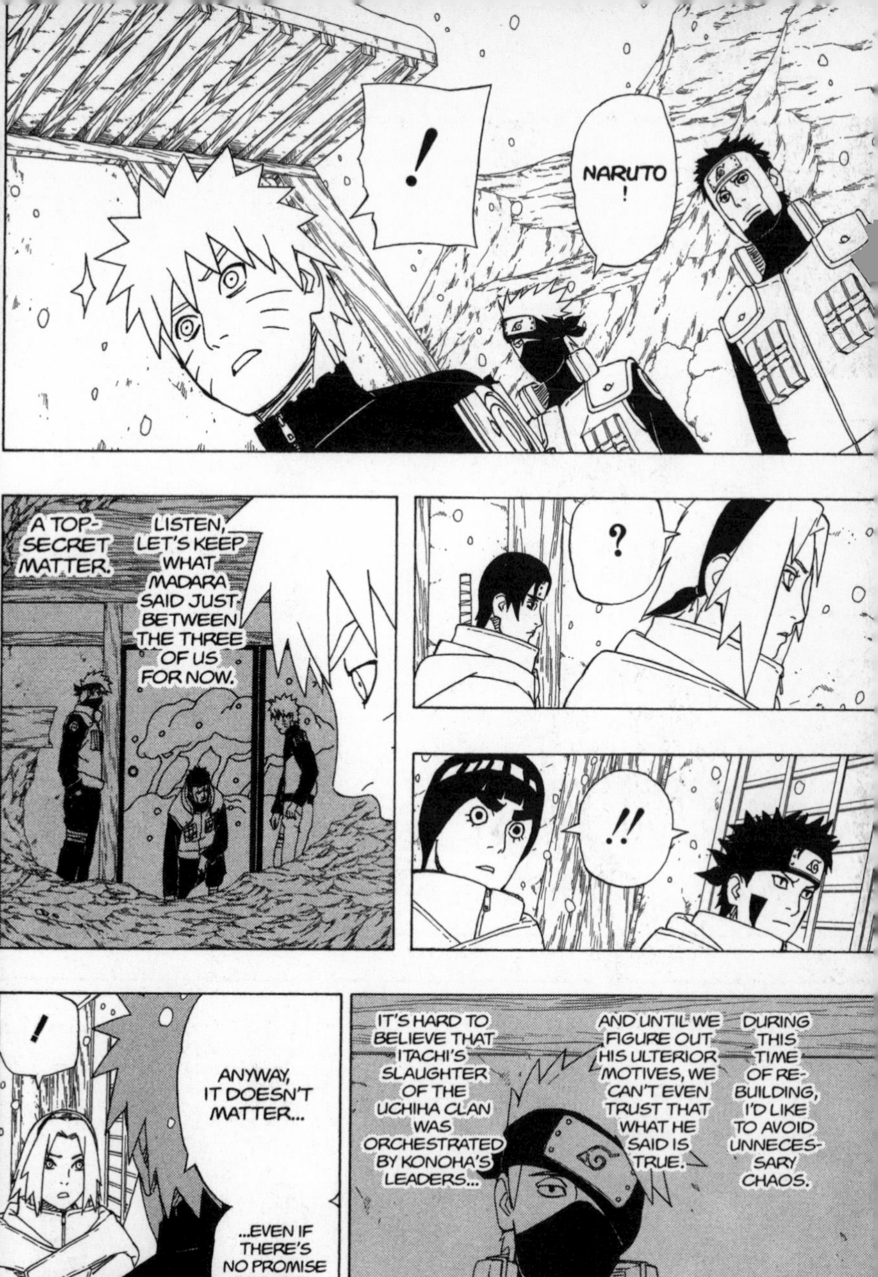

NARUTO !
!
?
!!
LISTEN, LET'S KEEP WHAT MADARA SAID JUST BETWEEN THE THREE OF US FOR NOW.
A TOP-SECRET MATTER.
DURING THIS TIME OF RE-BUILDING, I'D LIKE TO AVOID UNNECES-SARY CHAOS.
AND UNTIL WE FIGURE OUT HIS ULTERIOR MOTIVES, WE CAN'T EVEN TRUST THAT WHAT HE SAID IS TRUE.
IT'S HARD TO BELIEVE THAT ITACHI'S SLAUGHTER OF THE UCHIHA CLAN WAS ORCHESTRATED BY KONOHA'S LEADERS...
ANYWAY, IT DOESN'T MATTER...
...EVEN IF THERE'S NO PROMISE BETWEEN US ANY-MORE.
!

READ THIS WAY

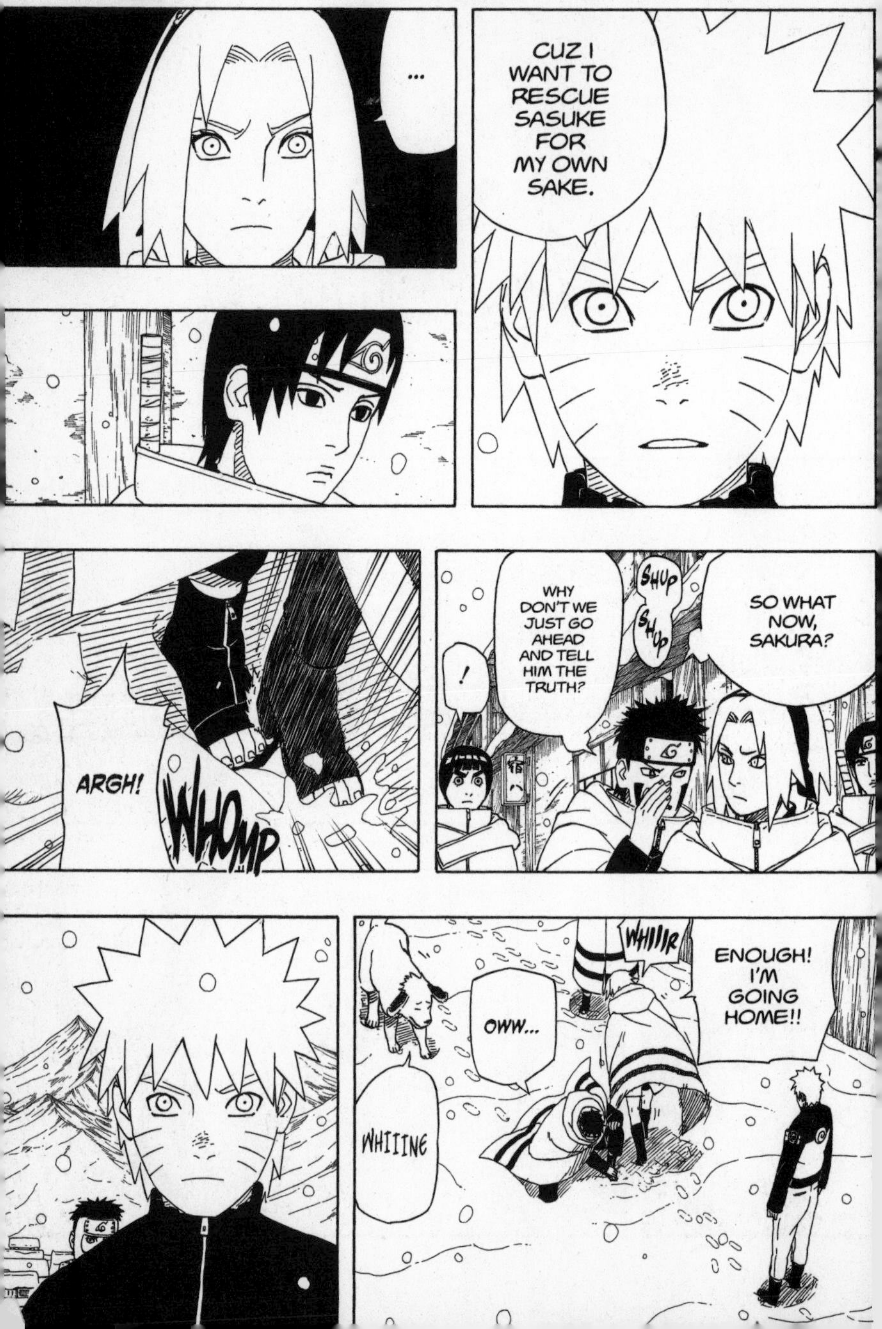
CUZ I WANT TO RESCUE SASUKE FOR MY OWN SAKE.
...
SO WHAT NOW, SAKURA?
SHUP
SHUP
WHY DON'T WE JUST GO AHEAD AND TELL HIM THE TRUTH?
!
WHOMP
ARGH!
ENOUGH! I'M GOING HOME!!
WHIIIR
OWW...
WHIIINE

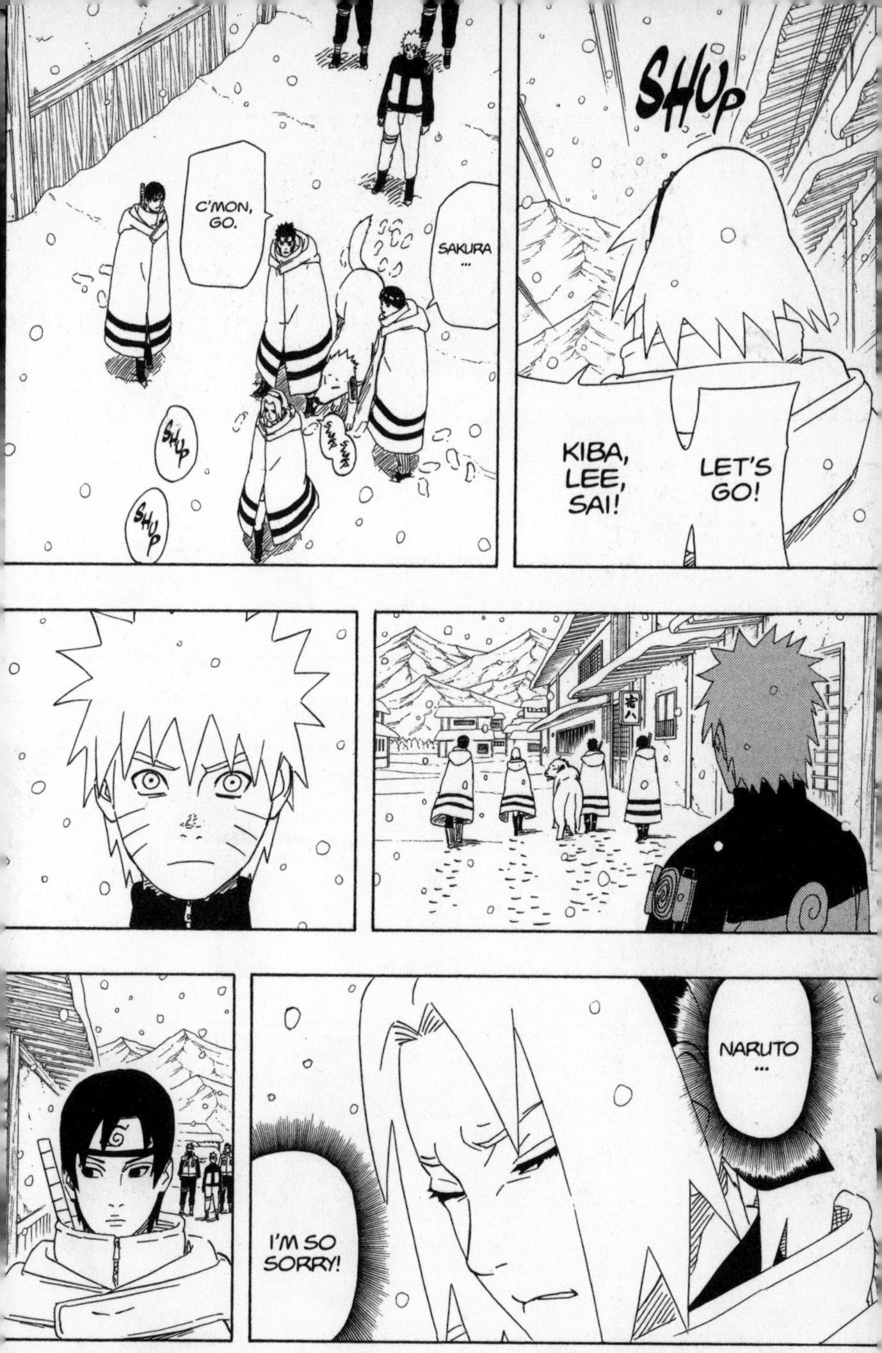
SHUP
LET'S GO!
KIBA, LEE, SAI!
SAKURA ...
C'MON, GO.
SHUP
SHUP
NARUTO ...
I'M SO SORRY!

READ THIS WAY

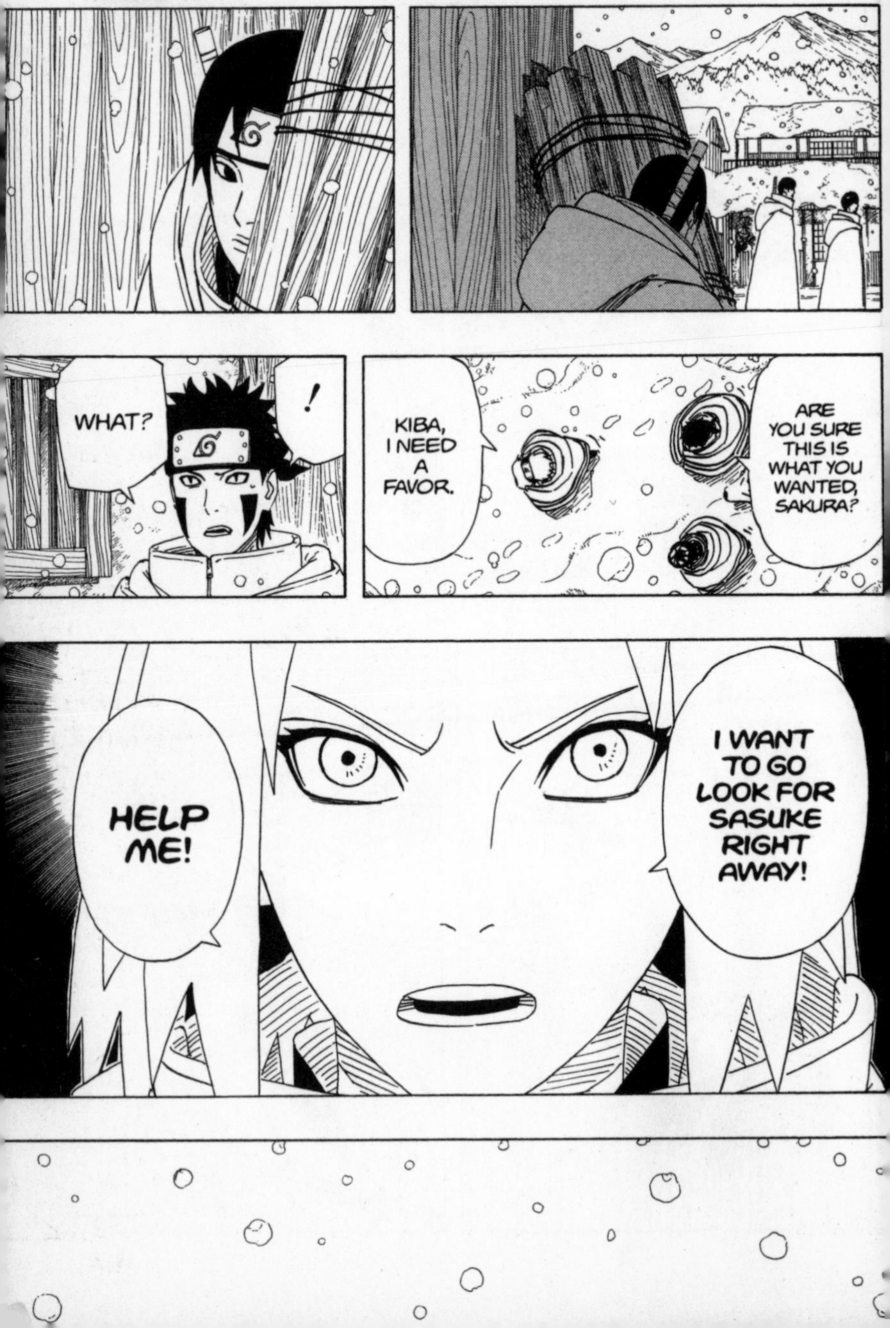
ARE YOU SURE THIS IS WHAT YOU WANTED, SAKURA?
KIBA, I NEED A FAVOR.
!
WHAT?
I WANT TO GO LOOK FOR SASUKE RIGHT AWAY!
HELP ME!

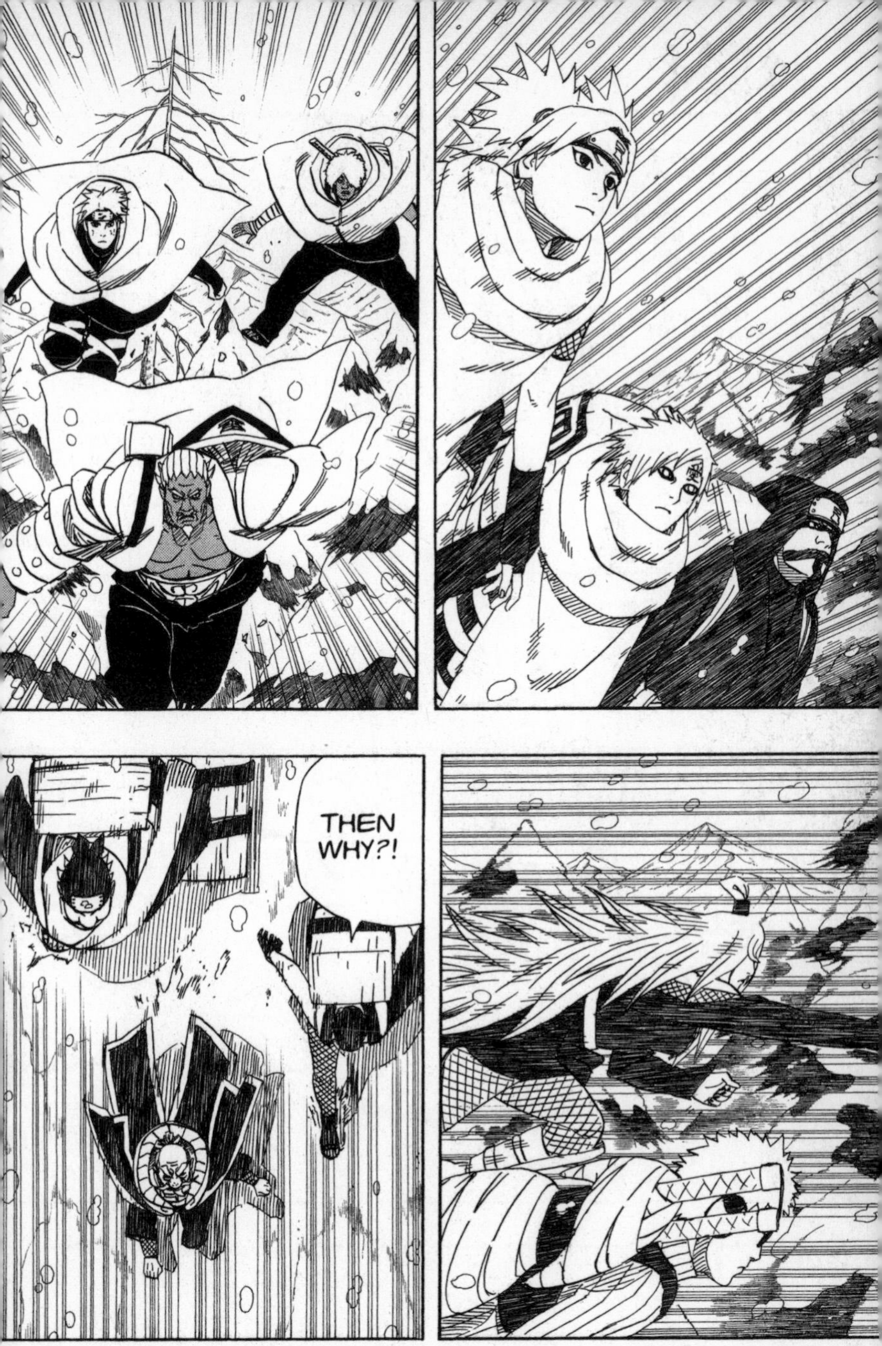
THEN WHY?!

READ THIS WAY

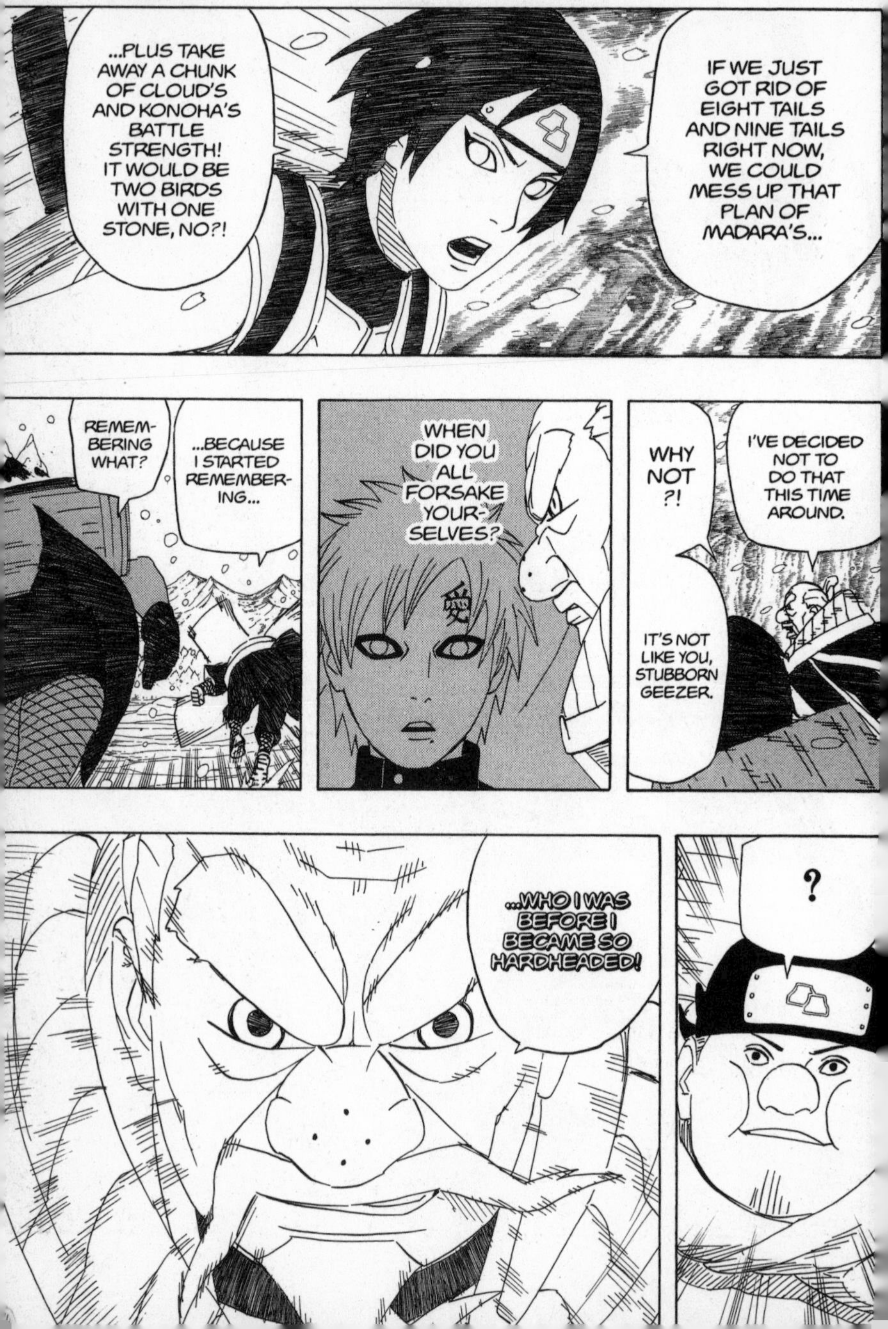
IF WE JUST GOT RID OF EIGHT TAILS AND NINE TAILS RIGHT NOW, WE COULD MESS UP THAT PLAN OF MADARA'S...
...PLUS TAKE AWAY A CHUNK OF CLOUD'S AND KONOHA'S BATTLE STRENGTH! IT WOULD BE TWO BIRDS WITH ONE STONE, NO?!
I'VE DECIDED NOT TO DO THAT THIS TIME AROUND.
WHY NOT?!
IT'S NOT LIKE YOU, STUBBORN GEEZER.
WHEN DID YOU ALL FORSAKE YOURSELVES?
...BECAUSE I STARTED REMEMBERING...
REMEMBERING WHAT?
?
...WHO I WAS BEFORE I BECAME SO HARDHEADED!

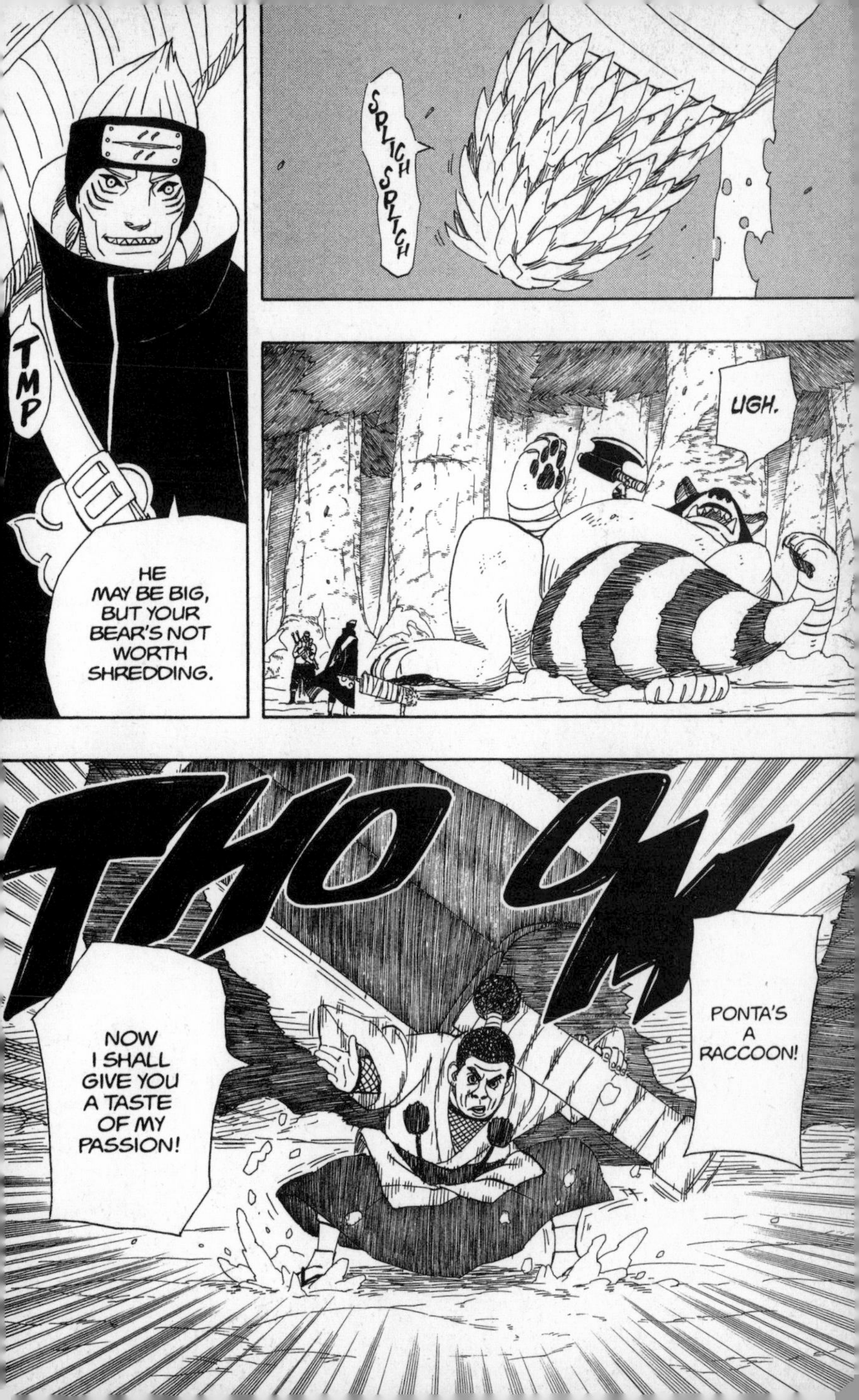
SPLICH SPLICH
UGH.
TMP
HE MAY BE BIG, BUT YOUR BEAR'S NOT WORTH SHREDDING.
THOCK
PONTA'S A RACCOON!
NOW I SHALL GIVE YOU A TASTE OF MY PASSION!

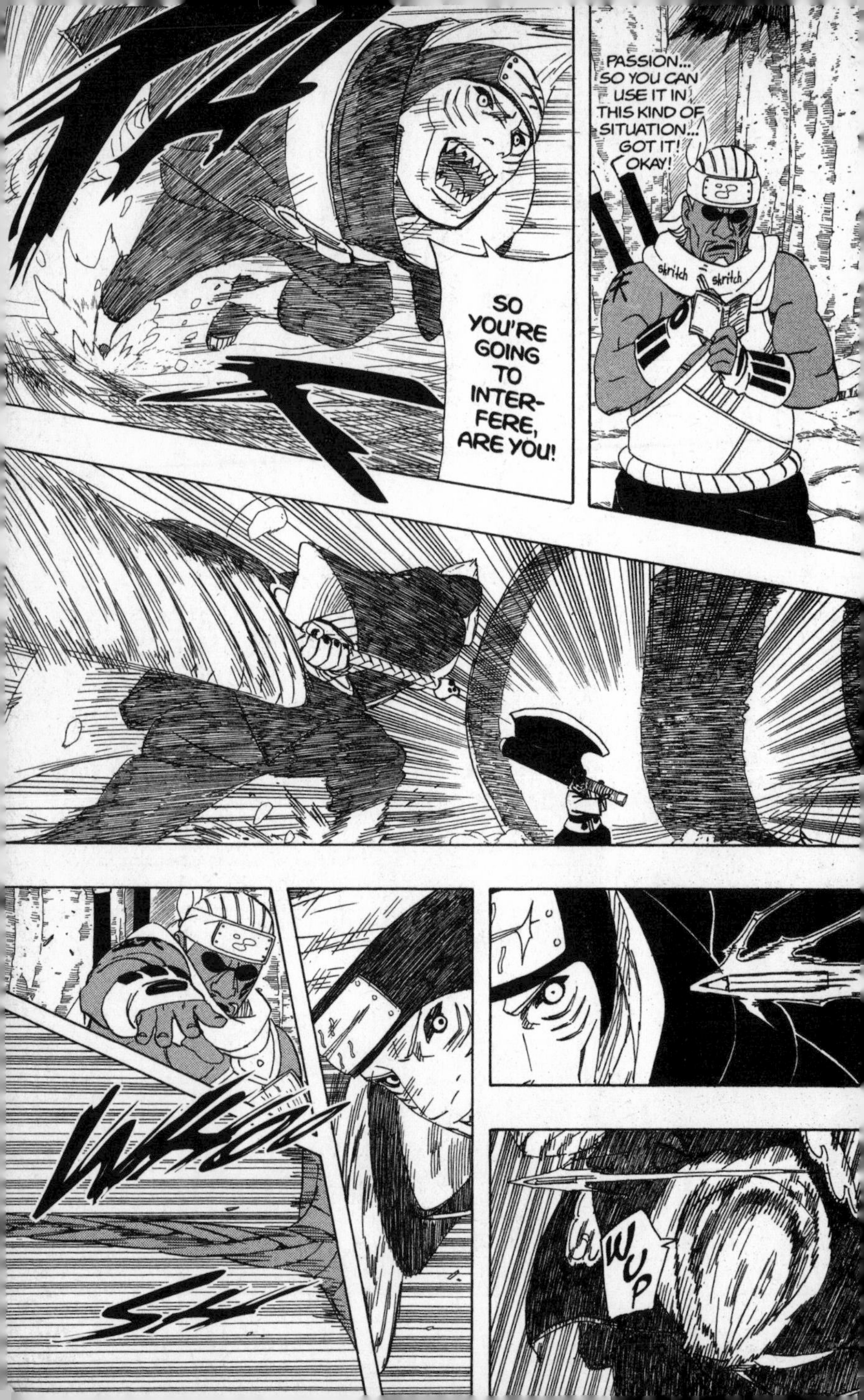
PASSION... SO YOU CAN USE IT IN THIS KIND OF SITUATION... GOT IT! OKAY!
skritch
skritch
SO YOU'RE GOING TO INTER-FERE, ARE YOU!
WUP

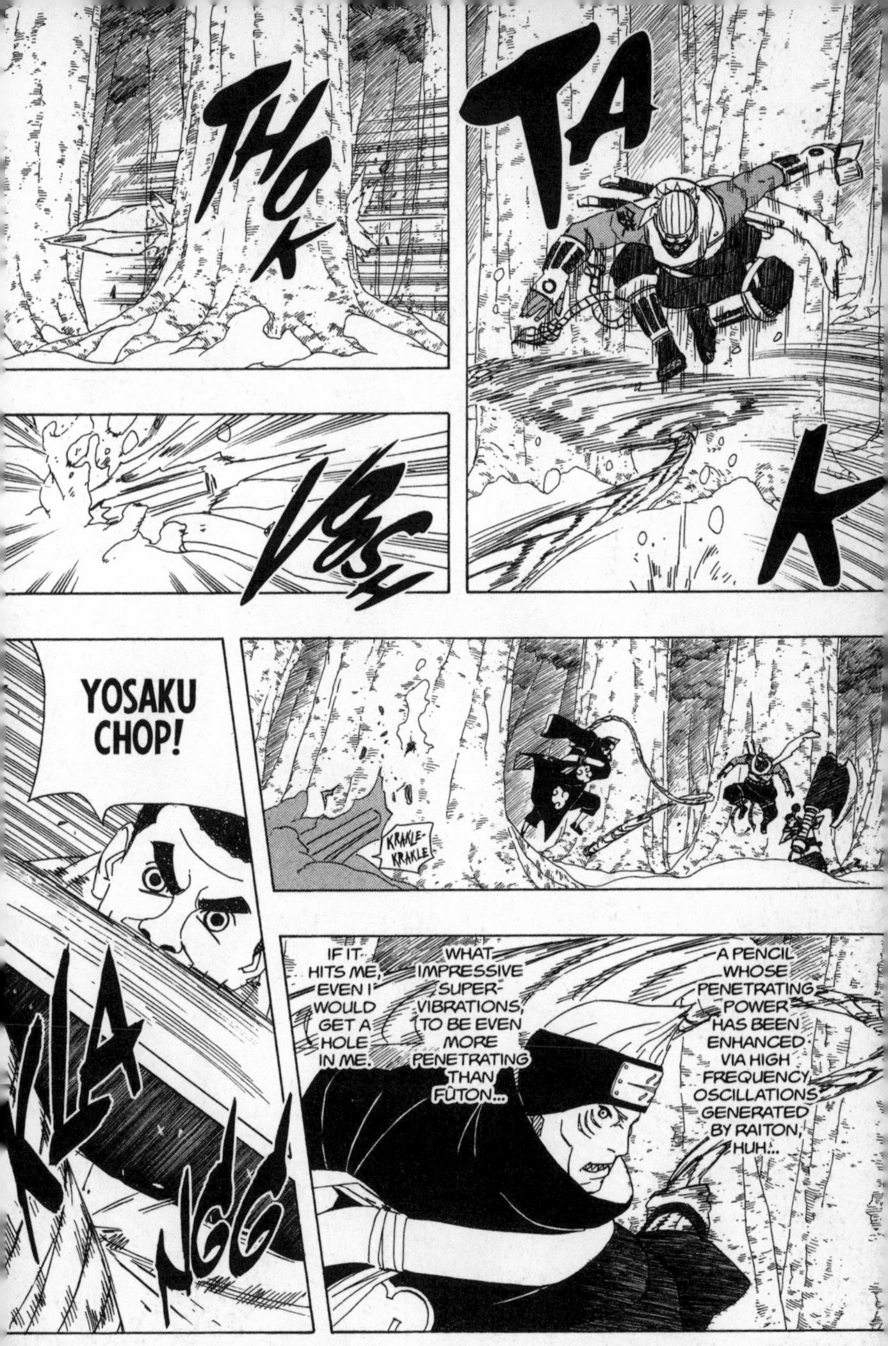
TA
K
THOK
VOSH
KRAKLE-KRAKLE
YOSAKU CHOP!
KLANGG
A PENCIL WHOSE PENETRATING POWER HAS BEEN ENHANCED VIA HIGH FREQUENCY OSCILLATIONS GENERATED BY RAITON, HUH...
WHAT IMPRESSIVE SUPER-VIBRATIONS, TO BE EVEN MORE PENETRATING THAN FÛTON...
IF IT HITS ME, EVEN I WOULD GET A HOLE IN ME.

READ THIS WAY

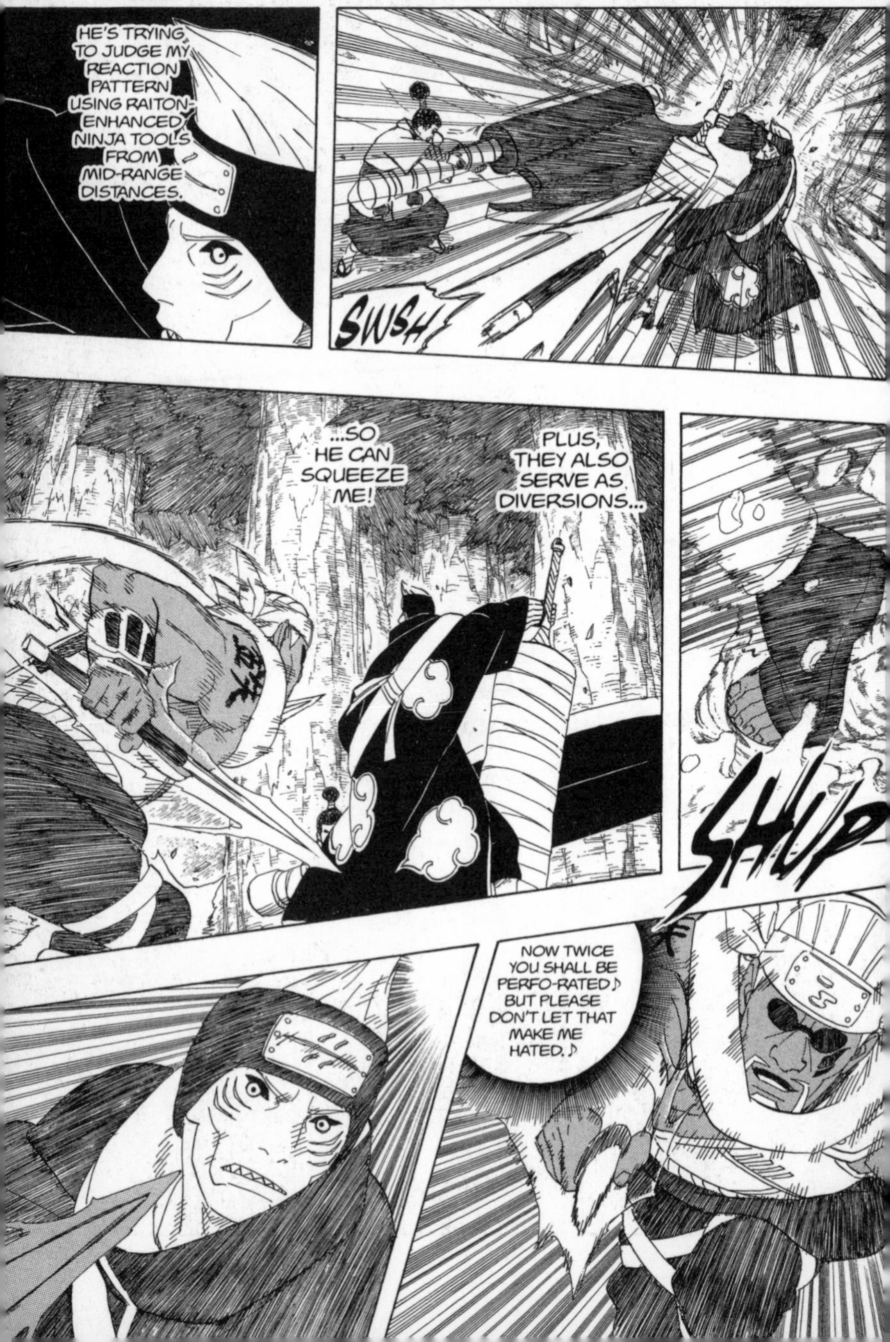

SWSH
HE'S TRYING TO JUDGE MY REACTION PATTERN USING RAITON-ENHANCED NINJA TOOLS FROM MID-RANGE DISTANCES.
SHUP
PLUS, THEY ALSO SERVE AS DIVERSIONS...
...SO HE CAN SQUEEZE ME!
NOW TWICE YOU SHALL BE PERFO-RATED♪ BUT PLEASE DON'T LET THAT MAKE ME HATED.♪

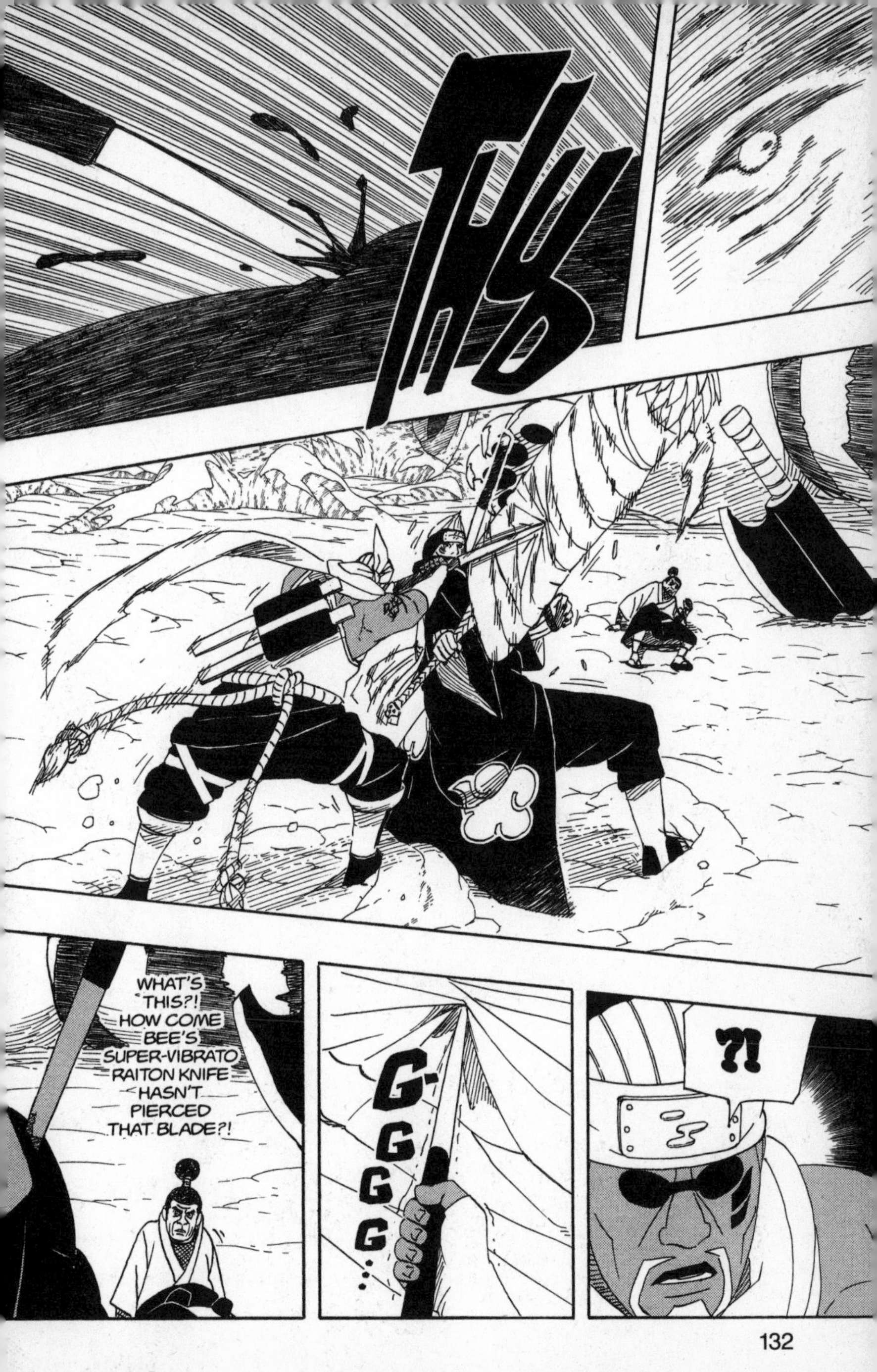
THUD
?!
G-GGG...
WHAT'S THIS?! HOW COME BEE'S SUPER-VIBRATO RAITON KNIFE HASN'T PIERCED THAT BLADE?!

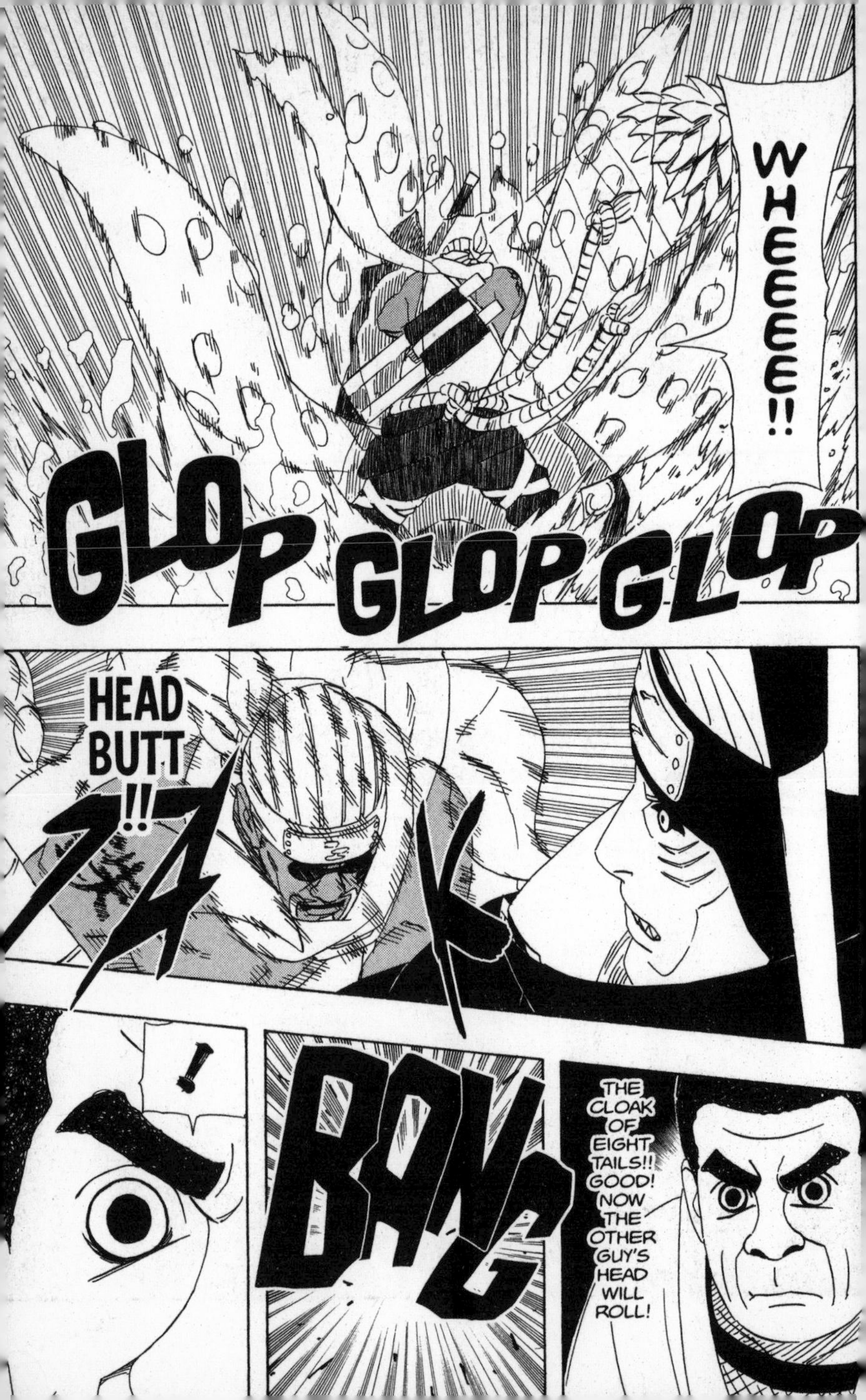
WHEEEE!!
GLOP GLOP GLOP
HEAD BUTT!!
THE CLOAK OF EIGHT TAILS!! GOOD! NOW THE OTHER GUY'S HEAD WILL ROLL!
BANG
!

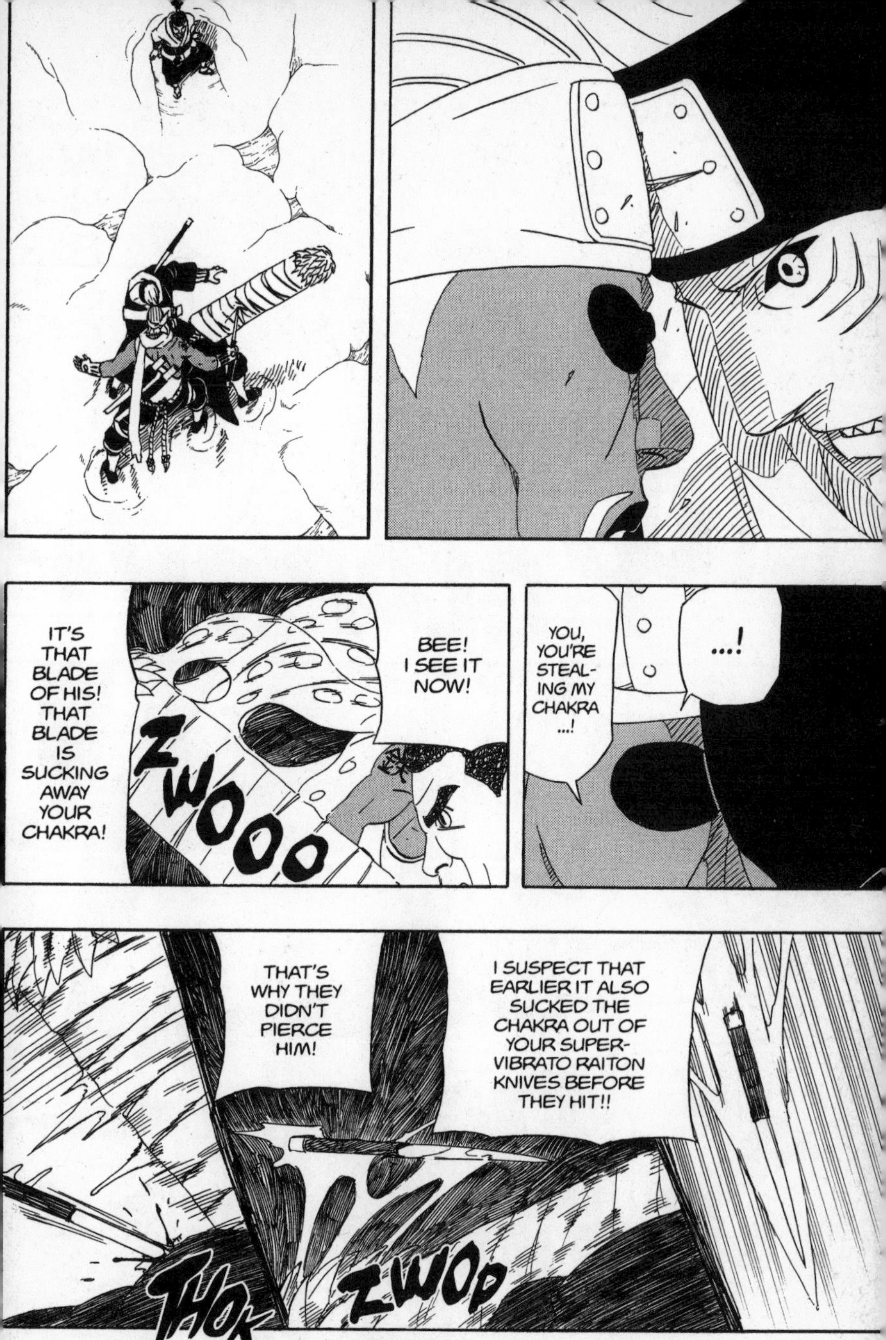
...!
YOU, YOU'RE STEALING MY CHAKRA ...!
BEE! I SEE IT NOW!
IT'S THAT BLADE OF HIS! THAT BLADE IS SUCKING AWAY YOUR CHAKRA!
ZWOOO
I SUSPECT THAT EARLIER IT ALSO SUCKED THE CHAKRA OUT OF YOUR SUPER-VIBRATO RAITON KNIVES BEFORE THEY HIT!!
THAT'S WHY THEY DIDN'T PIERCE HIM!
ZWOP
THOK

READ THIS WAY

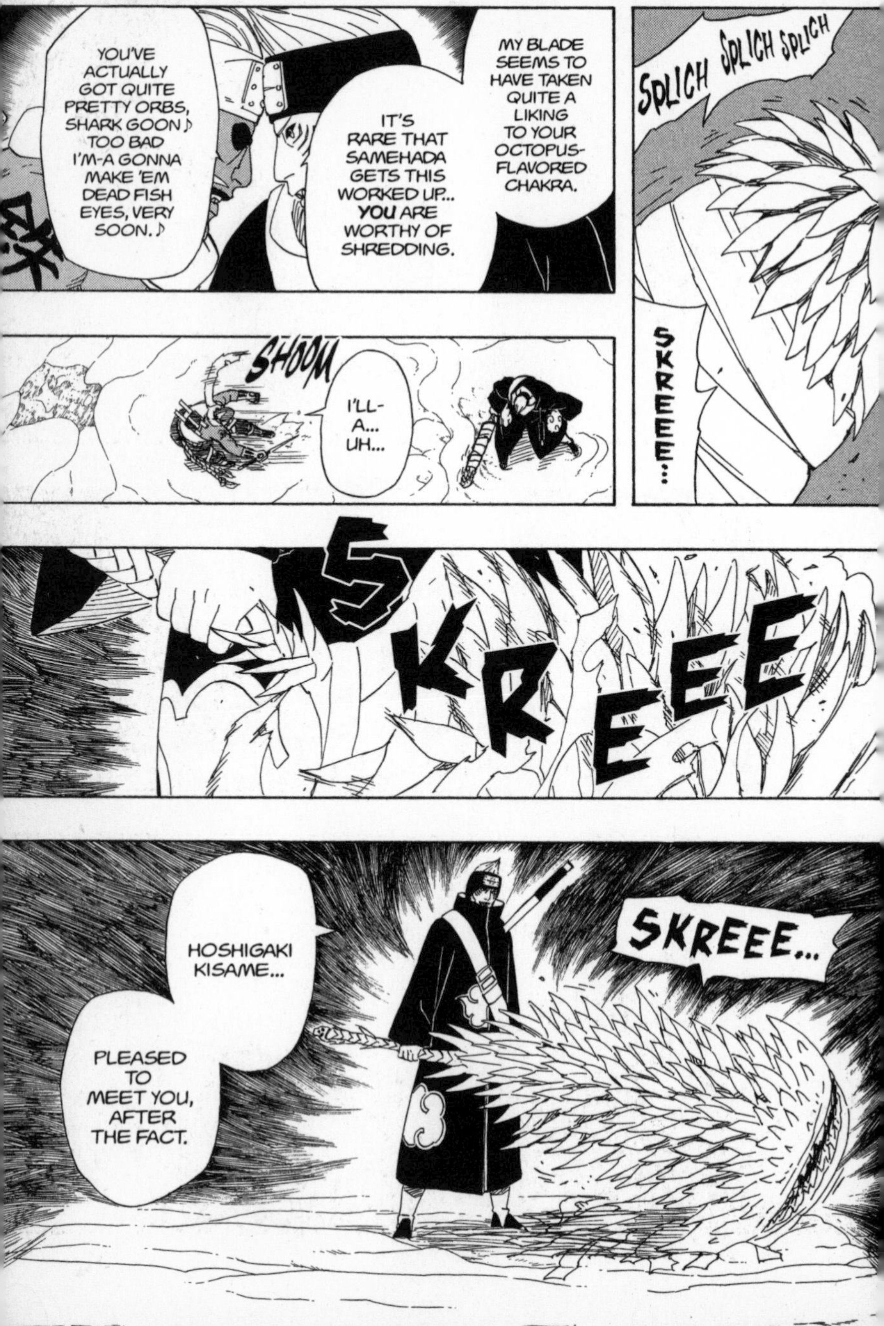
SPLICH SPLICH SPLICH
SKREEE...
MY BLADE SEEMS TO HAVE TAKEN QUITE A LIKING TO YOUR OCTOPUS-FLAVORED CHAKRA.
IT'S RARE THAT SAMEHADA GETS THIS WORKED UP... **YOU** ARE WORTHY OF SHREDDING.
YOU'VE ACTUALLY GOT QUITE PRETTY ORBS, SHARK GOON♪ TOO BAD I'M-A GONNA MAKE 'EM DEAD FISH EYES, VERY SOON.♪
SHOOM
I'LL-A... UH...
SKREEE
SKREEE...
HOSHIGAKI KISAME...
PLEASED TO MEET YOU, AFTER THE FACT.

NARUTO

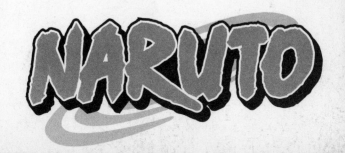

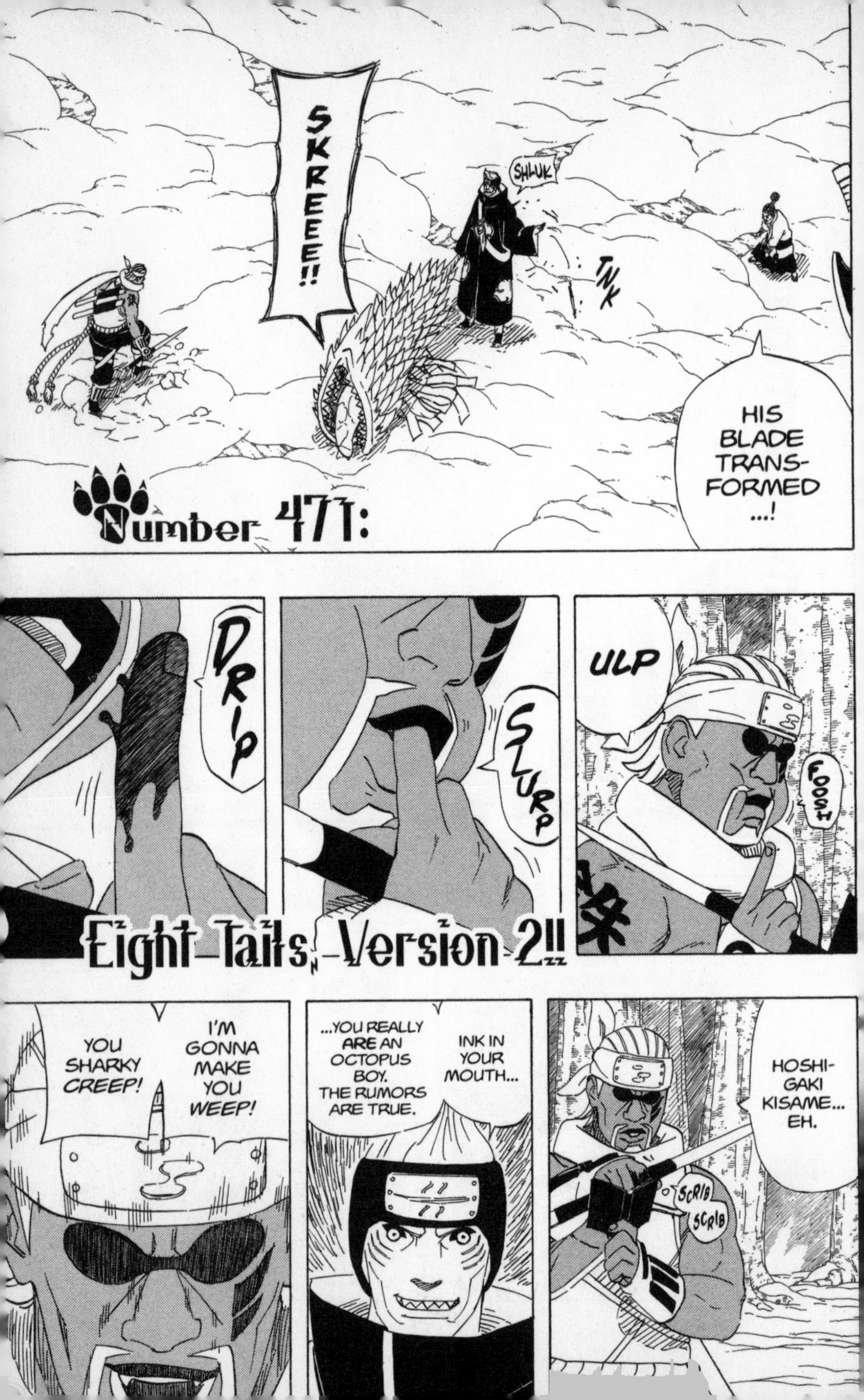
HIS BLADE TRANSFORMED...!
TNK
SHLUK
SKREEE!!
Number 471:
ULP
FOOSH
SLURP
DRIP
Eight Tails, Version 2!!
HOSHIGAKI KISAME... EH.
SCRIB
SCRIB
INK IN YOUR MOUTH...
...YOU REALLY ARE AN OCTOPUS BOY. THE RUMORS ARE TRUE.
I'M GONNA MAKE YOU WEEP!
YOU SHARKY CREEP!

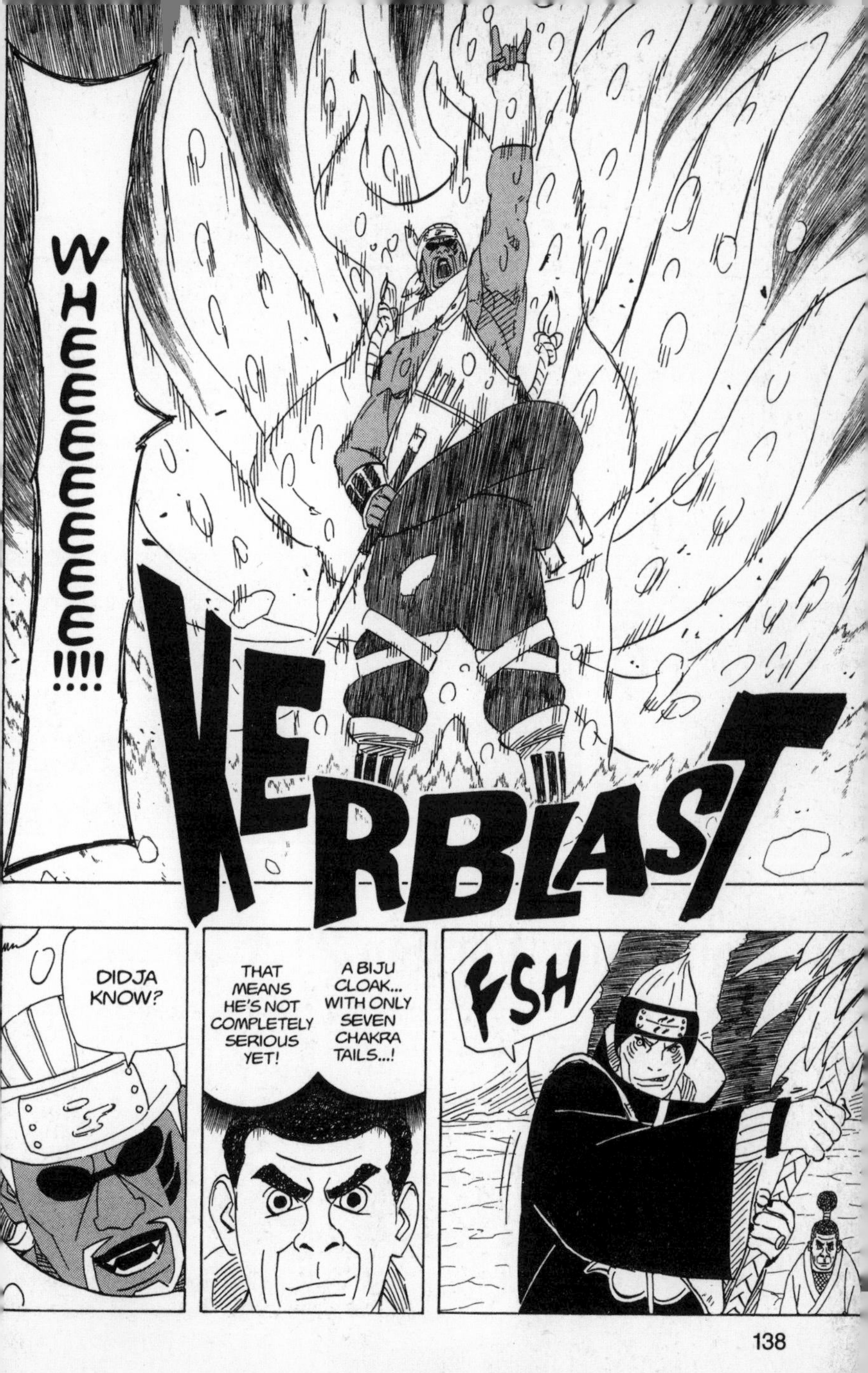
KERBLAST
WHEEEEEEEE!!!!
FSH
A BIJU CLOAK... WITH ONLY SEVEN CHAKRA TAILS...!
THAT MEANS HE'S NOT COMPLETELY SERIOUS YET!
DIDJA KNOW?

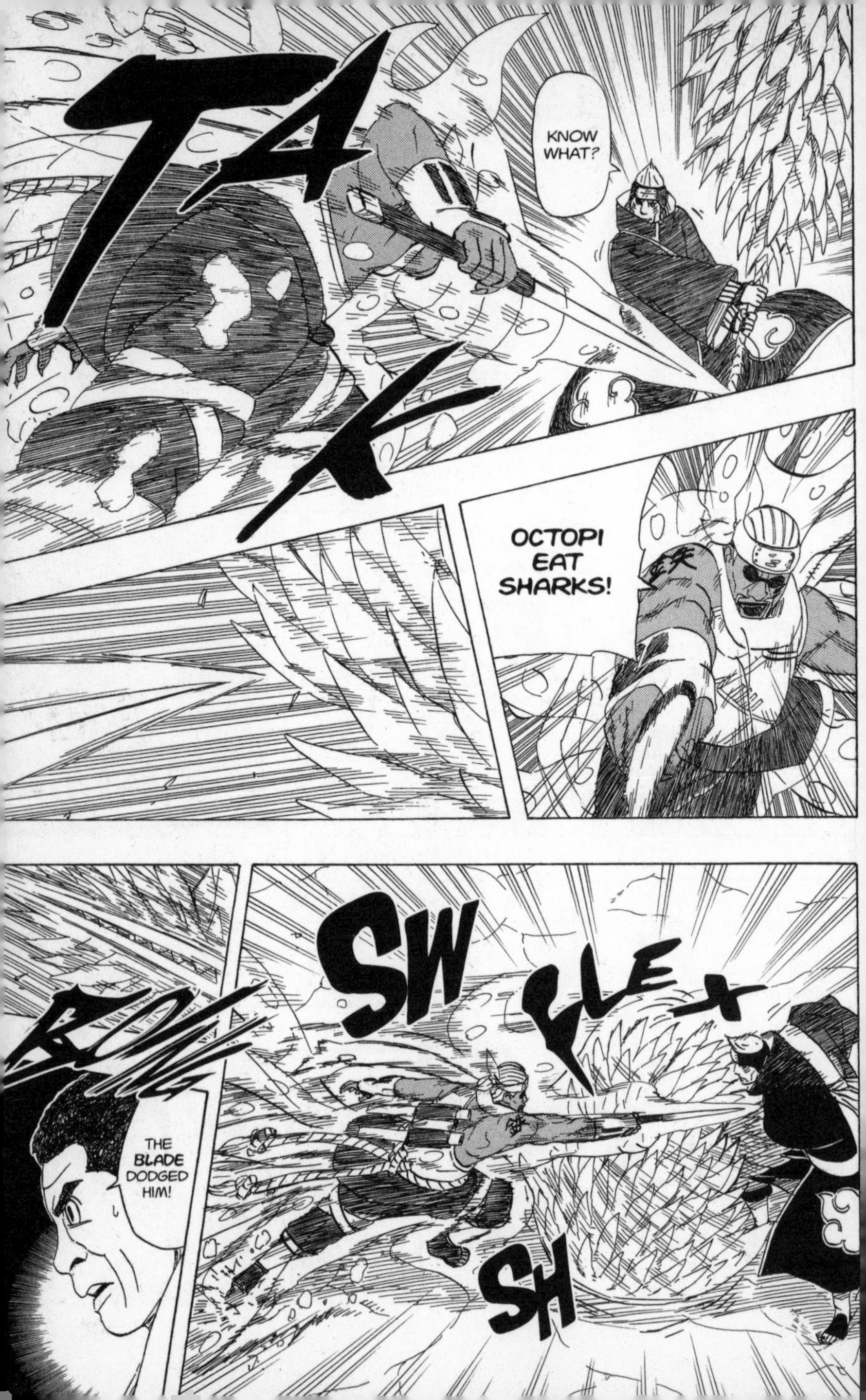
TAK
KNOW WHAT?
OCTOPI EAT SHARKS!
SW
FLEX
SH
THE BLADE DODGED HIM!

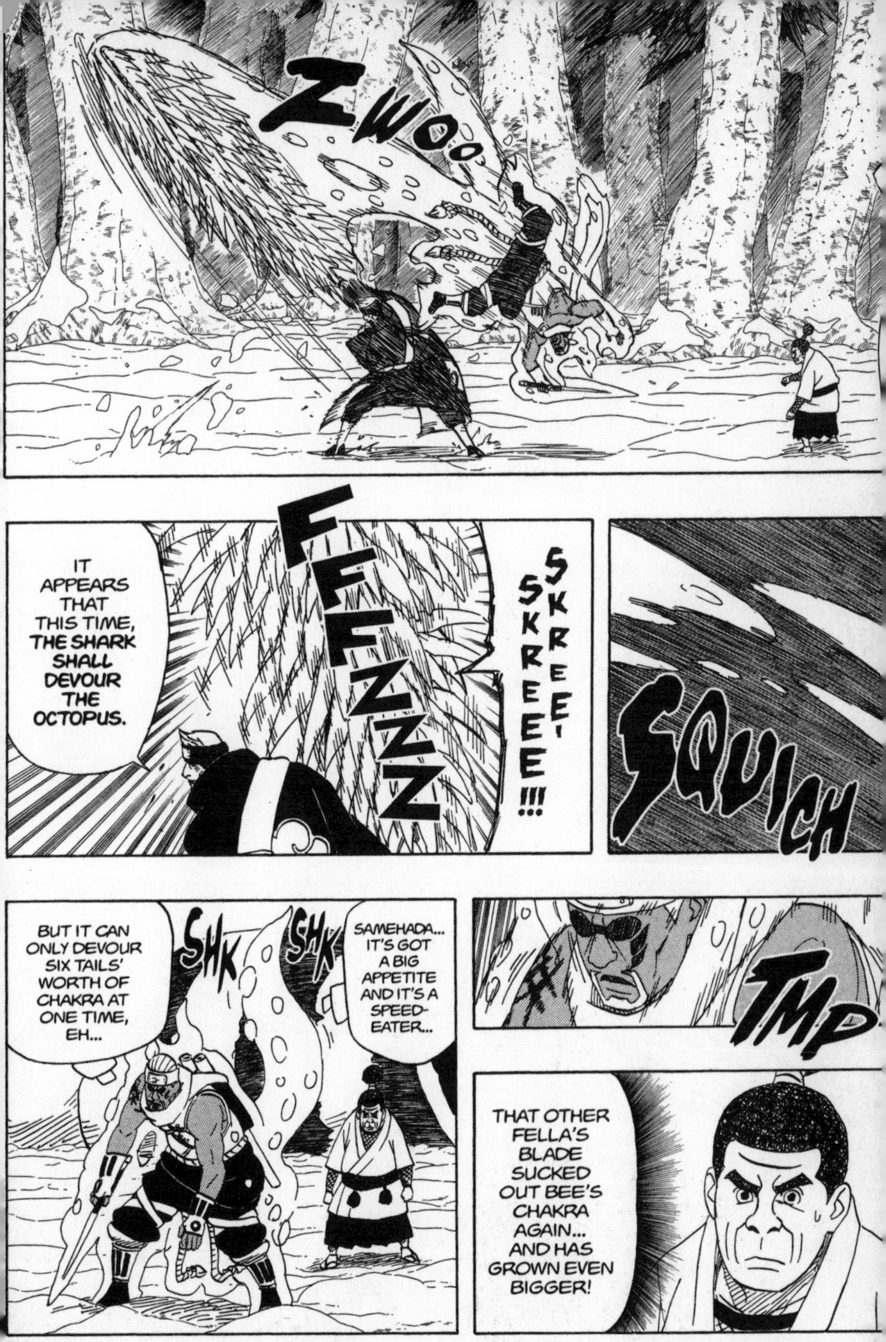
ZWOO
SQUICH
SKREE!
SKREEE!!!
FFFZZZ
IT APPEARS THAT THIS TIME, THE SHARK SHALL DEVOUR THE OCTOPUS.
TMP
THAT OTHER FELLA'S BLADE SUCKED OUT BEE'S CHAKRA AGAIN... AND HAS GROWN EVEN BIGGER!
SHK
SHK
SAMEHADA... IT'S GOT A BIG APPETITE AND IT'S A SPEED-EATER...
BUT IT CAN ONLY DEVOUR SIX TAILS' WORTH OF CHAKRA AT ONE TIME, EH...

READ THIS WAY

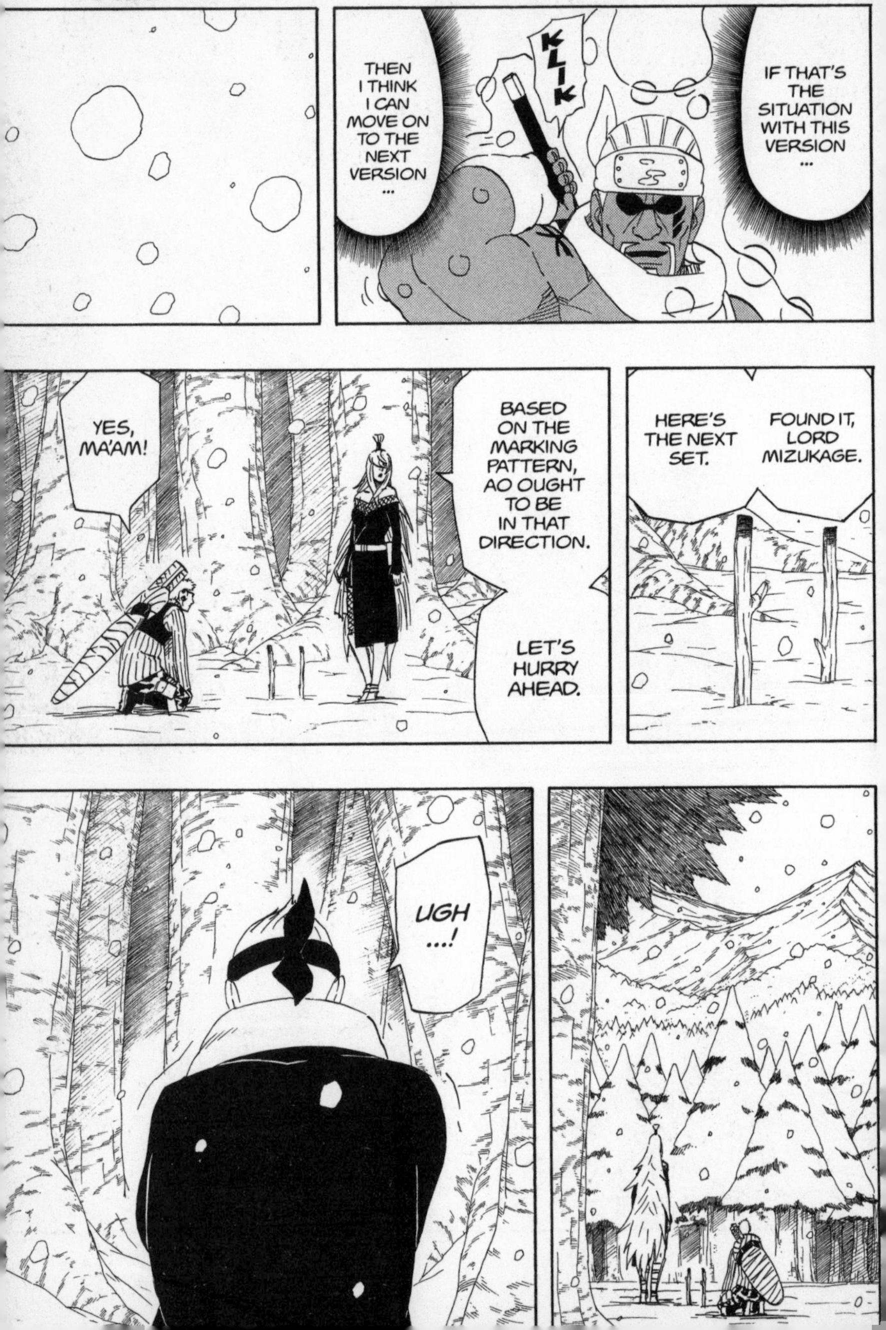
IF THAT'S THE SITUATION WITH THIS VERSION ...
KLIK
THEN I THINK I CAN MOVE ON TO THE NEXT VERSION ...
FOUND IT, LORD MIZUKAGE.
HERE'S THE NEXT SET.
BASED ON THE MARKING PATTERN, AO OUGHT TO BE IN THAT DIRECTION.
LET'S HURRY AHEAD.
YES, MA'AM!
UGH ...!

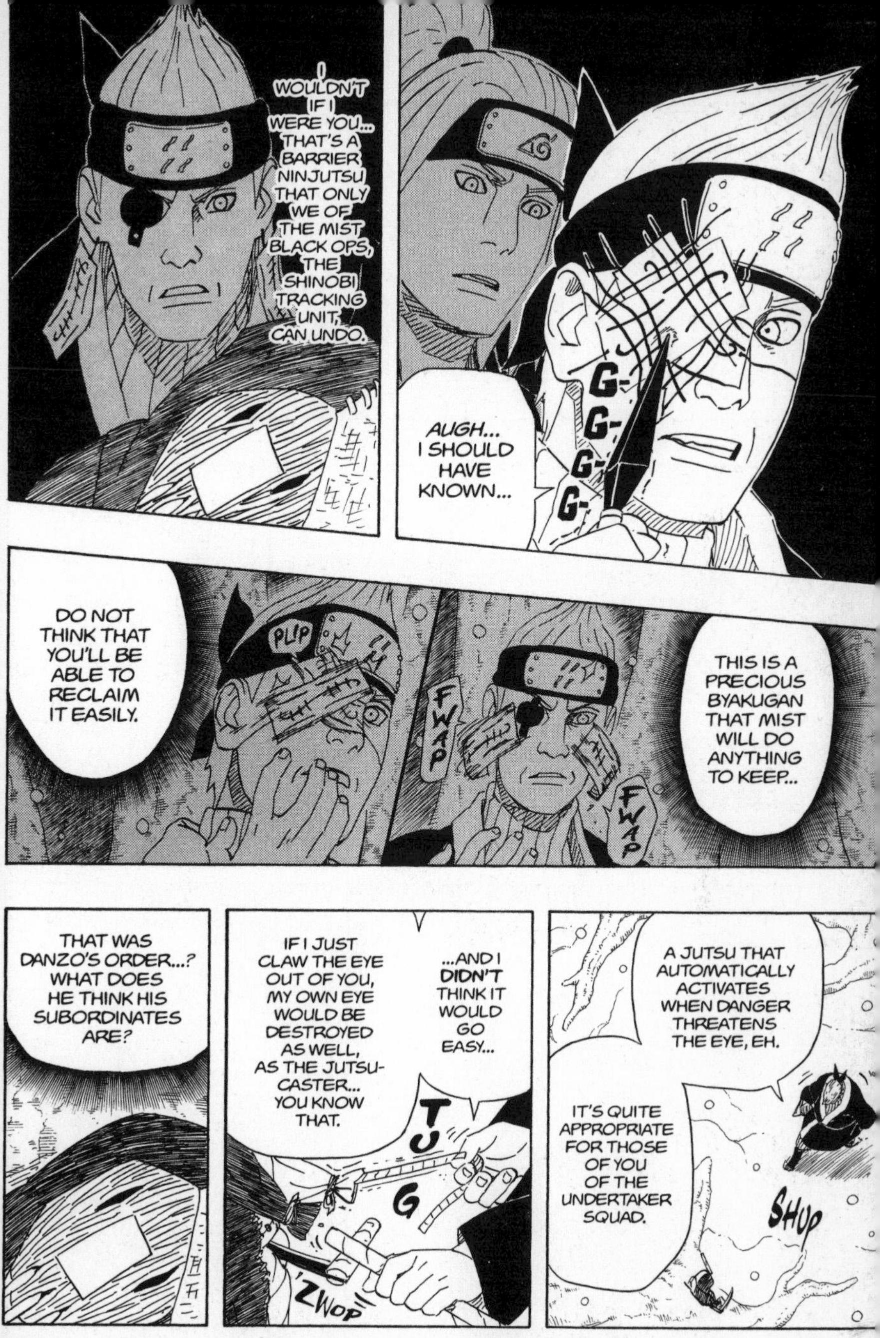
AUGH... I SHOULD HAVE KNOWN...
G-G-G-G-
I WOULDN'T IF I WERE YOU... THAT'S A BARRIER NINJUTSU THAT ONLY WE OF THE MIST BLACK OPS, THE SHINOBI TRACKING UNIT, CAN UNDO.
THIS IS A PRECIOUS BYAKUGAN THAT MIST WILL DO ANYTHING TO KEEP...
FWAP
FWAP
PLIP
DO NOT THINK THAT YOU'LL BE ABLE TO RECLAIM IT EASILY.
A JUTSU THAT AUTOMATICALLY ACTIVATES WHEN DANGER THREATENS THE EYE, EH.
IT'S QUITE APPROPRIATE FOR THOSE OF YOU OF THE UNDERTAKER SQUAD.
SHUP
...AND I DIDN'T THINK IT WOULD GO EASY...
IF I JUST CLAW THE EYE OUT OF YOU, MY OWN EYE WOULD BE DESTROYED AS WELL, AS THE JUTSU-CASTER... YOU KNOW THAT.
TUG
ZWOP
THAT WAS DANZO'S ORDER...? WHAT DOES HE THINK HIS SUBORDINATES ARE?

READ THIS WAY

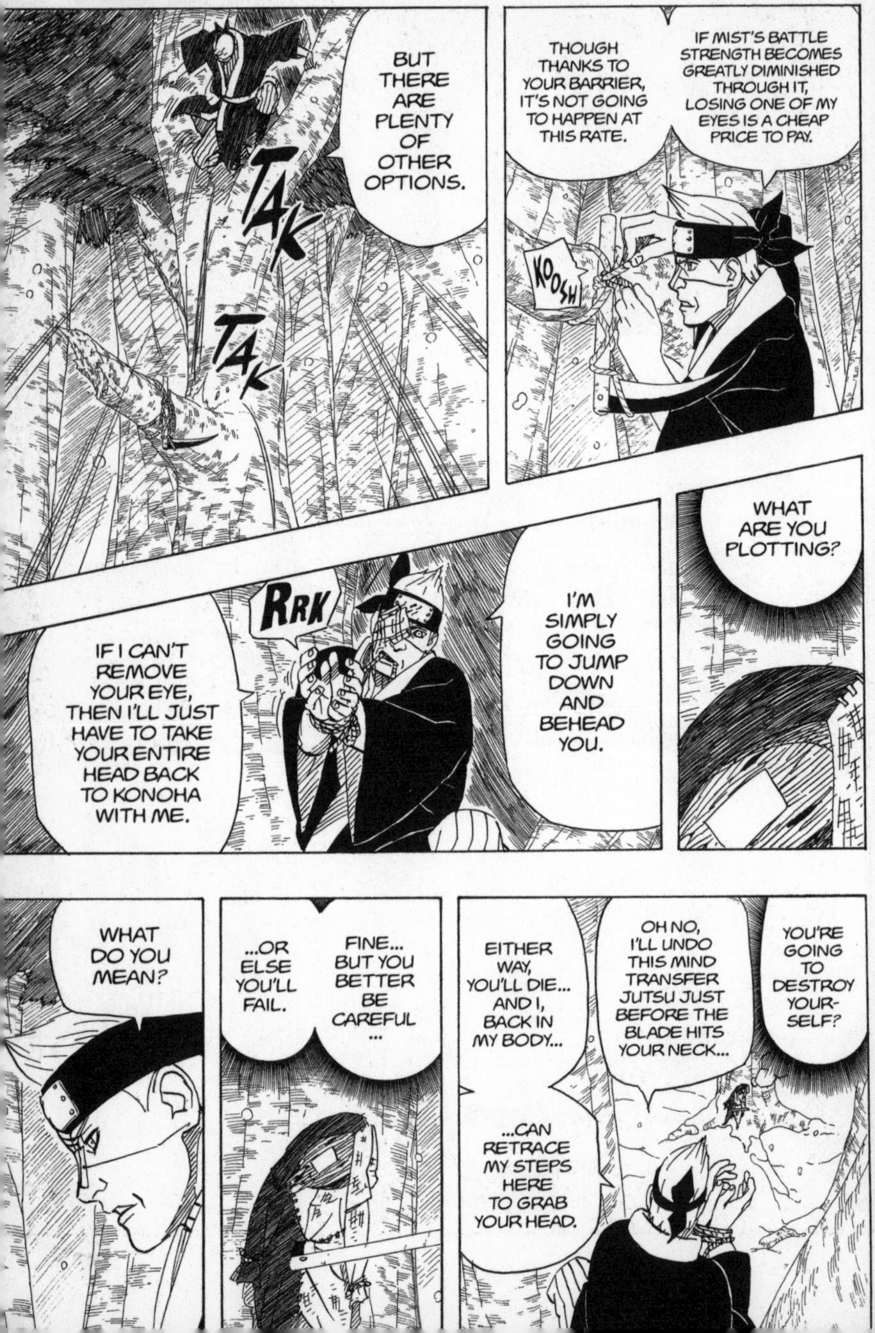
IF MIST'S BATTLE STRENGTH BECOMES GREATLY DIMINISHED THROUGH IT, LOSING ONE OF MY EYES IS A CHEAP PRICE TO PAY.
THOUGH THANKS TO YOUR BARRIER, IT'S NOT GOING TO HAPPEN AT THIS RATE.
KOOSH
BUT THERE ARE PLENTY OF OTHER OPTIONS.
TAK
TAK
WHAT ARE YOU PLOTTING?
I'M SIMPLY GOING TO JUMP DOWN AND BEHEAD YOU.
RRK
IF I CAN'T REMOVE YOUR EYE, THEN I'LL JUST HAVE TO TAKE YOUR ENTIRE HEAD BACK TO KONOHA WITH ME.
YOU'RE GOING TO DESTROY YOUR-SELF?
OH NO, I'LL UNDO THIS MIND TRANSFER JUTSU JUST BEFORE THE BLADE HITS YOUR NECK...
EITHER WAY, YOU'LL DIE... AND I, BACK IN MY BODY...
...CAN RETRACE MY STEPS HERE TO GRAB YOUR HEAD.
FINE... BUT YOU BETTER BE CAREFUL...
...OR ELSE YOU'LL FAIL.
WHAT DO YOU MEAN?

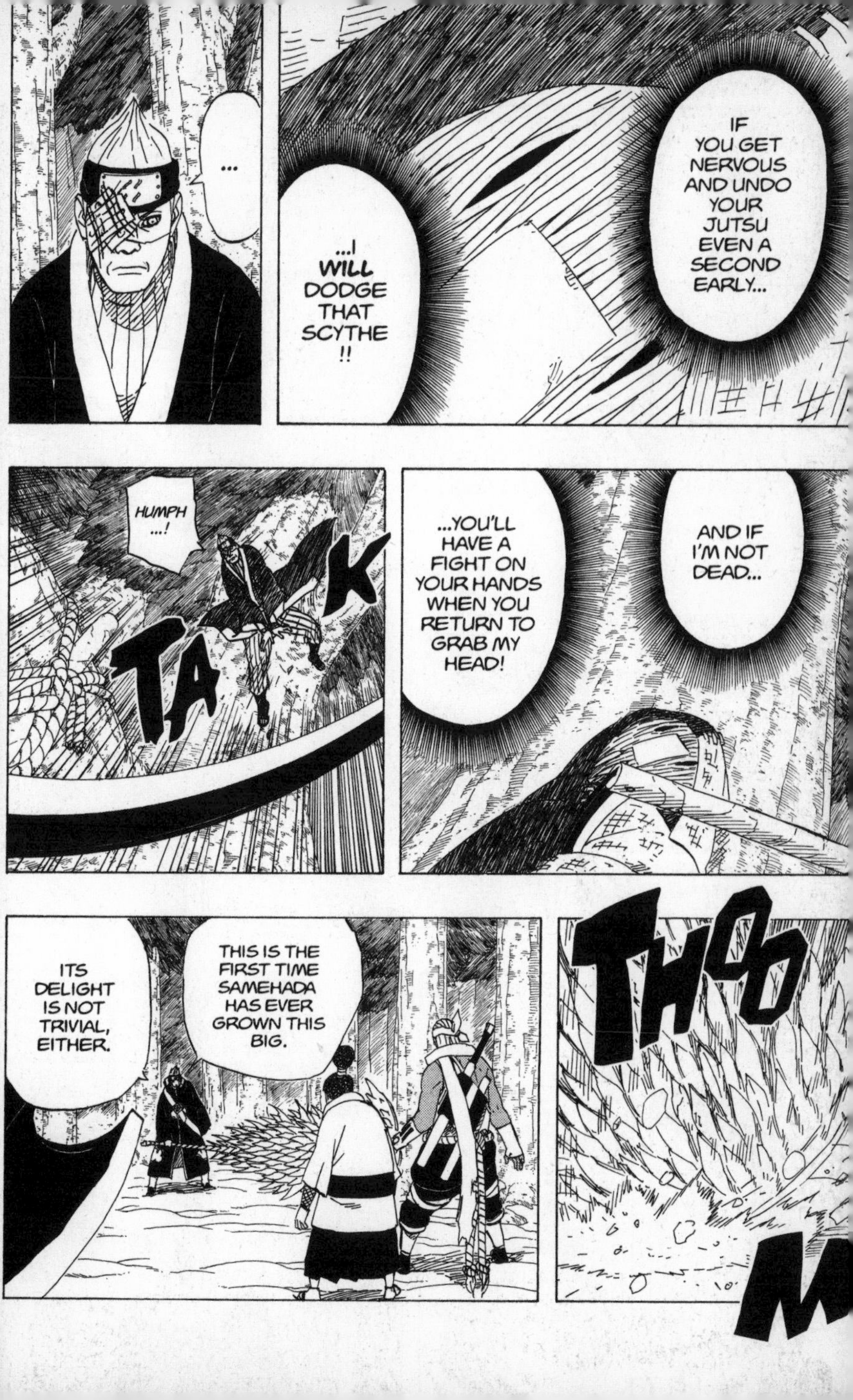
IF YOU GET NERVOUS AND UNDO YOUR JUTSU EVEN A SECOND EARLY...
...I WILL DODGE THAT SCYTHE!!
...
AND IF I'M NOT DEAD...
...YOU'LL HAVE A FIGHT ON YOUR HANDS WHEN YOU RETURN TO GRAB MY HEAD!
HUMPH...!
TAK
THOO
M
THIS IS THE FIRST TIME SAMEHADA HAS EVER GROWN THIS BIG.
ITS DELIGHT IS NOT TRIVIAL, EITHER.

READ THIS WAY

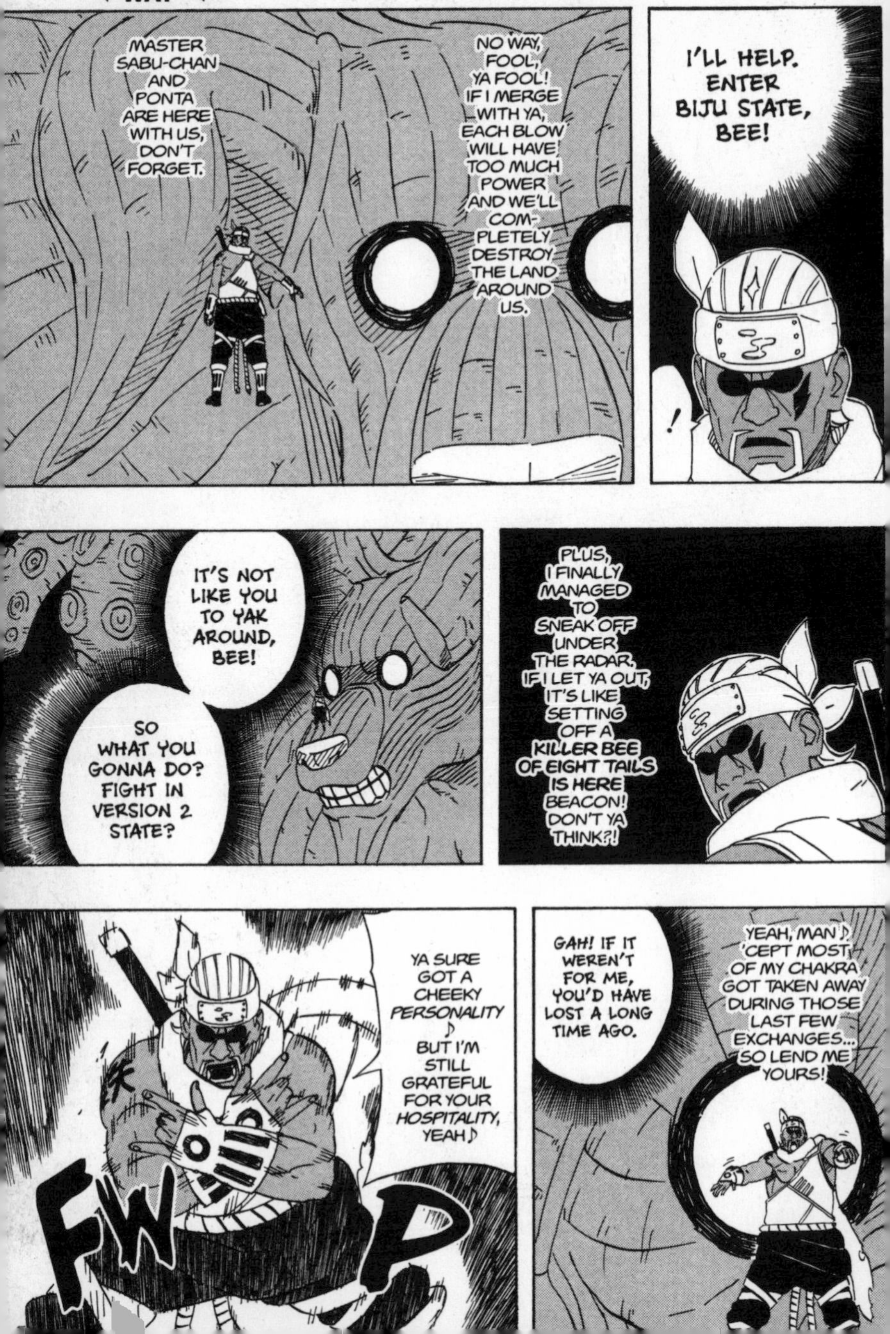
I'LL HELP. ENTER BIJU STATE, BEE!
!
NO WAY, FOOL, YA FOOL! IF I MERGE WITH YA, EACH BLOW WILL HAVE TOO MUCH POWER AND WE'LL COM- PLETELY DESTROY THE LAND AROUND US.
MASTER SABU-CHAN AND PONTA ARE HERE WITH US, DON'T FORGET.
PLUS, I FINALLY MANAGED TO SNEAK OFF UNDER THE RADAR. IF I LET YA OUT, IT'S LIKE SETTING OFF A **KILLER BEE OF EIGHT TAILS IS HERE** BEACON! DON'T YA THINK?!
IT'S NOT LIKE YOU TO YAK AROUND, BEE!
SO WHAT YOU GONNA DO? FIGHT IN VERSION 2 STATE?
YEAH, MAN♪ 'CEPT MOST OF MY CHAKRA GOT TAKEN AWAY DURING THOSE LAST FEW EXCHANGES... SO LEND ME YOURS!
GAH! IF IT WEREN'T FOR ME, YOU'D HAVE LOST A LONG TIME AGO.
YA SURE GOT A CHEEKY *PERSONALITY* ♪ BUT I'M STILL GRATEFUL FOR YOUR *HOSPITALITY*, YEAH♪
FW
D

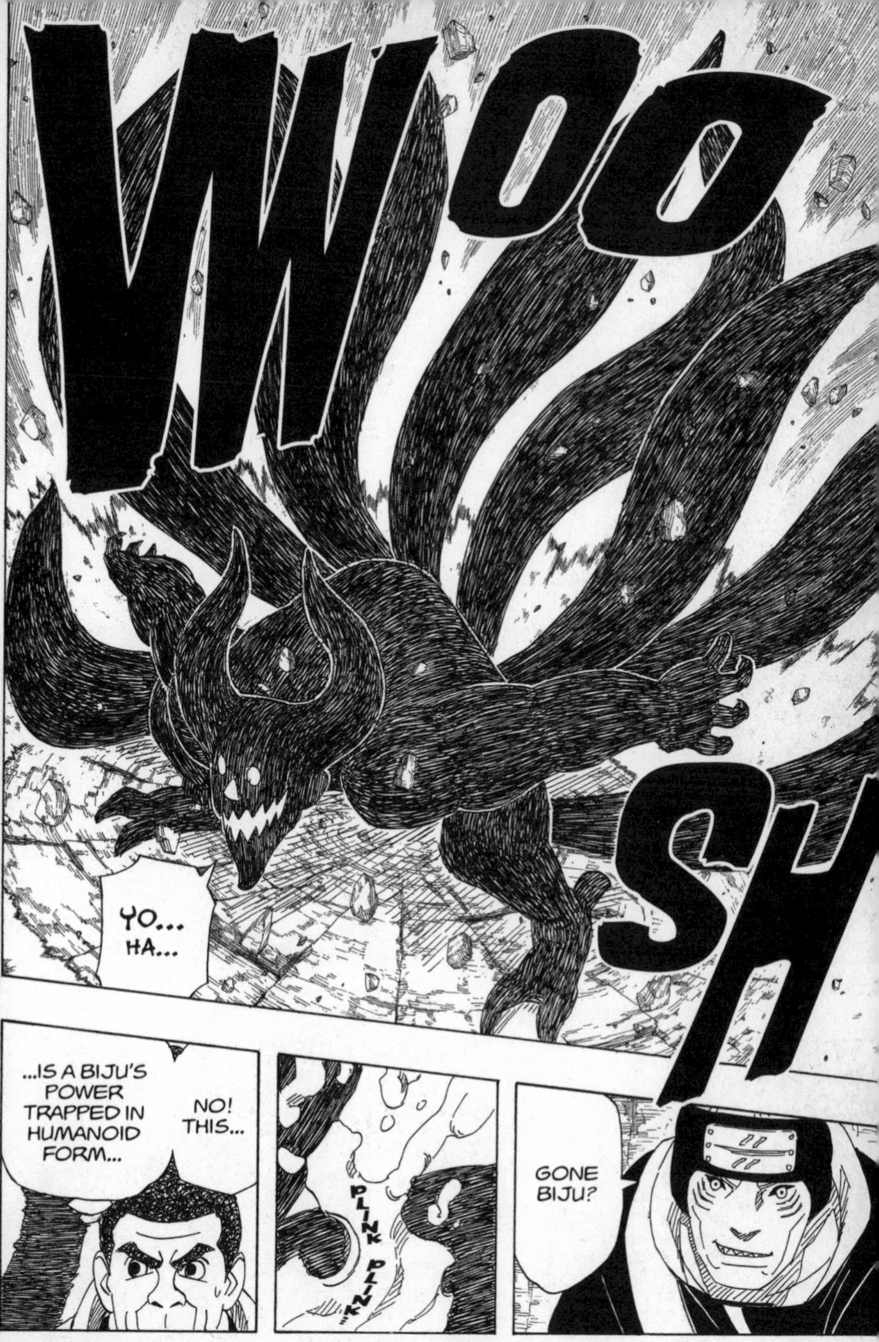
VWOOSH
YO... HA...
GONE BIJU?
PLINK PLINK
NO! THIS...
...IS A BIJU'S POWER TRAPPED IN HUMANOID FORM...

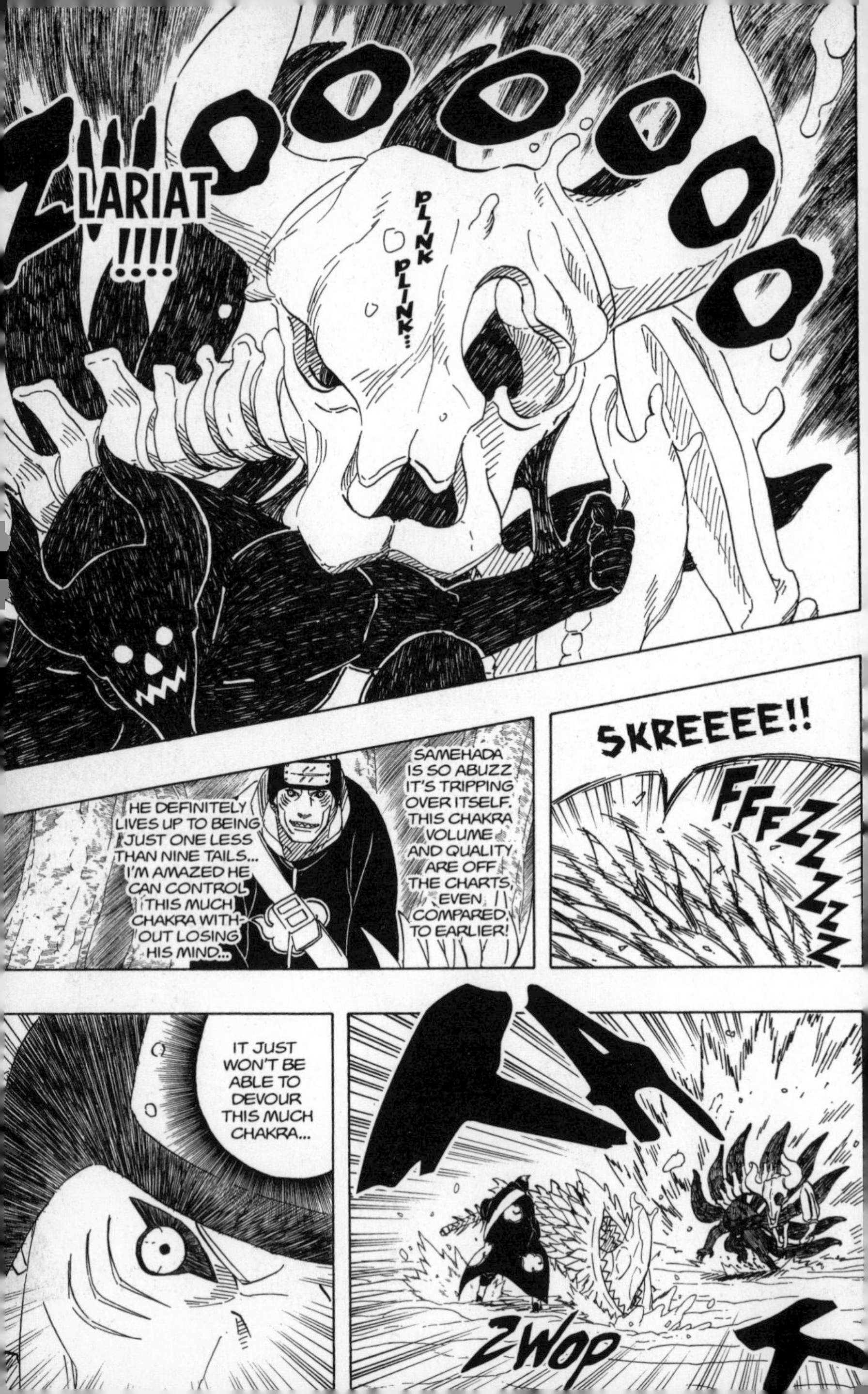
ZUDOOOOOOO
LARIAT!!!!
PLINK PLINK...
SKREEEE!!
FFFZZZZZZ
SAMEHADA IS SO ABUZZ IT'S TRIPPING OVER ITSELF. THIS CHAKRA VOLUME AND QUALITY ARE OFF THE CHARTS, EVEN COMPARED TO EARLIER!
HE DEFINITELY LIVES UP TO BEING JUST ONE LESS THAN NINE TAILS... I'M AMAZED HE CAN CONTROL THIS MUCH CHAKRA WITH-OUT LOSING HIS MIND...
ZWOP
IT JUST WON'T BE ABLE TO DEVOUR THIS MUCH CHAKRA...

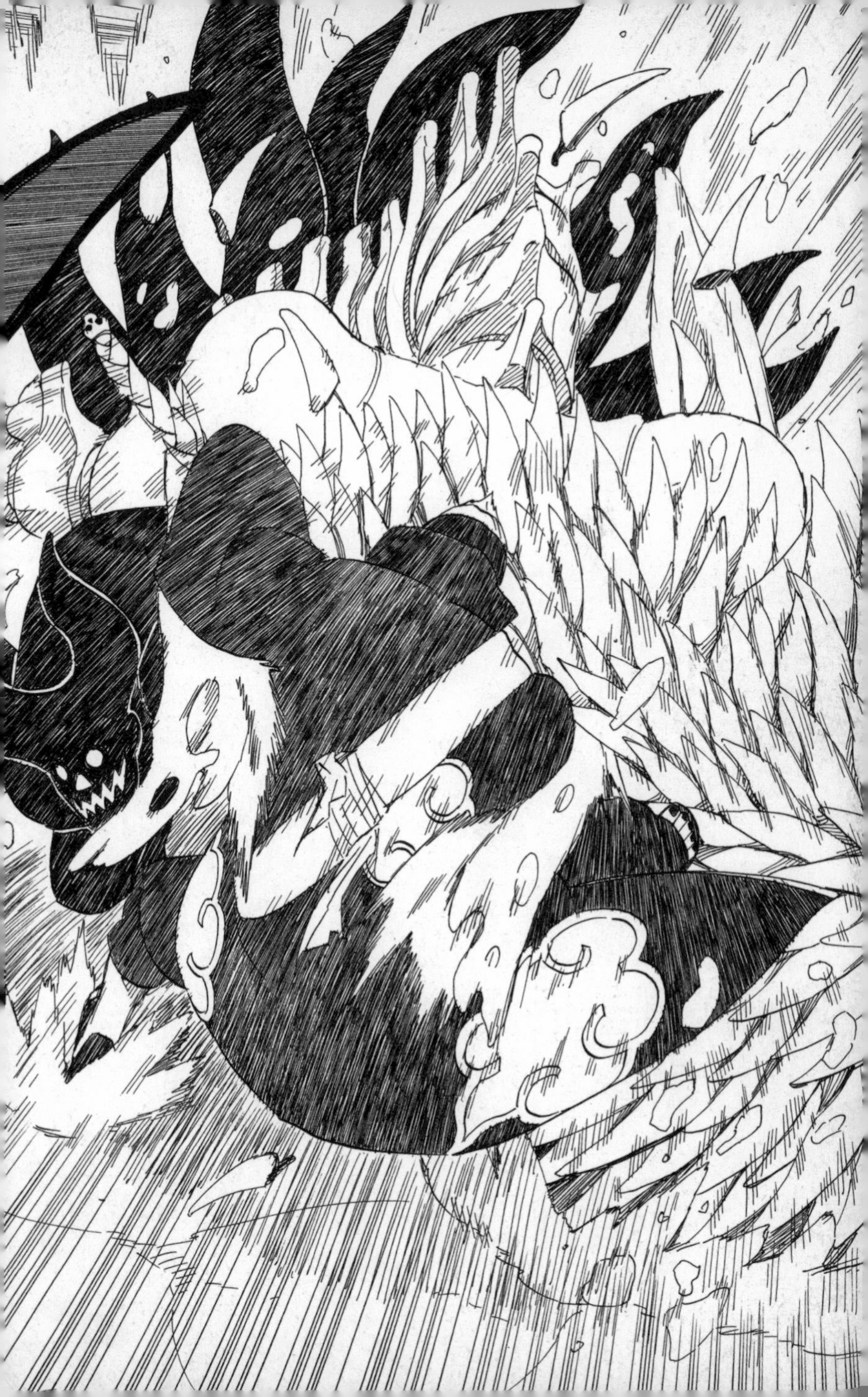

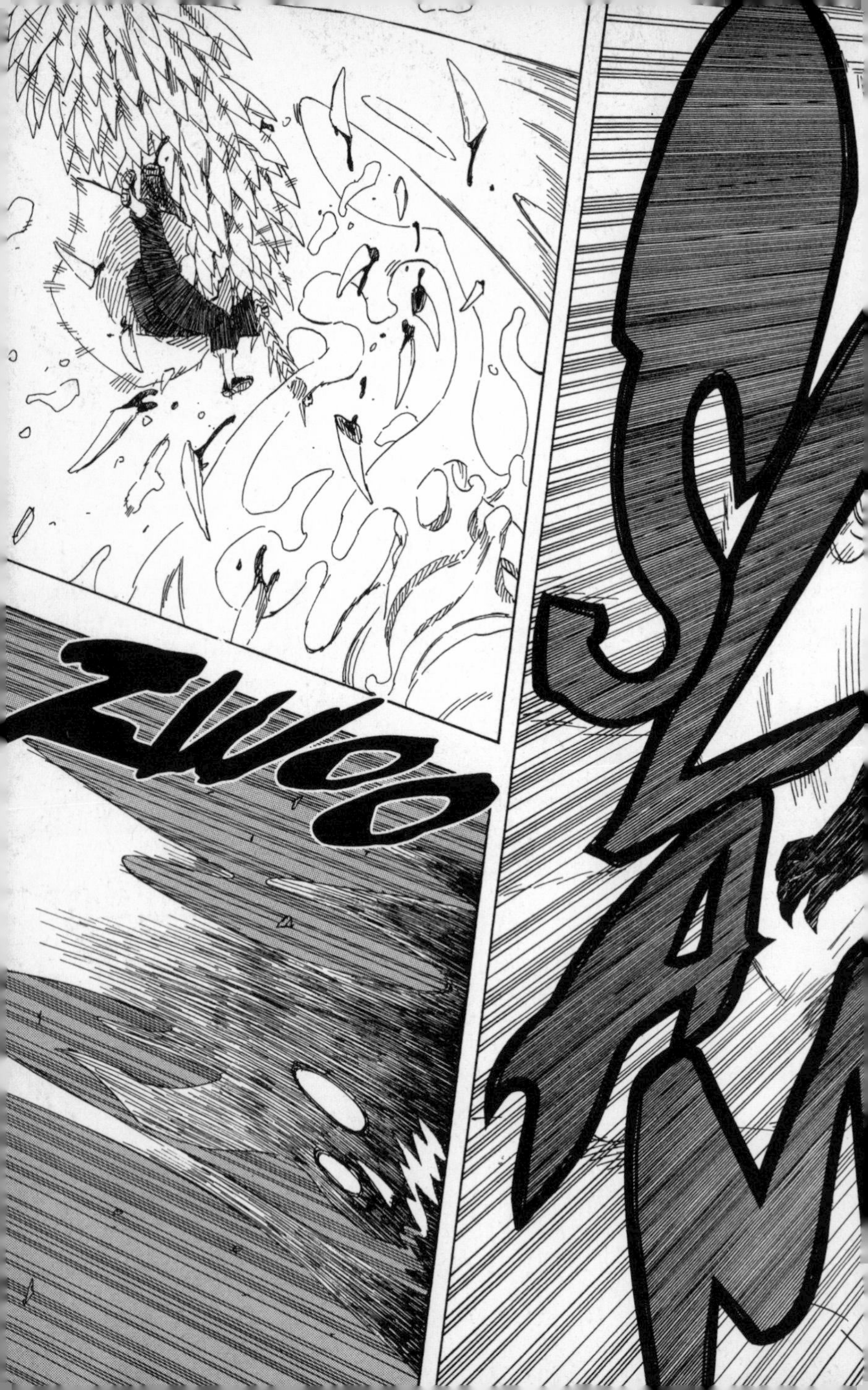
ZWOO

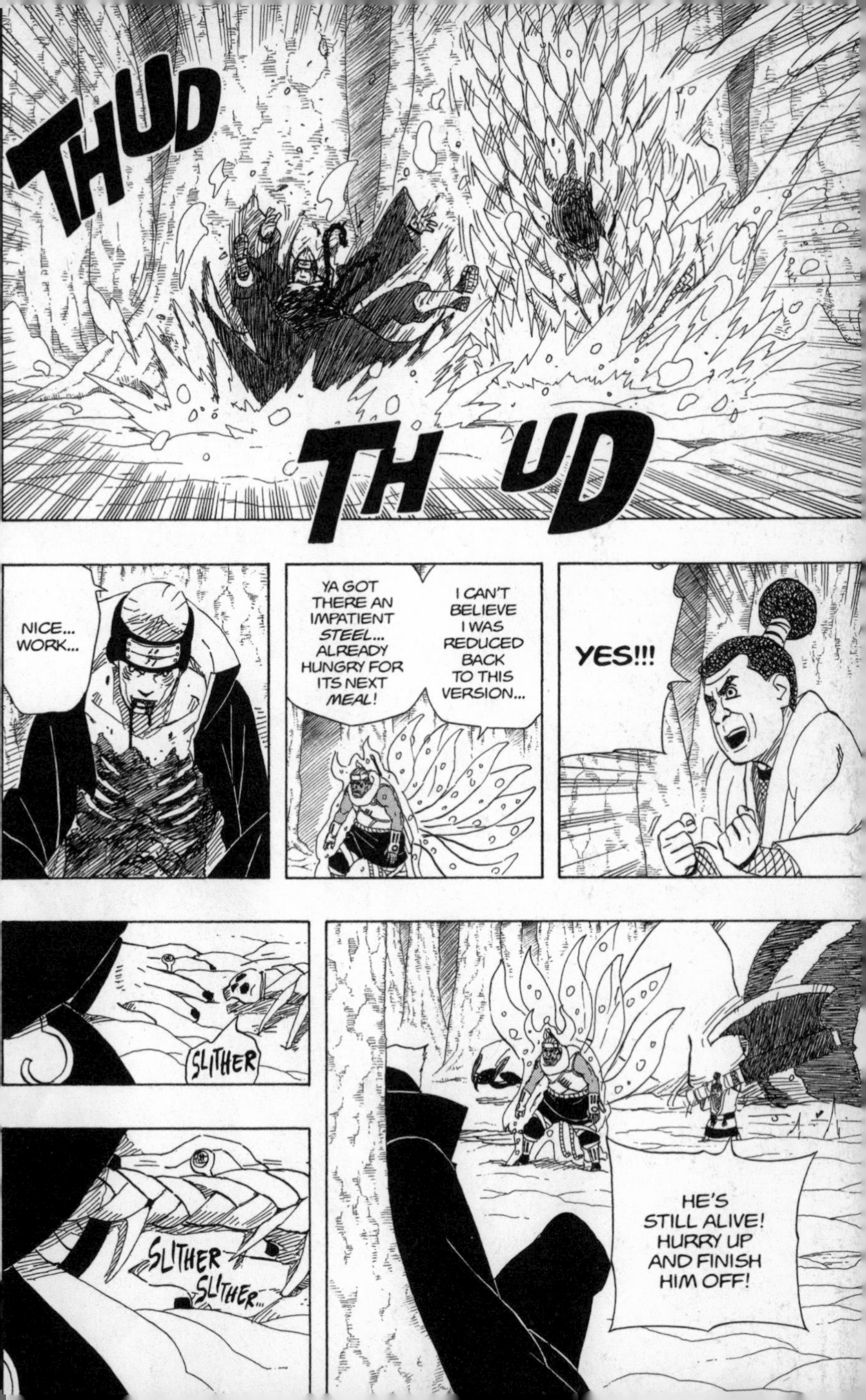
THUD
THUD
YES!!!
I CAN'T BELIEVE I WAS REDUCED BACK TO THIS VERSION...
YA GOT THERE AN IMPATIENT *STEEL*... ALREADY HUNGRY FOR ITS NEXT *MEAL*!
NICE... WORK...
HE'S STILL ALIVE! HURRY UP AND FINISH HIM OFF!
SLITHER
SLITHER
SLITHER...

READ THIS WAY

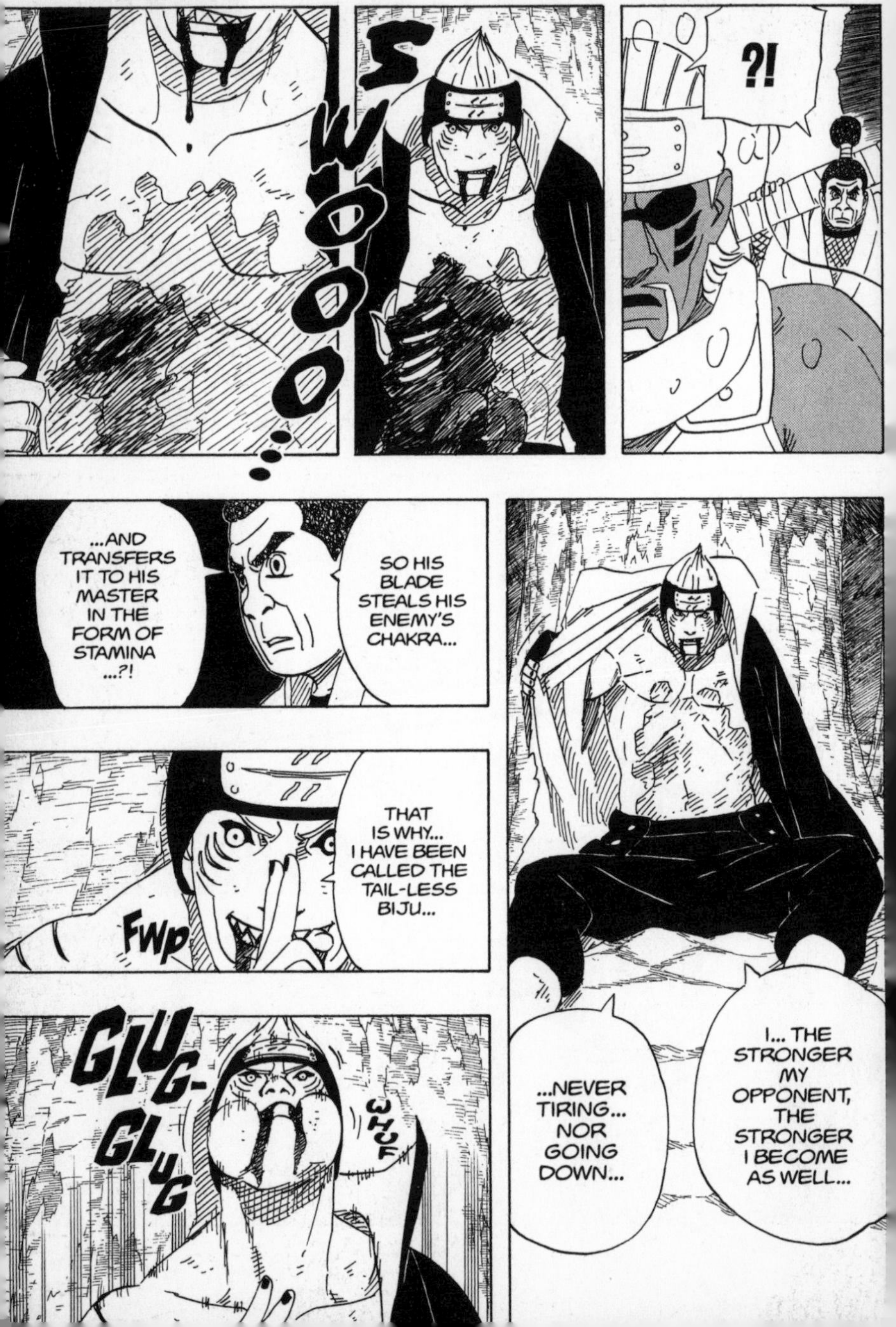
?!
SWOOOOOO...
I... THE STRONGER MY OPPONENT, THE STRONGER I BECOME AS WELL...
...NEVER TIRING... NOR GOING DOWN...
SO HIS BLADE STEALS HIS ENEMY'S CHAKRA...
...AND TRANSFERS IT TO HIS MASTER IN THE FORM OF STAMINA ...?!
THAT IS WHY... I HAVE BEEN CALLED THE TAIL-LESS BIJU...
FWP
GLUG-GLUG
WHUF

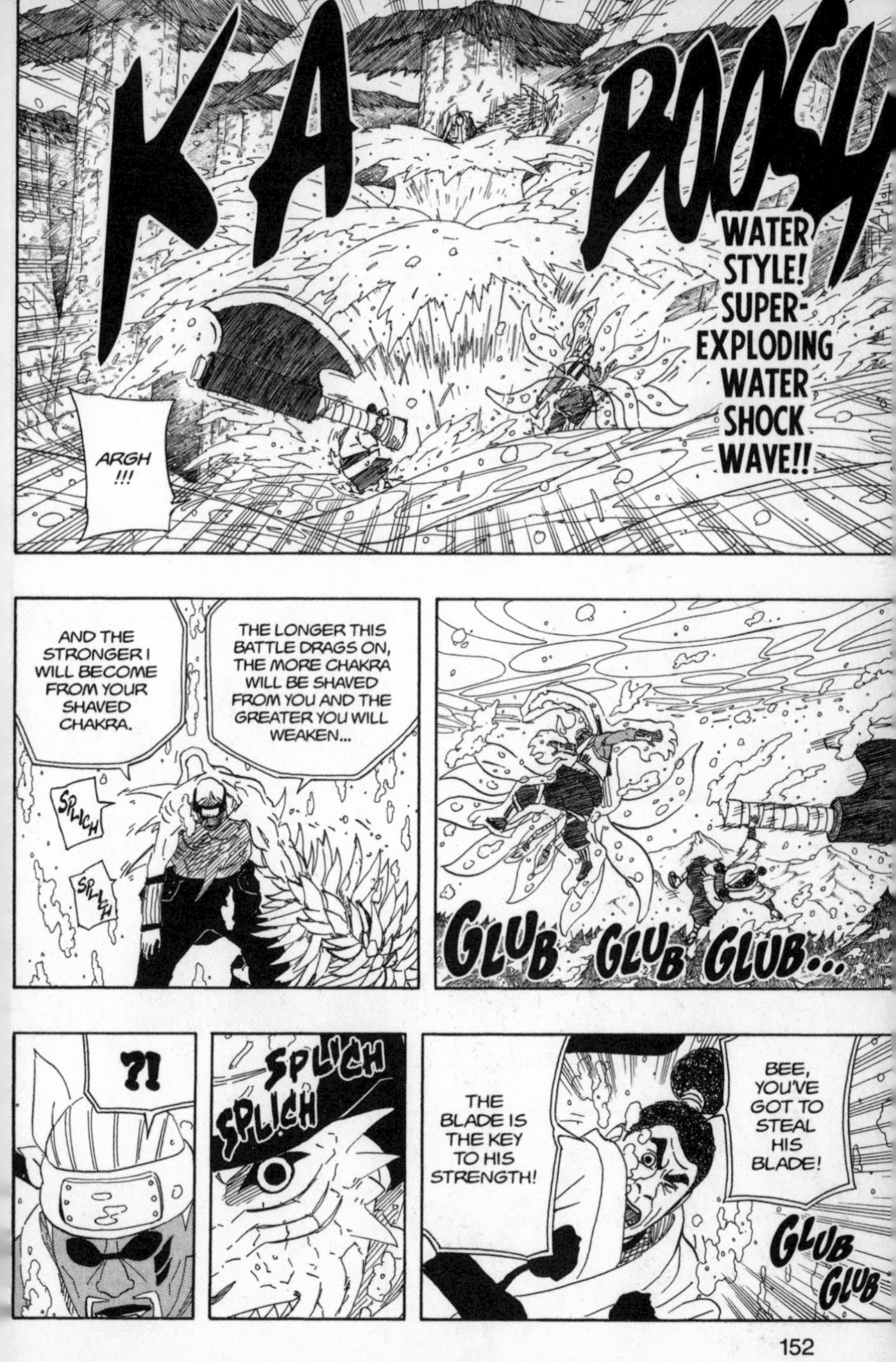
KA BOOM
WATER STYLE! SUPER-EXPLODING WATER SHOCK WAVE!!
ARGH !!!
GLUB GLUB GLUB...
THE LONGER THIS BATTLE DRAGS ON, THE MORE CHAKRA WILL BE SHAVED FROM YOU AND THE GREATER YOU WILL WEAKEN...
AND THE STRONGER I WILL BECOME FROM YOUR SHAVED CHAKRA.
SPLICH
SPLICH
BEE, YOU'VE GOT TO STEAL HIS BLADE!
THE BLADE IS THE KEY TO HIS STRENGTH!
GLUB GLUB
SPLICH
SPLICH
?!

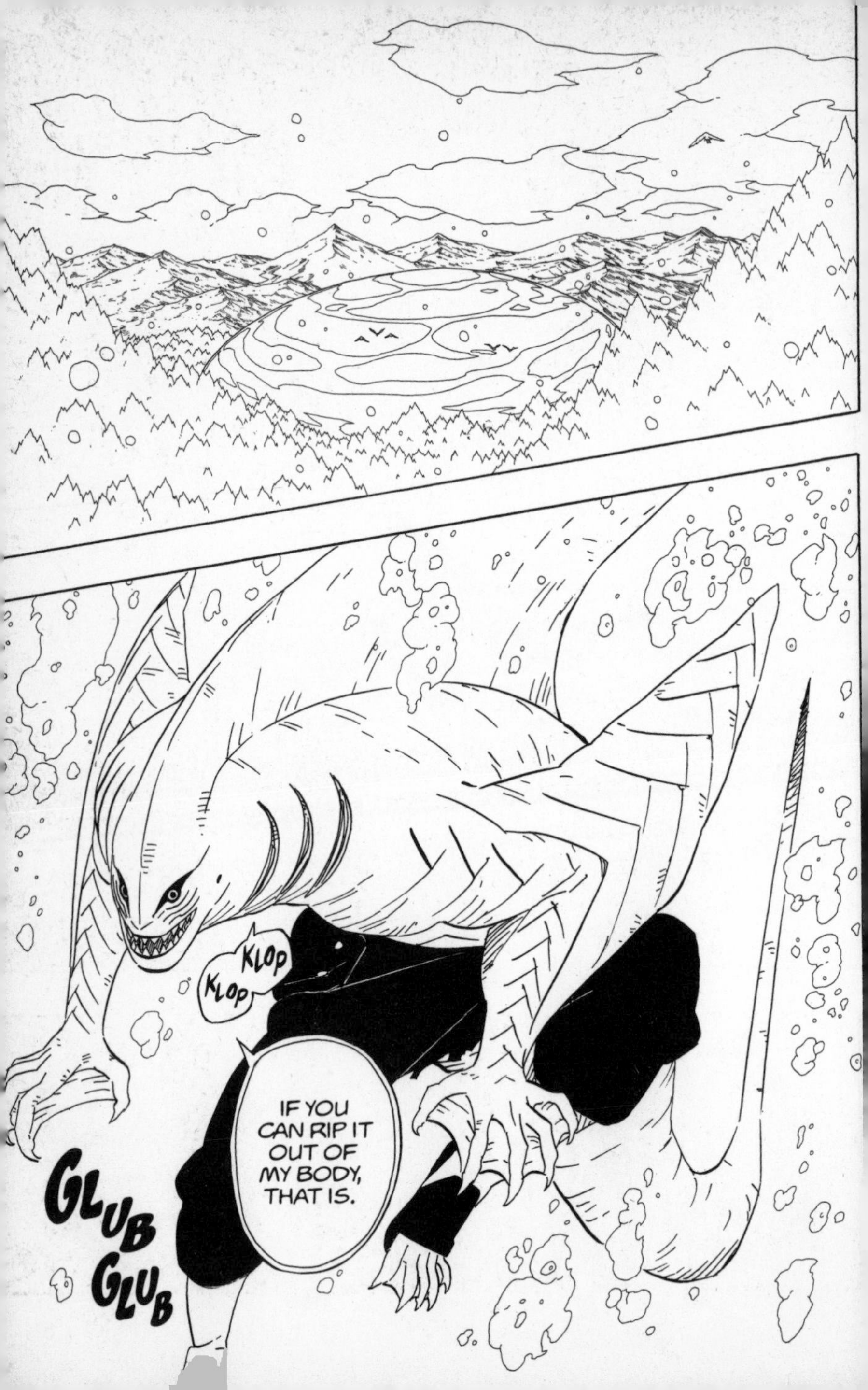
KLOP
KLOP
IF YOU CAN RIP IT OUT OF MY BODY, THAT IS.
GLUB GLUB

NARUTO

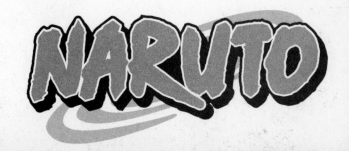

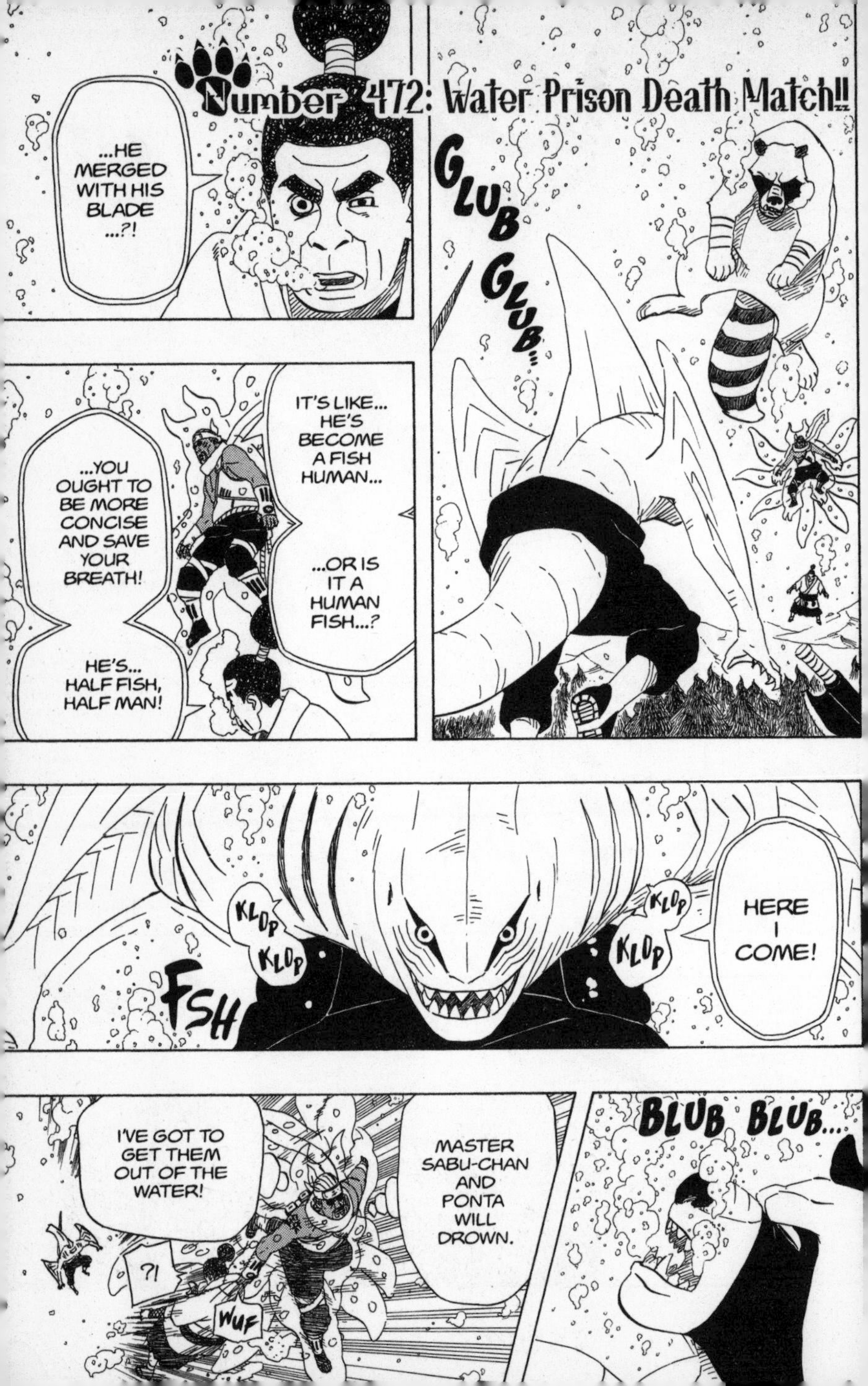
Number 472: Water Prison Death Match!!
GLUB GLUB...
...HE MERGED WITH HIS BLADE ...?!
IT'S LIKE... HE'S BECOME A FISH HUMAN...
...OR IS IT A HUMAN FISH...?
...YOU OUGHT TO BE MORE CONCISE AND SAVE YOUR BREATH!
HE'S... HALF FISH, HALF MAN!
HERE I COME!
KLOP
KLOP
KLOP
KLOP
FSH
BLUB BLUB...
MASTER SABU-CHAN AND PONTA WILL DROWN.
I'VE GOT TO GET THEM OUT OF THE WATER!
?!
WUF

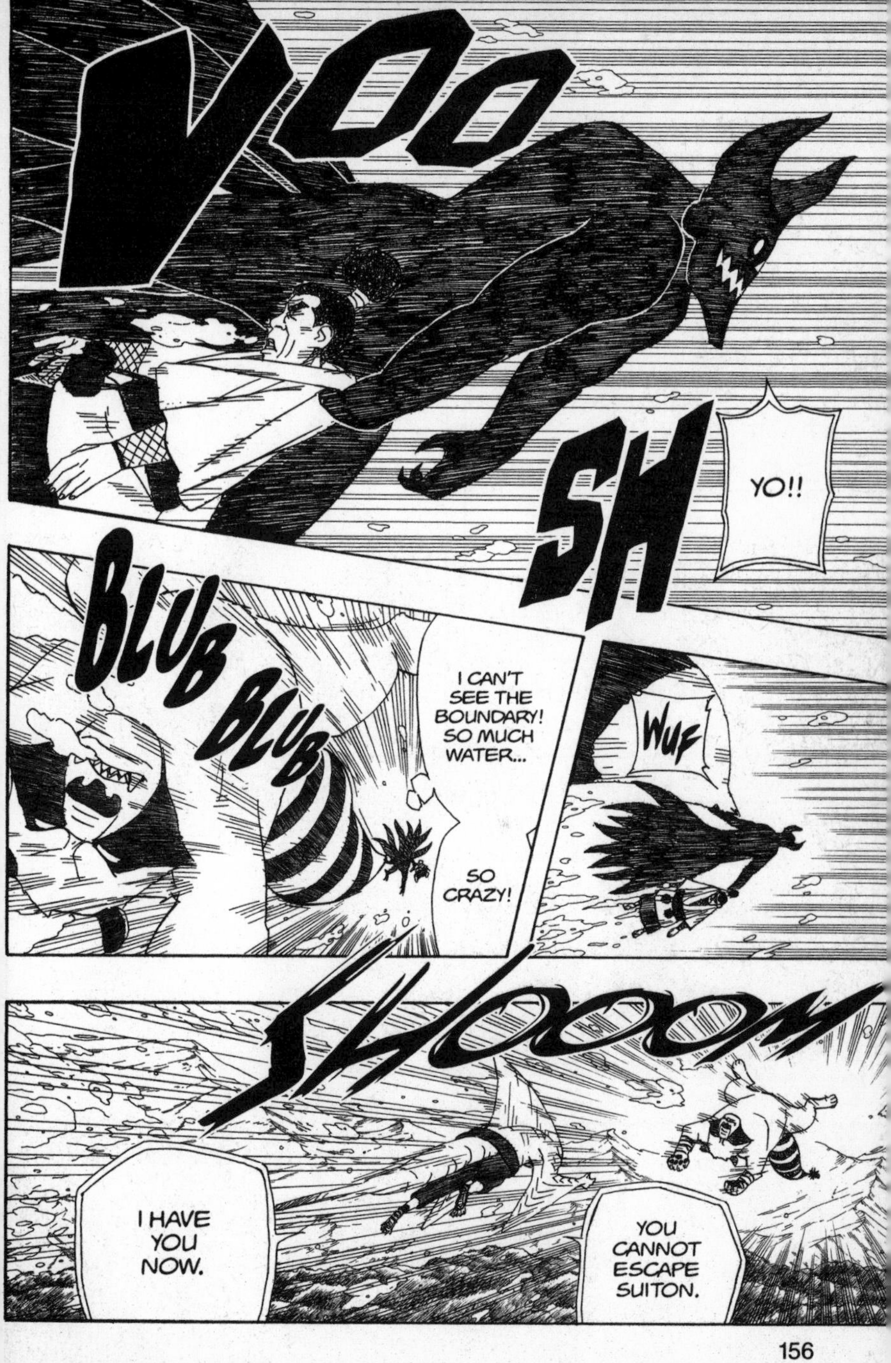
VOOO
SH
YO!!
WUF
BLUB BLUB
I CAN'T SEE THE BOUNDARY! SO MUCH WATER...
SO CRAZY!
SHOOOM
YOU CANNOT ESCAPE SUITON.
I HAVE YOU NOW.

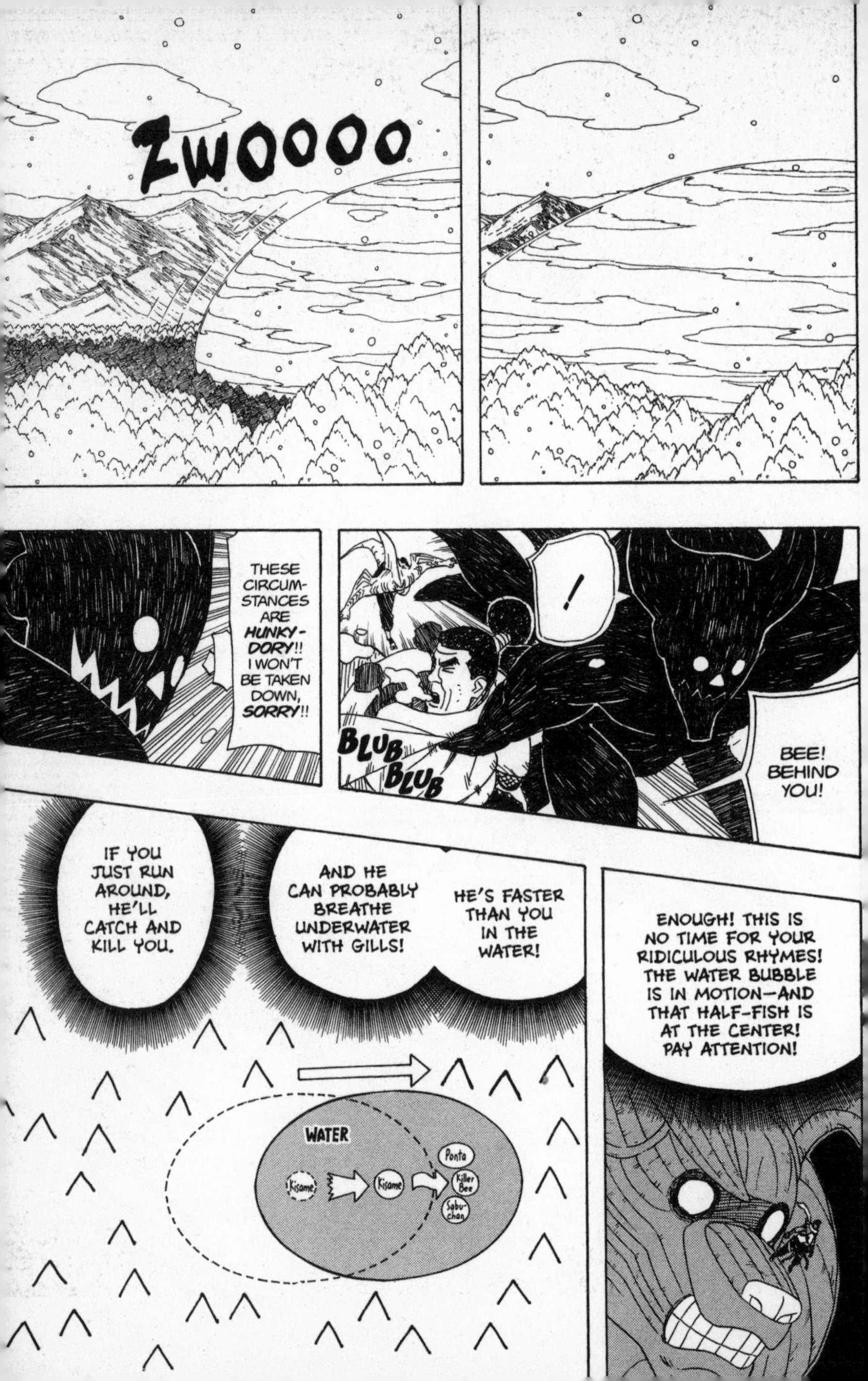
ZWOOOO
!
BEE! BEHIND YOU!
BLUB BLUB
THESE CIRCUM-STANCES ARE HUNKY-DORY!! I WON'T BE TAKEN DOWN, SORRY!!
ENOUGH! THIS IS NO TIME FOR YOUR RIDICULOUS RHYMES! THE WATER BUBBLE IS IN MOTION—AND THAT HALF-FISH IS AT THE CENTER! PAY ATTENTION!
HE'S FASTER THAN YOU IN THE WATER!
AND HE CAN PROBABLY BREATHE UNDERWATER WITH GILLS!
IF YOU JUST RUN AROUND, HE'LL CATCH AND KILL YOU.
WATER
Kisame
Kisame
Ponta
Killer Bee
Sabu-chan

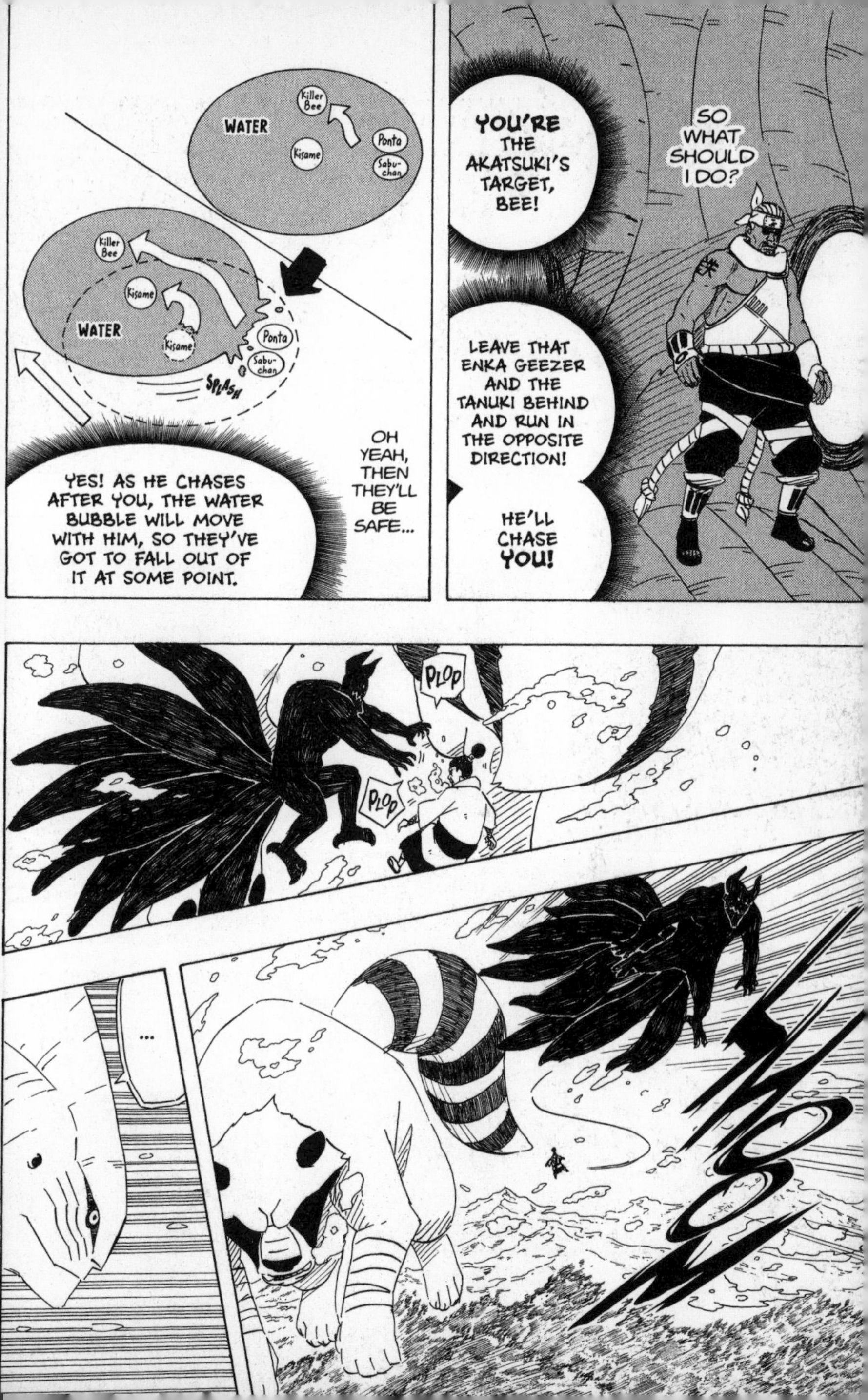
SO WHAT SHOULD I DO?
YOU'RE THE AKATSUKI'S TARGET, BEE!
LEAVE THAT ENKA GEEZER AND THE TANUKI BEHIND AND RUN IN THE OPPOSITE DIRECTION!
HE'LL CHASE YOU!
WATER
Killer Bee
Kisame
Ponta
Sabu-chan
WATER
Killer Bee
Kisame
Kisame
Ponta
Sabu-chan
SPLASH
OH YEAH, THEN THEY'LL BE SAFE...
YES! AS HE CHASES AFTER YOU, THE WATER BUBBLE WILL MOVE WITH HIM, SO THEY'VE GOT TO FALL OUT OF IT AT SOME POINT.
PLOP
PLOP
WHOOM
...

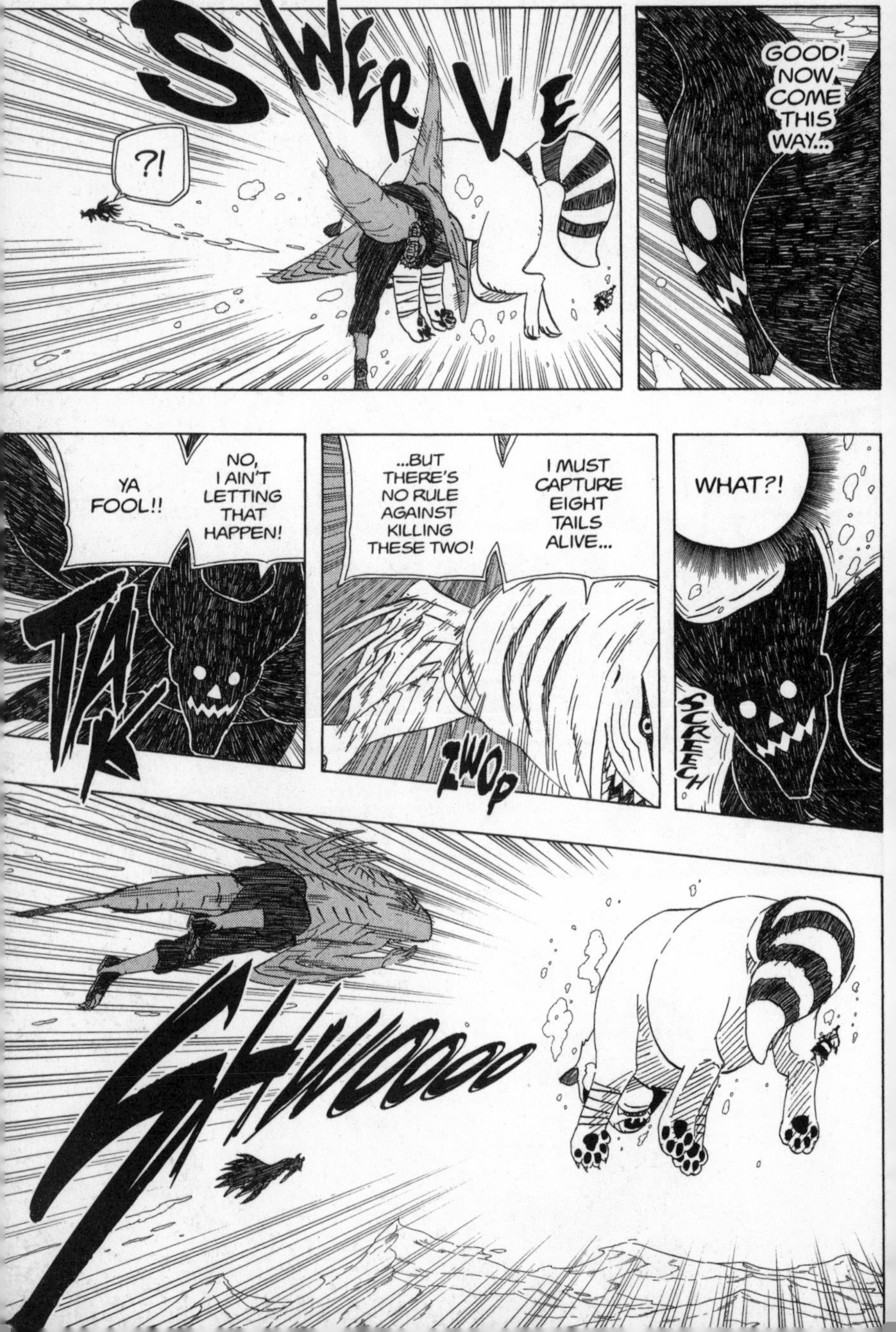
GOOD! NOW COME THIS WAY...
SWERVE
?!
WHAT?!
SCREECH
I MUST CAPTURE EIGHT TAILS ALIVE...
...BUT THERE'S NO RULE AGAINST KILLING THESE TWO!
ZWOP
NO, I AIN'T LETTING THAT HAPPEN!
YA FOOL!!
TAK
SHWOOOO

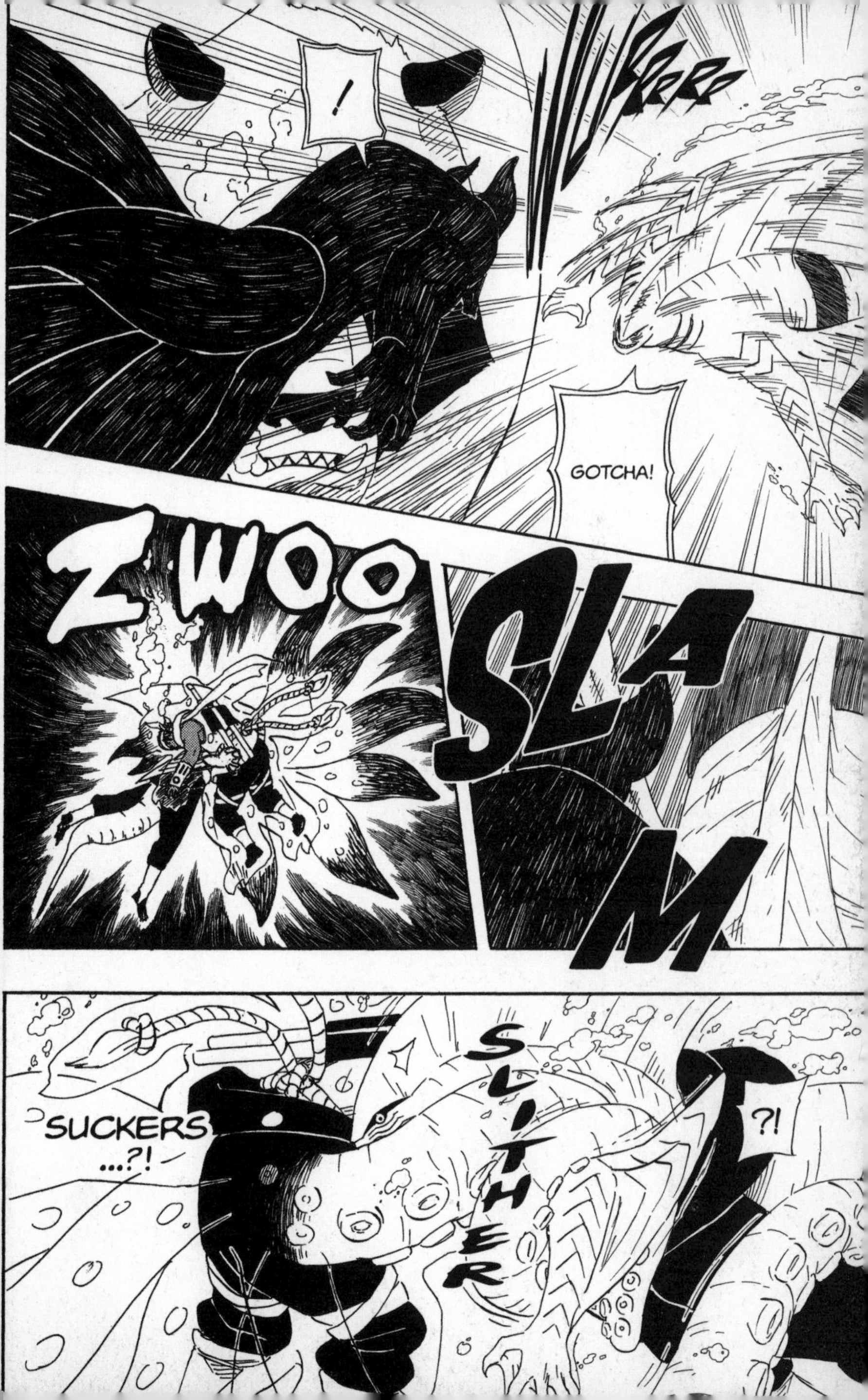
!
GOTCHA!
SLAM
ZWOO
?!
SLITHER
SUCKERS ...?!

READ THIS WAY

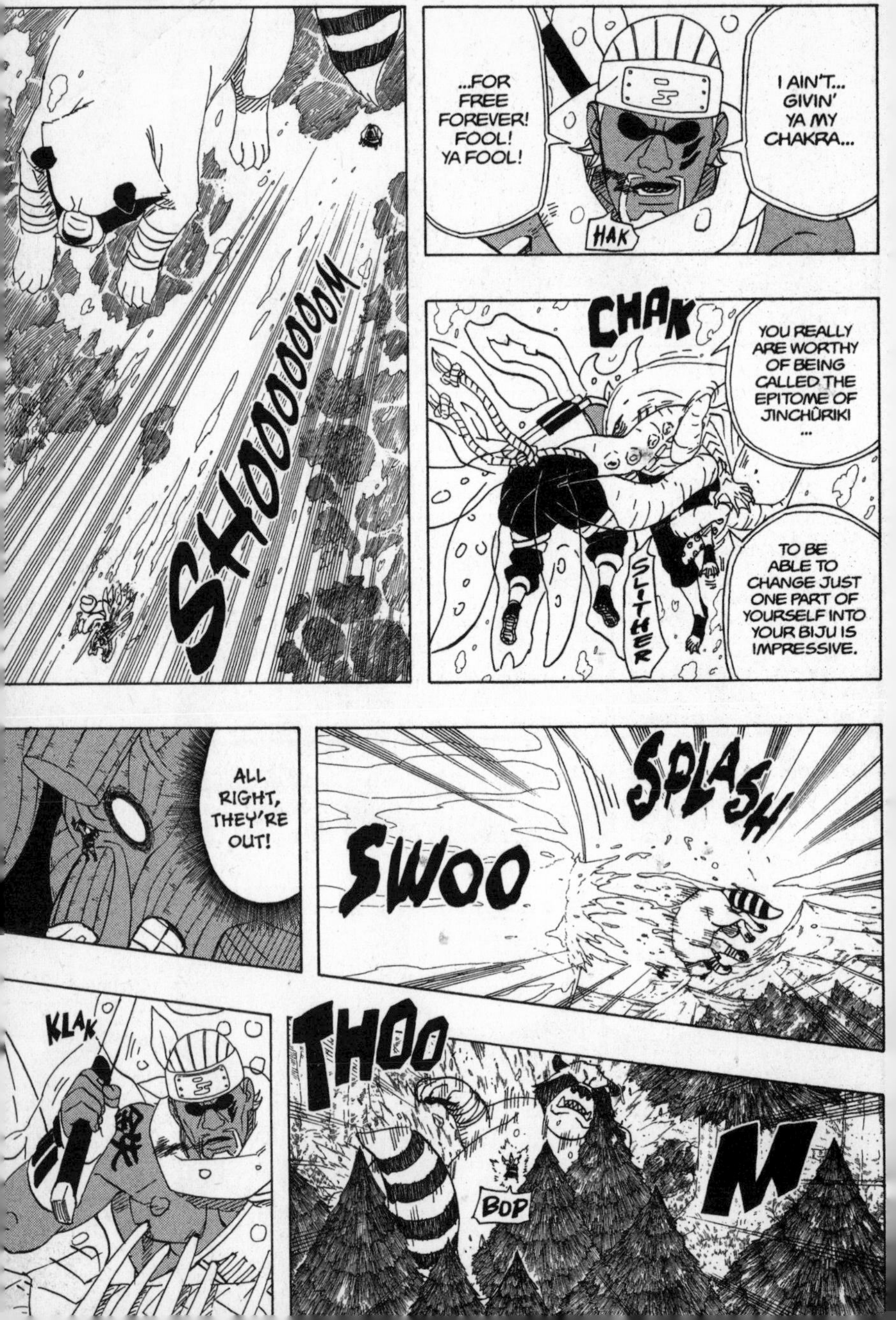
I AIN'T... GIVIN' YA MY CHAKRA...
...FOR FREE FOREVER! FOOL! YA FOOL!
HAK
CHAK
YOU REALLY ARE WORTHY OF BEING CALLED THE EPITOME OF JINCHÛRIKI ...
TO BE ABLE TO CHANGE JUST ONE PART OF YOURSELF INTO YOUR BIJU IS IMPRESSIVE.
SLITHER
SHOOOOOOOM
SPLASH
SWOO
ALL RIGHT, THEY'RE OUT!
THOO
M
BOP
KLAK

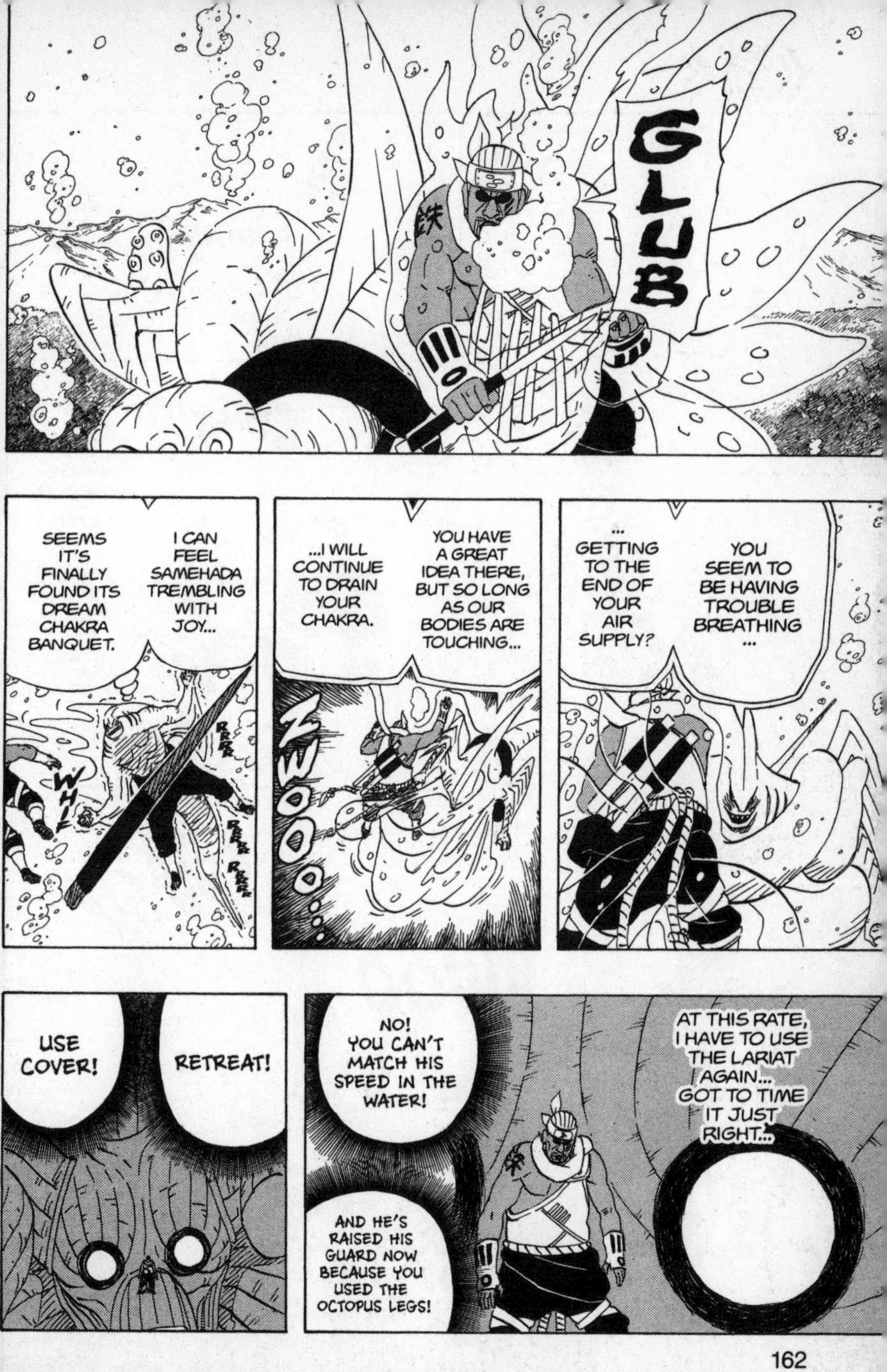
GLUB
YOU SEEM TO BE HAVING TROUBLE BREATHING...
...GETTING TO THE END OF YOUR AIR SUPPLY?
YOU HAVE A GREAT IDEA THERE, BUT SO LONG AS OUR BODIES ARE TOUCHING...
...I WILL CONTINUE TO DRAIN YOUR CHAKRA.
ZWOOO...
I CAN FEEL SAMEHADA TREMBLING WITH JOY...
SEEMS IT'S FINALLY FOUND ITS DREAM CHAKRA BANQUET.
AT THIS RATE, I HAVE TO USE THE LARIAT AGAIN... GOT TO TIME IT JUST RIGHT...
NO! YOU CAN'T MATCH HIS SPEED IN THE WATER!
AND HE'S RAISED HIS GUARD NOW BECAUSE YOU USED THE OCTOPUS LEGS!
RETREAT!
USE COVER!

READ THIS WAY

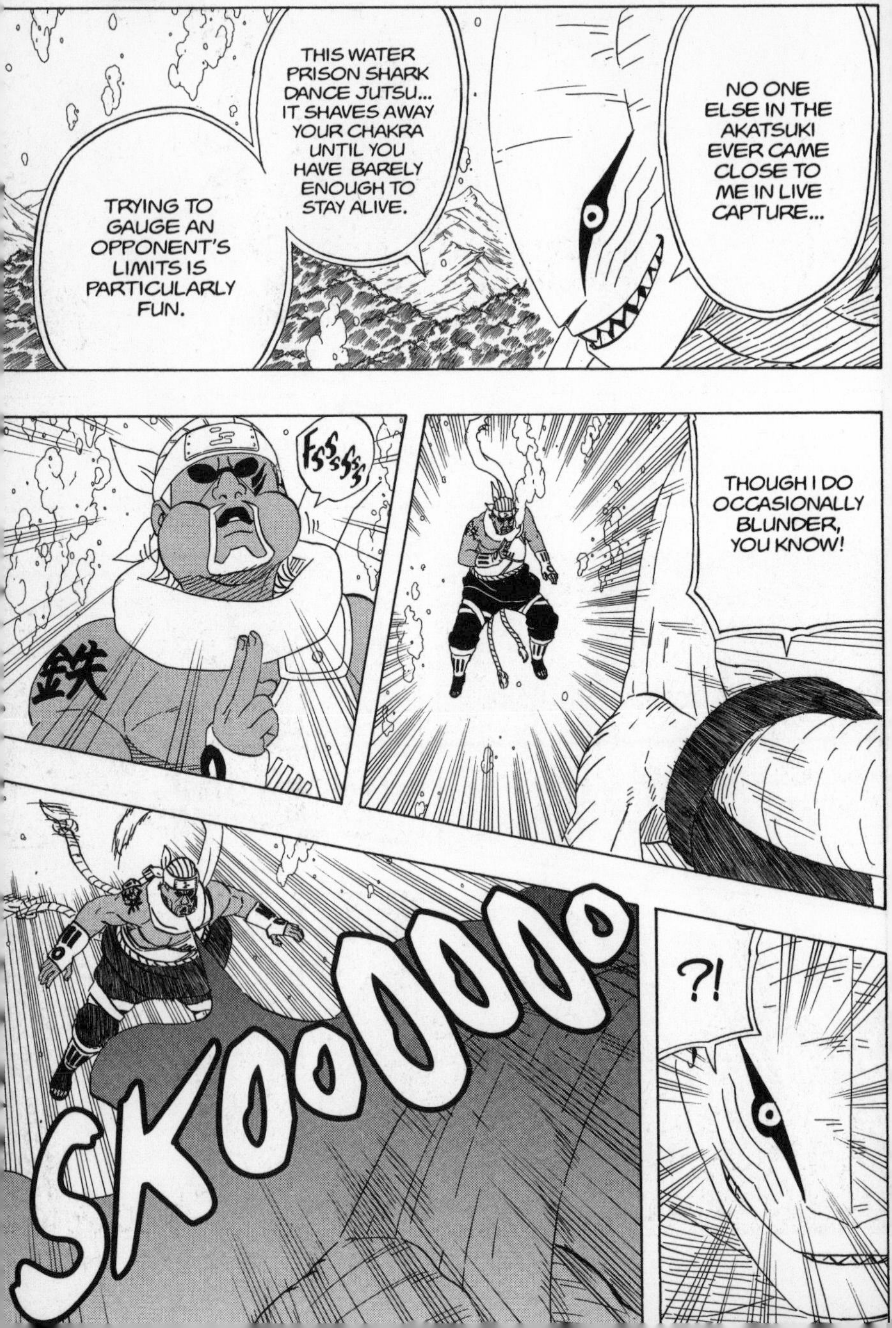

NO ONE ELSE IN THE AKATSUKI EVER CAME CLOSE TO ME IN LIVE CAPTURE...
THIS WATER PRISON SHARK DANCE JUTSU... IT SHAVES AWAY YOUR CHAKRA UNTIL YOU HAVE BARELY ENOUGH TO STAY ALIVE.
TRYING TO GAUGE AN OPPONENT'S LIMITS IS PARTICULARLY FUN.
THOUGH I DO OCCASIONALLY BLUNDER, YOU KNOW!
?!
SKOOOOOO

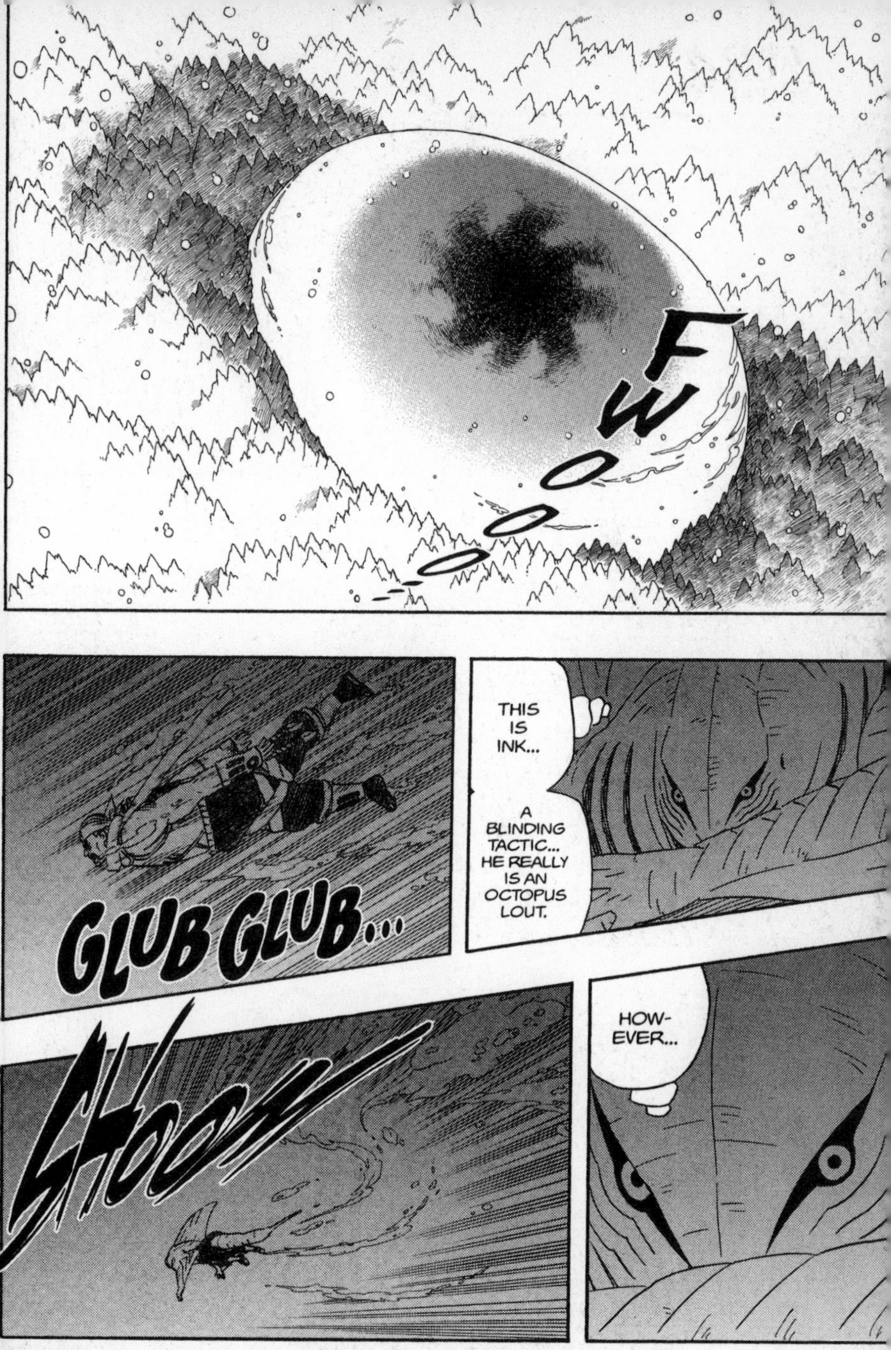
FWOOO
THIS IS INK...
A BLINDING TACTIC... HE REALLY IS AN OCTOPUS LOUT.
GLUB GLUB...
HOW-EVER...

READ THIS WAY

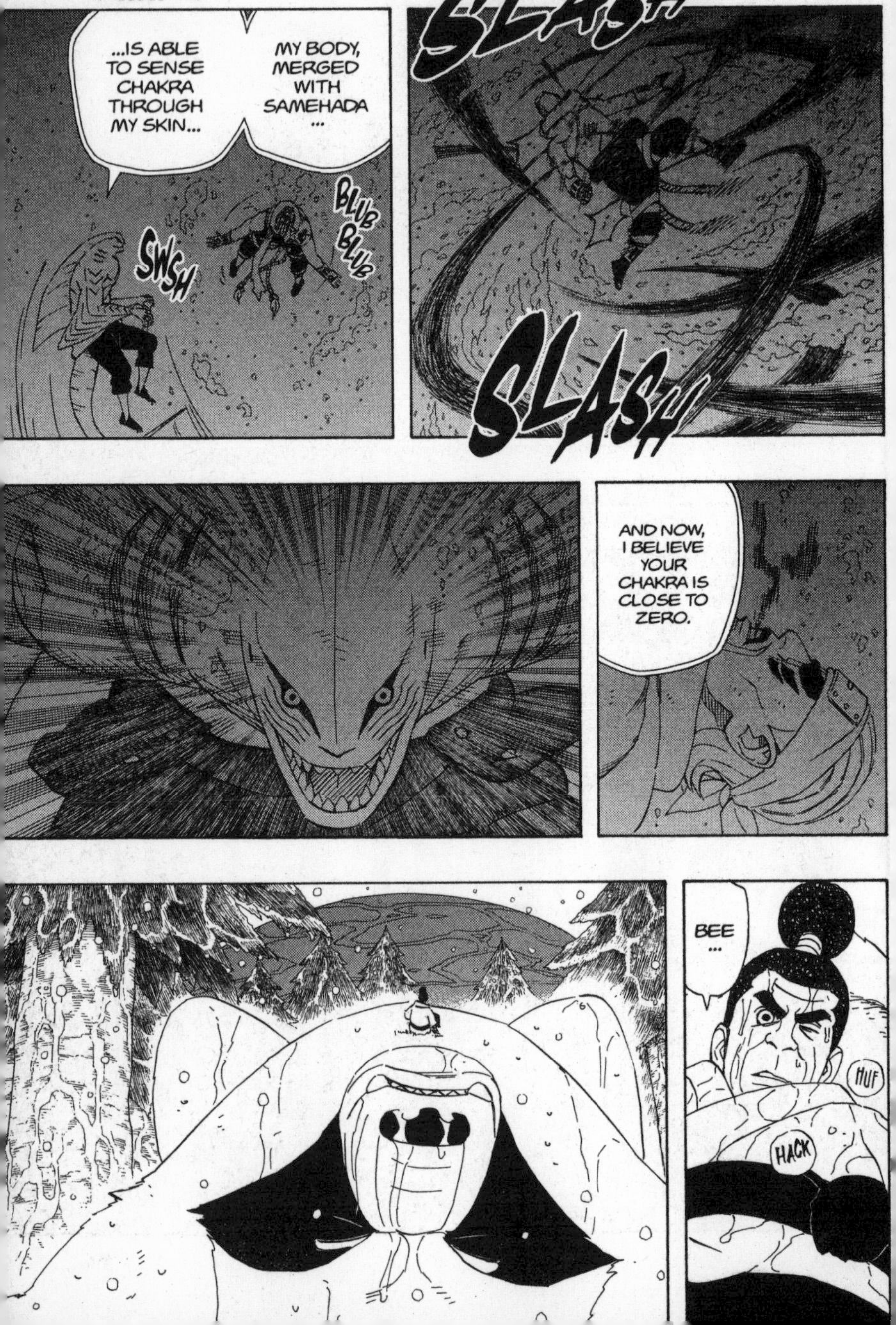
SLASH
SLASH
MY BODY, MERGED WITH SAMEHADA ...
...IS ABLE TO SENSE CHAKRA THROUGH MY SKIN...
BLUB BLUB
SWSH
AND NOW, I BELIEVE YOUR CHAKRA IS CLOSE TO ZERO.
BEE ...
HUF
HACK

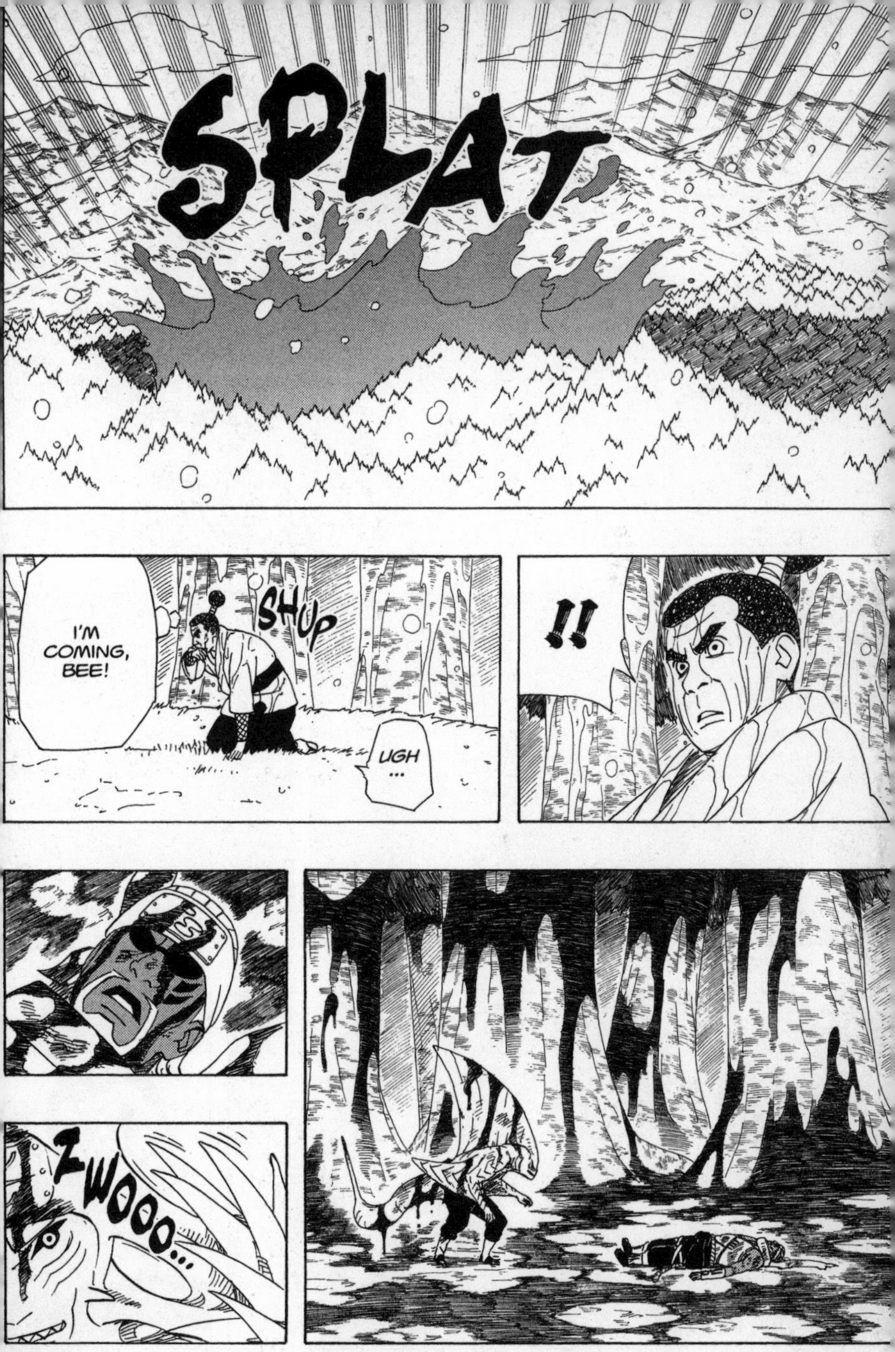
SPLAT
!!
SHUP
I'M COMING, BEE!
UGH ...
ZWOOO...

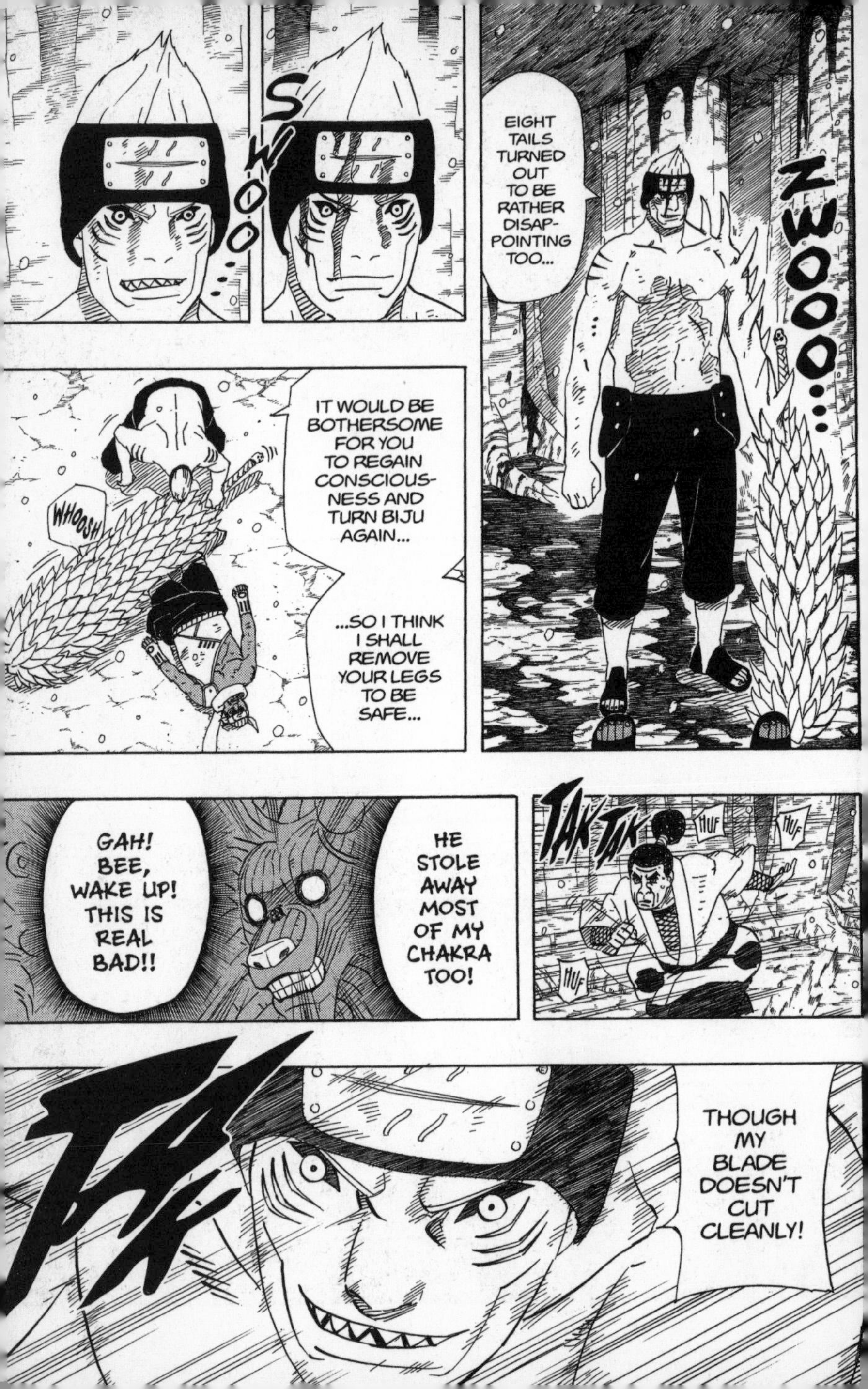
EIGHT TAILS TURNED OUT TO BE RATHER DISAP-POINTING TOO...
ZWOOOO...
SWOOO...
IT WOULD BE BOTHERSOME FOR YOU TO REGAIN CONSCIOUS-NESS AND TURN BIJU AGAIN...
...SO I THINK I SHALL REMOVE YOUR LEGS TO BE SAFE...
WHOOSH
TAK TAK
HUF
HUF
HUF
HE STOLE AWAY MOST OF MY CHAKRA TOO!
GAH! BEE, WAKE UP! THIS IS REAL BAD!!
THOUGH MY BLADE DOESN'T CUT CLEANLY!

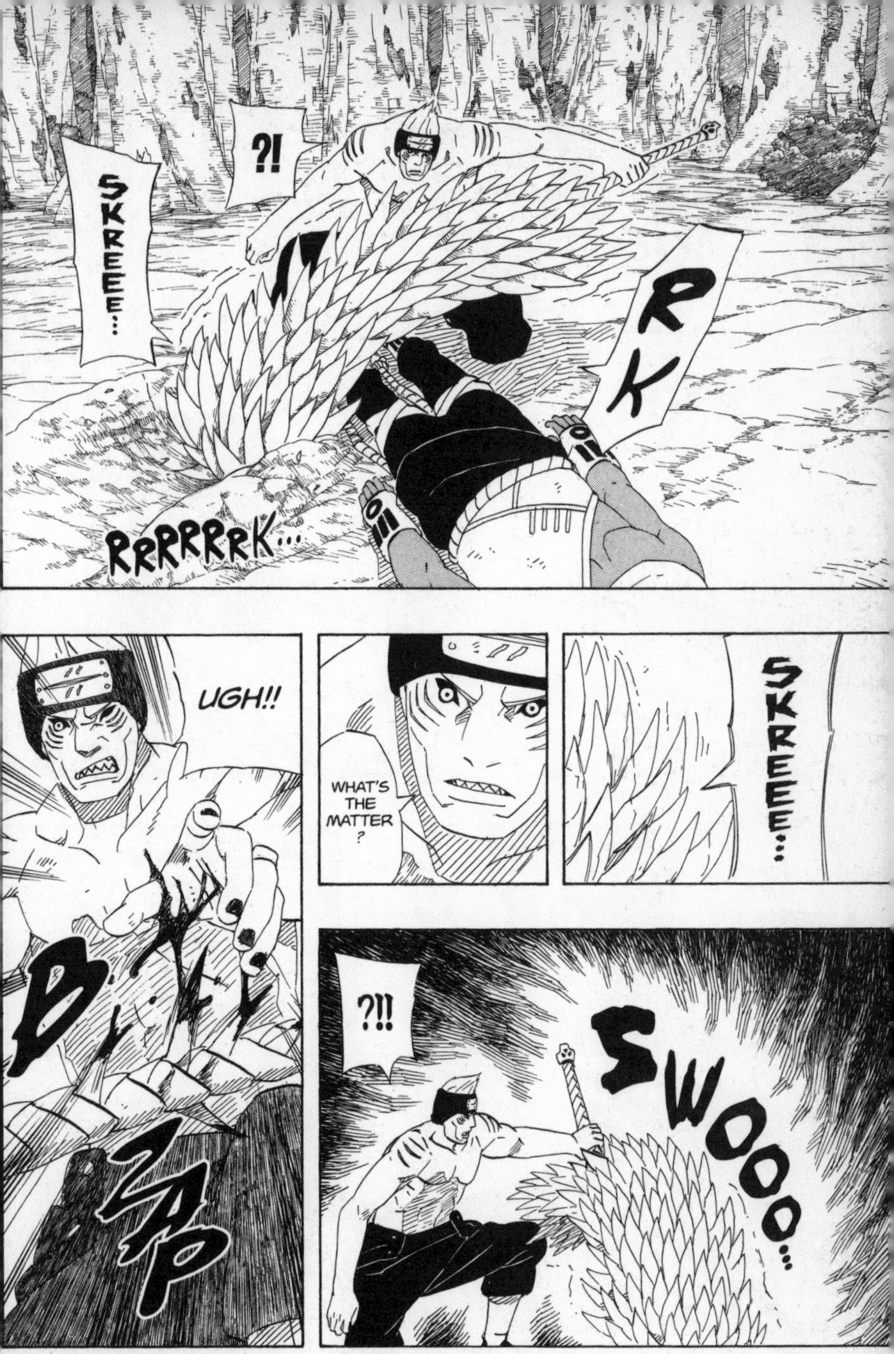
RK
?!
SKREEE...
RRRRRRK...
SKREEE...
WHAT'S THE MATTER?
?!!
SWOOO...
UGH!!
BZAP

READ THIS WAY

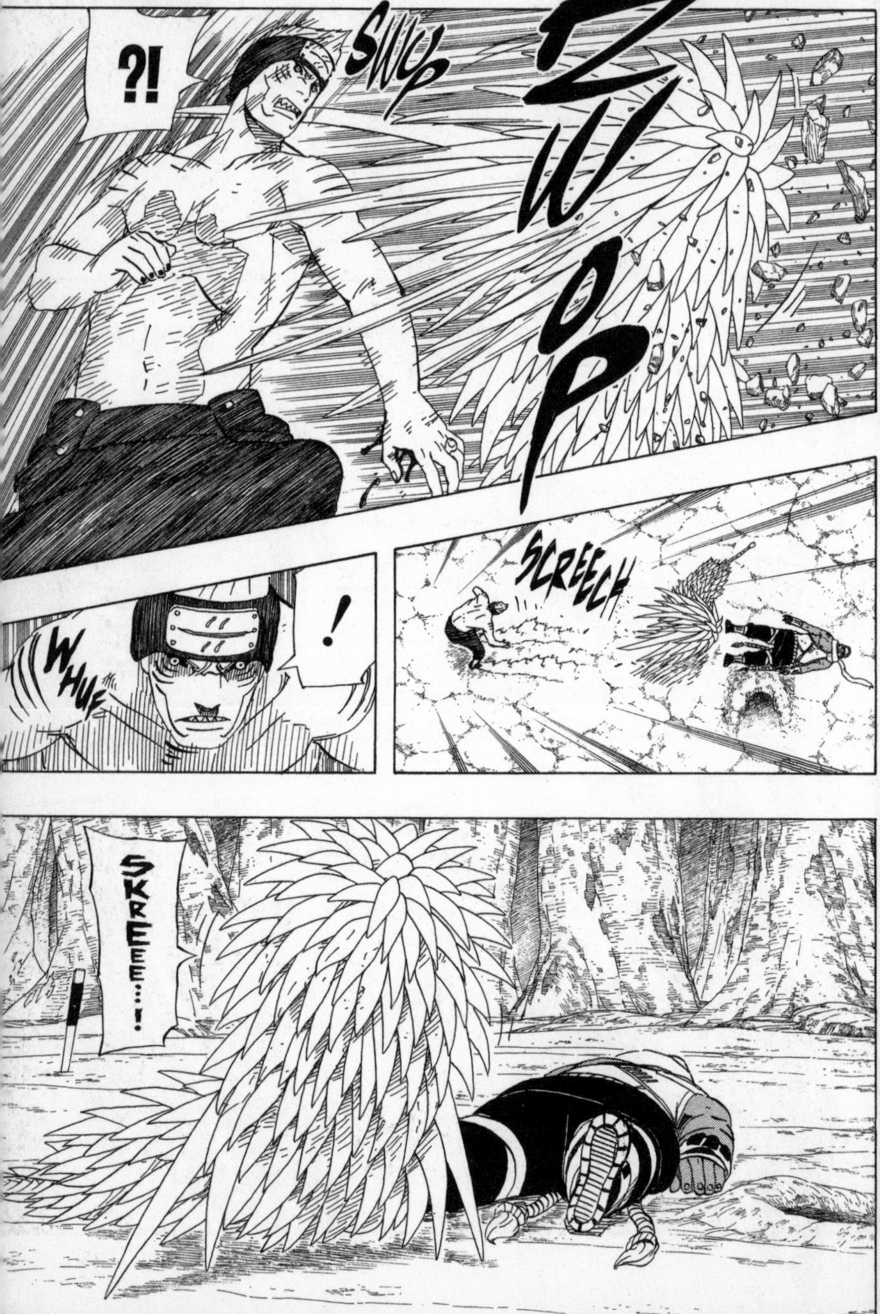
ZWOOP
SWUP
?!
SCREECH
!
WHUF
SKREEE...!!

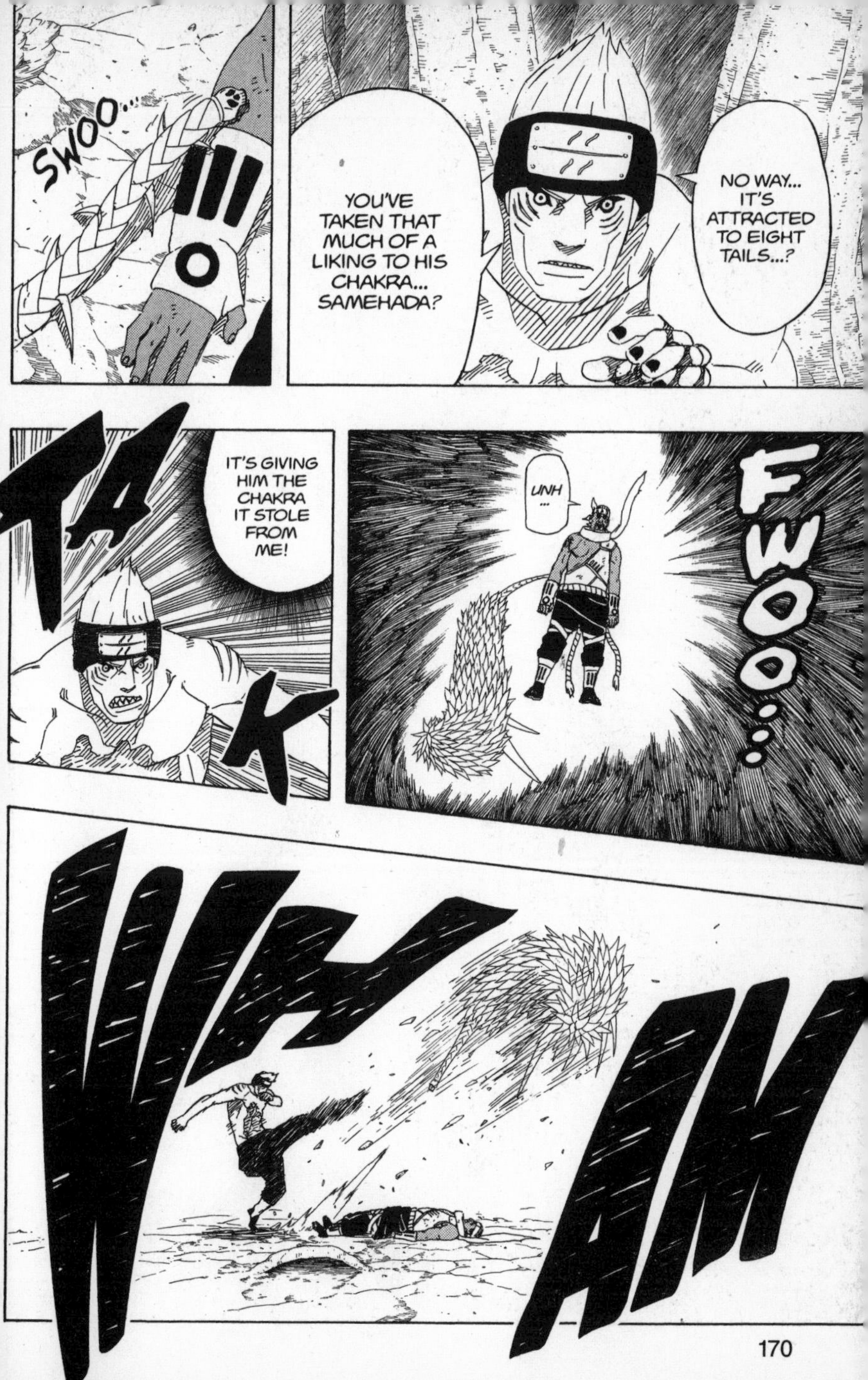
NO WAY... IT'S ATTRACTED TO EIGHT TAILS...?
YOU'VE TAKEN THAT MUCH OF A LIKING TO HIS CHAKRA... SAMEHADA?
SWOO...
FWOOO...
UNH...
IT'S GIVING HIM THE CHAKRA IT STOLE FROM ME!
TAK
WHAM

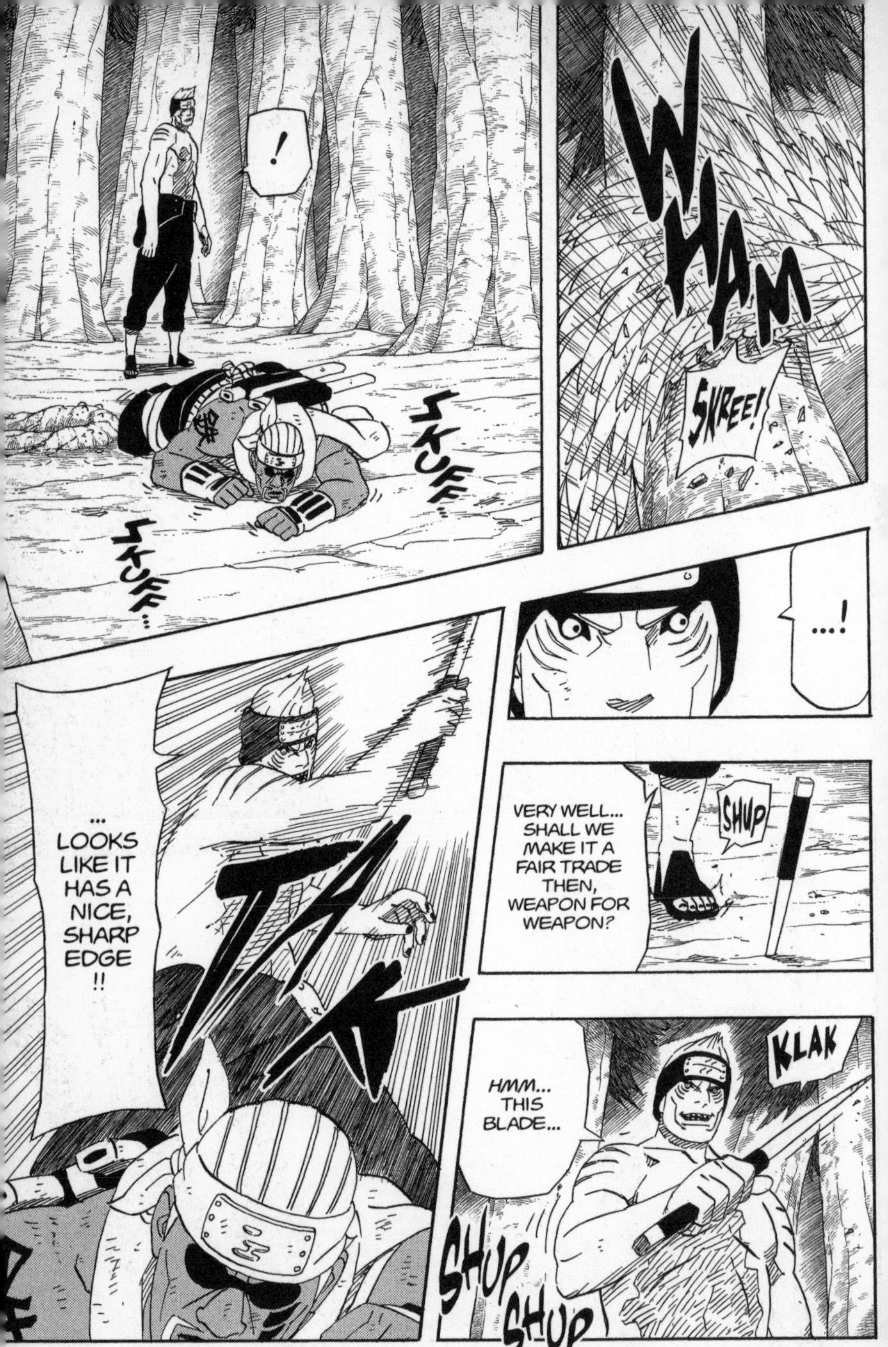
WHAM
SKREE!
!
SKUFF...
SKUFF...
...!
VERY WELL... SHALL WE MAKE IT A FAIR TRADE THEN, WEAPON FOR WEAPON?
SHUP
HMM... THIS BLADE...
KLAK
SHUP
SHUP
... LOOKS LIKE IT HAS A NICE, SHARP EDGE !!

NARUTO

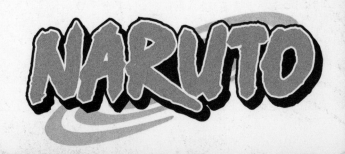

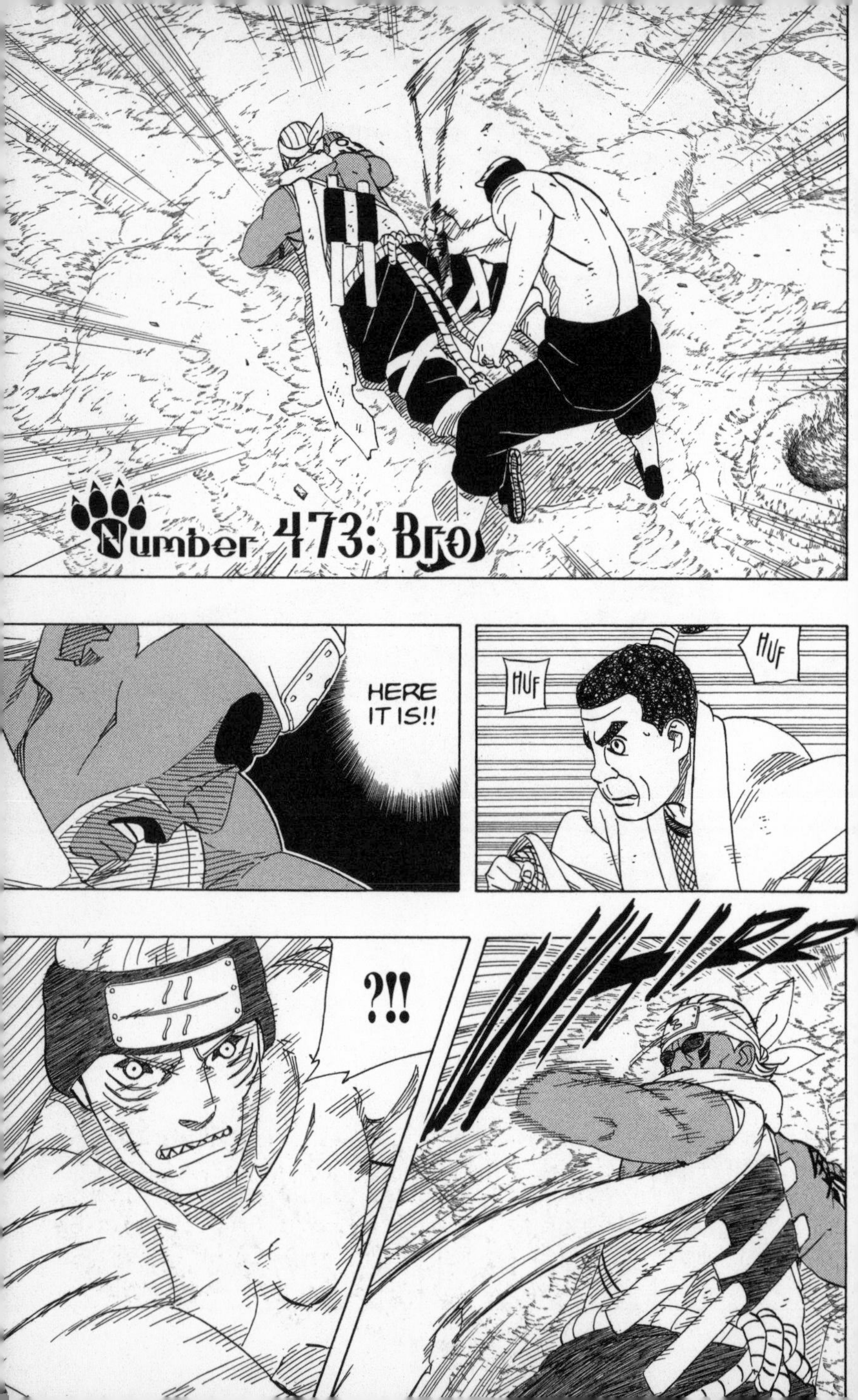
Number 473: Bro
HUF
HUF
HERE IT IS!!
WHIRR
?!!

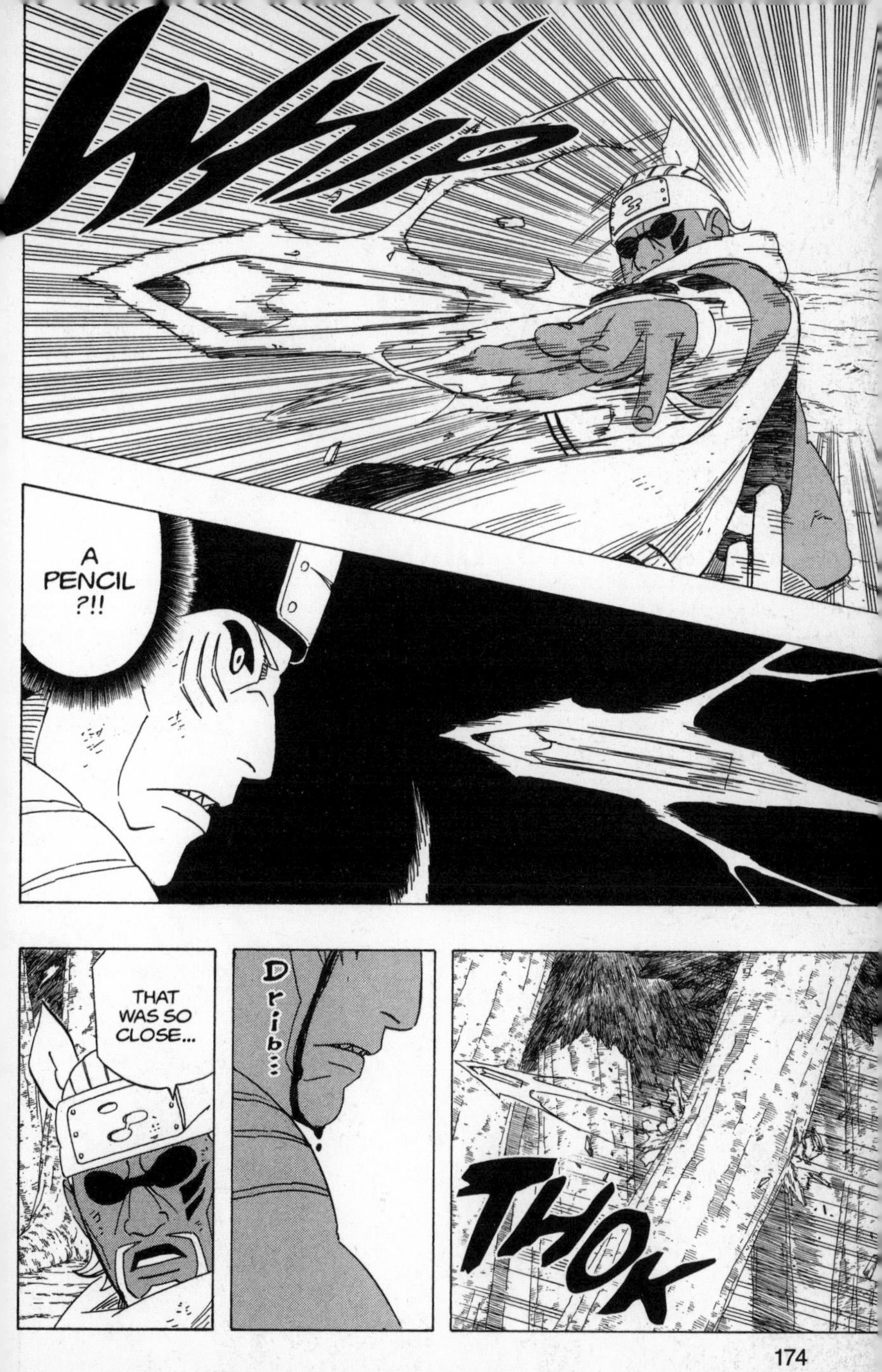
whip
A PENCIL ?!!
THOK
Drib...
THAT WAS SO CLOSE...

READ THIS WAY

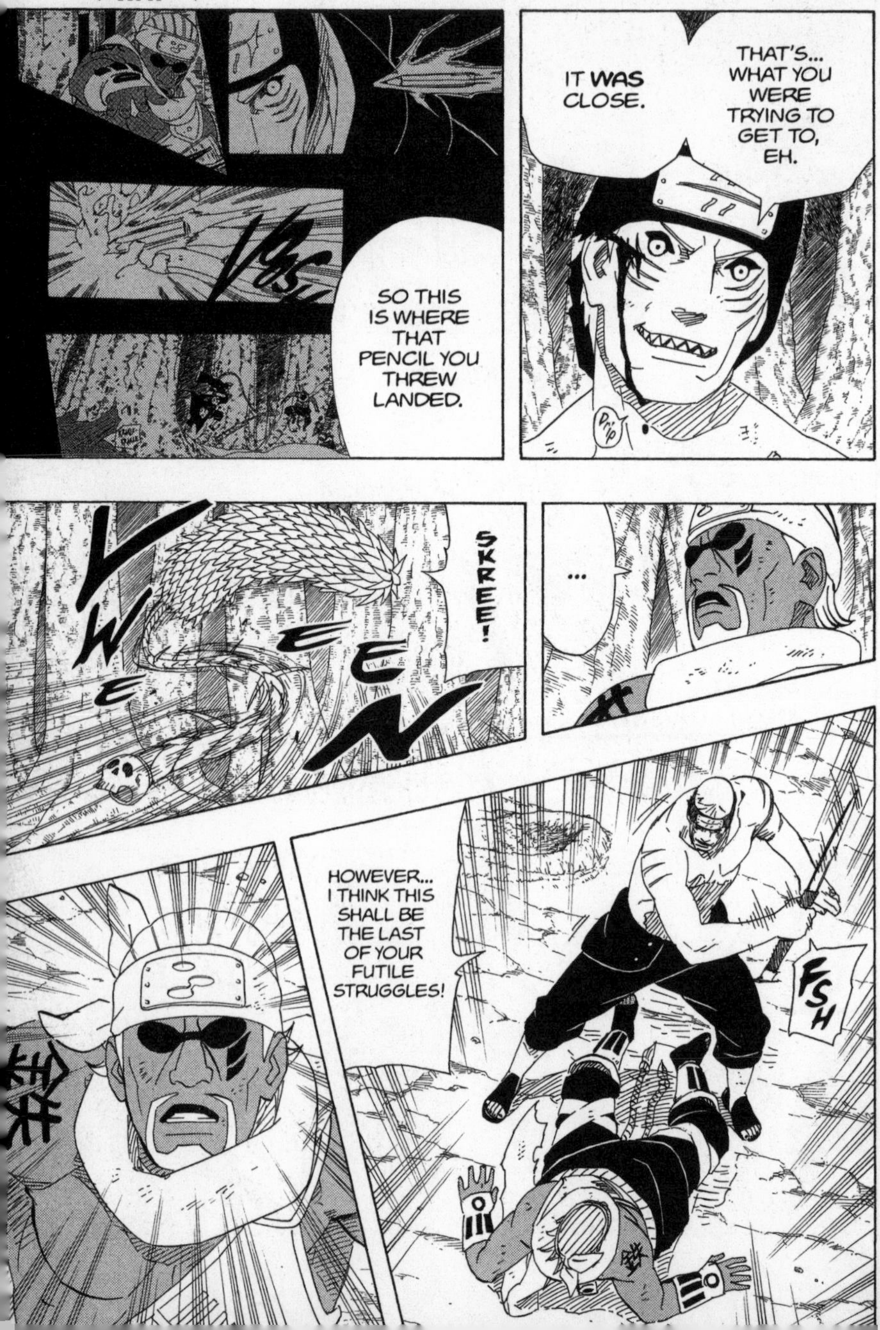

THAT'S... WHAT YOU WERE TRYING TO GET TO, EH.
IT WAS CLOSE.
Drip
SO THIS IS WHERE THAT PENCIL YOU THREW LANDED.
...
SKREE!
VWEEEEN
HOWEVER... I THINK THIS SHALL BE THE LAST OF YOUR FUTILE STRUGGLES!
FSH

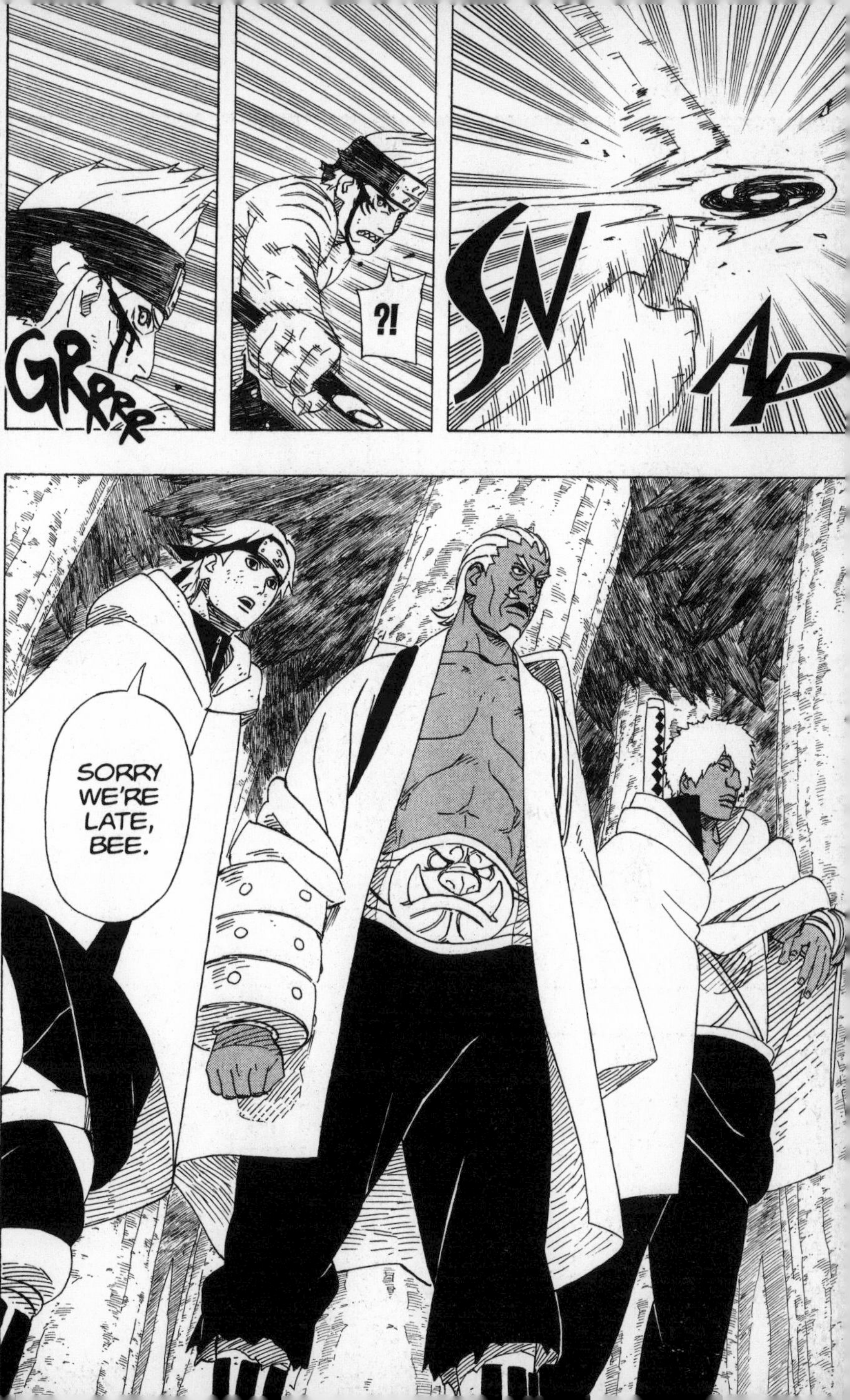
SWAD
?!
GRRRR
SORRY WE'RE LATE, BEE.

READ THIS WAY

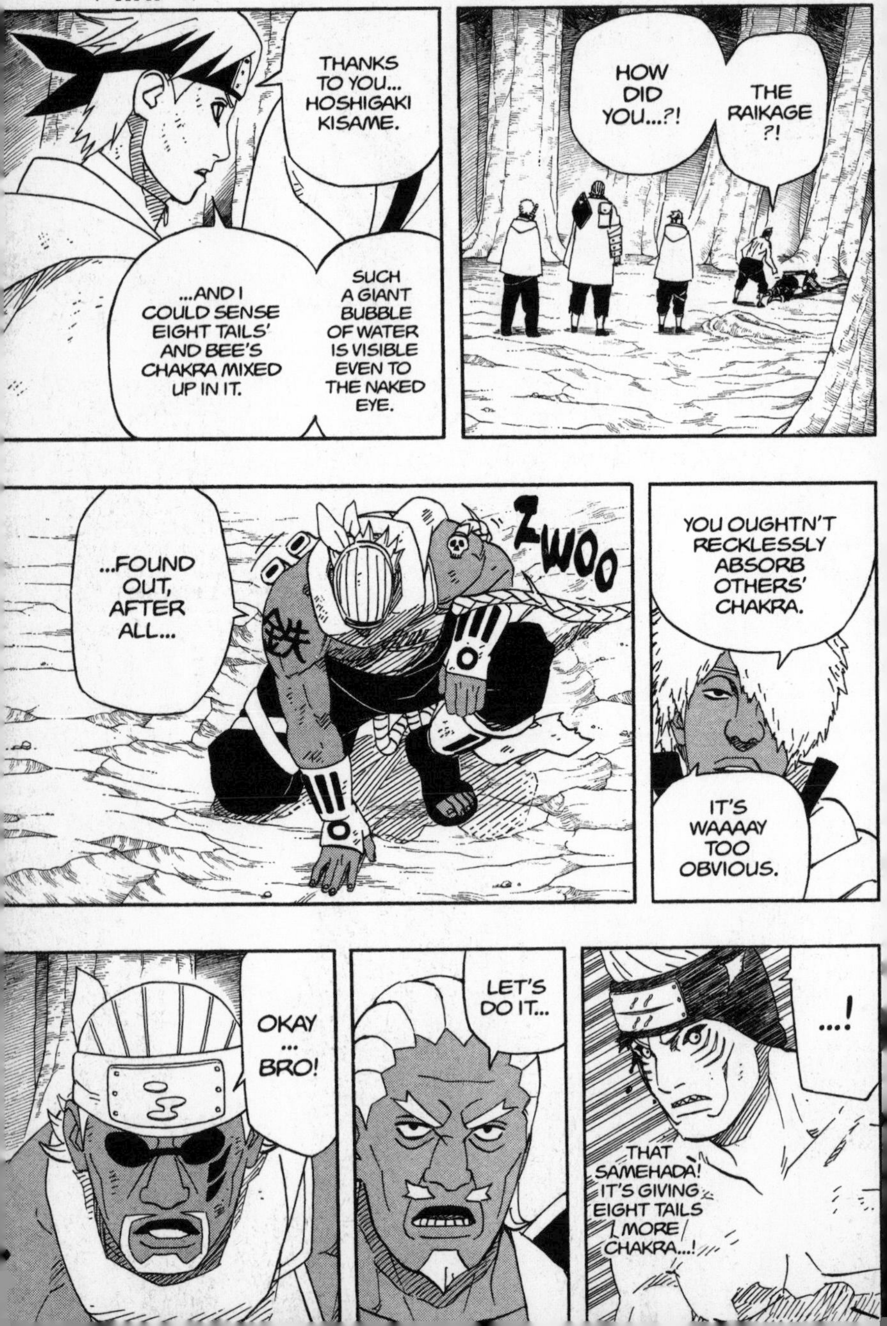
THE RAIKAGE?!
HOW DID YOU...?!
THANKS TO YOU... HOSHIGAKI KISAME.
SUCH A GIANT BUBBLE OF WATER IS VISIBLE EVEN TO THE NAKED EYE.
...AND I COULD SENSE EIGHT TAILS' AND BEE'S CHAKRA MIXED UP IN IT.
YOU OUGHTN'T RECKLESSLY ABSORB OTHERS' CHAKRA.
IT'S WAAAAY TOO OBVIOUS.
ZWOO
...FOUND OUT, AFTER ALL...
...!
THAT SAMEHADA! IT'S GIVING EIGHT TAILS MORE CHAKRA...!
LET'S DO IT...
OKAY ... BRO!

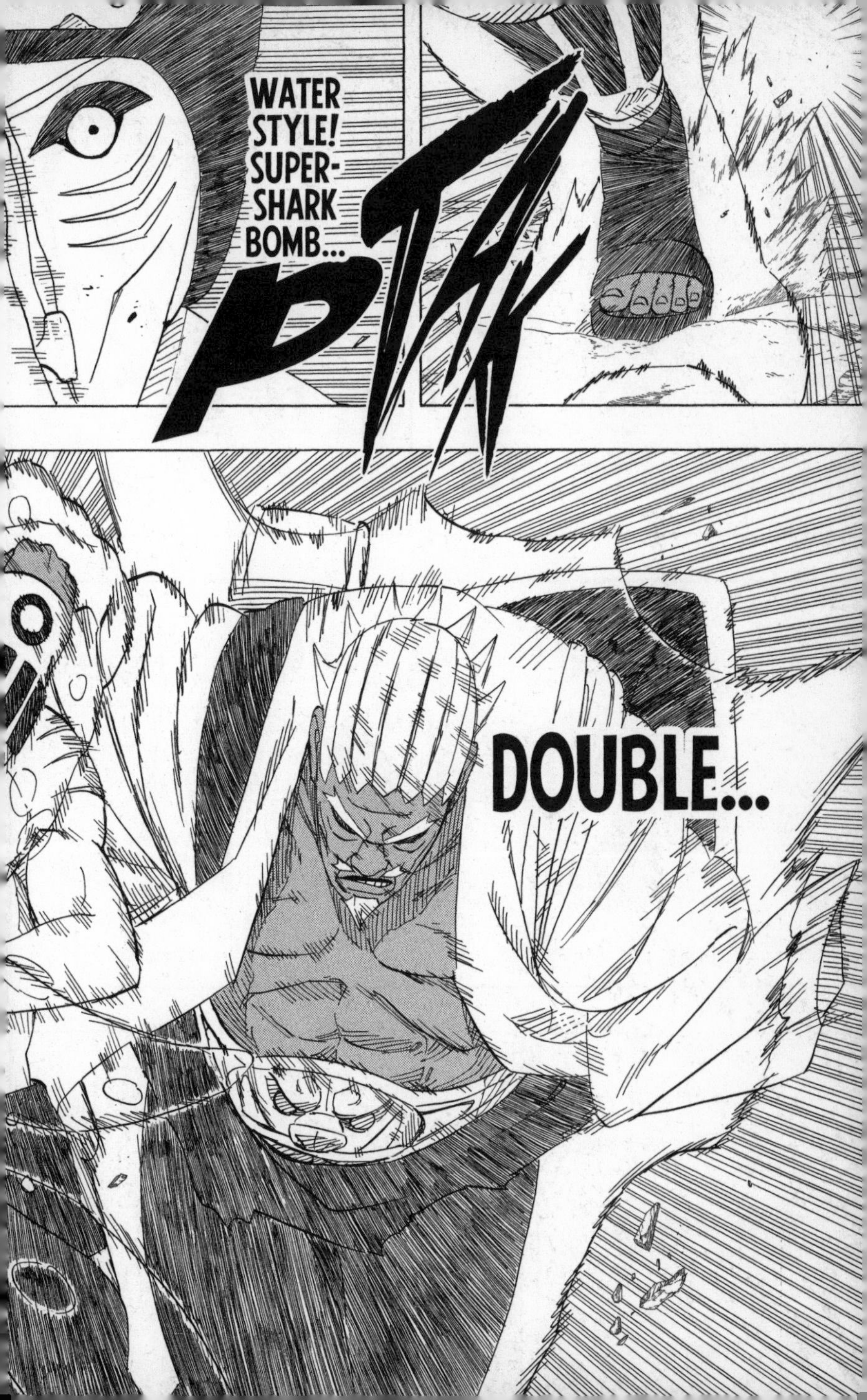
WATER STYLE! SUPER-SHARK BOMB...
PTAK
DOUBLE...

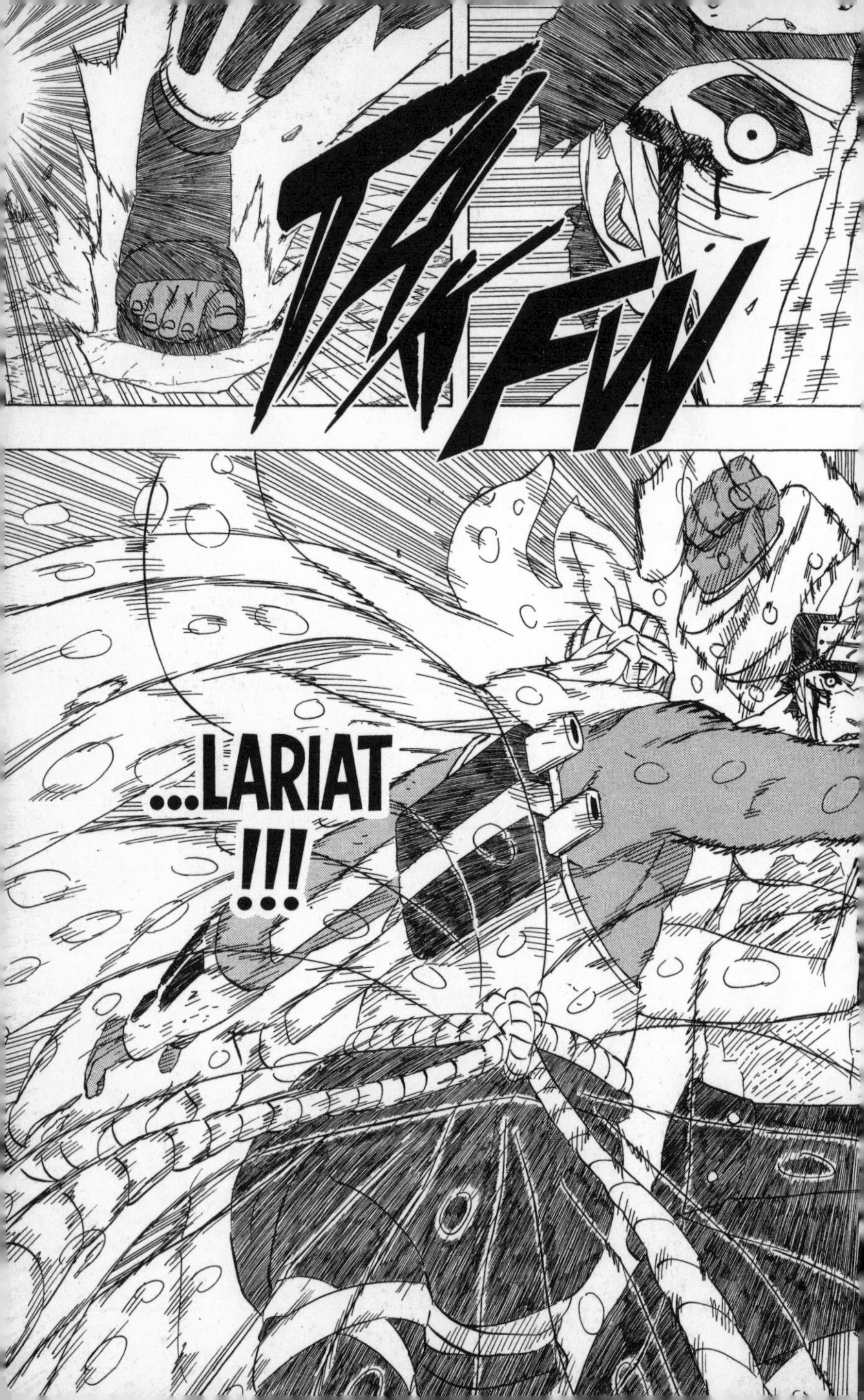

TMP FW
...LARIAT !!!

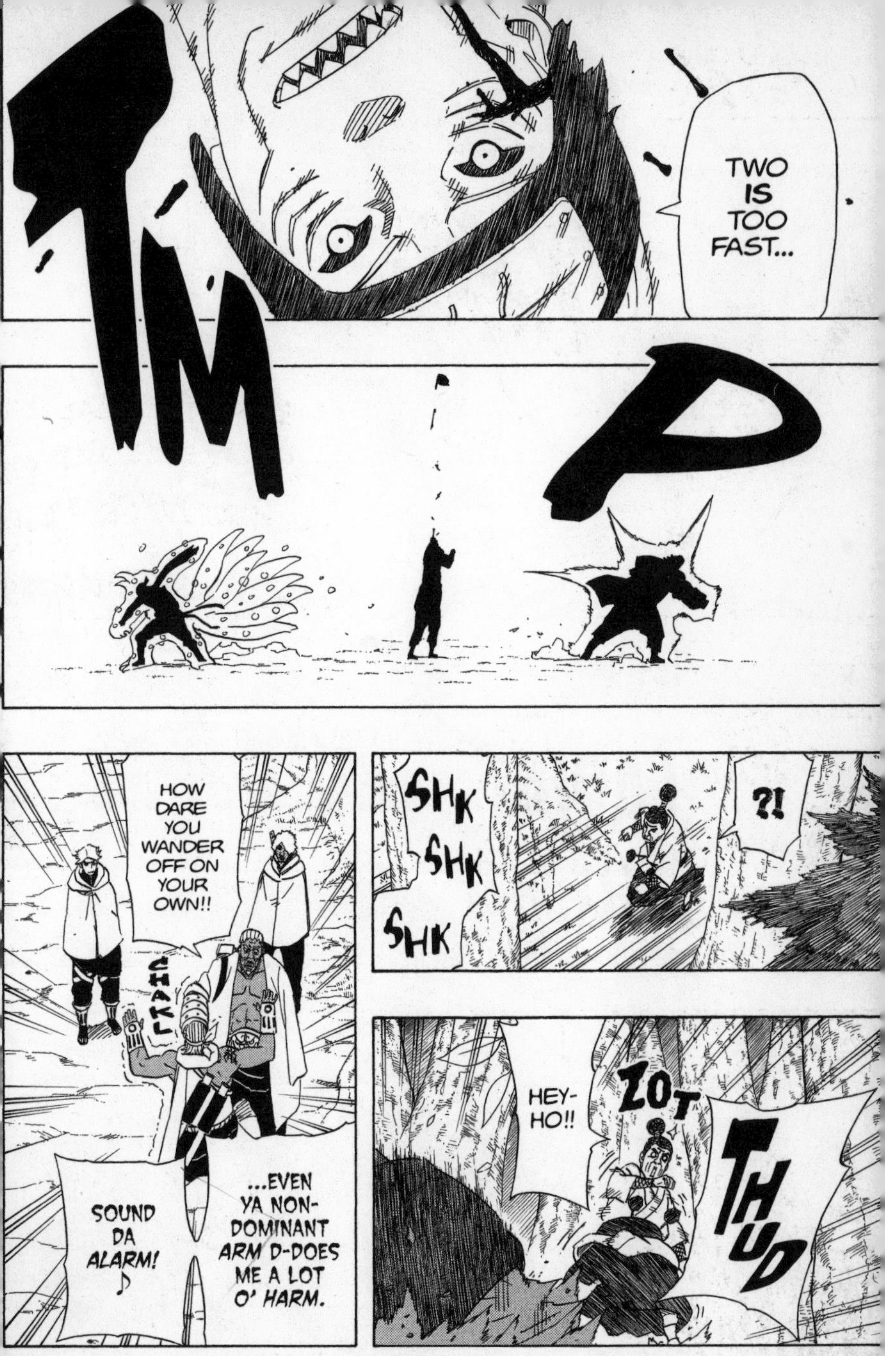

TWO IS TOO FAST...
TIMP
SHK SHK SHK
?!
HEY-HO!!
ZOT
THUD
HOW DARE YOU WANDER OFF ON YOUR OWN!!
CHAKL
...EVEN YA NON-DOMINANT ARM D-DOES ME A LOT O' HARM.
SOUND DA ALARM! ♪

READ THIS WAY

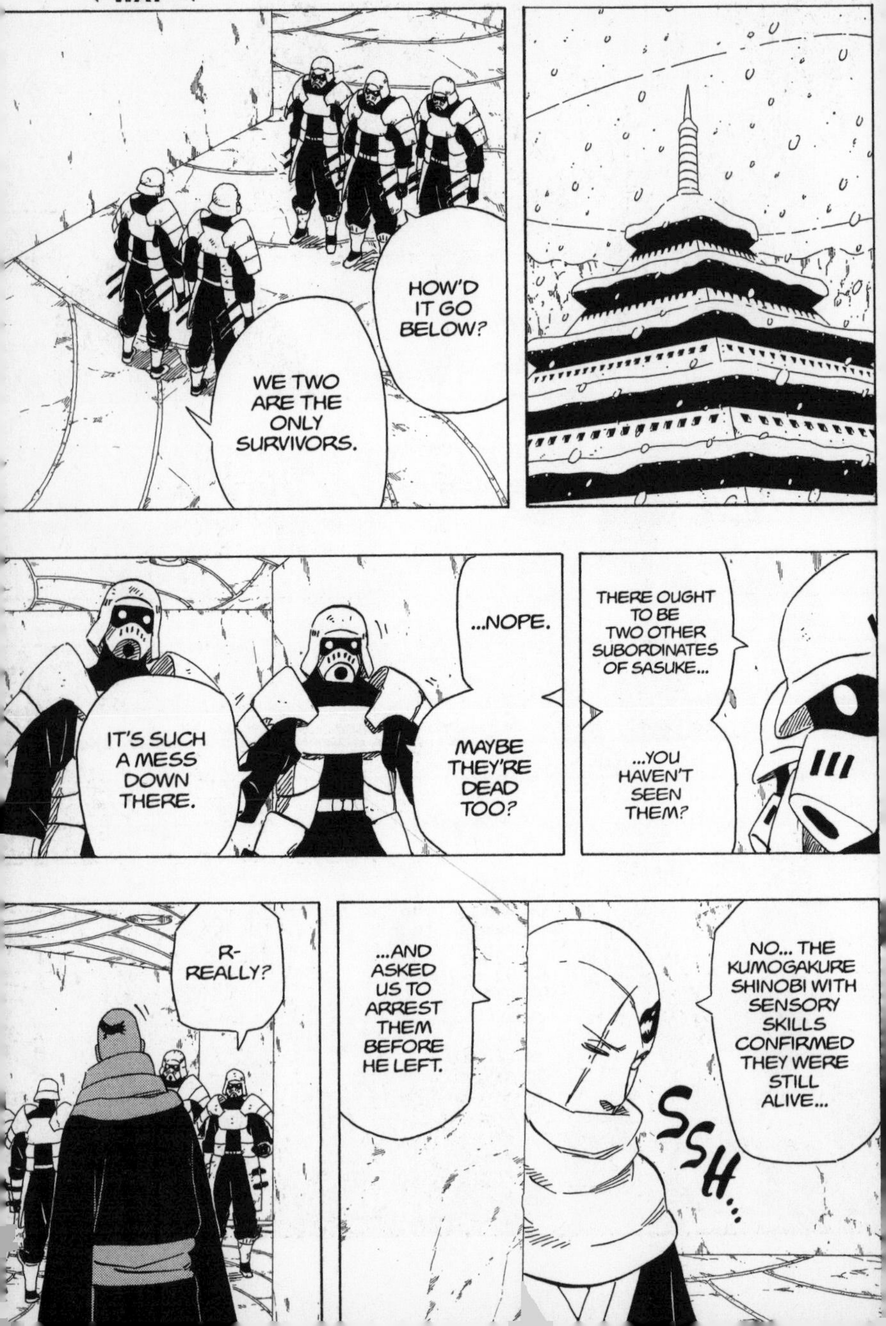
HOW'D IT GO BELOW?
WE TWO ARE THE ONLY SURVIVORS.
THERE OUGHT TO BE TWO OTHER SUBORDINATES OF SASUKE...
...YOU HAVEN'T SEEN THEM?
...NOPE.
MAYBE THEY'RE DEAD TOO?
IT'S SUCH A MESS DOWN THERE.
NO... THE KUMOGAKURE SHINOBI WITH SENSORY SKILLS CONFIRMED THEY WERE STILL ALIVE...
SSH...
...AND ASKED US TO ARREST THEM BEFORE HE LEFT.
R-REALLY?

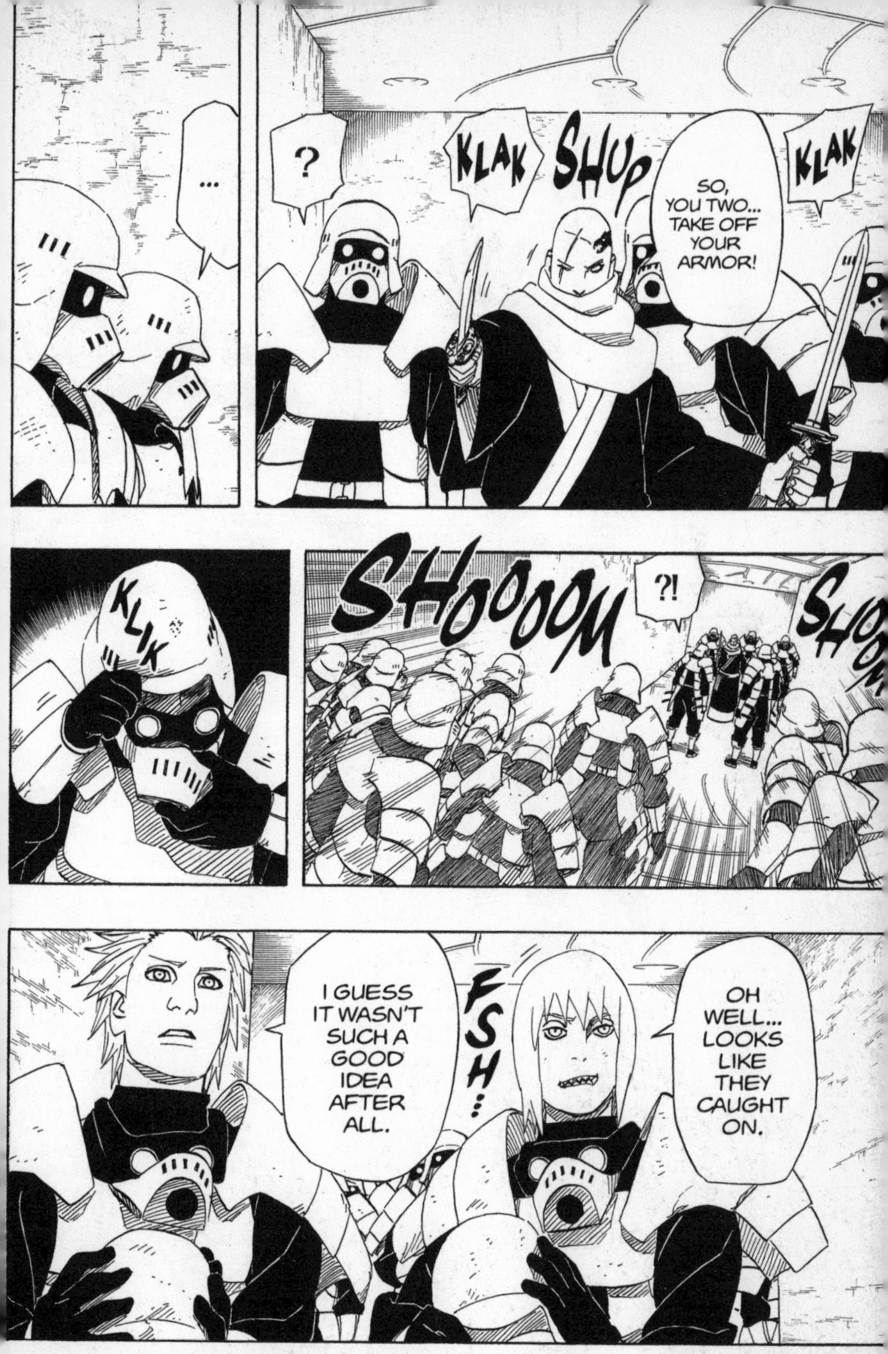
KLAK
SO, YOU TWO... TAKE OFF YOUR ARMOR!
SHUP
KLAK
?
...
?!
SHOOOOM
KLIK
OH WELL... LOOKS LIKE THEY CAUGHT ON.
FSH...
I GUESS IT WASN'T SUCH A GOOD IDEA AFTER ALL.

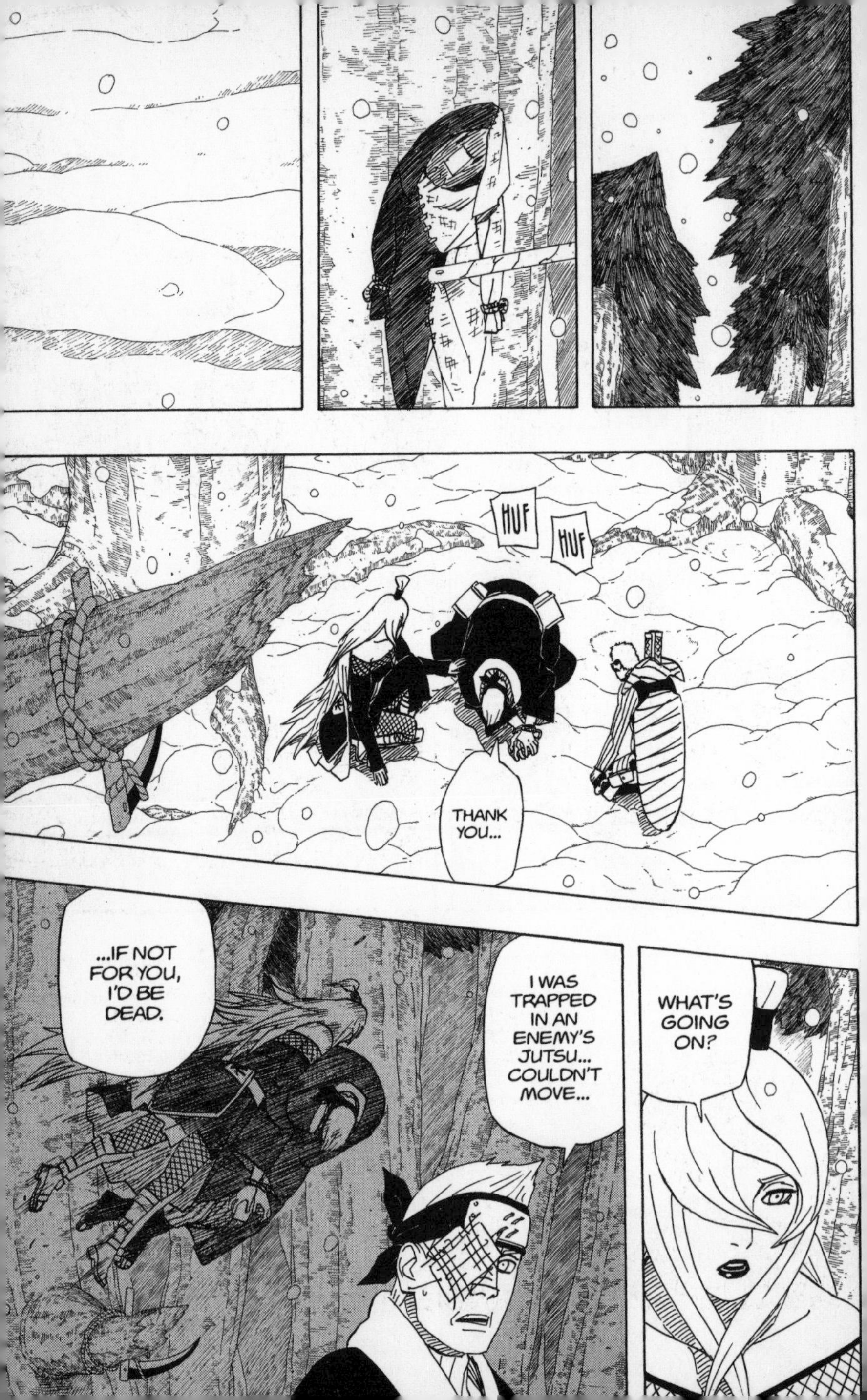
HUF
HUF
THANK YOU...
WHAT'S GOING ON?
I WAS TRAPPED IN AN ENEMY'S JUTSU... COULDN'T MOVE...
...IF NOT FOR YOU, I'D BE DEAD.

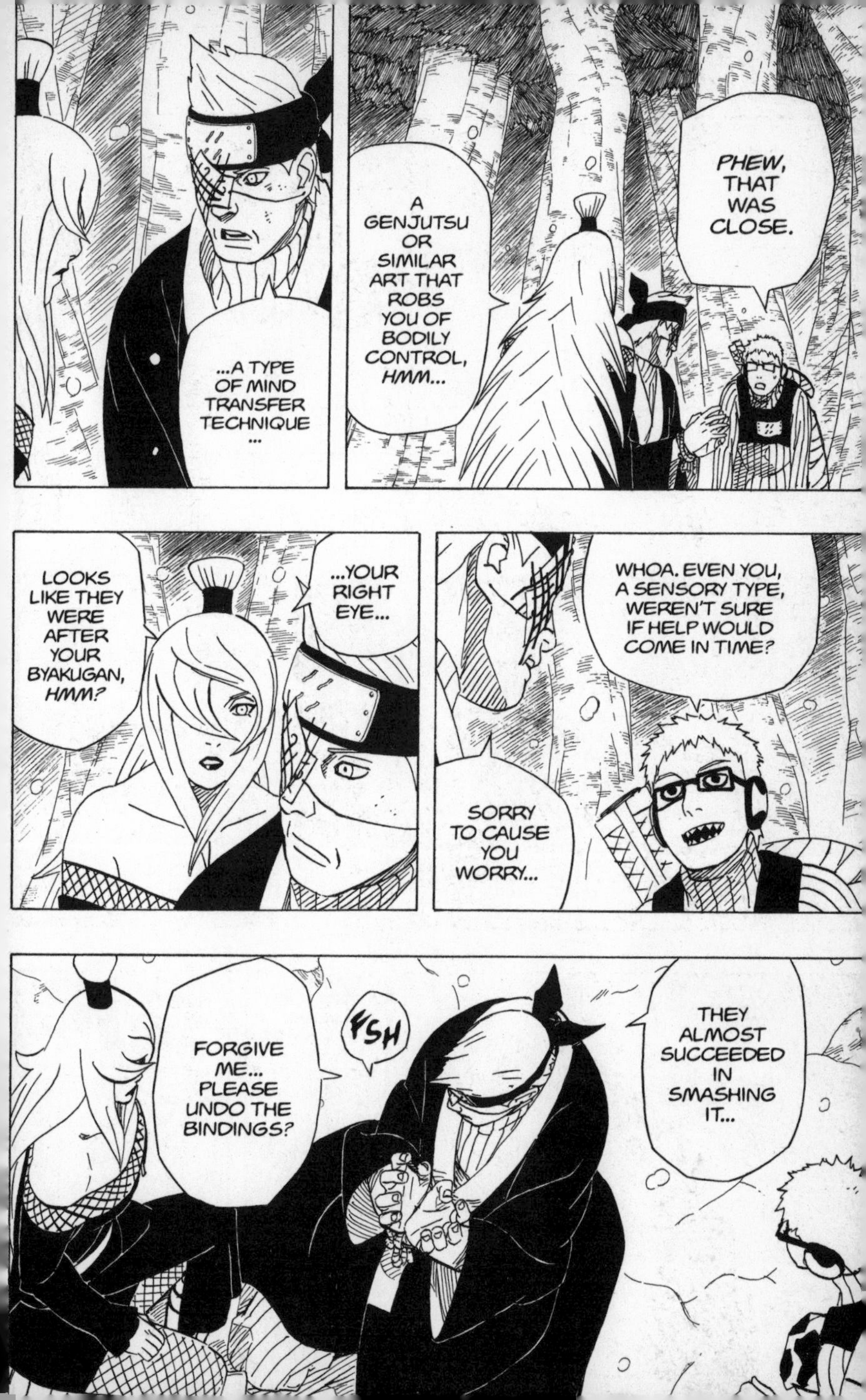
PHEW, THAT WAS CLOSE.
A GENJUTSU OR SIMILAR ART THAT ROBS YOU OF BODILY CONTROL, *HMM*...
...A TYPE OF MIND TRANSFER TECHNIQUE ...
WHOA. EVEN YOU, A SENSORY TYPE, WEREN'T SURE IF HELP WOULD COME IN TIME?
SORRY TO CAUSE YOU WORRY...
...YOUR RIGHT EYE...
LOOKS LIKE THEY WERE AFTER YOUR BYAKUGAN, *HMM?*
THEY ALMOST SUCCEEDED IN SMASHING IT...
YSH
FORGIVE ME... PLEASE UNDO THE BINDINGS?

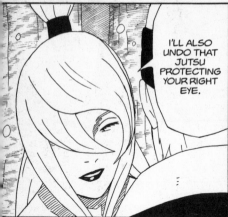

I'LL ALSO UNDO THAT JUTSU PROTECTING YOUR RIGHT EYE.

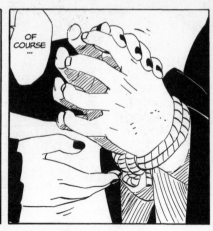

OF COURSE...

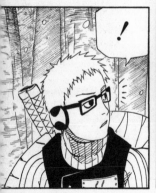

!

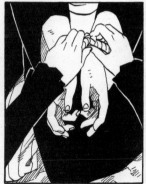

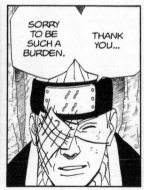

SORRY TO BE SUCH A BURDEN.

THANK YOU...

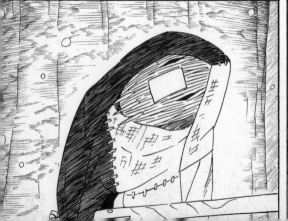

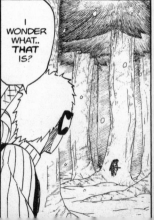

I WONDER WHAT.. THAT IS?

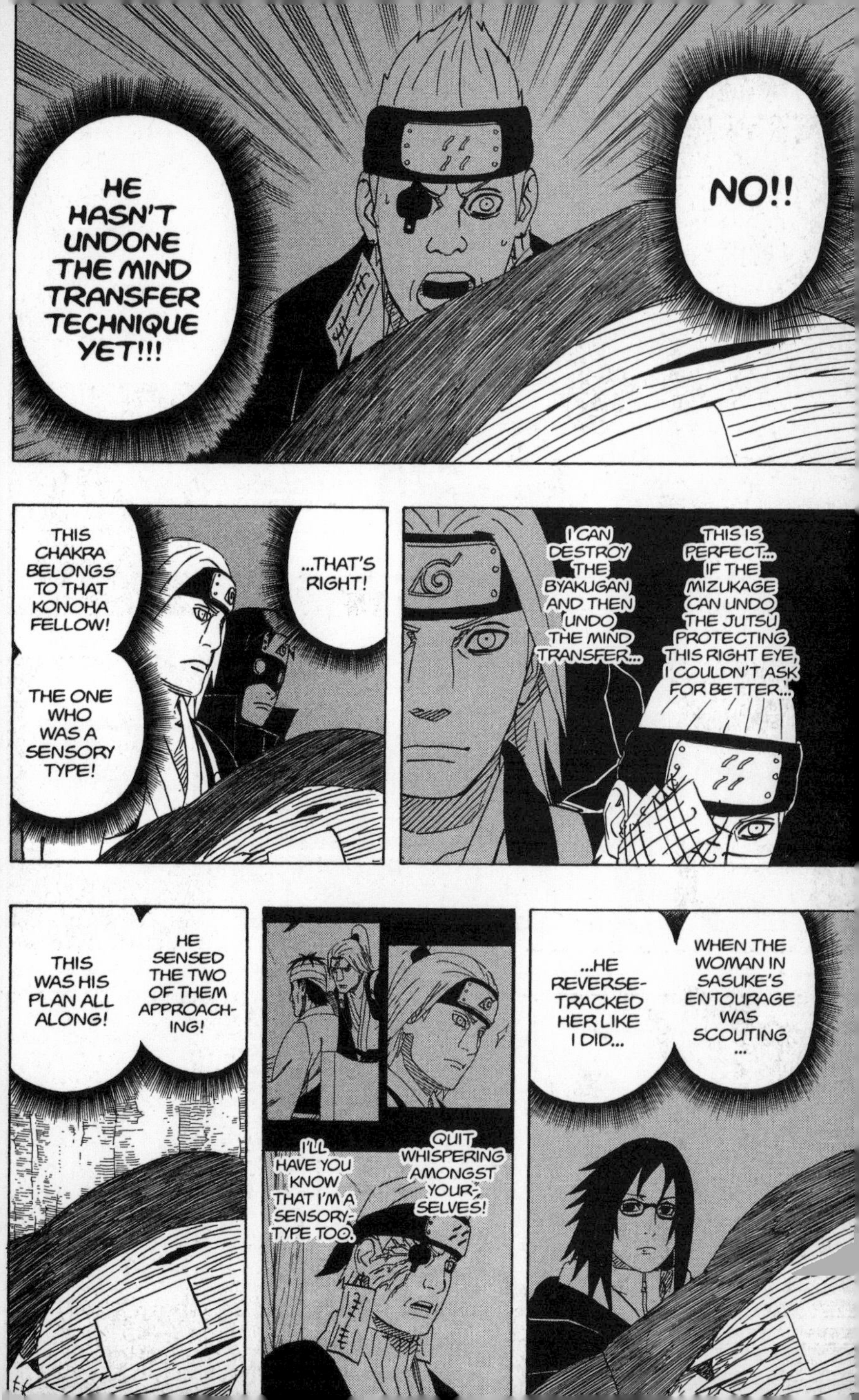
NO!!
HE HASN'T UNDONE THE MIND TRANSFER TECHNIQUE YET!!!
THIS IS PERFECT... IF THE MIZUKAGE CAN UNDO THE JUTSU PROTECTING THIS RIGHT EYE, I COULDN'T ASK FOR BETTER...
I CAN DESTROY THE BYAKUGAN AND THEN UNDO THE MIND TRANSFER...
...THAT'S RIGHT!
THIS CHAKRA BELONGS TO THAT KONOHA FELLOW!
THE ONE WHO WAS A SENSORY TYPE!
WHEN THE WOMAN IN SASUKE'S ENTOURAGE WAS SCOUTING...
...HE REVERSE-TRACKED HER LIKE I DID...
QUIT WHISPERING AMONGST YOUR-SELVES!
I'LL HAVE YOU KNOW THAT I'M A SENSORY-TYPE TOO.
HE SENSED THE TWO OF THEM APPROACH-ING!
THIS WAS HIS PLAN ALL ALONG!

READ THIS WAY

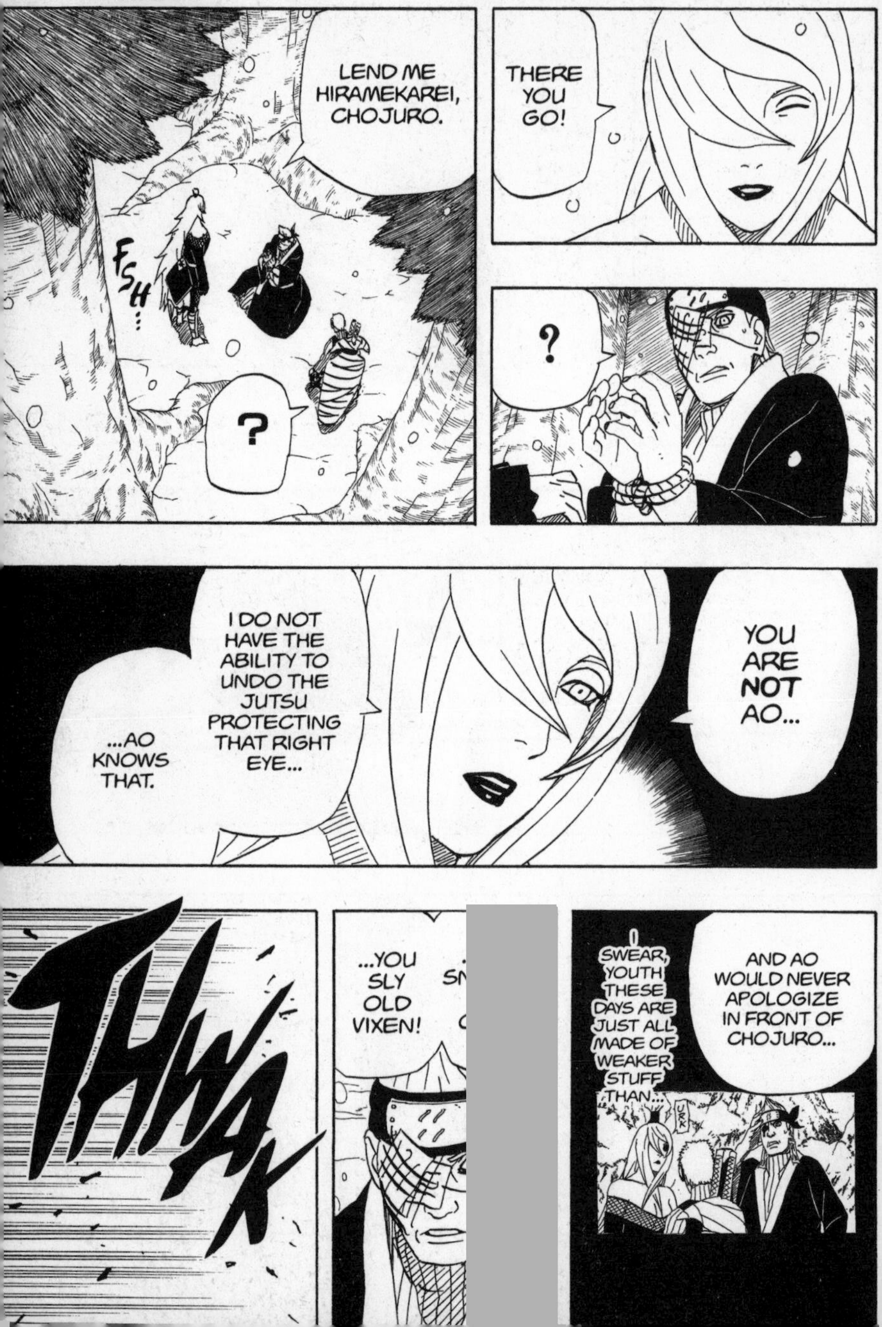
THERE YOU GO!
?
LEND ME HIRAMEKAREI, CHOJURO.
?
FSH...
YOU ARE NOT AO...
I DO NOT HAVE THE ABILITY TO UNDO THE JUTSU PROTECTING THAT RIGHT EYE...
...AO KNOWS THAT.
AND AO WOULD NEVER APOLOGIZE IN FRONT OF CHOJURO...
I SWEAR, YOUTH THESE DAYS ARE JUST ALL MADE OF WEAKER STUFF THAN...
URK
...YOU SLY OLD VIXEN!
THWAK

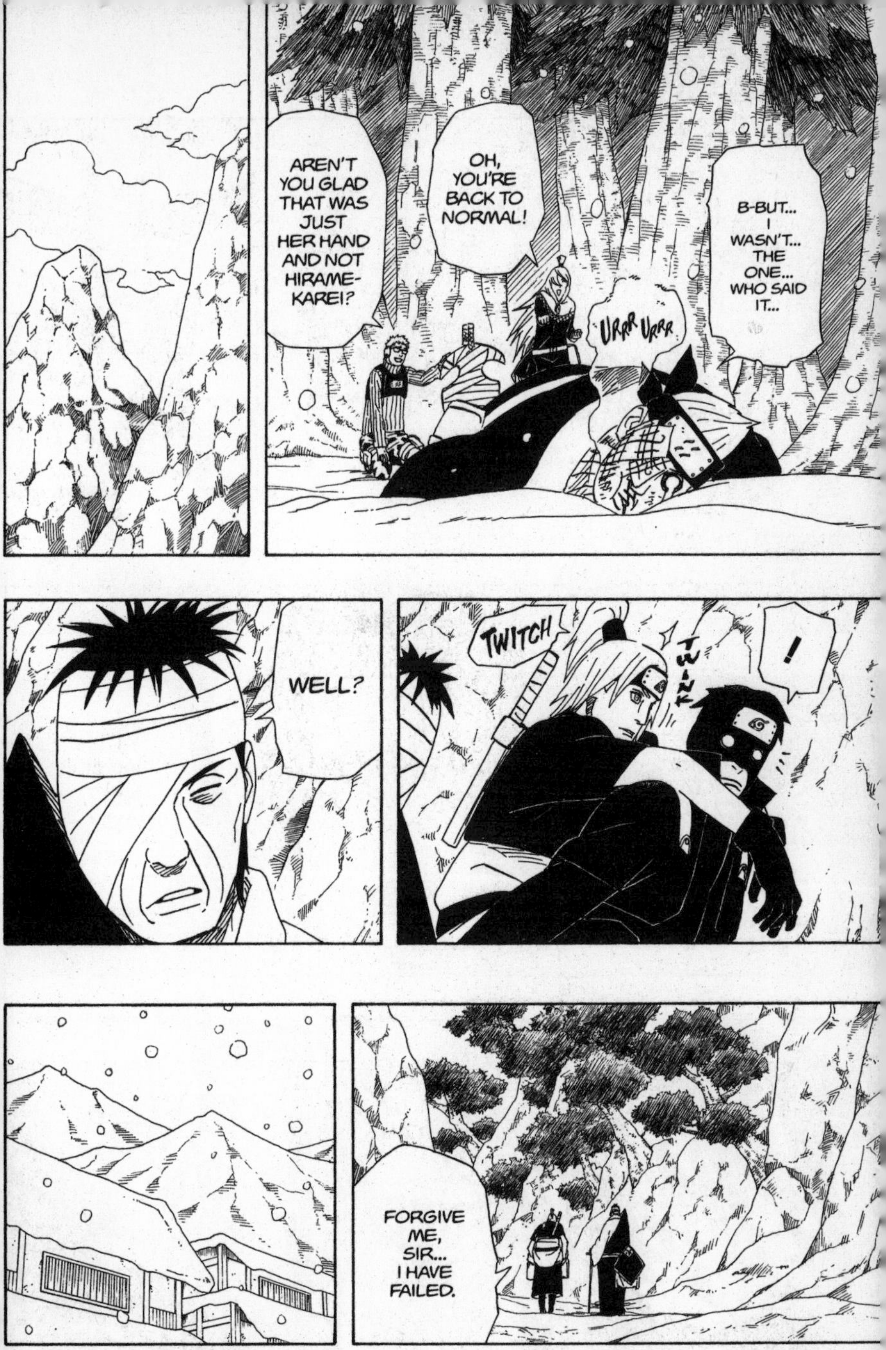
B-BUT... I WASN'T... THE ONE... WHO SAID IT...
URRR URRR
OH, YOU'RE BACK TO NORMAL!
AREN'T YOU GLAD THAT WAS JUST HER HAND AND NOT HIRAME-KAREI?
!
TWINK
TWITCH
WELL?
FORGIVE ME, SIR... I HAVE FAILED.

READ THIS WAY

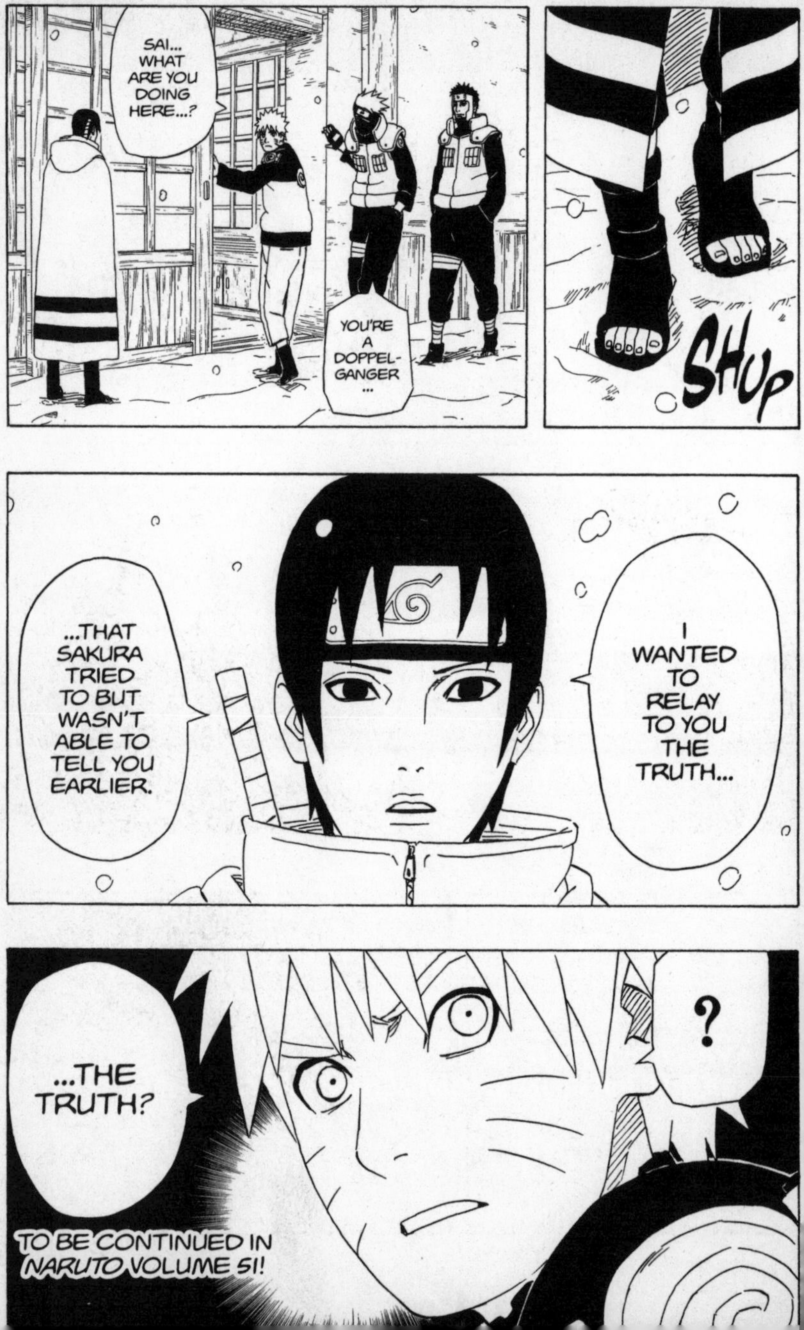
SHUP
SAI... WHAT ARE YOU DOING HERE...?
YOU'RE A DOPPEL-GANGER...
I WANTED TO RELAY TO YOU THE TRUTH...
...THAT SAKURA TRIED TO BUT WASN'T ABLE TO TELL YOU EARLIER.
?
...THE TRUTH?
TO BE CONTINUED IN NARUTO VOLUME 51!

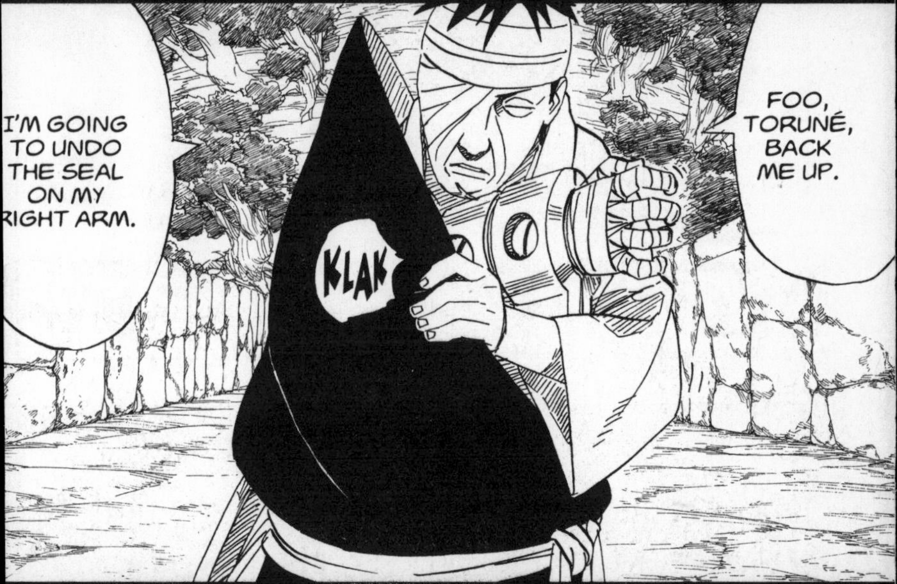
FOO, TORUNÉ, BACK ME UP.
KLAK
I'M GOING TO UNDO THE SEAL ON MY RIGHT ARM.

IN THE NEXT VOLUME...

A HOKAGE'S RESOLVE

Sasuke finally takes on Danzo, determined to interrogate him about the Uchiha clan and what really happened between the political factions of Konoha and his brother, Itachi. Sasuke has his team delving deep into the Hokage's past, but will what Sasuke uncovers help him bring about the Hokage's defeat? The battle that will ensue is going to be epic!

AVAILABLE JUNE 2011!
READ IT FIRST IN SHONEN JUMP MAGAZINE!

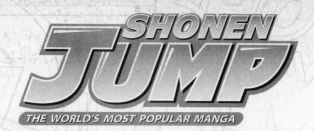
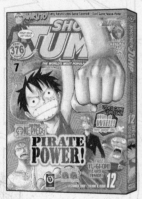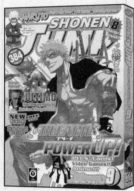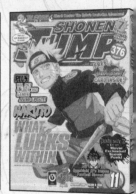

SAVE 50% OFF
THE COVER PRICE!

IT'S LIKE GETTING 6 ISSUES
FREE!

OVER 350+ PAGES PER ISSUE

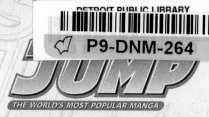

THE WORLD'S MOST POPULAR MANGA

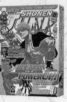

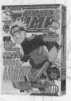

This monthly magazine contains 7 of the coolest manga available in the U.S., PLUS anime news, and info about video & card games, toys AND more!

❏ **I want 12 HUGE issues of SHONEN JUMP for only $29.95*!**

Zaire Harvey

NAME

20060

ADDRESS

CITY/STATE/ZIP

EMAIL ADDRESS   **DATE OF BIRTH**

❏ YES, send me via email information, advertising, offers, and promotions related to VIZ Media, SHONEN JUMP, and/or their business partners.

❏ **CHECK ENCLOSED** (payable to SHONEN JUMP)   ❏ **BILL ME LATER**

CREDIT CARD: ❏ Visa ❏ Mastercard

ACCOUNT NUMBER   **EXP. DATE**

SIGNATURE

CLIP&MAIL TO:
SHONEN JUMP Subscriptions Service Dept.
P.O. Box 515
Mount Morris, IL 61054-0515

P9GNC1

* Canada price: $41.95 USD, including GST, HST, and QST. US/CAN orders only. Allow 6-8 weeks for delivery.
ONE PIECE © 1997 by Eiichiro Oda/SHUEISHA Inc. BLEACH © 2001 by Tite Kubo/SHUEISHA Inc.
NARUTO © 1999 by Masashi Kishimoto/SHUEISHA Inc.